Israel's Military Operations in Gaza

Civilians in Gaza and Israel are caught up in complex, violent situations that have overstepped conventional battle lines. Both sides of the conflict have found ways to legitimate the use of violence, and continually swap accusations of violations of domestic and international humanitarian laws.

Israel's Military Operations in Gaza provides an ideological critique of the legal, military, and social media texts that have been used to legitimate historical incursions into Gaza, with special focus on Operation Protective Edge. It argues that both the Palestinians and the Israelis have deployed various forms of "telegenic" warfare. They have each used argumentative rhetorics based on competing interpretations of events, and are locked in a battle to convince international audiences and domestic constituencies of the righteousness of their causes. This critical genealogical study analyses a range of texts and images, from selfies circulated near the Gaza border to judicial opinions produced by the High Court of Israel.

With its multidisciplinary approach and original analysis of the Israel/Gaza situation, this book will be of interest to students and scholars of Middle East studies and the Arab–Israeli conflict, as well as security studies and communication studies.

Marouf Hasian, Jr. is Professor in the Department of Communication at the University of Utah. His research interests include critical security studies, critical legal studies, and post-colonial analyses.

Routledge studies in Middle Eastern politics

1. **Algeria in Transition**
   *Ahmed Aghrout with
   Redha M. Bougherira*

2. **Palestinian Refugee Repatriation**
   Edited by Michael Dumper

3. **The International Politics of the Persian Gulf**
   Arshin Adib-Moghaddam

4. **Israeli Politics and the First Palestinian Intifada**
   Eitan Y. Alimi

5. **Democratization in Morocco**
   Lise Storm

6. **Secular and Islamic Politics in Turkey**
   Ümit Cizre

7. **The United States and Iran**
   Sasan Fayazmanesh

8. **Civil Society in Algeria**
   Andrea Liverani

9. **Jordanian–Israeli Relations**
   Mutayyam al O'ran

10. **Kemalism in Turkish Politics**
    Sinan Ciddi

11. **Islamism, Democracy and Liberalism in Turkey**
    William Hale and Ergun Özbudun

12. **Politics and Violence in Israel/Palestine**
    Lev Luis Grinberg

13. **Intra-Jewish Conflict in Israel**
    Sami Shalom Chetrit

14. **Holy Places in the Israeli–Palestinian Conflict**
    *Edited by Marshall J. Breger,
    Yitzhak Reiter and
    Leonard Hammer*

15. **Plurality and Citizenship in Israel**
    *Edited by Dan Avnon and
    Yotam Benziman*

16. **Ethnic Politics in Israel**
    As'ad Ghanem

17. **Islamists and Secularists in Egypt**
    Dina Shehata

18. **Political Succession in the Arab World**
    Anthony Billingsley

19. **Turkey's Entente with Israel and Azerbaijan**
    Alexander Murinson

20 Europe and Tunisia
Brieg Powel and Larbi Sadiki

21 Turkish Politics and the Rise of the AKP
Arda Can Kumbaracibasi

22 Civil Society and Democratization in the Arab World
Francesco Cavatorta and Vincent Durac

23 Politics in Morocco
Anouar Boukhars

24 The Second Palestinian Intifada
Julie M. Norman

25 Democracy in Turkey
Ali Resul Usul

26 Nationalism and Politics in Turkey
Edited by Marlies Casier and Joost Jongerden

27 Democracy in the Arab World
Edited by Samir Makdisi and Ibrahim Elbadawi

28 Public Management in Israel
Itzhak Galnoor

29 Israeli Nationalism
Uri Ram

30 NATO and the Middle East
Mohammed Moustafa Orfy

31 The Kurds and US Foreign Policy
Marianna Charountaki

32 The Iran–Iraq War
Jerome Donovan

33 Surveillance and Control in Israel/Palestine
Edited by Elia Zureik, David Lyon and Yasmeen Abu-Laban

34 Conflict and Peacemaking in Israel–Palestine
Sapir Handelman

35 Arab Minority Nationalism in Israel
Amal Jamal

36 The Contradictions of Israeli Citizenship
Edited by Guy Ben-Porat and Bryan S. Turner

37 The Arab State and Women's Rights
Elham Manea

38 Saudi Maritime Policy
Hatim Al-Bisher, Selina Stead and Tim Gray

39 The Arab State
Adham Saouli

40 Regime Stability in Saudi Arabia
Stig Stenslie

41 Sacred Space in Israel and Palestine
Edited by Marshall J. Breger, Yitzhak Reiter and Leonard Hammer

42 The UN and the Arab–Israeli Conflict
Danilo Di Mauro

43 Sectarian Conflict in Egypt
Elizabeth Iskander

44 **Contemporary Morocco**
  Edited by Bruce Maddy-Weitzman and Daniel Zisenwine

45 **Political Regimes in the Arab World**
  Edited by Ferran Brichs

46 **Arms Control and Iranian Foreign Policy**
  Bobi Pirseyedi

47 **Everyday Arab Identity**
  Christopher Phillips

48 **Human Rights in Libya**
  Giacomina De Bona

49 **Negotiating Political Power in Turkey**
  Edited by Elise Massicard and Nicole Watts

50 **Environmental Politics in Egypt**
  Jeannie L. Sowers

51 **EU–Turkey Relations in the 21st Century**
  Birol Yesilada

52 **Patronage Politics in Egypt**
  Mohamed Fahmy Menza

53 **The Making of Lebanese Foreign Policy**
  Henrietta Wilkins

54 **The Golan Heights**
  Yigal Kipnis

55 **Iranian Foreign Policy since 2001**
  Edited by Thomas Juneau and Sam Razavi

56 **Modern Middle East Authoritarianism**
  Edited by Noureddine Jebnoun, Mehrdad Kia and Mimi Kirk

57 **Mobilizing Religion in Middle East Politics**
  Yusuf Sarfati

58 **Turkey's Democratization Process**
  Edited by Carmen Rodríguez, Antonio Avaloz, Hakan Yilmaz and Ana I. Planet

59 **The Formation of Kurdishness in Turkey**
  Ramazan Aras

60 **Egyptian Foreign Policy From Mubarak to Morsi**
  Nael Shama

61 **The Politics of Truth Management in Saudi Arabia**
  Afshin Shahi

62 **Transitional Justice and Human Rights in Morocco**
  Fadoua Loudiy

63 **Contemporary Kemalism**
  Toni Alaranta

64 **Urbicide in Palestine**
  Nurhan Abujidi

65 **The Circassian Diaspora in Turkey**
  Zeynel Abidin Besleney

66 **Multiculturalism and Democracy in North Africa**
  Edited by Moha Ennaji

67 **Strategic Relations Between the US and Turkey, 1979–2000**
Ekavi Athanassopoulou

68 **Ethnicity and Elections in Turkey**
Gül Arıkan Akdağ

69 **The Kurdish Liberation Movement in Iraq**
Yaniv Voller

70 **Arab Regionalism**
Silvia Ferabolli

71 **The Kurdish Issue in Turkey**
Edited by Zeynep Gambetti and Joost Jongerden

72 **The Turkish Deep State**
Mehtap Söyler

73 **Koreans in the Persian Gulf**
Shirzad Azad

74 **Europeanization of Turkey**
Ali Tekin and Aylin Güney

75 **Turkey's Kurdish Question**
H. Akin Unver

76 **The Israeli Conflict System**
Harvey Starr and Stanley Dubinsky

77 **Political Violence and Kurds in Turkey**
Mehmet Orhan

78 **The Europeanization of Turkish Public Policies**
Ali Tekin and Aylin Güney

79 **Diasporic Activism in the Israeli–Palestinian Conflict**
Svenja Gertheiss

80 **Israel's Military Operations in Gaza**
Marouf Hasian, Jr.

Israel's Military Operations in Gaza
Telegenic lawfare and warfare

Marouf Hasian, Jr.

LONDON AND NEW YORK

First published 2016 by Routledge

2 Park Square, Milton Park, Abingdon, Oxfordshire OX14 4RN
52 Vanderbilt Avenue, New York, NY 10017

Routledge is an imprint of the Taylor & Francis Group, an informa business

First issued in paperback 2019

Copyright © 2016 Marouf Hasian, Jr.

The right of Marouf Hasian, Jr. to be identified as author of this work has been asserted by him in accordance with sections 77 and 78 of the Copyright, Designs and Patents Act 1988.

All rights reserved. No part of this book may be reprinted or reproduced or utilized in any form or by any electronic, mechanical, or other means, now known or hereafter invented, including photocopying and recording, or in any information storage or retrieval system, without permission in writing from the publishers.

Notice:
Product or corporate names may be trademarks or registered trademarks, and are used only for identification and explanation without intent to infringe.

British Library Cataloguing in Publication Data
A catalogue record for this book is available from the British Library

Library of Congress Cataloging-in-Publication Data
Names: Hasian, Marouf Arif, author.
Title: Israel's military operations in Gaza : telegenic lawfare and warfare / Marouf Hasian, Jr.
Description: New York, NY : Routledge, [2016] | "2016 | Includes bibliographical references and index.
Identifiers: LCCN 2015039729 | ISBN 9781138125209 (hbk : alk. paper)
Subjects: LCSH: Arab-Israeli conflict. | Gaza Strip.
Classification: LCC DS119.76 .H3745 2016 | DDC 956.9405/4–dc23
LC record available at http://lccn.loc.gov/2015039729

ISBN: 978-1-138-12520-9 (hbk)
ISBN: 978-0-367-87641-8 (pbk)

Typeset in Times New Roman
by Wearset Ltd, Boldon, Tyne and Wear

Contents

Acknowledgments x

1 Telegenic lawfare and warfare and the rhetorical framing of Gaza conflicts 1

2 Domestic and international critiques of Israeli policies in Gaza, 2000–2013 31

3 Occupational hazards and the evolutionary, rhetorical development of Israeli targeted killing rationales 66

4 Disengagement from Gaza, "institutionalized impoverishment," and the biopolitics of Israeli pressuring of Gazans, 2005–2013 100

5 Arguing about the legality and legitimacy of Operation Protective Edge, 2014 120

6 Public diplomacy and the post-disengagement social media wars, 2005–2014 144

7 There are no "innocent civilians" in Gaza: coping with post-human framings of the Gaza Strip 182

Bibliography 214
Index 226

Acknowledgments

I would like to begin by thanking many of my colleagues in the Department of Communication at the University of Utah, who have helped create the type of academic environment that makes it easier to pursue what many here have called the "life of the mind." Our chair, Professor Kent Ono, tries to make sure we are all provided with both emotional and material support as we craft our essays and our books, and his very presence reminds us of the importance of scholarly inquiry. Our countless debates over lunch and in the hallways about the meaning of "critical rhetoric" or "vernacular" approaches to rhetorical situations has impacted the ways that I write about Gazan and Israeli populations. One of my other colleagues, Kevin DeLuca, has also been a constant source of inspiration as we have debated how to politicize Foucauldian genealogies or how to conceptualize public screens or how to operationalize rhetorical flows. Although we often disagree about social activism in the academy or the balancing of praxis and theory, his unique insights have helped me understand how to try to keep track of some of the intended and unintended consequences of social media coverage of Gaza conflicts.

Many of our present and former graduate students have also influenced the percolation and development of some of my ideas. Ammar S. Hussein always made sure that I kept this book on the front burner and that I took into account what was happening in the Gaza Strip, the West Bank, and other parts of the Middle East as I wrote about Operation Protective Edge. Dr. Megan McFarlane continually asked about the progress I was making on the book, and our shared interested in media representations of national security interests reminded me of the importance of media events as I wrote about the Israeli Iron Dome.

Dean Dianne Harris, the new dean of our College of Humanities, has provided me with a small research fund for books and other supplies that I needed as I worked weekly on this book. It is support like this from administrators that keeps faculty motivated, and I thank her for helping provide the funding for all the external hard drives and other back-up gear that I use for the storage of my research archives.

I would also like to thank Haneen Shafeeq Al-Ghabra, a doctoral candidate in the Communication Studies Department at the University of Denver, who has worked with me on several projects having to do with Palestinian identity and nationalism. Her critical feminist approach to the study of Middle East relations has influenced how I write about everything from the "separation" wall to the Palestinian BDS movement. She and I represent two different Palestinian generations working in the diaspora, but our common interests underscore the point that substantive change can only come through steadfastness, continual critique, and constant struggle.

There are several individuals or communities that provided me with some of the photographs, stills, infograms, and infographics that appear in this book, and I would like to thank them for allowing me to republish those materials in the various iterations of this book. I would also like to thank both Muhammad Sabah, the photographer who took some key pictures for B'Tselem, as well as Shirly Eran, for providing me with permission to reprint some of these images and for sending along the pictures of the destruction and ruins of parts of Beit Hanoun. I would also like to thank the Israel Defense Force (IDF) for allowing the open dissemination of many of the infographics and infograms that appear on IDF webpages. While some of these communities may not agree with some of my assessments and critiques of these materials, I nevertheless appreciate the open spirit of intellectual exchange that allows for the crafting of different interpretations of what happened during Operation Protective Edge.

I would just like to thank Ashleigh and the other project managers and copy editors who worked on this for helping improve the style and substance of the manuscript. There are several people who work for Routledge that I would like to thank. First of all, without Joe Whiting's early support this project would never have taken off. I would also like to thank Holly Jones, who sent along all of the needed forms and checked in with me to keep apprised of the progress I was making on the book during the last few months. It is a pleasure to work with professionals who also care about the details that need to go into the final production of books like this.

1 Telegenic lawfare and warfare and the rhetorical framing of Gaza conflicts

For Charles Krauthammer and many other defenders of Israeli policies in Gaza, it is absurd to believe that there is more than one moral story that needs to be told about the events that led up to what Israelis call Operation Protective Edge. We routinely hear this Israel–Gaza fighting described as a morally equivalent "cycle of violence," he noted, and he thought that this was "absurd." "What possible interest can Israel have in cross-border fighting?" he asked in July 2014, as he commented on how Hamas' rockets were producing "dead Palestinians for international television."[1]

In his narration of events, Israel, a magnanimous nation, left Gaza in 2005, pulled die-hard settlers off synagogue roofs, expelled its own citizens, and handed the Palestinians in Gaza greenhouses in a symbolic gesture of peace. For those who believe in his mythic world, the Israelis are the morally superior social actors who have done more than their fair share in granting political concessions to terrorist organizations like Hamas. Figurative olive branches have been handed to those who once talked of destroying Israel.

In this very popular American variation of the tale, Israeli utopias can be contrasted with Palestinian dystopias, and, by implication, moral clarity supposedly comes when international communities learn to leave Israel alone, to the point where viewers are not swayed by all of this telegenic propaganda. In other words, world audiences who see images of Palestinian dead are not supposed to let Hamas off the hook.

For those who are interested in the study of the ideological relationships that exist between textual argumentation and visual representation, Krauthammer's statement provides an example of what Rebecca Stein has called "inverted empathy," where "purity of arms mythology" is used to supply exculpatory images of Israeli humanity that "reiterates the central tenets of dominant Israeli discourses."[2] This is a fascinating phenomenon, for as Aeyal Gross and others have argued, it means that human rights talk can be appropriated by those who want to underscore the importance of the "security" rights of settlers or the national security "interests" of the Israeli State. Gross contends that this rhetorical posturing is used to create moral equivalence between the rights of settlers and the rights of Palestinians, and this in turn undermines the provisions of the Geneva Convention that were aimed at *protecting non-citizens* who have to live under the laws of occupying powers.[3] In order to rationalize the protection of select precious bodies and populations, the "other" has to die, or at least be dispossessed, in these legal, military, and biopolitical and thanatopolitical (politics of death) struggles.[4]

This book is written with the intention of showing readers that the Israelis are not the only victims who suffer from these episodic twenty-first-century Israeli–Palestinian conflicts, and that the people of Gaza are caught up in the maelstrom of war as Hamas tries to legitimate its terrorist strikes while Israelis respond with violent counterterrorist actions.[5] As I hope to show throughout this book, this is an incredibly complex situation, filled with competing narrations and interpretations of historical and contemporary events, and no one side has a monopoly on virtue. Both sides are trying to convince international audiences that their rights are being violated, and their deployment of "weaponized" social media has expanded the boundaries of those in the blogosphere who have to hear about the role that "international humanitarian law" (IHL) or the "law of armed conflict" (LOAC) should play in these Gazan conflicts.

Reading and writing about international law used to be the prerogative of a few select experts in the fields of law or international relations, but no more. The blogosphere is filled with commentaries on these topics from citizen-journalists, citizen-soldiers, and others who want to write or talk about the legality, legitimacy, or morality of Israeli strikes in Gaza.

As I write this book, journalists are publishing material on the prospects for lasting peace in the region, Egyptians are monitoring border closures in Gaza, critics comment on how Israeli youngsters circulate selfies showing support for the Israel Defense Forces (IDF), bloggers are still writing about the existential dangers posed by "terror" tunnels and Hamas rockets, and more than a few pundits worry about the viability of two-state solutions in Palestinian–Israeli contexts. Many recall the ceasefire that put an end to some 50 days of fighting, and mainstream newspapers contain stories about the legitimacy of targeting Gazan "infrastructure," the impact of social media wars, and the UN investigations that are reviewing potential violations of Geneva Convention regulations or principles.[6] This is just the tip of the iceberg when it comes to locating the tropes, *topoi*, narratives, myths, visuals, and countervisuals that are being circulated in countless transnational spheres, and Krauthammer's supposed "moral clarity" can only come from intentional or unintentional bracketing out of many complex factors in some difficult geopolitical situations.

Individuals like Krauthammer, who argue that Israel could not have any "possible interest" in cross-border fighting, are missing all of the short-term and long-term benefits that come from periodically terrorizing Gazan civilians, and these individuals conveniently forget that the firing of rockets has something to do with decades of occupation, blockades, and the restriction of mobility of entire populations. One UK newspaper described Gaza as "the world's largest outdoor prison," and this was before the latest round of fighting in that area.[7] National pride, expansionist sentiments, collective punishment of enemies, demographic pressures, and scarcity of resources have everything to do with this tragedy.

Gazan citizens, after all, can easily be blamed for the firing of those rockets and their own suffering. In the name of military necessity, Israelis have been able to maintain the "visual" and "virtual" occupation of Gaza, control Gazan sea, air, and land, turn electricity on and off, and use information from "good" West Bank collaborators to help with the carrying out of drone or helicopter attacks on "bad" terrorist leaders. At the same time, Hamas leaders, cognizant of their precarious position, have been handing out thousands of dollars to the Gazan families whose homes were destroyed during the latest Israeli incursion. Hamas supporters have their own narratives and mythologies, and they like to argue that their very survival is demonstrative evidence of Palestinian determination and steadfastness.

Myths and realities blur as Gazan civilians try to rebuild their lives while international communities, NGOs, and others write and talk about Hamas war crimes, the power of Israeli tanks, the blockading by Israeli naval vessels, and the F-16s that pound away at mosques, hospitals, schools, UN buildings, refugee camps, and police stations. The Israelis defend some of these practices by alleging that Hamas uses civilians as "human shields," and IDF websites and YouTube videos are supposed to render visible the complicity of those who hide the terrorists who fire rockets at Tel Aviv or Sderot.[8]

This raises a host of questions regarding disparate power relationships, and given the relative disempowerment of Mahmoud Abbas' Palestinian Authority and the vilification of Hamas, the Israelis are now in full control of the military and diplomatic fronts, and they have no incentive to negotiate with Palestinians or sign any peace treaties. The international communities who produce document after document complaining about Israeli practices during Operational Protective Edge have done little to end Israeli blockades, closures, or military incursions, and the Israelis know that time is on their side. Israelis often complain about the lawfare of their opponents, or the politicized use of courts, but the Israelis are themselves master rhetors who spend millions of shekels to train military lawyers in the art and science of strategic legal communication.

None of this happened overnight, and this book explains how, over the years (especially between 2001 and 2014), Israelis patrolled the Mediterranean Sea, formed economic blockades, fought off a "peace" flotilla, built a fence in Gaza, and helped distribute "humanitarian aid" during times of emergency in Gaza. Social media outlets were used to justify Israeli initiatives at the same time that military forces search for "terror" tunnels and rockets in Gaza. It is telling that in 2012, when the Israelis launched Operation Pillar Defense, they began their offensive by tweeting and posting videos about the targeted killing of Al-Jabari, a Palestinian militant.

At one time, before the second Intifada, there were many Israeli leftists who expressed the hope that Palestinians might become good neighbors after the end of what was called a "belligerent" occupation, but growing worries about violent terrorism dashed many of these plans. Separatist rhetorics replaced the earlier integrative discourses as hardline politicians like Ariel Sharon and Benjamin Netanyahu showed their constituents that they, too, were steadfast, and that they were determined to stop all sorts of terrorist threats.

4 *Telegenic lawfare and warfare*

The growing power of Hamas, and the apparent unwillingness of Gazan populations to follow the edicts of the West Bank Palestinian Authority, complicated matters for Israeli peace activists and others who supported Palestinian independence. By 2000, it could be argued that Israel's growing military and economic power was put on full display, and exasperated international critics made little headway as they tried to lobby for the formation of a "two-state" solution or alter Israeli securitization policies toward civilian populations. The very quest for Palestinian human rights, or calls for Gazan food security or economic freedom, were oftentimes viewed by Israelis as measures that only aided Hamas.

Israelis, who were convinced that the spread of their type of Zionist democracy represented the best hope for despairing Gazans, have learned to argue that Hamas, and Islamic fundamentalism, are the root causes of terrorist threats.

The rationale for this book

This book is intended to provide readers with a detailed, critical rhetorical study of Israel–Gaza relationships between 2000 and 2014, and it investigates the question of how elite and public audiences in Israel have gradually come to accept the militarizing narratives that focus attention on the social agency of Hamas. As I note below, countless military and legal arguments are used by those who have trouble expressing open sympathy with the more than 1.8 million Gazans who refuse to bow to Israeli will, and the "Hamas regime" becomes a cipher for all of the ills that are posed by recalcitrant Palestinians.

Again, talk about moral clarity becomes myopic when defenders of the seventh largest military force in the world act as if the Israelis are the only victims in these complex affairs. There is a reason why Benny Morris, one of the most famous historians writing on some of these conflicts, titled one of his books *Righteous Victims*.[9] Morris traced how competing mythologies—that go back to the time of the Haganah—have influenced the trajectory of Israeli reactions to Palestinian–Israeli and Arab–Israeli affairs. Benny Morris often writes about how Jews are the real victims who have suffered for 2,000 years, and he likes to frame his history using a rhetorical lens that sees Israelis as a small minority surrounded by a large number of threatening Arabs. Morris' partisan historiography at least tries to do more than provide simplistic or reductionist pictures of the causes of episodic violence in this region. As Rashid Khalidi has recently argued, the problems in Gaza, and the "question of Palestine," have been deeply imbricated in the domestic histories that are told of the great colonial powers, and he notes that Israel's "absolute control of Jerusalem, security, settlements, Israeli settlers, water, and land" shows that today there is "not even an intimation of parity" as Palestinians still fight for their self-determination or independence.[10] Yet the Israelis, through their militarist and humanistic rationales for Operation Protective Edge, are busy rhetorically crafting the *appearance of parity*.

A review of the elite and vernacular arguments that have been deployed between 2000 and 2014 illustrates how Israelis were gradually moving away from thinking about the "police" control of Palestinian populations in the West Bank and Gaza as they saw themselves involved in what they called "a new kind of conflict." Many foreigners criticized the Israelis for their treatment of Palestinians who live in a region that outsiders viewed as "occupied" territory, but the Israelis themselves counter this by arguing that they are simply "recovering" those promised lands that have belonged to indigenous Jews since at least the time of King David. As many readers are aware, Israelis use the term "disputed" territory when they debate with their detractors, and instead of mentioning the "West Bank" they talk about "Judea" or "Samaria," and their legal texts often mention how Israeli courts use their "Basic" laws as they regulate the daily affairs of those who have to fight off terrorist foes.

In some cases defenders of Israeli policies go so far as to argue that the Israeli Supreme Court, as well as the IDF's International Law Branch (DABLA), have helped reign in the Israeli militaries as they tried to protect Palestinians and their rights. Amichai Cohen and Stuart A. Cohen, for example, writing in 2011, could even outline examples of these efforts:

> Under his [Justice Aharon Barak] influence, from the year 2000 the Court began to hand down several decisions declaring military actions and decisions to be void, on the grounds of their incompatibility with IHL. Notable examples include: the neighbor policy decision (2002; declaring illegal the IDF's use of non-combatant Palestinian neighbors and relatives to help arrest wanted suspects in the territories); the cluster of Rafah decisions ... the separation barrier decisions ... and the targeting killing decisions ... allowing the use of targeted killings only if certain strict conditions are fulfilled.[11]

What Cohen and Cohen glossed over, however, were the ways that this Israeli court took for granted that it had the right to decide these matters, and how minor concessions based on what they called "soft power" legal acceptability contributed to settler expansionism and other forms of dispossession. Their work does, however, represent fairly typical ways of legitimating Israeli warfare and lawfare.

During the first and second decades of the twenty-first century many Israelis have argued that their leftist critics simply do not understand the nature and scope of the existential threats that are posed by organizations like Hezbollah in Lebanon or Hamas in Gaza, and they claim that their own High Court's (IHC) interpretation of IHL ought to provide a model for other nations. This, in effect, has meant that for some 15 years most Israeli newspapers, journal articles, law reviews, military reports, Ministry of Foreign Affairs blogs, and other persuasive texts were crafted by those who assume that Israelis were *always* on a war footing with Palestinian populations that were once regarded as potential neighbors.

What I will argue here is that this paradigmatic shift in argumentation, which focuses on militarization or securitization, and not on policing, has also impacted the ways we talk and write about the protection of Gazan civilian populations. In the name of fighting terrorism we are asked to adopt conceptual paradigms that invite us to forget that many of the Gazans are refugees, or communities that might be covered by the "law of occupation." Instead of studying the historical and contemporary causes of their wretched conditions, we are supposed to see them as the "voluntary" human shields who enable Hamas to fire rockets into Israel "proper" or into Israeli settlements. By the time of the ceasefire in August 2014, more than 2,050 Palestinians had died during Operation Protective Edge, and some estimate that it may take decades before Gazans can recover from this particular incursion.

When we read essays like Krauthammer's, and other texts that have been written by those who share his views, we may recognize what looks like familiar and naturalized ways of thinking about the "facts" regarding Hamas and linkages to terrorism, but I contend that decision-makers and publics often forget about the discursive formations, the erasures, and the selective usage of rhetorics that helped usher in these cycles of violence. We therefore need critical decodings and demystifications that can help readers see the cumulative, long-term instantiation and effect of that paradigmatic shift away from thinking about peaceful resolutions to Israeli–Palestinian problems. This is the only way we can see how the Gazans are caught between the terrorism of Hamas and the counterterrorism of the Israelis.

Countless Israelis, American supporters of Israeli policies, and others who accept the vilification of Hamas or Palestinian Gazans have essentially given up on the idea of "territory for security" solutions, and in the rest of this book I try to explain how this happened in such a short span of time. Granted, many of the textual fragments and visual arguments that I will be studying in various chapters draw on "always already" and overdetermined historical shards of Israeli and Palestinian memories, but between 2000 and 2014 we witnessed an increased volume of the shrill advocacy that parallels that escalation of violence in Gaza.

What were the motivations of those who contributed to this sad affair, and what were some of the vectors of politicized legal arguments that were used by Israeli jurists, military legal advisers, and American law review authors when they read commentaries like Krauthammer's? What have been some of the dominant stories that mention various causes and effects of terrorism, and why haven't international actors, who claim they have a "responsibility to protect" (R2P), interceded in these Gazan conflicts? Is all of this talk of "international law" constraints just one more example of what Walter Benjamin, Jacques Derrida, and Judith Butler called lawmaking or law preserving violence?[12] Are these "terrorist" frames of analysis helping with the securitization of Israel?

A growing number of commentators have noted how many of these questions are being posed in jurisprudential contexts where both the Israelis and their detractors discuss the legality of particular military strategies, tactics, and operations in places like the Gaza Strip. For example, when bloggers write about the Israeli "Dahiya Doctrine," are they referring to a military doctrine that advocates the harsh treatment of Lebanese civilian populations in order to pressure those who needed to turn against Hezbollah? Is Darryl Li being fair when he argues that, since 2005, Israel has sought to turn Gaza into a place of experimentation for "colonial management," where Benjamin Netanyahu tries to secure as "much land as possible" with "as few Palestinians as possible"?[13] If Israel's detractors are going to complain about blockades, targeted killings, the formation of buffer zones, fences, the "separation barrier," etc. then what are they suggesting the IDF or Shin Bet (the secret service) do about suicide bombers and the firing of rockets by Hamas?

I am convinced that readers need to understand the influential nature of the arguments that are now used to turn Gazan civilians into Hamas' "infrastructure." If experts, academics, and lay persons are going to study the post-second Intifada shift toward the adoption of "armed conflict" paradigms, then we need to see these changes from multiple vantage points. As Matthew Cohen and Charles Freilich recently noted in their essay, "The Delegitimation of Israel, Diplomatic Warfare, Sanctions, and Lawfare," Israel has "repeatedly been a prime target of delegitimation" since 1948.[14] What they don't of course acknowledge is that some of this is due to the fact that Israelis use war footings to legitimate the taking over of East Jerusalem, the maintenance of a controversial separation wall, the denial of rights of return for Palestinians in the diaspora, and incursions into Gaza.

During this same period Gazans have had to deal with a host of cultural, structural and material factors that have influenced the constitutive co-production of many partial, contingent, motivated, and contradictory rhetorics. For example, there are cultural and tactical reasons why the Israelis have not adopted the US "hearts and minds" counterinsurgency (COIN) strategies that were popularized by former General David Patraeus and his followers in Iraq, and reactionary Israeli policies were not things that were dreamed up by solitary individual Israeli hardliners like Ariel Sharon or Benjamin Netanyahu. This move away from talk of "belligerent occupation" is a *communal, transgenerational and populist change* within Israel that reflects and refracts both elite and popular Israeli opinion. As I note in many of my chapters, these empowered audiences are dangerously close to configuring all Gazans as terrorists.

As one analyzes the mounds of material that have been produced since 2000 one realizes that fewer and fewer Israelis are listening to the voices of leftist critics who, ironically, are gaining more of a voice in international circles. Organizations like B'Tselem, one of the most prominent of the Israeli human rights groups, have produced countless statistics, photographic images, and other materials for international critics of Israel policies, but some Israeli television audiences have recently been told that B'Tselem has "crossed the line in wartime [by] campaigning and inciting against the state of Israel and the Israel Defence Force, which is the most moral of armies."[15] The recent revelations in 2015 from soldiers testifying about their Operation Protective Edge experiences for Breaking the Silence, as well as the mainstream reactions to those revelations, is telling, as ordinary Israeli citizens join their military generals and political leaders in denouncing those who do not understand Hamas prevarications.[16]

8 *Telegenic lawfare and warfare*

After years of hearing about Arafat's "missed opportunities" for peace during the Oslo Accords or the Cairo meetings, and after witnessing countless debates about how to best stop the firing of Qassam missiles and the digging of tunnels in Gaza, Israelis seem to have given up hope that this generation, or any other generation, can peacefully resolve what appear to be intractable problems. Everything from the celebration of the building of the "Iron Dome" to the public acceptance of "liquidation" killing rationales speak volumes about the ineffectiveness of the arguments of the leftists. Given asymmetric power relations, moderate and conservative Israelis can ignore the clarion calls of those NGOs, foreign national states, and others who have been complaining about Israeli policies throughout the early decades of the twenty-first century.

If I am right, it is not a stretch to argue that at the same time Israelis have been able to fend off attacks on their actions—like their containment of the infamous Goldstone Report that critiqued Operation Cast Lead (2008–2009)—they have also been able to create the impression that their unique Zionist form of democracy should light the way for other nations who are looking for efficacious counterterrorism policies. In other words, Israelis are not shy about arguing that they can outsource their legal decisions on occupation or counterterrorism so that other nations can profit from the wisdom that is dispensed by the IHC and IDF. What outsiders view as indiscriminate attacks on helpless Gazan civilians are treated by Israelis as "precise" attacks on the homes, schools, and mosques that house dangerous Hamas weaponry. This all assumes that Israeli "situational awareness" comes from decades of fighting terrorism, and that within Israel one finds the neo-realists, and the legal and military experts in the art and science of "deterring" terrorism. Permutations of this metanarrative can then be disseminated though countless official and non-official social media outlets. This is part of the "hasbara," or strategic diplomacy, that will be discussed in more detail in later chapters.

The chapters in this book are meant to provide readers with an explanation of how this Israeli pride in counterterrorism developed, and I unpack the constitutive rhetorics that went into the formulation of what some scholars and journalists call "Israeli exceptionalism."[17] As an activist by the name of Brad Parker argues, if the Israeli Ambassador to the UN, Eviatar Manor, hopes to get across his messages regarding the "deep-rooted notion of Israeli exceptionalism," then Israeli leaders will have to take "responsibility for what is truly exceptional; a 46-year-old occupation where systematic discrimination and persistent human rights violations are deeply entrenched and impunity reigns."[18]

This obviously is not the way that Israelis talk about the situation, and Israelis can counter this by arguing that they actually have minimal control over Gaza. They contend that a review of their actions since 2005 will show that they have worked to reduce suffering in the refugee camps by allowing in "humanitarian aid," and they often juxtapose this with the efforts of a Hamas regime that wastes its money on rockets and weaponry.

Some of this disputation migrates into legal realms, and there are some formalists and positivists who would like to believe that all of this violence, and at least some of this acrimonious disputation, could be contained by those who work away at trying to define, describe, and explain the IHL principles of "proportionality" that should be used in debates about *jus ad bellum* (reasons to go to war in the first place) or *jus in bello* (modes of war, or how we act once we go to war) doctrines. These are important concepts, but they are malleable and indeterminate, and simply reciting their importance does not help us understand the ideological nature of their application by foreign governments or the UN Security Council in Gazan contexts. Why, for example, haven't these vaunted principles been used to spur interventionist practices? How has this IHL rights talk constrained the efforts of Israelis who can *always magnify the existential threats of terrorism* so that they can argue that their strikes in Gaza are proportional, in that their military gains outweigh the potential civilian losses?

In other words, until we see how these philosophical ideas are put into actual practice, then we miss the ways that everyone in these disputes is referencing the same IHL materials. Rights talk can enable, as well as constrain, warfare.

This is why we need a book that focuses on the argumentative features of these controversies, so that we can see how both formalistic jurisprudential arguments, as well as IDF social media messages, are converging in ways that allow elite and public Israeli audiences to feel good about the justness of their cause. For example, a critical genealogical approach to argumentation, that traces the migration of "lawfare" arguments in several different venues, allows us to see how military colonels and young Israeli audiences share similar scopic visions of Hamas and civilian social agency in Gaza. Again, all of this helps those who want to claim that most, or all, Gazan citizens can become thanatopolitical bodies living in "infrastructures" who lost their Geneva Conventions protections when they were "participating" in "armed conflict." It is the rhetorical nature of these types of lexical and visual shifts that are often missed in other arhetorical studies and traditional analyses of these conflicts.

It is no coincidence that some of the same law review writers who want to give counterterrorist armies latitude in their characterization of these participants are some of the most vocal defenders of drone attacks on enemies in Afghanistan, Pakistan, or Gaza. Many of these writers like to follow the lead of military authors who talk about how "new" wartime conditions call for changes in the rules of engagement or the "lessons learned" from early incursions, and patriotic legal authors similarly try to influence the interpretations of the IHL that could be applied in German, Spanish, or Belgian courts that may put in the docks those who bomb Gazan civilians. Depending on one's rhetorical situation, select interpretations of the IHL can serve as swords or shields.[19]

Again, we do need to familiarize ourselves with some of the legalese that circulates in legal opinions, treatises or law reviews, but it would be a mistake to think that an *exclusive* focus on Israeli judicial opinions or texts on international interpretations of the IHL is going to help us understand all of the rhetorical dynamics of these situations. We should also value theories and perspectival approaches that underscore the importance of studying the cultural, economic, political, and social views of the average Israeli citizen or Gazan who may never read an entire IHC opinion. Diverse audiences care about the framing of the actions of the "most moral army" in the world, and they keep track of IDF activities, but these interpretive communities use modes of argumentation and social networking that look nothing like the formalistic reasoning that appears in traditional IHL or international relations analyses.

Since 2000 many branches of the Israeli government, including the IDF and the Israeli Foreign Ministry, have become heavily invested in social media and "public diplomacy," and some of the bombings in Gaza are now shown in "real time" as many Israelis and others are invited to become witnesses to the securitizing wars that have to be fought in the name of destroying those who allegedly seek Israel's destruction. Note, for example, how Rebecca Stein, in her essay on "How Israeli Militarized Social Media,"[20] underscores the point that the Israeli mainstream media dealt with the presence of the telegenically Palestinian dead of Operation Protective Edge by "removing most traces" of them from national news broadcasts.[21] As Professor Stein explains, images like these are produced because:

> Today, Israelis are also concerned about losing the media war. But they tell the story differently. In their rending, the Israeli media problem is a by-product of damning or doctored images ... of Palestinian media manipulation, or global anti-Israel cum anti-Semitic bias.... As in Gaza campaigns of the past, many Israelis deem their [Palestinian dead] tantamount to national slander.... And for mainstream Israeli publics, who overwhelming back the current operation, @IDFSpokesman tweets will continue to resound convincingly: the only moral army, their existential threat, we had no choice, #IsraelUnderFire.[22]

All of this creates incredible difficulties for the Israeli leftists and others in Israel who want to form alliances with outside critics who worry about the episodic violence that is destroying so many Gazan homes, social bonds, and economies.

A critical rhetorical approach that extends the work of Michel Foucault and others interested in genealogical studies may provide a fruitful way of organizing the research so that readers can see why post-2000 conversations about terrorism in the Middle East resonate with so many pro-Israel audiences. It would be a mistake to be summarily dismissive of the emotive, often Kafkaesque ways that purveyors of just war rhetorics or "armed conflict" scenarios justify dispensing violence in the name of searching for peace.

No one scholar can exhaustively cover every key historical incident that may have contributed to the discursive or visual formation of provocative *epistemes* and *dispositifs*, but a critical researcher interested in genealogical studies can provide helpful and representative examples of how select argumentative fragments have been used in evolutionary and incremental ways to further the cause of those who would militarize Gaza while they solidify their hold on Judea and Samaria.

I am convinced that a comprehensive, critical rhetorical study of multiple fragments circulating in myriad venues will allow us to see the protean, and the dynamic nature of the rhetorical flows that my colleague Kevin DeLuca calls "image events."[23] These types of genealogical studies, that trace the repetitive and argumentative nature of military flows and legal contestations, enable us to see the persuasive gain or loss of adherents as various arguers debate about what should be done during times of war and peace. Again, the discovery of some mythic moral clarity is not the goal here, especially when that supposed moral clarity is used to rationalize the perennial destruction of Gaza.

With this in mind, let me briefly elaborate on what I mean when I talk about these perspectival approaches.

The heuristic value of humanistic, perspectival approaches to the study of Israeli counterterrorism

In this particular study, I extend the work of Michel Foucault,[24] Judith Butler, Jacques Derrida, Eyal Weizman, Neve Gordon, Derek Gregory, and others who have adopted post-structural or post-modern ways of viewing how societies and military cultures have dealt with twenty-first-century terrorism. This type of approach resembles functionalist ways of thinking of large-scale massacres, disasters, or genocides because it invites researchers to pay attention to massive numbers of fragmented and mobile texts instead of single public addresses, videos, or websites.

As I noted above, the assumption behind many post-structural approaches is that too many modernists commit the intentionalist fallacy when they focus on the discourse of a single rhetor or only one decision-maker, because that focus does not get at the power or epistemic dimensions that are created when large communities share motivations as they make key life and death decisions. Michel Foucault and Eyal Weizman, for example, have written about how states can deploy rhetorics aimed at the preservation of life (biopolitics) as well as discourses that politicize death (thanatopolitics). Many humanists have now extended this type of work as they analyze the treatment of detainees in Guantánamo, as they critique the CIA's infamous "torture memos," as they assess the use of drones over the skies of Iraq, Afghanistan, or Pakistan, or as they note the growing power of the US military's Joint Special Operations Command (JSOC). There may be times when those who adopt these perspectival ways of conceptualizing power do analyze single documents, tweets, military reports, etc., but these are then linked to the larger "discursive production" of various journalistic, military, or "pseudo-judicial" processes.[25]

Those interdisciplinary scholars who deploy these types of perspectival approaches are constantly paying attention to what might be included or excluded in particular discourses or visualities, and oftentimes they are interested in tracing the evolutionary nature of arguments, or genealogies, that show us the historical "winners" and "losers" of rhetorical disputation. This orientation reminds us that our archives, libraries, think-tanks, and blogosphere are filled with the accretions and relics of bygone discursive and iconic battles. Regardless of the issue or topic we are studying, the complexities of life, and the existence of countless motives, national anxieties, individual subject positions, and changing life situations means that we are born into a prefigurative world that is "always already" there.

One of the best illustrations of the heuristic value of this type of approach, that is directly related to many of the topics that I cover in this book, appears in an incredibly insightful essay written by Neve Gordon, entitled "Rationalising Extra-Judicial Executions." In that essay, Professor Gordon studied literally hundreds of articles that appeared in Israel's three major newspapers—*Yedioth Ahronoth*, *Ma'ariv*, and *Ha'aretz*—so that he could show some of the major "emplotments" and other rhetorical devices that were used by Israelis in the aftermath of the second Intifada to justify and rationalize Israel's targeted killing policies. Professor Gordon argued that his study of the journalistic coverage of the targeting of Ahmad Khalil As'ad, Thabet Thabet, and many other Palestinian dead could show how the Israeli newspapers were often recirculating materials and emplotments that came from the IDF as they constructed partial, contingent, and patriot narratives. For example, the newspaper outlets that he studied used a spectrum of details, data, and figures as they crafted narratives that vindicated Israeli decision-making regarding assassinations, and he shows that some of the same rhetorical figurations appeared over and over again as these outlets helped establish the guilt of those who were targeted. Professor Gordon argued that the connection of many Palestinians to the attacks on the Dolphinarium discothèque in Tele-Aviv, or the Sbarro Pizza establishment in Jerusalem, or the Park Hotel in Netanya during the Passover, helped prove that many of those killed either "had blood on their hands" or were "ticking time bombs."[26] Gordon concludes that the strategic usage of these employments, or sense-making narratives, created a situation where "Israel is absolved of wrongdoing since it [targeted killing] saves Israeli lives while at the same time carrying out those executions in a moral way."[27] I want to show that this type of operative logic *migrated* into other contexts as decisions had to be made about the bombing of Gazan homes, mosques, schools, and hospitals.

In order to reach his conclusions Gordon had to pay attention to the way the arrest records of thousands of Palestinians were being handled and categorized after the first and second Intifada, and he had to keep track of what was emphasized and de-emphasized in order to come up with coherent and persuasive tales that became a part of Israeli "collective memory." This, I contend, is an excellent model for those of us who want to use genealogical analyses.

Adopting this type of perspectival approach is challenging because the critic is trying to keep track of both micro-features of grammars and smaller artifacts as well as more macro-*epistemes*, or sedimented knowledges that circulated in military, legal, diplomatic, or public cultures. The goal here is be able to discover, and to explain, the existence of dominant rhetorical themes as well as the potential motivations of large communities *who act on the basis* of those themes. For example, I will be arguing that many different generations of Israeli social agents, including IDF leaders and former Air Force colonels and generals, were just some of those who helped co-produce the infamous "Dahiya Doctrine" that I mentioned above.[28]

From a post-structuralist perspective, those who commit the intentionalist fallacy of linking the Dahiya doctrine to thoughts or words of just one or two individuals miss the cultural resonance of this phrase and the power dynamics of a situation that allowed many Israelis to fight against Hezbollah in Lebanon in particular ways. Unlike more modernist approaches that might treat Richard Goldstone as the primary "author" of the famous Goldstone Report,[29] a critical genealogical approach would view this as just an "apparently finished" text that contains many fragmentary arguments.[30] While such an approach would acknowledge the limited social agency and the material constraints that were faced by the four members of the "fact-finding mission on the Gaza Conflict" who were appointed by the Human Rights Council of the UN General Assembly, it would recognize the fact that this report was just a compendium, a typical condensation symbol of the many other arguments. The Goldstone Report, for example, can be viewed as a *symbolic text* that represented the arguments that had been produced by NGO observers and others who lived alongside Gazans and could testify about the same potential violations that were discussed in this text.

This is important because the attempted discrediting of the Goldstone report, by pointing to a single retraction by Richard Goldstone, does not mean that the entire report was flawed or that Operation Cast Lead was some legal military operation. The material realities in Gaza were *not* going to be physically altered by the acceptance or rejection of the representations of these realities that appeared in the Goldstone Report.

In other words, from a post-structuralist standpoint, the critics of the Goldstone Report were confusing the epistemic coverage of these material events with the ontological existence of the violence that was perpetrated in Gaza.

From a post-structuralist vantage point the Goldstone Report was simply a persuasive text that stitched together many of the complaints that had been lodged against Israeli militarists by Gazan refugees, Israeli peace advocates, Palestinians living in the West Bank, writers in the diaspora, NGOs and others *for more than a decade*.

In this particular book one of my challenges will be to convince readers that incremental, micro-changes have been made in the ways that Israelis have talked and written about Palestinian terrorists, politicians, and civilians between 2000 and 2014, and that these smaller changes were linked to larger securitization rhetorics and other military or legal emplotments. This is why you will see me referring to mini- and macro-Israeli stories and paradigms that were used to convince domestic and international audiences that the Israelis were the aggrieved parties who were forced to use military tactics in the "disputed territories" during a continued "armed conflict."

As noted above, critical rhetoricians who adopt these genealogical approaches are looking for *recurring patterns of argumentation* that serve as the grammatical scaffolding of some of these emplotments, and a review of the Israeli arguments that swirled around Gaza between 2000 and 2014 shows this evolutionary trajectory:

1   In the beginning of the twenty-first century we were left with residual pre-2000 descriptions of discriminating attacks on clearly identified, individual terrorist leaders, but this was gradually replaced with;
2   talk of discriminating attacks on terrorist leaders, bomb-makers, terrorist financiers, that expanded in the direction of;
3   discriminating attacks on all of the above as well as Fatah, Hamas, or Hezbollah "politicians" who occupied multiple subject positions. These new Israeli targets appeared by day to be innocent civilians, while at night they engaged in nefarious terrorist activities. By 2006, Israelis were willing to write defenses of;
4   indiscriminate attacks on collective Gazan civilian populations who were either
    a   terrorists themselves,
    b   persons who helped use the embargo, tunnels, etc., or people who bought in supplies to terrorists, or
    c   collectives that allowed themselves to be used as "human shields," as evidenced by their continued election of Hamas officials or their obstinate refusal to leave their homes after receiving Israeli warnings.

What the adoption of my perspectival approach will help explain are the ways that the evolution of these types of arguments was appearing at the same time that Israeli decision-makers and citizens were re-characterizing Gaza. Before 2005 it was the land that might be another place where the Israelis could make the "desert bloom," filled with settlements, but all of this changed as they recycling a permutation of an old adage—"a land without a people for a people without a land."[31] Talk of the complicity of Gazan civilians just happened to coincide with the 2006 takeover of Gaza by Hamas, and this in turn emboldened some of the Israeli hardliners who openly declared that it was not in the best interest of Gazan citizens to stay in Gaza.

While Israelis are often willing to admit that thanatopolitical representations of Gazan dead are problematic, they accuse Hamas and their supporters of performing terrorist acts that perpetuate this state of affairs. Some academics who critique some of this discourse, including Achille Mbembe, have a different way of talking about the responsibilities and the limits of state sovereignty. Mbembe, in his famous "Necropolitics" essay, once argued:

> Gaza and the West Bank presents three major characteristics in relation to the working of the specific terror formation I have called necropolitics. First is the dynamics of territorial fragmentation, the sealing off and the expansion of settlements ... contemporary forms of subjugation of life to the power of death (necropolitics) profoundly reconfigure the relations among resistance, sacrifice, and terror ... occupation of the skies therefore acquires a critical importance.... Killing becomes precisely targeted. Such precision is combined with the tactics of medieval siege warfare adapted to the networked sprawl of urban refugee camps ... in other words, *infrastructural warfare* [emphasis in the original].[32]

Telegenic lawfare and warfare 15

This type of critique is incredibly prescient, in that the term "infrastructure" became one of those 2014 buzzwords that was used by those who wanted to use infographics and other mediums to argue that Gazan civilian homes became legitimate military targets.

Mbembe's approach infuriates many Israelis, because it focuses on the social agency of the IDF or other empowered Israeli decision-makers, and Israelis believe that this deflects attention away from the decisions that are made by Hamas, terrorist supporters, or those who elect terrorists to political positions of power.

Rhetorical status and epistemic authority are at the heart of many of these contentious debates. Outside critics may try to paint Israelis as colonial or neo-colonial reactionaries, but the Israelis themselves see their post-2005 Gaza incursions as experiences that turned them into realists. This, in turn, allows them to gain the moral high ground as they give talks in the United States and elsewhere on how to deal with the misperceptions of those who do not know how to leave behind their antiquated policing paradigms.

For those who hold these views, some enlightened Americans have gotten the picture, and more US law review authors and conference planners understand the real problems with critics' usage of "telegenically dead," but many Europeans, members of the African Union, the Arab League, NGOs, etc. simply don't get it.

Besides explaining some of the structural and material features of the seemingly interminable debates that take place regarding who is, and who is not a civilian or terrorist "target" in Gaza contexts, this book also underscores the importance of the geopolitical dynamics of the arguments that take place as observers debate about the meanings of concepts such as "occupation," state sovereignty, disengagement, and buffer zones. All of this touches on what Eyal Weizman has conceptualized as the "forensic architectures" that are used for Israeli Zionist projects.[33]

Weizman explains that since the 1967 War, the Israeli occupation of the West Bank and Gaza has involved a massive project of strategic, territorial planning that has involved everything from the architectural building of walls to the use of lawfare that rationalizes the fragmentation and control of scarce resources. Weizman invites us to leave behind our traditional "two-dimensional" way of thinking about the Palestinian–Israeli conflicts so that we can see more multidimensional displays of power that involve the layering of "strategic, religious and political strata."[34] Given Prime Minister Netanyahu's commentary on the persuasive power of telegenic argument, this seems to be an apt way of helping me frame my analyses.

What is fascinating to observe in these academic debates about territories, occupations, and other geopolitical configurations are the ways that both Israeli defenders of incursions into Gaza, as well as their detractors, have been influenced by some intriguing post-structural, post-modern, and post-colonial ideas. For example, when brigadier generals of the Israel Armed Forces, Aviv Kokhavi and Shimon Havey, tried to explain some of the ways the IDF was going to conduct future urban warfare in some of the occupied territories, they turned to the work of thinkers like Bernard Tschumi, Guy Debord, Gilles Deleuze, and Felix Guattari as they engaged in new "micro-tactical actions."[35] After watching maneuvers in places like Nablus, some of these innovative Israeli military planners began to alter the ways they fought in streets, roads, alleys, or courtyards. Instead of following the traditional, linear, and orderly pathways that might lead to excessive Israeli casualties, the innovators thought outside the box as they moved horizontally through walls of civilian homes so that they could fight the "infestation" of terrorists. "The IDF's strategy of 'walking-through walls,'" argued Eyal Weizman, "involved a conceptualization of the city as not just the site, but the very medium of warfare—a flexible, almost liquid medium that is forever contingent and in flux."[36] Ironically, education in the humanities—often "believed to be the most powerful weapon against imperialism" was being "appropriated as a powerful weapon of imperialism."[37]

One of the key geopolitical difficulties, of course, has to do with the issue of whether these types of "post-human" framings of micro-activities are an inherent aspect of Israeli control and surveillance of Gaza. While the Israelis see themselves as reluctant interveners who are merely trespassing so that they can defend their nation from Hamas missiles, many other parts of the world see some of this telegenic warfare through very different lenses.

By the time of the August 5, 2014 withdrawal of Israel troops from Gaza, so that the Israelis could get to their "defensive positions" outside the Palestinian territory, some 1,800 Palestinians and 67 Israelis had been killed.[38] Places like Shuja'iyya, a neighborhood district of Gaza City that was east of the city center, were leveled.

Shuja'iyya would be one of the Gazan communities that witnessed some of the most intense fighting between Hamas forces and the Israeli military, and this horrific violence resulted in the deaths of 72 Palestinians and 13 Israel soldiers. Israeli critics posted a video that allegedly showed an Israeli sniper killing a wounded Palestinian, and images of what became known as the "Shuja'iyya massacre"[39] went viral as all the sides in this conflict used both mainstream and alternative press outlets to tell their competing sides of what was happening. Israeli critics commented on how Israeli troops were firing on 65-year-old Ahmed Suleiman Akram Al-'Atawai and his ten-year-old grandchild, Tala, who were running away from the onslaught, and others were said to have been killed when shells either hit their homes or when they tried to rescue the wounded. Eran Efrati, a former combat soldier in the Israeli army turned whistleblower, was valorized by Israeli detractors when he was reportedly arrested after posting "Israel troops killed Gaza citizens in revenge" on *Facebook*.[40]

Israeli framings of what was happening in places like Shuya'iyya focused on the "limited" nature of the ground operation. What supposedly began as the "specific" targeting of the tunnels that were in a "relatively narrow strip of around 1.5 kilometers from the border fence" suddenly "expanded 48 hours later into a full-scale onslaught on Shuya'iyya and its environs."[41] The Israeli focus on what many military experts call the "fog of war" provides one more horrific example of the horrors, the ambiguities, and the general messes of what Antoine Bousquet calls "chaoplexic warfare."[42]

When Israeli officials drop leaflets or send email messages about impending strikes on Hamas targets that are in civilian regions, does this provide sufficient indication that they are complying with some of the basic tenets of IHL? Or does the practice of giving civilian residents in Gaza a little time to vacate their homes only provide a "self-sanitizing gesture"[43] that assuages the guilt of Israeli domestic audiences but does little to mute the criticisms of international detractors who complain about neo-colonial adventurism or violations of the letter and spirit of IHL principles? When Israelis go after the Hamas tunnels in Gaza are they fairly exercising their inherent rights of self-defense under the UN Charter, or is all of this rhetoric masking illegitimate forms of collective punishment against Palestinian populations? What do readers and decision-makers do in situations where both Hamas and the Israelis may be involved in the perpetration of war crimes or crimes against humanity?

Who should be blamed, and who should have the most responsibility, in situations like this? Is it really fair to call Israel one of the last "settler" colonies,[44] or to argue that Israelis are engaging in a form of collective punishment in order to force Palestinians to dissociate themselves from Hamas? Is this another example of the generative productive of "necessary suffering," or what Joseph Pugliese calls the "tutelary architecture" of the empowered who can detain at will?[45]

Granted, Israeli frames of these events have some resonance, but at various times since 2001 the Gaza Strip has been characterized as a massive prison, a "laboratory,"[46] or a humanitarian disaster. Some go so far as to talk about the presence or absence of jurisprudential norms, where Gaza is configured as some "black hole" or state of exception, a place populated by unruly Hamas fighters and IDF forces who set aside their scruples as they fight totalizing battles that catch civilians in crossfires and crosshairs.

One of the most intriguing claims that I need to grapple with in this book is Helga Tawil-Souri's contention that Israelis may feel that they have physically left Gaza behind, when in fact they continue what she calls Israel's "digital occupation."[47] Professor Tawil-Souri had this to say two years before the 2014 Gaza incursion:

> Disengagement has not meant an end of Israel occupation. Rather, Israel's balancing act "of maximum control and minimum" responsibility has meant that the occupation of Gaza has been increasingly technologized. Unmanned aerial reconnaissance and attack drones, remote-controlled machine guns, closed-circuit television, sonic imagery, gamma-radiation detectors, remote-controlled bulldozers and boats, electrified fences, among many other examples, are increasingly used for control and surveillance. One way to conceptualize disengagement, then, is to recognize it as a moment marking Israel's move from a traditional military occupation toward a high-tech one.[48]

All of this sounds remarkable, especially when we juxtapose this commentary with Prime Minister Netanyahu's commentary on the telegenically dead. Given the *realpolitik* nature of his subject position, we can readily understand why Netanyahu may not have wanted to admit Israel's own active role in all of these perceptual wars.

In sum, it could be argued that Hamas and the IDF have been waging physical, psychological, and perceptual warfare, and over the years the circulation of information about this warfare has gotten increasingly sophisticated. Each side claims to be conducting warfare in scrupulous ways that conform to their religious tenets.

Sometimes these complex battles are fought on jurisprudential terrains. For example, more and more lawyers comment on how the IDF follows the changing rules of engagement that can be found in their nation's judicial precedents, evolving military "operational" doctrines, and cultural norms. By November 2012, when Israel launched Operation Pillar of Defense, Israeli citizens could buy an app for their phones, called Red Alert Israel, that sent out a harrowing alert whenever a rocket was being fired into Israel.[49]

Other rocket attacks that targeted Israel—for example the Hezbollah rockets that were sent out in 2006 from Lebanon—may have caused many more Israeli casualties—but in these perceptual wars the 2012 threats were magnified when new telegenic vulnerabilities appeared on the literal and metaphoric screens of the Israelis. John Timpane, a reporter for the *Philadelphia Inquirer*, admitted that media campaigns had "gone to war since before the Sumerians," but by July 2014 it was becoming evident that the scale and the nature of these campaigns was changing. Timpane quotes Lawrence Husick, a senior fellow at the Center for the Study of Terrorism at the Foreign Research Policy Institute, who argued that Red Alert Israel brought a "punch in the gut" that gave "a dramatic sense of what it's like to live in a state of threat."[50] By the time of Operation Protective Edge, explained Husick, many of the sides in this dispute had become "remarkably more sophisticated in how they use social media to engage with the rest of the world."[51]

The deployment of all of this telegenic warfare was obviously not the only factor in this complex, multi-factorial situation, but it was an important one. One could argue that Israeli settlers were not the only ones feeling threatened, which may help explain why polls showed that some 85 percent of Israelis supported the prime minister's escalation of the 2014 conflict when he went after the tunnels. Polls that were conducted by both the Sarid Institute and the University of Haifa showed that many Israelis thought the latest Gaza incursion was just, and that they opposed any immediate unilateral withdrawal. The Sarid poll found that only 4 percent of those polled thought the Israel military was using *excessive* force. When William Booth and Ruth Eglash of the *Washington Post* looked at these data near the end of July 2014, they concluding that there was "deep support among Israelis, both left and right, for the military's Gaza offensive and Netanyahu's leadership."[52] If precious Israeli blood was going to have to be spilled, then it needed to be spent in decisive fashion as the Air Force, Navy, and Army tried to take out all of the Hamas fighters and their "infrastructure."

The Israeli public, tired of hearing the lamentations of international cosmopolitan critics who did not have to deal with Red Alert Israel or share these perceived risks, were now willing to support their armed forces as they fired away at civilian homes that were purportedly hiding Hamas terrorists or their weapons. By this point in time a growing number of Israelis, and US defenders of Netanyahu's policies, were willing to argue that vast gulfs existed between the rights of innocent civilians who did not support Hamas and those who implicitly or explicitly condoned their actions.

By the second decade of the twenty-first century visually minded audiences need to be able to see, as well as hear, about some of these perceived dangers, and one of the most influential of the academic critics who have kept track of the "digital occupation" of Gaza has been Professor Derek Gregory. His blog site, *Geographical Imaginations*, has become a key nodal point for those who wish to critique Israel's Operation Protective Edge. Gregory's circulation of his own academic work, as well as his hyperlinking of various geopolitical maps, social media conversations, and assessments of the "real war" behind some of these "virtual" contestations has constantly reminded many of us of the horrors that are suffered by those living in this "all too material firestorm."[53]

All of this focus on visuality put on display the plight of Gazan populations, but who is going to protect those who put together the "liquidation" lists, or carried out the F-16 raids, or fired the long-range missiles from Israeli naval vessels? The word and the image would come together to exonerate those who "deterred" perfidious foes.

As I note below, all of these visualities that circulated in vernacular, public spheres complemented the more elite discourse that was circulated by military lawyers, international law scholars, and others who complained about the "lawfare" directed at Israeli policies.

Israeli lawfare and the jurisprudential arguments that circulated before Operation Protective Edge

The term "lawfare" references the ways that courts, or other legal institutions, become venues or forums for those who complain about particular counterterrorism practices, and the word now appears in many discussions about "Islamic" terrorism. Note, for example, how Brooke Goldstein, a former White House consultant, has written about lawfare:

> The Islamist movement has two wings—one violent and one lawful.... Islamists with financial means have launched a "legal jihad," filing frivolous and malicious lawsuits with the aim of abolishing public discourse critical of Islam and the goal of establishing principles of Sharia law ... as the governing political and legal authority in the West. Islamists' lawfare is often predatory, filed without a serious expectation of winning, and undertaken as a means to intimidate, demoralize and bankrupt defendants.[54]

What is interesting to note here are the ways that Goldstein's description of legal battles of attrition in the courts sounds very much like what Eafraim Inbar and Eitan Shamir in 2014 called Israel's policy of "mowing the grass."[55] From a post-structural vantage point, the supporters of terrorists in Goldstein's narrative, and the Israelis in Inbar and Shamir's tale, seemed to be using parallel, and similar, tactics and strategies as they fight on the battlefield and in courtrooms in protracted geopolitical conflicts.

Goldstein was writing about the usage of defamation or access-to-information cases when she was commenting on lawfare, but this would become just the tip of the proverbial iceberg when it comes to uncovering the diverse ways that "the enemy" might be employing legal arsenals that can be found in our own backyard. During the same month that Americans sent Coalition Forces to Iraq, an essayist for the Council of Foreign Relations had this to say in an essay entitled "Lawfare, the Latest of Asymmetries":

> The intersection of globalization and the emergence of international law has resulted in a variant of warfare described by some as lawfare. Lawfare is a strategy of using or misusing law as a substitute for traditional military means to achieve military objectives. Each operation conducted by the US military results in new and expanded efforts by groups and countries to use lawfare to respond to military force. Although not a symmetrical threat to American military power, lawfare can be used to undercut American objectives. For example, it can be used … [to] encourage peasants to file human rights suits with few grounds against military figures.[56]

According to its detractors, lawfare was one of the weapons of the weak, something to be avoided by those living in modern democracies who understood the real importance of fairer usages of the "rule of law."

Debates about lawfare usually privilege militaristic framings of counterterrorist policies. For example, then-Colonel Charles Dunlap Jr. (later Major General Dunlap, and after that, a Duke law professor), would note that as early as 2001 some NGOs who complained about excessive violence during wartime simply did not understand that those who waged war for this country were doing everything possible to avoid unnecessary loss of civilian life. Dunlap averred that anyone who had any passing familiarity with the lessons from "Clausewitz" or other military strategists would quickly realize that critics of some counterterrorist practices should not be trying to undermine the government's political support during wartime. This was because loss of public support during the Vietnam years had shown that this "center of gravity" was strategically important, and he excoriated the "international lawyers" who waged this type of lawfare in their critiques of American GWOT policies.[57] This sounds remarkably like the attacks on B'Tselem that I mentioned earlier in this chapter.

Depending on how readers feel about the connotative meaning of "lawfare," some complaints about targeted killings could be considered to be either lawfare or counterlawfare. Defenders of what Israeli newspapers sometimes called "liquidation" had to discursively battle with those who wrote about the "extra-judicial," arbitrary, self-serving, or unreasonableness of the Israeli acceptance of assassination strategies and tactics. For example, after the outbreak of the al-Aqsa "armed conflict," many Israeli military figures wanted to show publics and jurists that some Fatah or Hamas politicians were actually engaging in acts that warranted targeting, and they also invited conversations regarding the difficulty of capturing them, the incompetence of the Palestinian Authority officials who let detainees go, and the "proportional" responses of the Israeli Air Force pilots who were doing all they could to avoid excessive collateral damage in Gaza. These very *topoi* drift into colloquial, idiomatic ways of talking about some of the major principles of the law of armed conflict.

All of these various micro-arguments were also a part of those emplotments that Neve Gordon was talking about, in that they became fragments in much larger, and very resonate, nationalistic tales that could be told of how Israeli targeted killing (TK) policies were the model that needed to be emulated by US military planners and other counterterrorist strategists. In many ways, this was the ultimate lawfare, in that the law was indeed placed at the disposal of those who dispensed violence, a perfect example of what Walter Benjamin long ago called the violence-making, as well as violence-preserving, powers of law.[58]

There are also historical reasons why so many mainstream and blogging commentators on lawfare, especially from the political right, treat lawfare as a pejorative term, that represents the efforts of misguided Israeli detractors. As John and Jean Camaroff observed in 2006:

> what imperialism is being indicted for, above all, is its commission of lawfare; its use of its own rules—of its duly enacted penal codes, its administrative law, its states of emergency, its charters and mandates and warrants, its norms of engagement—to impose a sense of order upon its subordinates by means of violence rendered legible, legal, and legitimate by its own sovereign word. And also to commit its own ever-so-civilized, patronizing, high-minded forms of kleptocracy.[59]

This obviously is not the way that most Israelis would think about their own lawfare, or counterlawfare, in Israel "proper" or in the "disputed territories."

Throughout this book I will be deploying a perspectival way of thinking about lawfare that considers how all of the parties in disputes on Gaza use jurisprudential arguments in their debates about relevant rules of engagement, law of armed conflict principles, or interpretations of materials like the Geneva Conventions. My usage of that term will be used to describe *all militarized legal rhetorics*. I realize that this will not be accepted by some scholars or lay persons who read this, because over the last several years this has become a pejorative term with a specific valence, a label that is used selectively by some to name what are viewed as transgressive—often foreign—strategies and tactics.

Ironically, the very pejorative labeling of select lawfare is itself a Kafkaesque tactic that *hides the rhetorical nature of all jurisprudence*, especially when it is artistry that parades in the guise of legal science supplementing military science. As Stephen Humphreys has insightfully observed, "the double-binding of humanitarianism and the military through shared legal narratives" have become entangled in linguistic contests where theories about strategies, tactics, and operations are used to contextualize the ways that we think about managerial decisions. Elites and publics have to listen to a "progression of cost–benefit analyses and moral balancing acts" that put on display "differentiated weapons, forms of cruelty or coercion" or "military tactics."[60]

Is it any surprise that much of what passes for "counterlawfare" just happens to end up rationalizing the building of "separation barriers" in the West Bank, the blockading of ports, the use of drones, targeted killings, etc.? David Luban, operating from a more liberal framework, contends that "lawfare" is a "way of waging war through law."[61] Luban's heroes are the JAG officers who make incredible career sacrifices as they try to preserve the rights of foreign detainees as Guantánamo, and he works mightily at fashioning for us a select history that puts on display the micro-rules that are used to regulate the behavior of humanitarian lawyers who try their best to preserve legal freedoms. We need to remember, however, that he himself is engaged in storytelling and employment.

While micro- and macro-debates about lawfare will appear in many guises, there is little question that one of the key issues in Gazan contexts has to do with the ways that lawyers, jurists, and other participants in jurisprudential debates configure the relative power of "combatants" and "civilians." It is often said that the principles of IHL or the law of armed conflict are the rhetorical substances that help prevent just and measured wars from turning into unregulated and violent campaigns of indiscriminate slaughter. For example, it could be argued that those who believe in the constraining powers of laws and moral codes were trying to answer the type of claims that were used by the Athenians when they were fighting the weaker Melians during the Peloponnesian War (around 400 BC). Thucydides records for posterity that the Athenians answered the entreats of the Melians by averring that "rights are in question between equals in power, while the strong do what they can and the weak suffer what they must."[62]

On December 13, 2006 the Supreme Court of the State of Israel handed down an opinion on the legality and legitimacy of the targeted killing of terrorists that made it clear that Israeli jurists were not going to argue that might makes right. In *Public Committee Against Torture in Israel et al.* v. *Government of Israel et al.*,[63] Chief Justice Aharon Barak, along with two other Israeli jurists, used a balancing test to set conditions for when Israeli military and security forces were going to be allowed to attack terrorist targets. While Chief Justice Barak would argue that combatants and military objectives were going to be legitimate targets for Israeli military attacks, he was going to use a framework that took fragments from international human rights law and IHL to argue that civilians who did not directly participate in hostilities were going to be protected. Helen Keller and Magdalene Forowicz contend that the Israeli Supreme Court's opinion in *Public Committee against Torture* was a "tremendous development in the field of state responsibility" or potential "criminal responsibility" for some targeted killings, in that this all translated into more "legal certainty."[64] I would disagree, and note that this belief in achieving supposed legal certainty is itself a rhetorical achievement that depends on how military planners, Israel civil servants, and many others think of the "balancing" test and "prongs" that appear in the Barak opinion.

The Keller and Forowicz essay is filled with abstract, formalistic discussions that provide us with many examples of how IHL experts argue about provisions of the Geneva Convention and the traditional law of war principles, but what they do not provide is any cultural, contextual, rhetorical explanation for why Barak and other members of the Israeli Court came up with certain examples about snipers, bombers, and terrorists who either did, or did not, act in ways that triggered potential violations. What I put on display in later chapters are some of the Israeli cultural norms, and some of the IDL planning, that went into the framing of the second Intifada, that infused these abstract provisions with substantive meaning for many Israeli readers of Barak's opinion.

If lawfare and counterlawfare involves the study of the politics behind the formation of jurisprudential rules, statutes, precedents, or principles, then we should not treat the "rule of law" in Gazan contexts as some non-rhetorical entities that supposedly guide neutral arbiters. Instead, we need to view Chief Justice Aharon Barak as a motivated social agent who *was refusing to ban all targeted killings*—a stance that was taken by many IHL experts outside of Israel who viewed these acts as "extra"-judicial assassinations. Moreover, given the genealogies that hover around targeted killings—that Adam Stahl has traced back to the time of the Yishuv in the 1920s[65]—we cannot ignore how members of the IDF were disagreeing among themselves regarding the ratio of acceptable civilian to terrorist losses (some thought around 3:1) that would be regarded as parts of the "proportionate" calculus that would guide acceptable risk-taking. In other words, we can never understand the legal application of these rules in places like Gaza if we stay within the formalistic "four corners" of legal texts.

Although countless essays have now been written about the relevance of international law and the need for humanitarian intervention or UN peacekeeping in Gaza, there are some observers who appear to have lost hope that anything can be done by members of the Arab League or the European Union to stem Israeli aggression in Gaza. Richard Falk explained why he was so concerned that so few were doing anything to help end this "infernal entrapment of the innocent":

> International law has little to say. International refugee law avoids issues associated with any right to escape from a war zone and does impose a duty on belligerent parties to provide civilians with an exit and/or a temporary place of sanctuary. International humanitarian law offers little more by way of protection to an entrapped people, despite the seeming relevance of the Fourth Geneva Convention devoted to the Protection of Civilians in Time of War. There is accorded to *foreign* nationals a right of departure with the onset of war, including even repatriation to an enemy country, but no right

of nationals to leave their own country if under attack. And the generalized obligation of an Occupying Power to protect the civilian population is legally subordinated to its security needs, including military necessity, and so is generally of little practical use during an ongoing military operation.[66]

For Falk, the unique characteristics of the Gaza occupation, and the lack of international political will, had created a situation where there were jurisprudential gaps in all of the applicable legal architectures. This, in turn, allowed those who did not feel any self-imposed moral restraints to turn the other way as entrapped populations prayed for an end to the latest cycle of violence.

The rest of the chapters in this book are intended to provide nuanced explanations for how Gazan citizens have been turned into biopolitical targets, and how many strands of military, legal, and cultural argumentative threads are woven into a thanatopolitical tapestry that traps those living in the Gaza Strip.

The trajectory for this book and the contents of each chapter

Each of the chapters in this book supplies readers with some essential information regarding the Israeli lawfare, political argumentation, military disputation or telegenics that has been used in Gazan contexts.

Chapter 2 sets the stage for the rest of the book by outlining the domestic and international criticisms of Israeli military and civil decision-making in Gaza, and this portion of the book highlights many of the challenges that enable and constrain Israeli argumentation. Here I mention the Turkish and international reactions to the Israeli commando boarding of the *Mavi Marmara*, a ship that was part of a flotilla that was heading toward Gazan shores, as well as critics' usage of the Goldstone Report, which implied that Israelis "intentionally" targeted Gazans civilians during Operation Case Lead in 2008–2008. This chapter also provides readers with more information about the activist role the IHC has played in Palestinian–Israeli affairs, and also includes materials on how international communities reacted to Dror Moreh's film, *The Gatekeepers*. That documentary highlighted the testimony of six former directors of Shin Bet, and it was used to promote the idea that Israelis needed to reconsider the potential of "two-state" solutions to the "Palestinian problem."

In Chapter 3 I explore in much more detail some of the rhetorical functions of the Israeli defenses of targeted killing that are used to rationalize the "liquidation" of members of both the military and political wings of Hamas. This chapter illustrates how frustrations with the handling of the second Intifada were being expressed just months before Americans were traumatized by the events of 9/11, and how, over the years, Israelis have prided themselves on how the Americans seem to have recognized what Israelis regard as the evolutionary and progressive nature of their targeted killing regimes. This portion of the book explains how Israeli elites and publics have reacted to President Aharon Barak's decision in *The Public Committee Against Torture in Israel* v. *The Government of Israel Case* (2006). In that part of the book I argue that many of these arguments about targeted killings would migrate into Israeli defenses of "necessitous" attacks on Gazan civilian infrastructures.

Chapter 4 extends this analysis by unpacking and critiquing the Israeli positions on their 2005 "disengagement" for Gaza. While the Israelis have argued, in cases like *Al Bassiouini* v. *The Prime Minister of Israel*, that they only retain a few "certain obligations" after the withdrawal of Israeli troops from Gaza,[67] such as supplying electricity or fuel for humanitarian purposes, researchers like Douglas Guilfoyle point out that the overwhelming majority of countries around the world have expressed the view that "Israel remains the occupying power."[68] This has not deterred the Israelis from advancing some fairly sophisticated biopolitical arguments regarding occupation law, refugee law, and the civil and military responsibilities of what they regard as the "Hamas regime" in Gaza. Chapter 4 ends with the Israeli discourse that was circulating just before the beginning of Operation Protective Edge in 2014.

All of Chapter 5 is devoted to the Israeli framings of how to justify Operation Protective Edge, the 2014 conflict with Hamas that was geared toward *finally* taking out the terrorist threats that were posed by Qassam rockets and enemy tunnels. That particular chapter begins by explaining the material and symbolic importance of the vaunted Iron Dome, and there I show that after about ten days the public rationales for this operation shifted from a focus on rockets to the dangers that were posed by dozens of "terror" tunnels. The armed incursion into Gaza, that resulted in the regrettable loss of so many Palestinian lives, was deemed a military success.

Chapter 6 invites readers to see how Israelis and Palestinians are locked in social media wars as they try to "win" the support of domestic and international communities. This is the world of hashtags and YouTube, where ordinary citizens as well as experts deploy various types of strategic communication as they help move the Gaza conflicts into the blogosphere. As Rebecca Stein has explained, during some of the earlier conflicts Israelis tried to prevent journalists from entering some of the battlegrounds of Operation Cast Lead, or they tried to filter the international commentaries that appeared on Israeli television.[69] Now they use complementary techniques as they produce infographics or other images for social media outlets. The Israelis use these social media outlets so they can circulate their own persuasive messages on such topics as the terrorist usage of human shields, the dangers of rockets, or the traumas that are suffered by the Israeli children in settlements who live in states of constant fear.

Chapter 7, the concluding chapter, is a speculative portion of the book that explores how future Israeli and international advocates may want to debate about the issue of civilian involvement in Gaza affairs. This chapter, for example, explains some of the strengths and weaknesses of various domestic and cosmopolitan schemes that have been suggested for resolving these Israeli–Hamas conflicts, and it covers everything from having the United Nations intervene on the basis of the doctrine of R2P to some of the controversial "one-state" solutions that are offered by some members of the growing Palestinian boycott, divestment, and sanctions (BDS) campaign.

Conclusion

In sum, this book has been written with the hopes that an argumentative, critical genealogical study of Israeli texts and visualities about Gazans will help readers understand why Israelis have consistently used what Yonatan Mendel calls the "forced to" narrative to justify their treatment of Gazan citizens. Mendel reminds us of the countless times that defenders of Israeli policies have quoted former Prime Minister Golda Meir, who in 1969 said: "We can forgive the Arabs for killing our children, but we cannot forgive them for forcing us to kill their children."[70] Mendel is curious about how Israelis can "tighten the screws on 1.8 million people already living under the harshest conditions in the most densely populated place on earth," and yet make it look as though Hamas is laying siege or bombing Israel from the air.[71]

By defining "intentionality," "terrorism," and the "Nakba" in particular ways, Israelis have convinced themselves, and many others, that their system of "deterrence" is the only way to simultaneously maintain the integrity of their nation while fighting off those they believe are out to destroy them.

As strange as this may seem, by the end of the book readers will get the sense that, in many ways, Israelis feel much more at home coping with the headaches posed by Mahmoud Abbas and the PA in the West Bank than they do trying to reason with the Palestinians living in Gaza. The only way we can come to understand the symbolic, structural, and material factors that have contributed to this dysfunctional relationship is by taking both a macro- and micro-look at the complex rhetorics that have been circling in Israeli circles between the time of the second Intifada and Operation Protective Edge in 2014.

In the next chapter, I decode some of the dominant narratives and arguments that are circulated by international detractors of Israeli policies so that readers get some sense of why Israelis feel that their "hasbara" will help the world understand what they are doing in Gaza.

Notes

1 Charles Krauthammer, "Moral Clarity in Gaza," *Washington Post*, last modified July 17, 2014, www.washingtonpost.com/opinions/charles-krauthammer-moral-clarity-in-gaza/2014/07/17/0adabe0c-0de4-11e4-8c9a-923ecc0c7d23_story.html.
2 Rebecca L. Stein, "Impossible Witness: Israeli Visuality, Palestinian Testimony and the Gaza War," *Journal for Cultural Research* 16, no. 2 (2012): 135–153, 150.
3 Aeyal M. Gross, "Human Proportions: Are Human Rights the Emperor's New Clothes of the International Law of Occupation?" *The European Journal of International Law* 18, no. 1 (2007): 1–35.
4 Stuart J. Murray, "Thanatopolitics: On the Use of Death for Mobilizing Political Life," *Polygraph* 18 (2006): 191–215. For more on the suasory power of thanatopolitics, see Miguel Vatter, "Eternal Life and Biopower," *CR: The New Centennial Review* 10, no. 3 (2010): 217–240, DOI: 10.1353/ncr.2010.0035.
5 Elsewhere I will write on the impact that all of this has had on Fatah, the PA, and the Palestinians who live on the West Bank, but this particular book will concentrate attention on the plight of the Gazans, and the suspected terrorist leaders who were targeted for assassination. Long before the advent of the second Intifada many of the

refugees and others were already suffering from a host of privations, but responses to the Al-Asqa Intifada added to their woes.
6 For a discussion of how the Israelis are preparing themselves for some UN investigative reports, see Josef Federman, "Israel Bolstering Legal Team Ahead of U.N. Gaza Probe," *The Times of Israel*, last modified September 5, 2014, www.timesofisrael.com/israel-bolstering-legal-team-ahead-of-un-gaza-probe.
7 Alistair Dawber, "Tales From Gaza: What is Life Really Like in 'The World's Largest Outdoor Prison'?" *Independent*, April 13, 2013, www.independent.co.uk/news/world/middle-east/tales-from-gaza-what-is-life-really-like-in-the-worlds-largest-outdoor-prison-8567611.html.
8 See, for example, Idfnadesk, "12 Examples of Hamas Firing Rockets From Civilians Areas," YouTube, published July 31, 2014, www.youtube.com/watch?v=IUrDAEgisXM.
9 Benny Morris, *Righteous Victims: A History of the Zionist–Arab Conflict, 1881–1999* (New York: Vintage Books, 2001). For a contrasting historiographic account that provides a different tale on the causes of suffering, see Ilan Pappe, *A History of Modern Palestine: One Land, Two Peoples* (Cambridge: Cambridge University Press, 2004).
10 Rashid Khalidi, "1948 and After in Palestine: Universal Themes?" *Critical Inquiry* 40, no. 4 (2014): 313–331, 315, 317.
11 Amichai Cohen and Stuart A. Cohen, "Israel and International Humanitarian Law: Between the Neo-Realism of State Security and the 'Soft Power' of Legal Acceptability," *Israel Studies* 16, no. 2 (2011): 1–23, 11.
12 For an excellent overview of how the work of Walter Benjamin, Jacques Derrida, and Judith Butler could be applied to the decisions that have been reached by President Barak in the 2006 targeted killings case, *The Public Committee Against Torture in Israel and Palestinian Society for the Protection of Human Rights and the Environment* v. *The Government of Israel et al.* (PCATI), see Markus Gunneflo, "The Targeted Killing Judgment of the Israeli Supreme Court and the Critique of Legal Violence," January 2012, *Selected Works of Markus Gunneflo*, http://works.bepress.com/cgi/viewcontent.cgi?article=1007&context=markus_gunneflo.
13 Darryl Li, quoted in The European Institute for International Law and International Relations Staff, "Israel's Dahiya Doctrine: Terror Tactics to Ensure Colonial Domination of Gaza," *The European Institute for International Law and International Relations*, last modified July 31, 2014, www.eiilir.eu/politics-strategies/topics/actual-topics/128-israel-s-dahiya-doctrine-terror-tactics-to-ensure-colonial-domination-in-gaza.
14 Matthew S. Cohen and Charles D. Freilich, "The Delegitimation of Israel, Diplomatic Warfare, Sanctions, and Lawfare," *Israel Journal of Foreign Affairs* 9, no. 1 (2015): 29–48, 29.
15 Sar-Shalom Jerbi, talking to *Channel 2 TV* in Israel about B'Tselem, quoted in Orlando Crowcroft, "Israel Bans National Service with Rights Group B'Tselem in Gaza Row," *Guardian*, last modified August 15, 2014, www.theguardian.com/world/2014/aug/15/israel-btselem-service-aid-gaza-human-rights.
16 For a general overview of some of this criticism, see Associated Press, "Israeli Veterans Group Breaking the Silence Comes Under Criticism Amid Boycott Threat," Fox News, last modified June 14, 2015, www.foxnews.com/world/2015/06/14/israeli-veterans-group-breaking-silence-comes-under-criticism-amid-boycott. "So long as we are in uniform and we are going to kill and die for settlements and for the occupation," explains Breaking the Silence co-founder Yehuda Shaul, "everything is fine," but "the moment we break the silence, suddenly we are traitors. That's the hypocrisy of the Israeli right-wing" (paragraph 12).
17 For illustrative examples of critiques of this Israeli exceptionalism, see M. Shahid Alam, *Israeli Exceptionalism: The Destabilizing Logic of Zionism* (Basingstoke: Palgrave Macmillan, 2009); Gil Merom, "Israel's National Security and the Myth of Exceptionalism," *Political Science Quarterly* 114, no. 3 (1999): 409–434. For a study

of how various generations of young Israelis learn about this Israeli exceptionalism, see Phillip L. Hammack, "Exploring the Reproduction of Conflict Through Narrative: Israeli Youth Motivated to Participate in a Coexistence Program," *Peace and Conflict: Journal of Peace Psychology* 15, no. 1 (2009): 49–74, DOI: 10.1080/1078 1910802589923. For a critique of how contemporary films deal with Israel exceptionalism, see Gil Hochberg, "Soldiers as Filmmakers: On the Prospect of 'Shooting War', and the Question of Ethical Spectatorship," *Screen* 54, no. 1 (2013): 44–61.
18 Brad Parker, "Israeli Exceptionalism at the United Nations," *972 Magazine*, last modified November 14, 2013, paragraph 3, http://972mag.com/israeli-exceptionalism-at-the-united-nations/81857.
19 See Gross, "Human Proportions," 1–35.
20 Rebecca L. Stein, "How Israel Militarized Social Media," *Mondoweiss*, last modified July 24, 2014, http://mondoweiss.net/2014/07/israel-militarized-social.html.
21 Ibid., paragraph 11.
22 Ibid., paragraph 11.
23 Kevin Michael DeLuca, "Unmoored: The Force of Images as Events," *Journal of Advanced Composition*, 28, no. 3–4 (2008): 663–673.
24 Michel Foucault, *The History of Sexuality, Volume One* (New York: Vintage Books, 1990).
25 Neve Gordon, "Rationalising Extra-Judicial Executions: The Israeli Press and the Legitimation of Abuse," *International Journal of Human Rights* 8, no. 3 (2004): 305–324.
26 Gordon, "Rationalising Extra-Judicial Executions," 309–324.
27 Ibid., 309.
28 Yaakov Katz, "The Dahiya Doctrine: Fighting Dirty or a Knock-out Punch," *The Jerusalem Post*, last modified January 28, 2010, www.jpost.com/Features/FrontLines/The-Dahiya-Doctrine-Fighting-dirty-or-a-knock-out-punch.
29 UN Fact-Finding Mission, *Report of the United Nation Fact-Finding Mission on the Gaza Conflict* (New York: United Nations General Assembly, 2009).
30 Here I have been influenced by the work of Michael Calvin McGee, "Text, Context, and the Fragmentation of Contemporary Culture," *Western Journal of Speech Communication* 54 (1990): 274–289.
31 Diana Muir, "A Land Without a People for a People Without a Land," *Middle East Quarterly*, Spring (2008): 55–62, www.meforum.org/1877/a-land-without-a-people-for-a-people-without.
32 Achille Mbembe, "Necropolitics," *Public Culture* 15, no. 1 (2003): 11–40, 27–29.
33 Eyal Weizman, *Hollow Land: Israel's Architecture of Occupation* (London: Verson, 2007).
34 Eyal Weizman, "Introduction to the Politics of Verticality," *Open Democracy*, last modified April 24, 2002, www.opendemocracy.net/ecology-politicsverticality/article_801.jsp.
35 Eyal Weizman, "Lethal Theory," *Open* 18 (2009): 80–99, 81.
36 Ibid., 81.
37 Ibid., 95.
38 BBC News, "Israel Pulls Troops Out of Gaza," *BBC News*, last modified August 5, 2014, www.bbc.com/news/world-middle-east-28654229.
39 See, for example, Ben White, "Premeditated Murder: The Shuja'iyya Massacre and Israeli Criminality," *Middle East Monitor*, last modified July 22, 2014, www.middleeastmonitor.com/articles/debate/12996-premeditated-murder-the-shujaiyya-massacre-and-israeli-criminality.
40 Joey Ayoub, "Israel Army Whistle-Blower Gets Arrested After Posting 'Israeli Troops Killed Gaza Civilians in Revenge' on Facebook," *Global Voices*, last modified August 3, 2014, http://globalvoicesonline.org/2014/08/03/israeli-army-whistle-blower-leaks-account-of-revenge-attacks-against-civilians-by-israeli-troops-in-gazas-shujaiyya.

41 Anshel Pfeffer, "In Gaza, a War of Two Narratives," *Ha'aretz*, last modified July 20, 2014, www.haaretz.com/news/diplomacy-defense/.premium-1.606178.
42 Antoine Bousquet, "Chaoplexic Warfare or the Future of Military Organization," *International Affairs* 84, no. 5 (2008): 915–929.
43 Richard Falk, "No Exit From Gaza: A New War Crime?" Richard Falk Word Press, last modified July 16, 2014, paragraph 11, https://richardfalk.wordpress.com/2014/07/16/no-exit-from-gaza-a-new-war-crime.
44 Nadera Shahoub-Kevorkian, "Human Suffering in Colonial Contexts: Reflections from Palestine," *Settler Colonial Studies* 4, no. 3 (2014): 277–290. DOI: 10.1080/2201473X.2013.859979.
45 Joseph Pugliese, "The Tutelary Architecture of Immigration Detention Prisons and the Spectacle of 'Necessary Suffering,'" *Architectural Theory Review* 13, no. 2 (2008): 206–221, DOI: 10.1080/13264820802216841.
46 Darryl Li, "The Gaza Strip as Laboratory: Notes in the Wake of Disengagement," *Journal of Palestine Studies* 35, no. 2 (2006): 38–55.
47 Helga Tawil-Souri, "Hacking Palestine: A Digital Occupation," *Aljazeera*, last modified November 9 2011, www.aljazeera.com/indepth/opinion/2011/11/2011117151559601957.html.
48 Helga Tawil-Souri, "Digital Occupation: Gaza's High Tech Enclosure," *Journal of Palestine Studies* 41, no. 2 (2012): 27–43, 27.
49 John Timpane, "The Social-Media Side of War," *Philly.com*, last modified July 20, 2014, paragraphs 1–2, http://articles.philly.com/2014-07-20/news/51749894_1_social-media-war-ahmed-al-jabari-social-media.
50 Lawrence Husick, quoted in Timpane, "The Social-Media Side," paragraph 3.
51 Ibid., paragraph 6.
52 William Booth and Ruth Eglash, "Israelis Support Netanyahu and Gaza War, Despite Rising Deaths on Both Sides," *Washington Post*, last modified July 29, 2014, paragraph 3, www.washingtonpost.com/world/middle_east/israelis-support-netanyahu-and-gaza-war-despite-rising-deaths-on-both-sides/2014/07/29/0d562c44-1748-11e4-9349-84d4a85be981_story.html.
53 Derek Gregory, "Virtual Gaza," *Geographical Imaginations*, July 27, 2014, http://geographicalimaginations.com/2014/07/27/virtual-gaza.
54 Brooke Goldstein, "Welcome to 'Lawfare': A New Type of Jihad," *Family Security Matters*, April 14, 2008, paragraphs 1–3, www.familysecuritymatters.org/index.php?i=1387239.
55 Efraim Inbar and Eitan Shamir, "'Mowing the Grass': Israel's Strategy for Protracted Intractable Conflict," *Journal of Strategic Studies* 37, no. 1 (2014): 65–90.
56 Council on Foreign Relations, "Lawfare, the Latest in Asymmetries," March 18, 2003, paragraphs 1–3, www.cfr.org/publications.html?id=5772.
57 Charles J. Dunlap, Jr., *Law and Military Interventions: Preserving Humanitarian Values in 21st Century Conflicts*, Humanitarian Challenges in Military Intervention Conference (Washington, DC, Kennedy School of Government, Harvard, November 29, 2001), 14–15. http://people.duke.edu/~pfeaver/dunlap.pdf.
58 See Massimiliano Tomba, "Another Kind of *Gewalt*: Beyond Law, Re-Reading Walter Benjamin," *Historical Materialism* 17 (2009): 126–144.
59 Jean Comaroff and John Comaroff, "Law and Disorder in the Postcolony: An Introduction," in *Law and Disorder in the Postcolony*, ed., Jean Comaroff and John L. Comaroff (Chicago: University of Chicago Press, 2006), 24.
60 Stephen Humphreys, "The Emptiness of Empire and Other Hazards of Theory," *International and Comparative Law Quarterly* 57, no. 1 (2008): 225–242, 229.
61 David Luban, "Lawfare and Legal Ethics in Guantánamo," *Stanford Law Review* 60 (2008): 1981–2026.
62 Nimer Sultany, "Repetition and Death in the Colony: On the Israeli Attacks on Gaza," *Critical Legal Thinking*, last modified July 11, 2014, paragraph 6, http://criticallegalthinking.com/2014/07/11/repetition-death-colony.

63 Supreme Court of Israel, *Public Committee Against Torture in Israel et al.* v. *Government of Israel et al.*, JCJ 769/02 (December 13, 2006).
64 Helen Keller and Magdalena Forowicz, "A Tightrope Walk Between Legality and Legitimacy: An Analysis of the Israeli Supreme Court's Judgment on Targeted Killing," *Leiden Journal of International Law* 21, no. 1 (2008): 185–221, 219.
65 Adam Stahl, "The Evolution of Israeli Targeted Operations: Consequences of the Thabet Thabet Operations," *Studies in Conflict & Terrorism* 22 (2010): 111–133, 111.
66 Falk, "No Exit From Gaza," paragraph 25.
67 See Supreme Court of Israel, *Al Bassiouni* v. *Prime Minister*, HCJ 9132/07, January 30, 2008, http://elyon1.court.gov.il/Files_ENG/07/320/091/n25/07091320.n25.pdf; Yuval Shany, "The Law Applicable to Non-Occupied Gaza: A Comment on *Bassiouni* v. *The Prime Minister of Israel*," *Israel Law Review* 42 (2009): 101–116. DOI: 10.1017/S0021223700000467.
68 Douglas Guilfoyle, "The *Mavi Marmara* Incident and Blockade in Armed Conflict," *British Yearbook of International Law* 2011 (2011): 13.
69 Stein, "Impossible Witness," 135–153.
70 Golda Meir, quoted in Yonatan Mendel, "Forced to…," *London Review of Books*, last modified July 25, 2014, www.lrb.co.uk/blog/2014/07/25/yonatan-mendel/forced-to.
71 Mendel, "Forced to …," paragraph 2.

2 Domestic and international critiques of Israeli policies in Gaza, 2000–2013

As I indicated in Chapter 1, there is no shortage of cynicism regarding Israeli or Palestinian willingness to negotiate and implement either one-state or two-state solutions for what look like intractable political problems, but I think most readers would agree that any sliver of hope regarding peaceful resolutions has to be better than the status quo's militarized and security *dispositifs*. We must overcome those hurdles because demographic pressures, resource scarcity, the spread of hatred, and the proliferation of both conventional and unconventional weapons in the region are just some of the material factors that will converge to make life even more miserable for Gazans. As I will argue in more detail in Chapter 7, this is not the type of regional conflict that can be resolved without outside interference, and there needs to be some mutual understandings of the fears and insecurities that exist on many sides before there can be any non-violent resolution to these Palestinian conflicts.

Many Israelis who send letters to the editors of their newspapers, or who put up blog sites commenting on the second Intifada, Operation Cast Lead, or the actions of the Israel Defense Force (IDF) in the West Bank often take the position that the world needs to know that the Israelis feel they are surrounded by hostile forces as they defend the land of their ancestors. They argue that they face unique threats that are misunderstood by Latin Americans, Europeans, and other critics. In their minds this is no "Masada complex"[1] or collective pathology, but rather the harsh realities of a world where expansion of settlements has little to do with stealing land from anyone. Aharon Barak, the former President of the Israeli Supreme Court, spoke for many when he intoned that Israel had "suffered continuous, non-stop security tensions since the day of its establishment."[2] This created a situation in which Israel became one of the few nations that had municipal courts that dealt with IHL and belligerent occupation issues, and Barak claimed that he became an expert in the study of IHL. How readers feel about the various edicts that have been handed down by Barak and his colleagues has much to say about how readers feel about Israeli claims regarding "disputed" territory, "recovery" of biblical lands, separation practices, and myriad numbers of Israeli counterterrorist practices.

The question of just how many foreigners would agree with Barak will always be a source of contention, but there is little question that long before

32 Domestic and international critiques

Operation Protective Edge domestic gadflies like Gideon Levy[3] and B'Tselem have consistently complained about everything from Palestinian detention policies to the cycles of violence that were witnessed in both the West Bank and Gaza. Other observers who write or talk about peaceful protest do not hesitate to join the chorus of those who believe that both the Israelis and Hamas are involved in threat inflation.

Israelis may think it is naive to have peace activists talking about negotiating with Hezbollah or Hamas, and they view their securitization and militarization framing of Israeli–Palestinian relations as prudential acts. Note, for example, how Avi Kober, in 2015, contrasted the ways that Israelis lived in a "postheroic" age during asymmetric conflicts while their enemies operated from less noble frameworks:

> the fact that Israel's enemies have refused to abide by postheroic rules has created an asymmetry that has been detrimental to Israeli conduct of war. Since at least the early 1980s, Israel's non-state enemies—the PLO, Hezbollah, and Hamas—have aimed their rockets at Israeli populated areas in order to incur casualties that would demoralize the Israeli rear. At the same time, they have tried to kill Israeli troops, being aware of the fact that in Israel the lives of soldiers have often been considered more precious than the lives of residents of peripheral areas.... The rich evidence on Israeli statements, decisions, and military action substantiates the fact that Israel has been behaving postheroically since the late 1970s.[4]

The message seemed to be clear by 2015 for those who shared Avi Kober's concerns—reforms were needed so that casualty aversion and love of Israel's sons and daughters did not stand in the way of what he called "mission fulfillment."

Avi Kober was a political scientist who worked in Tel Aviv, but his academic commentaries appeared to have reflected the taken-for-granted wisdom that was circulating in diplomatic and political circles as well. Note how Kober's notions meshed with Prime Minister Netanyahu's plans for an Israeli "two state solution," a future roadmap that envisioned having Israel keep all of Jerusalem, keep all of the settlements and land in "Samaria" and "Judea," maintain the separation barriers, end talk of any Palestinian right of return, and reserve the right to have Israeli militaries police the demilitarization of Palestinian states.[5] This, in effect, would leave the Palestinians with tiny slivers of land in Gaza and the West Bank, and this would theoretically reduce the friction that might lead to Israeli casualties.

By 2015 it looked as though Israeli politicians and IDF forces had indeed implemented the type of plan that was outlined by both academics like Avi Kober and politicians like "Bibi" Netanyahu.

Israeli critics often argue that they are convinced that Israelis over the years have overreacted to the second Intifada and that they have underestimated the role that Ariel Sharon and others played in stirring up new waves of violence. Israeli journalists, military experts, diplomats, and others have had to listen to those who seemed to be incessantly complaining about expansion in the West Bank, the "separation barrier," Israelis' Basic Laws, Israelis' alleged "settler complex,"[6] their use of white phosphorus during Operation Cast Lead, and their valorization of their own High Court's interpretations of international humanitarian law (IHL) that did not mirror the views of writers in Geneva or The Hague.

One of the most frequent complaints that Israelis have had to hear is that their judiciary liked to create the impression that they were dispensing egalitarian social justice by hearing "petitions" from settlers and Palestinians and accepting jurisdiction over military commanders, when in fact functionalists or consequentialists could point out that the decisions that were handed down by the Israeli High Court (IHC) often rubber-stamped, in *post-hoc* fashion, the decisions that were made by the Israeli security officials or the military that wanted to bulldoze, detain, deport, dehumanize, or kill Palestinians. For example, Israeli cases allowed for the legitimation of the very naming of occupied territories as "disputed" land, and the IHC aided the incremental Judeazation of these spaces by using the phrases "Judea" and "Samaria" in referencing those lands. These grammatical choices, in turn, could be linked to all types of securitization or martial rhetorics.

How do Israelis handle the complaints of those who constantly underscore the differential treatment of Palestinians and Israelis? Adi Ophir, Michal Givoni, and Sari Hanifi call this the power of "inclusive exclusion," where a study of various "genealogies of power" illustrates how formalistic jurisprudential pronouncements are used to track down those who do not follow the checkpoint rules, who quibble with eviction notices, or who have to cope with investigations of Palestinians who are "illegal" residents of Eretz Israel.[7] All of this appears in the guise of "noninterference" in Palestinian affairs.[8]

Israeli jurists may self-identify as non-political social actors who cater to the needs of neither the far left nor the far right in Israel, but they are nevertheless empowered participants in an incremental process of dispossession that uses the petitions of aggrieved individuals to serve as didactic vehicles for teaching everyone else lessons about the lines that need to be drawn between human rights and military needs. When we take into account the material consequences of the decisions that are made by the IHC, the very fact that they arrogate to themselves the right to "interpret" rules created, produced, and circulated by the Israeli military or civil authorities can be viewed as just more evidence of the pervasive belief in Israeli exceptionalism.

What many international critics are trying to point out is that a careful review of many Israeli military orders and jurisprudential decisions illustrates how similar patterns of argumentation are used to justify and naturalize the territorial growth of Israel, the control of scarce water, gas, and other resources, and the administrative, civilian, and military control of the mobility of the Palestinians. In this Kafkaesque world, talk of disengagement leads to more interventionism; commentaries on the Israeli dispensation of humanitarian aid are used to explain why water or electricity can be cut off; and bombs are used to convince Gazans that they need to make peace.

More than a few cosmopolitan critics have pointed out that Israelis take for granted their own decisionism that provides them with the regional power to make these types of rulings in the first place. The Israelis are said to add insult to injury when they argue that Israeli policies are being used to protect the Palestinians themselves from Hamas and Hezbollah.

Outside of Israel and the United States, relatively few participants in these transglobal conversations about Palestinian–Israeli affairs use the terms "Judea" or "Samaria," and these foreigners use the term "apartheid wall" instead of "separation barrier" when they reference what is supposed to be a "temporary" anti-terrorist architectural wonder. Rhetors in places like South Africa or Argentina continue to talk about illegal or temporary occupations, as well as *state terrorism*, and this vilification contributes to the polarization of positions.[9] Even more controversial, and infuriating to many Israelis, is all of this foreign talk of "apartheid," and this has elicited heated responses from Israeli jurists and other writers who were convinced that this unfairly represented the nature of their unique Zionist and democratic nation.

Throughout this chapter I supply readers with what might be called rhetorical vignettes, that have been purposively selected because of their evocative and representative nature. For example, I want to comment on how the global communities configured Turkish support for the flotilla that included the *Mavi Marmara*, and how international audiences reacted to the supposed "factual" revelations that were found in the now infamous Goldstone Report.

These are some obvious choices for decoding recognizable diplomatic situations, but I also want to provide readers with vignettes that would not be obvious choices for the study of Israeli argumentation, including a review of how international viewers reacted to Gaza buffer zones, and how audiences responded to the arguments that appeared in Dror Moreh's 2012 documentary, *The Gatekeepers*.[10] That particular film was based on interviews with former members of Israel's secret service who expressed reservations about some of Israel's militarist and exclusionary policies, and *The Gatekeepers* would be nominated for Best Documentary Feature at the 85th Academy Awards.

Critical studies of these vignettes should provide readers with a good range of rhetorical situations and mediums, and when we study Israeli reactions to these incidents we get a fairly representative picture of the type of repetitive arguments that circulate in Israeli military, legal, and public circles.

Each of the incidents I have selected for analysis in this chapter has raised its own firestorms of protest, but when we see the *cumulative effect* of these critiques I think we can understand just why Israelis pride themselves on remaining "steadfast" in the face of all of this domestic and international pressure.

As an entrée point into this discussion of the growing power of the Israeli right and middle portions of the political spectrum, and the challenges that they face as they hear from their detractors, let me begin by introducing one of the topics that has captured the imagination of key international critics, the Gaza Freedom Flotilla and the boarding of the *Mavi Marmara*.[11]

Critiques of Israeli blockades of Gaza and remembrances of the *Mavi Marmara* incident

On August 11, 2014 Palestinians living in Turkey joined hands with some of their Turkish brothers and sisters as it was announced during the middle of an Operation Protective Edge ceasefire that a new Turkish humanitarian flotilla was set to travel to Gaza in defiance of an Israeli blockade. Journalists for *Reuters* reported that the Turkish aid organization, the Humanitarian Relief Foundation (IHH) had supervised the collection of materials from representatives of 12 different countries that had met in Istanbul, and those who paid for the loaded ships sent out a missive indicating that they were sending humanitarian aid in the "shadow of the latest Israeli aggression on Gaza."[12]

Idealists may celebrate this latest venture as some meaningful international attempt at breaking the blockade, but it is possible that Israeli realists will dismiss this as a publicity stunt that may placate Palestinian anger at the cost of misreading terrorist threats. For example, in June 2015, when a flotilla of some four boats carried along former Tunisian president Moncef Marzouki and others who wanted to try to reach Gaza, Prime Minister Netanyahu sent a sarcastic missive to the flotilla indicating that they surely must have gotten lost and meant to help the Syrians who were being killed. Israeli authorities reiterated the point that they had no intention of allowing any boats to reach Gaza, and that the organization of this latest flotilla must have known that the Israelis had put in place a legal naval blockade. All humanitarian aid, they argued, needed to pass through established channels.[13] When the IDF heard about these latest flotilla plans they indicated that they would continue to prevent any vessel from breaching their blockage of the Gaza Strip.

Since at least 2005 Israelis may have unilaterally proclaimed their "disengagement" from Gaza, but this did not mean they were uninterested parties when it came to the mobility of people or the flow of goods and services that came in and out of Gaza. From birth to death, even in the midst of Operation Protective Edge, the Israelis had a great deal of say about the transfer of goods and services that impacted the daily lives of Gazan populations. This all became a part of what Gil Hochberg has recently called the "violence and visibility in a conflict zone."[14]

Israelis can link all types of humanitarian organizations or dissenters to any number of terrorist activities or groups, and this is especially the case when it comes to the organizations that were held responsible for the promotion of the 2010 Gaza Flotilla. For example, in January 2014 Ariel Ben Solomon would write an essay for *The Jerusalem Post* that explained how the Turkish police had been carrying out raids and ransacking the offices of the IHH. Solomon recalled that the IHH had helped instigate the *Mavi Marmara* incident, and it was reported that members of the IHH were now caught up in an "al-Qaida sweep."[15] Readers could follow the syllogistic reasoning that assumed that if the IHH was involved with terrorism today, then they must have been involved with similar groups in 2010.

On May 31, 2010 a Turkish vessel, the *Mavi Marmara* was moving in international waters and heading to the Gaza coast when it was boarded by Israeli commandos. Nine passengers were killed (eight Turks and one Turkish-American), and many more were wounded. Both the United Nations Rights Council and the Israelis produced reports that provided contradictory framings of what happened that day.[16]

The *Mavi Marmara* was a part of what mainstream and alternative presses called the "Gaza Freedom Flotilla," that itself was a part of the broader "Free Gaza Movement." The UN National Rights Council contended that the six ships that set out on this voyage were trying to draw international public attention to the plight of the Gazans, as well as break the blockade that had been put in place by both the Israelis and the Egyptians, and it was noted that the *Mavi Marmara* was trying to deliver humanitarian assistance and supplies to Gaza.[17]

As Ufuk Ulutaş has explained, Turkish observers took the lead in criticizing the action of the Israeli commandos, and they arguing that the Israelis had violated international law under the "pretext" of exercising Israeli self-defense rights,[18] but the Turks were not the only international commentators on the actions of Israel's Navy. Russell Buchan, writing in the *Netherlands International Law Review*, noted that on May 31, 2010 Israel was not engaged in any international armed conflict with Hamas, and since customary international law prohibited the use of blockades that were intended to deny civilian populations objects that were needed for survival, the Israelis needed to come up with reasonable arguments regarding the anticipated military advantages that they were getting.[19] Buchan concluded that the blockade was already causing a severe humanitarian crisis, and that enforcement of the blockade, as demonstrated by the excessive use of force during the *Mavi Marmara* incident, went far beyond what was necessary under the circumstances.

For many years the unilateral Israeli decisions regarding the blockading of the Gaza Strip made little sense to cosmopolitans and other critics of Israeli policies. If poverty, dehumanization, lack of economic development, political stability, etc. contributed to the rise of radical organizations like Hamas, then wasn't it possible that all of this blockading was actually undermining Israeli national security interests?

Organizations provided Israeli detractors with mounds of information and statistics regarding the adverse impact that the blockade was having on the Gaza Strip, and in 2010 select members of the UN's Human Rights Council circulated their version of what happened during the *Mavi Marmara* boarding.[20]

The Israeli forces did more than just board a ship. They also jammed the signals of *Al-Jazeera* and *Press TV* before the Israeli commandos boarded the *Mavi Marmara*, and after this boarding the raiders confiscated all the video footage and any recorded materials from the passengers. The passengers would remain in Israeli custody for three days, and during that time the Israelis took advantage of their social media spending and produced their own edited footage, which showed the Israelis being attacked by some of the Turkish passengers. This footage put on display the commandos who were descending from the top deck of the *Mavi Marmara* and it shows that they were attacked, and the edited Israeli footage was then uploaded to YouTube at the same time that it was made available to members of the international press.[21]

The Israelis also started three different internal investigations so that they could preempt some of the inevitable fallout that would come from Turkey, Europe, and other places. For a time it looked as though some of the Turkish authorities were going to file criminal charges against a group of former Israeli military commanders, including former Chief-of-Staff Lieutenant General Gabi Ashkenazi.[22]

In September 2010 Haroon Siddique of the UK's *Guardian* would report that the UN General Rights Council's fact-finding mission on the *Mavi Marmara* incident had determined that the Israeli forces had violated IHL as well as human rights law during their "lethal" attack on a "flotilla of ships."[23] Those who prepared this UN report assumed that there was indeed a humanitarian crisis going on at the time of the incident, and this was something that the Israelis denied. Moreover, the Israelis argued that five years earlier they left Gaza, so if the Palestinian people were suffering this was because the "Hamas regime" was misspending funds on missiles and tunnels and not working on alleviating the hunger or the malnutrition of its citizens.

From a rhetorical vantage point the Israeli prisms that emphasized the terrorist linkages to everything clashed with the humanitarian prisms that blamed Israeli actions for the Gazan economic, political, and social problems. The authors of the UN report angered many Israelis when they concluded that the Israeli military response to the flotilla's attempts to break the blockade "betrayed an unacceptable level of brutality" that was "disproportionate."[24]

The team of investigators that worked for the UN Human Rights Council would be led by Karl Hudson Phillips, a retired judge from Trinidad and Tobago. His team concluded that there was "clear evidence" of willful killing, torture, inhumane treatment, as well as the willful causing of great suffering or serious injury to body or health.

The Israeli editing of their video materials allowed them to argue, and to show, that they were not the first parties who fired their weapons, and they contextualized this combat as one more example of the existential dangers that were posed by Islamic terrorism. The commandos used their video materials to create the impression that they had peaceful intentions when they landed their helicopter on the upper deck of the *Mavi Marmara*, and dominant, hegemonic Israeli narratives of this boarding transformed some of the passengers into enemy aggressors who forced the commandos to defend themselves.[25]

The Israelis, of course, were assuming that they had a right to blockade an entire region, and that they had the right to interpret maritime or naval law in ways that allowed them to come armed and board a peaceful vessel. In what Shahira Fahmy and Britain Eakin would call the "dominant official Israeli narrative,"[26] the Israelis would say that the Turkish loss of life was tragic, but unavoidable.

With the passage of time, as Israelis started to sense that their own investigations had blunted some of the rhetorical impact of foreign investigations into the

Mavi Mamara incident, they continued to treat the commandos' rights of self-defense as metonymic markers of Israel's *larger national right to maintain the blockade* in the continuous war that it was waging with Hamas. More than three years after the event, a contributor to *The Jerusalem Post* took these inherent self-defense rights for granted when that person wrote that the "Israel Navy commandos" who boarded that ship "were attacked," and that the commandos were forced to kill nine "of the attackers."[27] Prime Minister Benjamin Netanyahu would eventually apologize to the Turkish people for these deaths, but he also used the occasion to note that the loss of life had not been intended, and he remarked that by 2014 Israel had already started to allow the passage of some goods and people into the Palestinian territories.[28]

The Israelis, however, refused to concede that there might be anything problematic about the blockade itself, or that they were violating any human rights laws or IHL by maintaining the blockade. The indefatigable Gideon Levy called this the "curse of the *Mavi Marmara*," in that the Israelis, with all of their investigations and inquiries, and all of their press coverage of the incident, refused (before Netanyahu's apology) to tell the world that they were sorry. Levy ridiculed the idea that the protesters on the *Mavi Marmara* threatened Israel's security, or that Israel had the right to place a total maritime embargo on the Gaza Strip. His arguments resembled those of many of the outside critics when he claimed that Israelis didn't have any right to use live weapons against "unarmed citizens."[29] In one key section of his essay Levy elaborated by noting:

> The inquiry by the Shayetet 13 naval commando unit pointed to defects in the way the force operated. The committee headed by Maj. Gen. (res.) Giora Eiland said there were no defects regarding the main issues. The Turkel committee said the commandos had acted reasonably. And the state comptroller declared last week that there were defects in the decision-making process. On the face of it, everything has been investigated, but in fact nothing has been investigated. So no one has paid the price, and the damage keeps piling up. Worst of all, the whitewashing by the investigators ensures one thing: Israel will learn nothing. Next time, too, force will be the first method, the concept that Israel is allowed to do anything won't change, and not a soul will ask what's legal, what's moral, what's appropriate and what serves Israel's interests.... Even after the nine Turkish citizens were killed, Israel kept to its path.[30]

At one point it even looked as though some of the Israeli peace activists were going to be ones that would have to appear before Israeli judges. Michael Ben-Ari and Itamar Ben-Gvir, two right-wing activists, tried to petition the IHC so that they could indict Haneen Zoabi, who had been a passenger in the flotilla, for her involvement in the *Mavi Marmara* incident. When the state announced that they had closed the investigation against Zoabi and had decided not to indict her, Ben-Givr told journalists working for *The Jerusalem Post* that he was "very disappointed" that the IHC was "giving immunity to terrorists."[31] These counterterrorist

Domestic and international critiques 39

framings that were used to characterize the blockade, and the boarding of the *Mavi Marmara*, looked nothing like some of the international critiques that accused the Israelis of using the blockade to "strangle" Palestinian autonomy, economic growth, or statehood.[32]

In the next portion of the chapter, I want to provide a genealogical critique that shows how responses to international lamentations about buffer zones in Gaza put on display how talk of land rights mirrored Israeli commentaries on sea rights.

International critiques of Israeli production of buffer zones

One of the often overlooked topics that needs to be explored in Israeli geopolitical narratives about Gaza are the rationales that are used for the establishment of what are called "buffer" zones. During February of 2002 Israeli Prime Minister Ariel Sharon announced that his government was going to set up buffer zones that were intended to achieve "security separation" so that Israelis could be protected from Palestinian attacks in the Gaza Strip. When he was pressed by reporters Sharon did not provide many details about what he called "border zones," but he argued that Israelis would continue to fight terrorists with all of their strength.[33]

It did not take long before global audiences learned what Sharon and his generals had in mind. As Darryl Li would write in 2006:

> Israel's notion of "security" is inherently expansive: security of the Jewish population demands that Arab movement be controlled and that Arabs be kept away from Jews. Securing this arrangement requires putting those Arabs behind a wall. And such a wall in turn demands its own protection. The ideal way to secure a barrier is through a vacant "buffer zone," whose emptiness allows a handful of soldiers to monitor relatively large areas and to respond quickly, decisively, and overwhelmingly to any perceived infiltrators, all while ensconced in fortified positions. In a place as tiny and as densely populated as the Gaza Strip, where Palestinian housing and agriculture are never too far away, such buffer zones had to be forcibly emptied of Arabs, houses, and agriculture.
> ...Maj. Gen. Doron Almog, who as head of the Southern Command of the Israeli military was the overall architect of Gaza Strip policy from 2000 to 2003, credited the near-impermeability of the fence between Israel and the Strip to the buffer zone's two "key elements"—mass property destruction and aggressive open-fire rules.[34]

During the second Intifada thousands of homes in the Gaza strip were razed as Israeli forces searched for terrorists and their smuggling tunnels, and as Li points out this was often done in incremental fashion so as to attenuate "international criticism."[35]

Organizations like Human Rights Watch contend that during the belligerent occupation years satellite images showed that the Israelis were demolishing

Palestinian homes "in the absence of military necessity."[36] The Israelis used armored Caterpillar D9 bulldozers to crash through walls and houses, and the IDF adopted Israeli interpretations of IHL that could rationalize all of this destruction as actions that were absolutely necessary for their military operations. B'Tselem researchers reported that some Israeli reports tried to create the impression that the razing of homes in places like Rafah was some "one time-act that was executed in response" to the killing of some Israel soldiers, but they noted that since the beginning of the al-Aqsa Intifada the Israel had uprooted thousands of trees and destroyed thousands of acres of land in the Gaza Strip.[37] By 2011 B'Tselem was estimating that since the time of the second Intifada the IDF had demolished some 1,800 housing units in the Rafah refugee camp alone.[38]

The Israeli military argued that their domestic and international critics were exaggerating the numbers of homes that had been destroyed, and during heated public debates the IDF noted that their destruction of parts of the Rafah refugee camp had everything to do with the prevention of smuggling of arms and materials that were dug under homes. Many of these same types of claims would be recycled during the "terror" tunnel debates that became a part of the mediated coverage of Operation Protective Edge (see Chapter 5).

In theory, the demolition of Palestinian homes and the creation of the buffer zones had nothing to do with revenge, even though some of the destruction that took place in May 2004 began immediately after the killing of eight Israeli soldiers.[39] The Israelis who carried out this destruction indicated that they were familiar with the rules of engagement and that they were complying with the law of armed conflict. For example, an analysis of the official transcript of the GOC Southern Command Regarding the Finding of the Investigation of the Demolition of the Buildings in Rafah (2002) (that may have been written by Almog or a member of his staff) reveals how at least one military commander configured the demotions of refugee camps. These supposedly fell within the "Pink line" rules that had been established by the Gaza-Jericho Agreement of 1994.[40]

The Pink line, argued this Israeli commander, was of strategic importance to enemies who wanted to relocate people belonging to terrorist organizations. The author of the GOC Southern Command military report claimed that Palestinians were active in this sector, near the Philadelphi route, and that they had thrown nearly 1,000 grenades. This military commander also argued that there were some 15 tunnel areas in this region, and that the Rafah crossing was symbolically important for Palestinians who wanted to transfer weapons or people without restriction or supervision. Given the fact that the IDF did not know exactly what is going on "underneath the surface," and that the commander had to be engaged in operational activity that protected the soldiers as if they were "our own sons and daughters," he argued that this particular military operation had to be carried out.[41]

In order to justify the demolition of so many homes the author of the GOC Southern Command Report had to rationalize his decisions, and he argued that the readers of his report needed to understand that the "houses were connected,

Domestic and international critiques 41

like honeycombs," and that nearly half of the structures were roofless. Some of the places that were razed were near the Termit outpost, and in many places these buildings were supposedly vacant. This military reporter then claimed that the Palestinians who lived in the area of the demolition "lied about the number of people that allegedly lived there," and he remarked that this was just "another of their manipulations."[42] Near the end of this GOC Southern Command Report one finds this conclusion:

> operationally, the activity was carried out well. We were not prepared, however, on the media front. We were prepared to defend the residents of Israel and the soldiers of the IDF, but we did not think about the way to present this to the media. Already during the following day tents were set up and film crews were brought in causing a huge media impact ... the number of buildings demolished were less than the planned number. Including this mishap, 21 complexes were razed. It must again be emphasized that the area was clear of people. The military necessity was clear and the rules of engagement are well known to me in this case. One of the basics of the rules of engagement states that operations need to stem from the military need of defending the people, and in this case the need to defend the residents of Israel and the soldiers of the IDF was absolutely clear. The security reality is better today.[43]

This type of military reportage serves several rhetorical functions. First of all, it assumes that it is the media coverage of the incident, and not the demolitions themselves, that led to the international complaints about these activities. Second, this military interpretation shows how military commanders who carried out this razing realized the importance of lawfare. Third, this Southern Command Report illustrates how talk of any kind of force protection of Israeli sons and daughters could be linked to military necessity. Fourth, the military comments regarding the "manipulations" of the Palestinians only underscored the point that the most moral army in the world was acting professionally as it demolished select homes. Finally, note how the talk of the supposed existence of a Gazan maze of tunnels under civilian homes—that was circulating almost a dozen years before Operation Protective Edge—provided the type of prefigurative, generic templates for the textual and visual arguments that would later reappear in 2014 talk of "terror" tunnels.

The Israeli military obviously tried to control the rhetorical frames that were used to discuss the creation of buffer zones and the demolition of homes and the razing of agricultural farms in Gaza. In spite of the fact that the Israelis claimed they have "disengaged" from Gaza, their military reserved the right to enforce the creation of restricted border zones between Israel and Gaza interiors. These buffer zones are no small matter because they include an area that would eventual cover more than 40 percent of the Gaza Strip, areas that contain the homes of some 250,000 people.[44]

There are different topographical layers of these buffer zones, and by the time of Operation Protective Edge one of these zones was made up of a 2 km long strip on the immediate outside of the border fence that separates Israel and Gaza, and this particular restricted area is a "no-go" zone for just about everyone, including Israelis. Israelis have also invented a second, 3 km deep zone that is inside the 2 km area, and that second zone is one that receives evacuation warnings.[45] The second strip is so deep into Gazan territory that it includes Gaza City's Shuja'iyya neighborhood. Sara Roy explains that this includes almost 50 percent of Gaza's total arable land.[46]

International critics complained that the unilateral decisions that were made about buffer zones provided more examples of "crimes against humanity" being committed by Israelis. Dennis Kuchinich, for example, writing in the *Guardian* on August 5, 2014, had to this say about the buffer zones:

> There is a land grab going on. The Israeli prime minister, Binjamin Netanyahu, has shrunk Gaza's habitable land mass by 44%, with an edict establishing a 3 km (1.8-mile) buffer zone, a "no-go" zone for Palestinians – and that's quite significant, because a good part of Gaza is only 3 to 4 miles wide. Over 250,000 Palestinians within this zone must leave their homes, or be bombed. As their territorial space collapses, 1.8m Gazans now living in 147 square miles will be compressed into 82 square miles. Gaza's entire social and physical infrastructure of housing, hospitals, places of worship, more than 130 of its schools, plus markets, water systems, sewer systems and roads are being destroyed. Under constant attack, without access to water, sanitary facilities, food and medical care, Gazans face an IDF-scripted apocalypse.[47]

While Kuchinich condemned the Hamas rocket attacks and argued that Israel had a right to exist, he also argued that that right was itself impaired when Israelis, like Moshe Feiglin, were arguing that Gaza needed to be part of "sovereign Israel" to ease the "house crisis in Israel." Kuchinich was convinced that Israel's own rights were endangered when they decided that Palestinians living in the buffer zones had no right to exist on their own lands. "It's time for us to stop paying for Israel's dubious, destructive self-righteousness," he argued, and time for the International Criminal Court to take a hard look at the "solipsism syndrome afflicting Israel's leaders" who established their new 3 km "buffer zone."[48]

Yet the International Criminal Court has not intervened in this situation, and Israel's buffer zone in Gaza remains. Perhaps the next section, which covers the international responses to the infamous "Goldstone Report," will help explain why so many states and NGOs encounter so many obstacles when they try to change Israeli hearts and minds.[49]

Explaining the Dahiya doctrine, and international responses to the Goldstone Report 2009–2010

After Operation Cast Lead, international communities were horrified to learn that some 1,400 Palestinian lives had been lost and thousands more had been injured.[50] This would involve an immense amount of warfare, lawfare, and social media activities, and it would provide the Israeli military and security forces with the opportunity to showcase what they had learned from their supposed mistakes during the wars against Hezbollah in Lebanon.

As many pundits have noted, UN employees have made a habit of complaining about Israeli policies in Gaza, and in April 2009 the President of the Human Rights Council of the UN established the UN Fact Finding Mission on the Gaza Conflict. This would be known as the "Goldstone" commission, and it was given the mandate to "investigate all violations of international human rights law and international humanitarian law" that might have been committed during the military operations that were conducted in Gaza between December 27, 2008 and January 18, 2009.[51]

This fact-finding mission went into great detail as they wrote about the Israeli shelling of the Gaza coast, and all of this was happening while Galani, Givati, and Paratrooper brigades joined five Armoured Corps Brigades as they prepared for land battles.[52] These would be some of the forces that would be accused of attacking the "foundations of civilian life in Gaza"—including "destruction of industrial infrastructure, food production, water installation, sewage treatment plants and housing."[53]

Claims like this would later add to the notoriety of the Goldstone Report, and UN investigators and Israeli military or legal experts clashed over how to interpret provisions of the Geneva Conventions or the addendums that were supposed to help discriminate between the treatment of combatants and non-combatants. The UN investigators usually cited authorities that demanded that soldiers avoid inflicting civilian casualties, and many of these writers assumed that Israeli soldiers needed to *place themselves at risk* instead of civilians. The Israelis countered with metanarratives that explained why Israeli blood was precious, and why it need not be spilled in an effort to spare those who harbored terrorists. As I noted in Chapter 1, the Goldstone Report thus needs to be viewed as an interventionist, polemic text that sutured together many of the arguments that had plenty of antecedent genres.[54]

The UN Fact Finding Mission on the Gaza Conflict, made up of Richard Goldstone, Christine Chinkin, Hina Jilani, and Desmond Travers, produced a document of about 2,000 pages. The Goldstone Report included everything from a historical preview to the study of attacks on UNRWA compounds and chicken farms, and it went so far as to accuse some Israelis of using Palestinian civilians—including Majdi Abd Rabbo, Abbas Ahmad Ibrahim Halawa, and Mahmoud Abd Rabbo al-Ajrami—as human shields.[55] This last accusation had important symbolic dimensions because for decades both American and Israeli legal scholars and military experts had been writing as if Palestinians were the only ones who ever used human shields in these conflicts.

Although the Goldstone Report did contain some brief commentary on potential Palestinian violations of the IHL, the bulk of the report was made up of detailed critiques of the goals, tactics, and strategies of the Israeli military forces as they detained and attacked Palestinian soldiers, civilians, and infrastructures.

When the Goldstone Report hit the blogosphere it went viral because anyone who wanted to vilify the Israelis could now turn to the report and find the facts that were needed to contradict the Israeli claims. The members of this fact-finding mission angered many Israelis because the authors of the Goldstone Report wrote about both the consequences of Operation Cast Lead and about the "intentions" of the Israelis. The Israelis could handle the first claims by arguing that all of this was unfair Monday-morning quarterbacking, but the second allegation stung those who believed they were fighting a moral and just war.

From a methodological standpoint, Goldstone, Chinkin, Jilani, and Travers tried to argue that they were using an inclusive approach that would help with all of this fact-finding, and they underscored the ways they reviewed diverse reports, interviewed victims, talked to witnesses, communicated with relevant parties, looked at video and photographic imagery, used satellite imagery, analyzed forensic analysis, sent out invitations to collect more information, and circulated calls for public hearings. On paper, this looked like an exhaustive effort. The Goldstone Committee reviewed some 10,000 pages of texts, looked at more than 30 videos, and gazed at some 1,200 photographs. The members of the UN Fact Finding Mission on the Gaza Conflict admitted they had initially intended to hold hearings in Gaza, Israel, and the West Bank, but they reported that they were denied access to potential witnesses who were living in Israel and in the West Bank. Richard Goldstone and the other co-authors of the report acknowledged that they had given "priority to the participation of victims and people from the affected communities."[56]

Although there were many other sub-arguments and sub-themes that were stitched together in the Goldstone Report, one of the most controversial claims that the authors advanced had to do with the allegation that the Israeli military was not just targeting the Hamas fighters or the military weapons of the enemy. Major parts of the Goldstone Report contained evidence that Israeli strategies, tactics, or operations were specifically and intentionally aimed at taking out what the IDF and others broadly defined as "Hamas terrorist infrastructure." This seemingly innocuous phrase could be used by the Israelis anytime anyone complained about their targeting of a hospital, a school, an electric plant, or a police station. For critics it denoted Israeli impunity and open disdain for constraining IHL provisions, while the Israelis viewed this as a pragmatic term that put on display how Hamas was trying to avoid Israeli attacks by hiding behind civilians. Israeli talk of "infrastructure" became an example of what Michel Foucault called a "technology" of the "self" employed by governments.[57]

After weighing the evidence, the UN Fact-Finding Mission on Israel's Operation Cast Lead concluded:

> While the Israeli Government has sought to portray its operations as essentially a response to rocket attacks in the exercise of its right to self defence, the Mission considers the plan to have been directed, at least in part, at a different target: The people of Gaza as a whole.[58]

The Goldstone Report seemed to be implying that the Israelis had been on the offensive, and that they were pursuing politics by other means.

The authors of the Goldstone Report appeared to be siding with those international critics who believed they could see through Israeli smokescreens and get to the underlying intentions; in this case they were arguing that Israeli texts and practices showed they were purposefully targeting civilians. By reading statements that came from the Israeli government or armed forces' representatives, and by comparing these texts with what they personally observed or heard when they collected testimony, the members of the Goldstone Mission found that the Israelis were attacking the Gaza prison, Gazan police stations, homes of Hamas leaders, and civilians in ways that violated customary IHL.

The authors of the Goldstone Report argued that the "facts" indicated that the Israeli military had committed grave breaches that were "not justified by military necessity" and that they were carried out unlawfully and wantonly.[59] For example, it was argued that on December 27, 2008 the Israelis had killed 27 policemen who were not directly participating in hostilities and therefore did not lose their civilian immunity from direct attack as civilians. The Israelis could, of course, counter that these were either Hamas operatives or they were trainees who would soon join the ranks of the terrorists. Obviously what I am trying to stress here is that the Goldstone Report, like any other text, has its own ideological gestures and inflections.

What really infuriated many supporters of the Israelis were the ways the authors of the Goldstone Report seemed to be accusing the IDF of using Palestinians as human shields while they simultaneously argued that there was little or no evidence that Hamas was using human shields. This was a *direct inversion* of popular Israeli narratives, a not-so-veiled critique of the ethos of those who kept harping on the problems associated with using human shields. Giving the fact that so many members of the international media kept writing about the "disproportionate" nature of the overwhelming amount of force that was being used by the Israelis, they could not afford to be accused of violating their own norms and standards.

In one key portion of the Goldstone Report the authors indicated that they found no evidence to "suggest that Palestinian armed groups either directed civilians to areas where attacks were launched or that they forced civilians to remain within the vicinity of the attack."[60] In other words, all of this anticipated, and tried to head off, the usual Israeli responses regarding Hamas usage of human shields.

In some cases those who produced the Goldstone Report critiqued the Israeli usage of artillery at the same time that they commented on aerial strikes. The authors of the Report claimed that intentionally or unintentionally, the Israeli policies that guided detention practices during Operation Cast Lead turned detainees into civilian shields for Israeli artillery. In the al-Atatra area in northwestern Gaza, for example, Israeli troops allegedly dug out sandpits and then detained Palestinian children, women, and men in those sandpits. Israeli tanks and artillery then fired from locations that were right next to these detainees.[61]

The Israelis have often singled out their military's usage of warnings as evidence of military practices that go above and beyond the customary calls of international law, but this did not impress the UN Fact Finding Mission on the Gaza Conflict. Goldstone, Chinkin, Jilani, and Travers acknowledged that the Israelis sent out civilian warnings that included telephone calls, leaflets and radio broadcasts, but the authors of report argued that some of these gestures were undermined by the actions of the IDF when the Israelis bombed city centers after warning Palestinians that they needed to move *toward* those very centers.[62] This would pave the wave for future arguers who later claimed that none of these warnings obviated the need to avoid the targeting of non-combatants.

As noted above, perhaps the most controversial claims that circulated in the Goldstone Report were those that argued that the Israelis—with all of their talk of precision warfare and careful planning—were acting in ways that evidenced that they were involved in "deliberate attacks against the civilian populations." For example, the Goldstone Report authors remarked that they had investigated 11 incidents in which the Israeli armed forces launched direct attacks against civilians with lethal outcomes. These incidents, according to the UN Fact Finding Mission, showed that the instructions that had been given to the Israeli armed forces had "provided for a low threshold for the use of lethal fire against the civilian population."[63] This was evidenced by their research that tended to show that a mosque had been targeted during early morning prayers, as a result killing 15 people, and their assessment of a later incident where some 22 family members died when the Israelis reportedly tried to target a neighboring house. All of this, argued Goldstone and the others, constituted grave breaches of the Fourth Geneva Convention that prohibited willful killings and willfully causing great suffering to protected persons.[64]

Various parts of the Goldstone Report covered many other alleged violations of all of the major IHL principles, including the principle of distinction. For example, the Israelis were accused of using white phosphorous, which creates severe and painful burns, and it was alleged that they were sending into Gaza flechette missiles that are an "area weapon" incapable of discriminating between objectives after detonation.[65] These missiles, the UN Fact-Finding Mission argued, were not precise weapons, and these Israeli weapons were configured as the types of munitions that were unsuitable for contemporary urban warfare.[66]

The Goldstone Report thus contained page after page of incriminating allegations, and for many years this dense and lengthy text served as an ideological archive for NGOs and other groups who wanted "facts" that they could use to support their critiques of Israeli wartime practices. All of this listing of horrors, including the usage of white phosphorus, were used to produce an inductively derived argumentative conclusion—that the Israelis were engaged in continuous and *systematic* abuse of civilians in an effort to inflict collective punishment on Palestinian terrorists in Gaza. By intimidating and terrorizing the Palestinians, argued the Goldstone Report authors, the Israelis were engaging in reprehensible types of arbitrary, cruel, and inhumane treatment. Others who read this report called this a prototypical example of "state terrorism."[67]

In some instances, the contributors to the Goldstone Report reviewed some of the written texts that contained information about Israeli military objectives and strategizing that had circulated years before Operation Cast Lead. After decoding and analyzing these written texts this UN Mission argued that the tactics that were used in late 2008 and early 2009 by the Israelis were "consistent with previous practices, most recently during the Lebanon war in 2006." At this point in their recital of allegations Richard Goldstone and the others explained to readers that during the war in Lebanon the Israelis had developed a concept known as the "Dahiya doctrine," and they elaborated by noting that this involved the application of disproportionate force, that caused great damage and destruction to civilian infrastructure and property. The Mission authors argued that the "facts on the ground that it witnessed for itself" showed that the Israelis were using the Dahiya doctrine during Operation Cast Lead, and that they were putting into practice what elite Israeli military experts had prescribed as the best strategy for dealing with Palestinian terrorists.[68] This type of argumentation downplayed the individualistic nature of support for the Dahiya doctrine while it magnified the alleged collectivist ratification of this doctrine.

In this ideological narration of events the second Israeli–Lebanese War in 2006 was sparked when a Hezbollah team crossed the border and attacked an Israeli Army patrol. In 2006, the Dahiya quarter of Beirut was a Hezbollah stronghold that Israeli forces flattened in sustained air raids that lasted some 34 days; these raids were designed to put an end to the troubles that were posed by Iranian-backed Shiite groups in the region. As noted above, the Israeli air raids created a situation in which the Israelis were accused of using "disproportionate" force in order to kill various enemies.[69]

Sometimes authors used the term "disproportionate" in a formalistic legal sense to argue that the Israelis were not getting that much benefit from their costly bombardments, while at other times that phrase was used in a more colloquial, military sense, to reference the use of overwhelming lethal force. Was it even possible that the circulation of talk about the doctrine was itself viewed as a possible deterrent, a type of warning to Hezbollah that might mitigate Lebanese civilian casualties?

This might be a plausible interpretation of the strategic usage of the Dahiya doctrine that did not appear in the Goldstone Report, but there is little doubt that the Israelis felt they had to respond to these types of accusations after 2006 by arguing that Hezbollah was firing rockets from civilian homes in southern Lebanon. This type of rhetorical framing meant that the Dahiya doctrine was simply one of many strategic plans that could be outlined by military analysts who were not that interested in debating about whether Israel was really that interested in regime change or in using military force to alter the Lebanese geopolitical landscape.

Critics of the Israelis could use conversations about the Dahiya doctrine as a way of placing the glare of international media spotlights on the legality and morality of the way the Israelis waged their campaign against Hezbollah—or Lebanon, depending on your interpretative frameworks.

Interestingly enough, given all the talk of security, the activities of the Israeli Army in 2006 could be attacked from both the left and right of the political spectrum. The leftists tried to argue that the Israeli soldiers were using too many aggressive warfighting tactics, while the right-wing critics of the Israeli military complained that these modern forces could not effectively halt the daily barrage of rockets that fell on some Israeli cities. In this political tug of war, one side wanted less interventionism while the other side wanted the Israelis to finish the job of wiping out Hezbollah. By the end of this Lebanese incursion some 1,200 Lebanese and more than 150 Israelis lost their lives and Prime Minister Ehud Olmert was asked to resign over his handling of the conflict.

Several pages of the Goldstone Report contain what communication scholars would call a "rhetorical analysis" of key Israeli military and diplomatic texts, and the authors of this report focused a great deal of attention on the ways the Israelis were ideologically deploying their concept of Hamas' "supporting infrastructure." Goldstone and the others explained that the IDF and other military forces were using this concept to "transform civilians and civilian objects into legitimate targets." By reviewing statements made by Israeli political and military leaders prior to, and during, Operation Cast Lead, the UN Fact-Finding Mission on the Gaza Conflict argued that the Israelis were deploying the Dahiya doctrine to justify "creating maximum disruption in the lives of many people as a legitimate means to achieve not only military but political goals."[70]

This particular wording, which attacked the Israelis' interpretations of "dual purpose" targets, was meant to highlight the ways that the Israelis were feigning military necessities so they could take out the political leadership of terrorists in Gaza. If this was accepted by international readers, then this would have meant that many Israelis had committed war crimes and that military leaders could be brought before dozens of foreign courts that wished to exercise "universal jurisdiction." This is why literally hundreds of academic essays and newspaper articles tried to delegitimize the Goldstone Report. In a host of ways the report seemed to be a frontal ideological attack on both the particular tactics that were used by the Israelis during Operation Case Lead as well as more general Israeli motivations, attitudes and strategies during wartime.

The authors of the Goldstone Report used all types of rhetorical strategies as they crafted their report, and one of their most intriguing claims appeared when they argued that the Israelis were choosing to use tactics for "area" bombing instead of the "precise" weapons that were at their disposal. In an attempt to add credibility and *gravitas* to their report, members of this UN Mission supplemented their rhetorical analysis of the Dahiya doctrine with critiques of the Israeli Air Force discourse that had lauded UAV drone precision. Goldstone and the others opined that if the Israelis really wanted to be taken at their own word that "almost no errors" occurred during the targeting stages, then this could only mean that *they purposely set aside this precision option* when the Israeli Air Force operationalized their own version of the Dahiya doctrine. This involved more than just the pilots, because there seemed to be "deliberate planning and policy decisions" being made throughout the Israeli chain-of-command, from the top down to the "standard operating procedures and instructions given to the troops on the ground."[71] This created the impression that *all of the Israelis*, regardless of rank, understood the ramifications of their decision-making or at least acquiesced in what looked to the Mission as intentional targeting of Palestinian civilians. Again, if true, this would have evidenced—for international audiences—the systematic violation of myriad *jus in bello* IHL principles that would have implicated thousands of Israelis.

The authors of the Goldstone Report combed through the archives as they looked for historical parallels that would highlight the repetitive nature of Israeli strategies, tactics, and operations. They were convinced that if one compared former Israeli operations in the West Bank with the Israeli strategizing that one found in Lebanon, then one had to conclude that these actions were following a consistent military roadmap that led them to Gaza. "The military operations from 27 December to 18 January did not occur in a vacuum," argued Goldstone and the others, "either in terms of proximate causes in relation to the Hamas/Israeli dynamics or in relation to the development of Israeli military thinking about how best to describe the nature of its military objectives." In theory, while many of the tactics remained the same, the Israelis were said to be engaged in qualitative shifts in strategic planning that moved from relatively focused operations to more "massive and deliberate destruction."[72] Critics who read between the lines could conclude that Israeli talk of precision was being used to paper over more imprecise area bombing and indiscriminate targeting.

Rhetoricians have often written about the ideological drift of arguments that move between public and legal or military venues, and in this case the authors of the Goldstone Report were able to collect both public statements made by reservists and more academic commentaries from active military planners as they tried to use the Israelis' own words to provide even more anecdotal evidence to support their empirical claims regarding the collective punishment and targeting of civilians. For years mainstream presses, alternative outlets, and the blogosphere had been filled with commentary about the mythic Dahiya doctrine, and many of those essays had been contextualized and recontextualized to document the discursive power of these *dispositifs*.

Regardless of whether one applauded or hated this doctrine it supposedly gained traction and spreadability as it moved across platforms. By the time the authors of the Goldstone Report collected these fragmentary comments on the Dahiya doctrine, they could easily contextualize the remarks that were made by then-Major General Gadi Eisenkot, retired Major General Giora Eiland, and retired Colonel Gabriel Siboni.

To be fair to the Israelis, one of the key issues that needs to be asked is whether the Dahiya doctrine was actually tailored to the specific needs of the Lebanon conflict, and then maybe *abandoned*, or whether it had an afterlife that lived on, an *episteme* or *dispositif* that represented a broader approach to dealing with Hamas or other types of Palestinian terrorism. Did the Dahiya doctrine provide a condensation symbol for the ways that most Israelis wanted to handle Hezbollah or Hamas foes?

50 *Domestic and international critiques*

During the fall of 2008, Gadi Eisenkot, the head of the IDF's northern division, warned Hezbollah that any all-out war against Israel might invite massive destruction. "What happened in the Dahiya quarter of Beirut," explained Eisenkot, "will happen in every village from which Israel is fired on."[73] To make himself perfectly clear Eisenkot elaborated in this fragment that appeared in the Israeli newspaper *Yedioth Ahronoth*:

> We will apply disproportionate force on it [village] and cause great damage and destruction there. From our standpoint, these are not civilian villages, they are military bases. This is not a recommendation. This is a plan. And it has been approved.[74]

In other words, if Lebanese villagers were going to tolerate Hezbollah's presence in their midst, then they were no longer going to be regarded as civilians but as participants in the war who helped form military bases.

We may never know whether Eisenkot's way of talking about the Dahiya "plan" represented the dominant theoretical positions of most Israeli military planners, but critics wearing a consequentialist lens could argue that events on the ground seemed to indicate that the Dahiya doctrine was put into practice in 2006. At the same time, *memes* with Gadi Eisenkot's words would recirculate countless times across the World Wide Web, and the Goldstone Report was just one of the texts that included commentaries from empowered Israelis who wrote or talked about disproportionate firepower. Eisenkot also warned that Syrian villages might also be attacked if they served as launching bases for Hezbollah rockets.[75]

General Eisenkot's reasoning seemed to make complete sense to those who were tired of trying to hunt and to track down *individual* carriers of rocket launchers. He explained that no one could hunt down the "thousands" of rockets, and existential fears about the rockets may have created a situation where many soldiers and members of the public not only accepted, but demanded, that the Dahiya doctrine become a reality. Dealing in collective threats against villages seemed an effective way of promoting military deterrence.

In spite of the fact that not everyone is willing to talk about, or publicly articulate their support for the Dahiya doctrine, there is little question that some Israelis were willing to defend the deployment of this strategizing. There is plenty of empirical and anecdotal evidence that many hardline Israeli military leaders did not enjoy hearing that they had "lost" a war in Lebanon. Giora Eiland, for example, in a 2008 essay entitled "The Third Lebanon War: Target Lebanon," would provide his honest assessment of what had to be done to avoid defeat in future struggles with Hezbollah. He argued that some of the softer policies that were "commended by the international community" were the ones where the Israelis struck at the individual "bad guys" (Hezbollah), but refrained from "striking the darlings of the West and the UN (The Lebanese state and its government)." This, according to Eiland, was going in the wrong direction, in that it might be "convenient and desirable for others, but for Israel it spells

Domestic and international critiques 51

disaster."[76] Part of this was perhaps putting on display the typical disdain for civilian and political interference in military affairs, but the public articulation of these types of arguments seemed to indicate that at least some Israeli leaders wanted to purposely blur the lines that existed between what other parts of the world configured as legitimate Hezbollah targets and illegitimate Lebanese targets. Eiland famously quipped: "People won't be going to the beach in Beirut while Haifa residents are in shelters."[77]

Commentaries like Eiland's provide an example of how the Israelis viewed some international interpretations of the law of war as antiquated vestiges of a Westphalian way of viewing state powers that bore no practical relationship to the actual lives of those who fought Hamas or Hezbollah.

As noted in Chapter 1, Israelis have argued for years that they represent the cutting-edge of counterterror thinking, and the promotion of ideas like the Dahiya doctrine shows that they are willing to think outside the box in all of this chaoplexic, irregular warfare. Eiland's plan provided one more typical example of how Israeli warhawks wanted to focus on military strategizing for Israel and not worry about foreign cosmopolitan concerns regarding potential diplomatic or political crises. What he suggested was just one of the most radical ways of implementing the Dahiya doctrine—why not treat the Lebanese as enemies instead of bystanders and make them share some of the suffering the Israelis were allegedly experiencing from rocket attacks? This *militarized way of thinking about strategic communication* assumed that the suffering of Lebanese populations would bring about the speedy ouster of Hezbollah.

Readers need to be aware that this appeared to be a key argumentative link within much larger chains of logical and cultural reasoning that circulated in these Israeli military metanarratives. For example, Eiland was convinced that his radical plan could prevent the third Lebanon War or win it for the Israelis, and he wanted to make it clear to "Lebanon's allies" that the next war would not be just between Israel and Hezbollah but between Israel and Lebanon. In one key passage that would be referenced by the authors of the Goldstone Report, Eiland noted:

> Such a war will lead to the elimination of the Lebanese military, the destruction of the national infrastructure, and intense suffering among the population.... Serious damage to the Republic of Lebanon, the destruction of homes and infrastructure, and the suffering of thousands of people are consequences that can influence Hezbollah's behavior more than anything else.... The Israeli message has to be clear and unequivocal.[78]

Note that the warnings about the suffering of thousands can be configured as a military necessity, providing the leverage that would be needed to save lives. In what might be called a necropolitical way of thinking about life and death, thousands of civilians who did not listen to these Israeli warnings suffered the potential consequences.

If Eiland had been the only person making these types of arguments it would have been difficult to make a case that Israelis really were trying to apply the Dahiya doctrine in Gazan contexts, but the authors of the Goldstone Report had other information that supported their claims. One colonel in the reserves, Gabriel Siboni, seemed to be on the same page as Eiland when Siboni talked about how future Israeli attacks needed to be aimed at both Hezbollah's military capabilities as well as the "economic interests and the centres of civilian power" in Lebanon that supported Hezbollah.[79] Siboni echoed Eisenkot's arguments when he wrote an essay on the Dahiya doctrine for Tel Aviv's Institute for National Security Studies (INSS). This was one of the most influential institutes that helped with Israeli wargaming and military strategizing, and Siboni argued in 2008 that there was a growing perception in Israel that Israelis needed an "updated response" to the rocket and missile threats that were coming from Syria, Lebanon, and the Gaza Strip.[80] Perhaps, just perhaps, that updated response came in the form of the Dahiya doctrine.

IHL scholars might cringe when they read Gabriel Siboni's discussion of "disproportionality" because it looks more like the military way of talking about "overwhelming" force instead of the legalistic, IHL way of defining disproportionality, but he was nevertheless defending a recognizable position when he argued that disproportionate strikes need to be designed so that they can hurt the enemy's weakest pressure points. Instead of worrying about the capacity of the missile launchers, the IDF was described as an organization that needed to hurt, and to punish, the support structures that would require long and expensive reconstruction. These types of strikes, explained Siboni, needed to be carried out as quickly as possible and they needed to prioritize the "damaging" of "assets" so that IDF soldiers would not have to take too many risks trying to take out each and every launcher. Siboni was convinced that the deployment of disproportionate force would create "lasting memory for decision-makers in Syria and Lebanon, thereby increasing Israeli deterrence."[81]

The authors of the Goldstone Report, by discovering some of the work of Eiland, Eisenkot, and Siboni, were not simply describing some of the "facts" as they waxed eloquently on what they saw when they reviewed what happened during Operation Cast Lead. They, like the members of the IHC, were also interventionists in these heated debates, and one can sense some of their fury as they juxtaposed talk of the Dahiya doctrine with the deaths of the Palestinian men, women, and children in Gaza. They, like many international observers, worried about the abstractions and decontextualization of Israeli strategies, tactics, and operations that were killing more than just the Hezbollah or Hamas fighters who were firing rockets.

Yet those Israeli leftists or other critics who armed themselves with the empirical evidence and argumentative summaries that were contained in the Goldstone Report faced the Sisyphean task of having to try to counter the rhetoric of Israeli hardliners who wanted to go after the civilians who were accused of helping or condoning attacks on Israeli populations. On February 2, 2009, Eli Yishai would argue that Israelis had to set a price on every rocket that was launched by Hamas. "Even if they fire at an open area or into the sea, we must damage their infrastructures and destroy 100 homes."[82]

Years later, Richard Goldstone went back to Israel with Eli Yishai after he reversed his position on the "intentional" nature of some of the Israeli targeting of civilians.[83]

Many Israelis attacked the conclusions of the Goldstone Report because they realized that it had established a template that was filled with allegations that would be recycled over and over again. The US Campaign to End Occupation, for example, argued that at various times it had been the Israelis who had been accused of using Palestinians as human shields. UN researchers later found that between January 2010 and March 2013 there had been a "continuous use of Palestinian children as human shields and informants." Palestinian children have been asked to open bags that were believed to contain bombs,[84] and some soldiers made youngsters stand in front of military vehicles in order to shield themselves from rock throwers. In some cases there were reports that children were forced to enter homes that were believed to be rigged with explosives.[85] Many of those soldiers who were involved in these incidents were reprimanded, but the clusters of arguments that were collected in the Goldstone Report drifted along and haunted the Israelis for many years.

The Israelis, and their American supporters, have succeeded in authoring many essays on "human shields" that resonate with many audiences who are used to hearing about the tactics of the Taliban or Al Qaeda, but international skeptics realized that the strategically ambiguous nature of the word "infrastructure" could hide the thanatopolitical nature of all of the devastation in Gaza. Even Aharon Barak, who prided himself on having the IHC require a thorough investigation of times when the Israelis may have erroneously determined that a Palestinian civilian was directly participating in hostilities, still believed that most of the time Israeli military authorities had the power of discernment in the fog of war.[86]

International critics might label Yishai's talk of destroying 100 homes for the firing of a Hamas missile as the advocacy of some unwarranted vengeance, but supporters of these hardline positions could respond that this just made military sense, constituted a form of force protection, and saved lives in the long run because it cut down on the loss of both Israeli and Palestinian lives.

Obviously the authors of the Goldstone Report did not accept all of those frames when they reviewed Operation Cast Lead, but as I note in the next section, the Israelis did not have to sit idly by and just accept what some UN Fact-Finding Mission had to say about the practices of the Israeli military forces.

Shin Bet critiques and the challenges posed by the circulation of Dror Moreh's *The Gatekeepers*

In other parts of this chapter I have focused on how Israelis have reacted to a host of outsider rhetorical texts that have been used to critique Israeli warfighting tactics or the strategizing that goes on in the "disputed territories"; in this section

I want to shift gears and provide readers with a vignette that illustrates how some Israeli leftists, or former militarists, have used the visual medium to critique some Israeli securitization practices.

Promoters of the notion of Israeli exceptionalism pride themselves on their tolerance of dissent, but there are always perceptual limits to this toleration. Note, for example, how Israeli diplomats, former security officers, members of the IDF, and Israeli citizens reacted to the 2012–2013 debates that were ignited in the aftermath of the release of Dror Moreh's *The Gatekeepers* (2012).[87] As Elisabeth Sydor noted in her review of this documentary, Israeli filmmaker Dror Moreh produced a "masterful" film that was framed around interviews that were conducted with six surviving former leaders of Shin Bet, the Israel secret security service. The central question at the heart of *The Gatekeepers*, explains Sydor, is the question: "What is morally appropriate in a wartime environment?"[88]

Observers disagree about how heavy-handed Dror Moreh might have been in guiding some of the questioning that goes on throughout this cinematic production, but those who watch this film get to hear former leaders of Israel's security agency talk as if they were the ones who chose these topics. At various points in the movie they are very open about the fact that they may have had to use harsh interrogation techniques or assassinate Palestinians as they tried to protect their country, but they hit a discordant note when they also start to pontificate on the question of whether any of these activities actually helped Israel in the long-run.

Many Israeli journalists and lay persons responded to some of the claims that were made by these six former directors of Shin Bet because they felt that these opinion leaders should have remained silent and kept their "political" opinions to themselves. At the same time, some Israelis accused Moreh of producing *The Gatekeepers* so he could advance his own political agenda as he sought out alliances with those who wanted to see "two-state" solutions to the Palestinian–Israeli conflict.

This advocacy of the two-state solution is something that viewers of *The Gatekeepers* are only gradually made aware of, because Moreh's documentary seems to be organized around moral questions that were posed by historical Shin Bet incidents. The documentary opens without any of the usual music tracks, and the stories that are told are initially contextualized by having a narrator ask this key question: "What do you do, hunting a terrorist? You can get him, but there are other people in the car."[89] Taken out of context, and isolated from the rest of the documentary, this might look like a typical question that would be asked by an Israeli legal adviser or an IDF commander who was concerned about the law of war doctrines of distinction and proportionality.

The aesthetics of *The Gatekeeper* have everything to do with the security conundrums and the moral queries that confront moviegoers, but as Gil Troy recognized, what might be going on here is that the "speaking spooks" are involved in a "coup d'etat."[90] In other words, there is something transgressive going on here, in that the six former leaders are going to be critiquing civilian superiors and former colleagues who were using counterterrorist rhetorics to justify their heavy-handed use of militarizing and securitizing tactics.

One of the ultimate messages that moviegoers take with them as they leave the theater is that even the most effective of the harsh security measures, that might protect the lives of security agents or the IDF, end up hindering, rather than facilitating, any chance of exchanging territory for security and finding lasting peace. This overarching message is extremely threatening to most patriotic Israelis because it implies that many of the tactics that were used by Shin Bet or the IDF contributed to the spread, rather than the containment, of Palestinian terrorist threats.

All of this interviewing of six directors was indeed being used to highlight the moral dilemmas that confronted those who had to kill or detain terrorist suspects, but Moreh was also trying to use this medium to get across other, larger, ideological messages. One of the interviewees, Amil Aylon, had this to say when American and Israeli commentators thought that it would have been a much better film if it had just tried to answer the moral questions without become "political":

> If it had, there would have been no point to the film.... Many Israelis and American Jews want to deny it, but this is our professional opinion. We are at the edge of an abyss, and if Israeli–Palestinian peace doesn't progress, it's the end of Zionism.[91]

Gil Troy characterized the major protagonists in *The Gatekeeper* as "anti-Israel activists" because it appears that all six of these former leaders of Shin Bet—who come from diverse political backgrounds—appear to be like-minded. Paul Byrnes, a writer for *The Sydney Morning Herald*, admitted that he did not know the specifics of how Dror Moreh was able to get all of them together, but he did think that *The Gatekeepers* was spreading the right idea at the right time. Moreover, Byrnes noted that this was not the first time some of these interviewees had gotten together. About a decade earlier, four of them had publicly urged "Ariel Sharon to make peace with the Palestinians *via* a two-state solution."[92]

Given the polysemic and polyvalent nature of filmic media, as well as the enduring desire to tell patriotic tales of Israeli exceptionalism, we can appreciate why many of Moreh's detractors argued that even the misleading features of *The Gatekeepers* couldn't keep out the illuminating light that came from the revelation of truth, where the film couldn't help showcasing "Israel's democratic vitality while seeking to undermine it."[93]

After many international screenings of the film, Israeli diplomats scrambled to find ways of effectively responding to the film, and in France, Yaron Gamburg, the spokesperson for the Israeli Embassy in Paris, wrote a telegram that stated that media coverage was placing Israel in a negative light.[94] Writing from Toronto, Canada, Hadas Wittenberg Silberstein sent the Israeli Foreign Ministry a missive that indicated that while she thought *The Gatekeepers* was a powerful film that put an Israeli face on some of the political-security dilemmas that confronted Shin Bet, it was "certainly tendentious in its portrayal of Palestinian suffering." Nevertheless, Silberstein concluded by arguing that the film could still be viewed as a "source of great pride because of its willingness to engage in soul-searching."[95]

Not all Israeli diplomats were willing to try to find that silver-lining when they thought about the potential suasory impact of Moreh's documentary. Michael Oren, Israel's Ambassador to the United States, was interviewed by the Israeli web portal *Ynet*, and he had this to say about why he worried about the film:

> The problem is that those interviewed are not Israeli citizens of a certain opinion, but rather former Shin Bet chiefs. One of them (Carmi Gilon) says that Israel causes daily suffering to millions of Palestinians. Then another former Shin Bet head (Avraham Shalom) compares Israel to Nazi Germany, not exactly, but kind of … and I've been hearing about Jews leaving the screen asking why we should keep supporting Israel.[96]

Oren thus worried that Moreh's film might adversely impact American Jewish support for Israeli causes.

Part of the evocative power of *The Gatekeepers* comes from the rhetorical ethos of these former leaders of Shin Bet, who cannot be summarily dismissed as Israeli leftists who don't understand Israel's existential dangers. During an interview with *Fathom*, Dror Moreh argued that Shin Bet was an organization that understands the "Israeli conflict better than anybody else," and he averred that these men had "walked in the alleys of the refugee camps" and knew the conflict "from the bottom of the sewers."[97]

One of the concrete historical examples of Moreh's documentary work that put on display some of this work from the "bottom" included the reenactment of the Bus 300 affair in 1984.[98] During that year, Majdi Abu Humma, one of the suspects involved in the hijacking of a bus, was said to have been killed earlier during a shootout, but it was later learned that the then-chief of Israel's secret service, Avraham Shalom, had ordered the Israeli secret services to kill two Palestinians who were captured after the attack on the Israeli bus.[99]

The no. 300 bus was hijacked by two Palestinians on its way from Tel Aviv to Ashkelon in April 1984, and we now know that Shin Bet was able to capture the hijackers. A chance photograph, taken by Alex Levac, that was published in an old daily, *Hadashot*, prevented Shin Bet from completely covering up the murder of the two Palestinians. Avraham Shalom had been forced to resign from his post in the wake of the coverage of this scandal, and all of this ended when President Herzog pardoned many of those who were involved in the incident. Shalom, who died just months before Operation Protective Edge, would serve as one of the founders of an organization called the Geneva Initiative, a group that brought together Israelis and Palestinians who were trying to find peaceful solutions to their conflicts.[100]

Dror Moreh may be using this medium to try to argue that the story of the no. 300 bus, and the treatment of Majdi Abu Humma, is emblematic of how Israelis have treated Palestinians during the occupation, and his documentary uses information about Alex Levac's photograph as a way of describing how handcuffed Palestinian prisoners were handled by Shin Bet agents. He, like others who have circulated this image over the years, protects the identity of the Shin Bet agents who carted Abu Humma away by blurring their faces, but it is evident that we know the identity of the prisoner. "Employing the sound effect of a snapshot," argues Tara Judah, "accompanied by a brief camera flash," Moreh "reverses the 'capturing' of a moment and instead uses the image as a phenomenological gateway to open up historical time and space."[101]

Many Israelis who watched and panned *The Gatekeepers* insisted that Dror Moreh and his former-Shin Bet interviewees had inaccurately represented both Israel's historical chronology and the contemporary conditions that led to the militarization and securitization of the disputed territories. Roz Rothstein and Roberta Seid, for example, argued that *The Gatekeepers* could have been a great film, but instead it became a documentary vehicle for telling a very "simplistic message" that implied that Israel's misguided occupation of the West Bank stood in the way of lasting peace.[102] While Rothstein and Seid acknowledged that the six former directors of Shin Bet "exude *gravitas*" as they are shown wrestling with moral quandaries, they thought that their genuine self-reflexivity and their willingness to speak was testament to Israel's "robust democracy."[103]

One of the Israelis' major concerns had to do with Moreh's historicizing of the causes of terrorism and perpetuation of the conflict, where the documentary appeared to blame Israel for the Palestinian hostility and violence that came in the wake of the 1967 Six-Day War. What Rothstein and Seid would have wanted to see would have been a film that would have allowed the viewer to learn more about the terrorism that had been "a regular feature of life since the pre-state days."[104] In theory, Moreh and his six interviews had confused cause with effect, and they had downplayed the existential dangers that always confronted Israel, and Rothstein and Seid were convinced that this had nothing to do with the Israeli administration of the West Bank.

These types of reviews of *The Gatekeepers* allowed Israelis to rummage through the past as they selectively chronicled historical events in ways that treated the Israeli–Palestinian conflict as one that was created by the Palestinians. For example, Rothstein and Seid, writing for *The Jerusalem Post*, deflected attention away from the horrors of detention and assassinations as they used this occasion to wax eloquently on the ways that Israelis were helping *rescue* Palestinians from their otherwise wretched conditions:

> Palestinian Arabs murdered over 1,000 Jews between 1920 and 1967, and they ethnically cleansed all Jewish communities from the areas they captured during the 1948 war, including the West Bank, Gaza and eastern Jerusalem. The pattern of terrorism simply continued after Israel's victory in its 1967 defensive war.... Visually and verbally, the film portrays Israel as a heartless occupier. Audiences get no information about how harsh life was for Palestinians under Egyptian and Jordanian rule between 1948 and 1967, with rampant childhood diseases, economic stagnation and restricted civil

and political rights. In addition, the documentary completely overlooks the big picture of positive Israeli–Palestinian relations after 1967. Even as Israel sought to stop terrorists, it also instituted Palestinian municipal self-government and administration, introduced freedom of speech and association, and vastly modernized the Palestinian economy as well as Palestinian health, welfare and education, turning the West Bank and Gaza into the world's fourth fastest growing economy in the 1970s and 1980s.[105]

Here, there is no discussion of Nakba, no commentary on the economic and political dismantling of Gaza, no conversation about refugees, no attention paid to the trauma and hatred that has been generated by an administrative system that privileged the rights of Israeli citizens and settlers. Note the absence of any thanatopolitical discussion of how many Palestinians may have been killed since 1948, or how many Palestinians would gladly give up all of that Israeli modernization in the name of their own independence.

Cinematic debates about *The Gatekeepers* also allowed Israelis to comment on the fact that Moreh and other critics of Israeli occupation policies were unfairly characterizing the settlers as extremists and intransigents. As Professor Sydor would explain in her trenchant summary of this portion of *The Gatekeepers*:

> Midway through the film, a bomb of another sort drops when the documentary reveals that Palestinians aren't the only terrorists at work. In fact, the Shin Bet considers them small potatoes compared to the Israeli extreme religious right, who are discovered plotting to blow up the Muslim shrine the Dome of the Rock, an act of such far-reaching proportions it could set off a world war. And when it is revealed that the Israeli government has effectively conspired with the convicted plotters by commuting their sentences, the security operatives become further disillusioned. Following Prime Minister Rabin's assassination by an Israeli, Ami Ayalon takes the Shin Bet helm, implementing an organizational shift that will transform the group.[106]

This type of contextualization would of course infuriate those who view the settlers as the Zionist pioneers of Eretz Yisrael, the brave souls willing to risk life and limb in order to help with the reclaiming of land that had been set aside for a chosen people.

Some Israelis got the feeling that Moreh was using this medium, and his interviewees, to create some type of moral equivalence by insinuating that many Jews, as well as Palestinians, became terrorists. Rothstein and Seid responded to these efforts by arguing that while a few Jewish settlers from Hebron had formed the "Jewish underground" in 1980, the overwhelming majority of Israeli settlers were law-abiding citizens.[107] These were contrasted with Hamas fighters, who were described as having a "genocidal ideology" that allegedly never showed up during the interview of the Shin Bet directors.[108]

The production of *The Gatekeepers* also provided Israelis with the chance to remind Moreh and other leftists that the second Intifada had brought with it waves of suicide bombings and the "fanatical hatred" of Israelis. The six Shin Bet directors were often thanked for their contributions as they tried to track down those who murdered and maimed Israelis, and many Israelis liked to focus attention on some key lines in *The Gatekeepers* that they thought explained some of the harshness behind controversial administrative measures. Avraham Shalom, when he was queried by Moreh about the potential immorality of what happened during his tenure (1981–1986), retorted: "This isn't about morality.... When the terrorists become moral, we'll be moral."

As I noted in Chapter 1, both sides in these Israeli–Palestinian debates often use what I've called "lost opportunities" types of arguments as they point fingers at those they believe allowed peace to slip through their fingers, and some of Moreh's interviewees don't mince words when they argue that Shin Bet operatives sometimes had to follow the orders of political leaders who knew little about the importance of negotiating with terrorist suspects or other Palestinians. Rothstein and Seid's critique of *The Gatekeepers* provided a typical Israeli chronology of lost opportunities when they explained that Moreh never allowed viewers to see that "Israel has repeatedly tried to do what Moreh advocates," and that the "film never mentions Israel's offers to trade land for peace in 1967, 1979, 2000, and 2008, or that Palestinian leaders systematically rejected these offers."[109]

As readers might imagine, Israeli commentators on *The Gatekeepers* had to find a way of linking the actions of the security leaders to the horrors and traumas of those who were worried about Hamas rockets in 2013. Morah is accused of trying to share his "wishful thinking" with audiences by conveniently leaving out "recent history," and this history is said to be one in which Israel has had to face threats from both Hezbollah and Hamas. For some Israelis, Moreh's attempt to blame either Israel or Shin Bet leaders for current hostilities was "like blaming the victim who is defending himself [*sic*] instead of blaming the perpetrator." If Moreh had really wanted to provide material that told the truth about Israel's "existential strategic challenges," then he would have told a story about Shin Bet heroism that would have put on full display life's hard realities.[110]

What this shows is that even hard-hitting, jarring visualities like *The Gatekeepers* can always be recontextualized by those who want to focus on using prisms that focus on Israeli rectitude and exceptionalism.

Conclusion

As I noted in the introduction to this chapter, I wanted to provide readers with a few vignettes that illustrated how domestic and international critics, between 2000 and 2013, were complaining about Israeli control of sea, land, and air spaces over the West Bank and Gaza. A critical genealogical study that brings together analyses of the synchronic and diachronic aspects of some of this foreign criticism underscores the repetitive nature of the arguments that were used in debates about the Dahiya doctrine from the Lebanon War, the Goldstone Report, and *The Gatekeepers*. Regardless of whether we were looking at the boarding of ships miles away from the Gazan coast or whether we were reviewing wartime decision-making during Operation Cast Lead, critics had little trouble tying these activities to occupational frames that highlighted the misery of the Palestinians. In each of these cases, the Israelis countered by recontextualizing each incident so that they could provide evidence of the existential dangers that confronted them.

One of the saddest conclusions that one reaches as one traces the historical trajectory of these vignettes is that one senses the growing frustration of both foreign skeptics and Israeli patriots who seem to be cognizant of the fact that they are presenting divergent metanarratives. These various camps accuse the other of misinterpreting IHL, misunderstanding the magnitude of the risk of terrorist threats from Hezbollah or Hamas, and misreading the prospects for achieving any viable "two-state" solutions to these problems.

In the next chapter, I begin to provide readers with a sense of just how far Israelis are willing to go in defending some of the most controversial of all of their policies, the targeted killing of Palestinian leaders who are suspected of being terrorists.

Notes

1 For critiques of Israeli "siege" mentalities or the "Masada" complex, see Daniel Bar-Tal and Dikla Antebi, "Siege Mentality in Israel," *International Journal of Intercultural Relations* 1, no. 1 (1992): 49–67; Yael Zerubavel, "The Death of Memory and the Memory of Death: Masada and the Holocaust as Historical Metaphors," *Representations*, 45 (1994): 72–100; Ruth Amossy, "From National Consensus to Political Dissent: The Rhetorical Uses of the Masada Myth in Israel," *Rivesta Italiana di Filosofia del Linguaggio* 6, no. 3 (2010): 1–15, DOI: 10.1080/14650040903486983.
2 Aharon Barak, "International Humanitarian Law and the Israeli Supreme Court," *Israel Law Review* 47, no. 2 (2014): 187.
3 Gideon Levy, *The Punishment of Gaza* (London: Verso, 2010).
4 Avi Kober, "From Heroic to Post-Heroic Warfare: Israel's Way of War in Asymmetrical Conflicts," *Armed Forces & Society* 41, no. 1 (2015): 96–122, 114. For more support of Kober's claims on the perceived value of the lives of single Israeli soldiers, see Yagil Levy, *Israel's Death Hierarchy: Casualty Aversion in a Militarized Democracy* (New York: New York University Press, 2012).
5 Benyamin Netanyahu, *A Durable Peace: Israel and its Place Among the Nations* (New York: Warner Books, 2000).
6 See Ariel Handel, "Gated/Gating Community: The Settlement Complex in the West Bank," *Transactions* 39, no. 4 (2014): 504–517, DOI: 10.1111/tran.12045.
7 Adi Opher, Michael Givoni, and Sara Hanif, eds., *The Power of Inclusive Exclusion: Anatomy of Israeli Rule in the Occupied Palestinian Territories* (Brooklyn, NY: Zone Books, 2009).
8 On this point note the work of François-Xavier Plasse-Couture, "Effective Abandonment: The Neoliberal Economy of Violence in Israel and the Occupied Territories," *Security Dialogue* 44, no. 5/6 (2013): 449–466.
9 See, for example, Ian S. Lustick, *Unsettled States, Disputed Lands: Britain and Ireland, France and Algeria, Israel and the West Bank-Gaza* (Ithaca, NY: Cornell University Press, 1993); Gillian Duncan, Orla Lynch, Gilbert Ramsay, and Alison M.S. Watson, *State Terrorism and Human Rights: International Responses Since the End of the Cold War* (New York: Routledge, 2013). For a recent critique of how

terms like "terrorism" or "terrorist" have become parts of social, political, and scholarly discourses, see Zohar Kampf, "News-Media and Terrorism: Changing Relationship, Changing Definitions," *Sociology Compass* 8, no. 1 (2014): 1–9.
10 Dror Moreh, *The Gatekeepers* (Mac Guff Ligne, Cinephil, and Dror Moreh Productions, 2012).
11 Moustafa Bayoumi, *Midnight on the Mavi Marmara: The Attack on the Gaza Freedom Flotilla and How It Changed the Course of the Israeli/Palestinian Conflict* (Chicago: Haymarket Books, 2010). For a representative example of how some UN observers framed this incident, see Geoffrey Palmer, Alvaro Uribe, and Joseph Ciechanover Itzhar, *Report of the Secretary-General's Panel of Inquiry on the 31 May 2010 Flotilla Incident, July 2011*, http://blog.unwatch.org/wp-content/uploads/Palmer-Committee-Final-report.pdf.
12 Damien Sharkov, "New Turkish Humanitarian Flotilla Set to Defy Blockade," *Newsweek*, last modified August 11, 2014, paragraphs 1–2, www.newsweek.com/new-turkish-humanitarian-flotilla-set-defy-gaza-blockade-263825.
13 Herb Keinon, "Netanyahu to Gaza Flotilla: Surely You Got Lost and Meant to Help the Syrians Being Butchered," *The Jerusalem Post*, last modified June 28, 2015, paragraphs 1–4, www.jpost.com/Arab-Israeli-Conflict/Netanyahu-to-flotilla-passengers-Surely-you-got-lost-and-meant-to-help-the-Syrians-being-butchered-40742.
14 Gil Z. Hochberg, *Visual Occupations: Violence and Visibility in a Conflict Zone* (Durham, NC: Duke University Press, 2015). For a different take on some of this state violence, see James Ron, *Frontiers and Ghettos: State Violence in Serbia and Israel* (Berkeley: University of California Press, 2003).
15 Ariel Ben-Solomon, "Turkish Organization Behind 'Mavi Marmara' Raided in Anti-al-Qaida Sweep," *The Jerusalem Post*, last modified January 13, 2014, www.jpost.com/Middle-East/Turkish-organization-behind-Mavi-Marmara-raided-in-anti-al-Qaida-sweep-338138.
16 For an analysis of how *Ha'aretz*, the *Guardian*, and the *New York Times* covered the *Mavi Marmara* incident, see Shahira Fahmy and Britain Eakin, "High Drama on the High Seas: Peace Versus War Journalism – Framing of an Israeli/Palestinian Related Incident," *The International Communication Gazette* 76, no. 1 (2014): 86–105.
17 UN Human Rights Council, *Report on the International Fact-Finding Mission to Investigate Violations of International Law, including International Humanitarian and Human Rights Law, Resulting from the Israel Attacks on the Flotilla of Ships Carrying Humanitarian Assistance* (New York: UN Human Rights Council, 2010), 20, www2.ohchr.org/english/bodies/hrcouncil/docs/15session/A.HRC.15.21_en.pdf.
18 Ufuk Ulutaş, *A Raid from the Sea: The Gaza Flotilla Attack and Blockade under Legal Scrutiny*, SETA Policy Brief, September 2011, http://arsiv.setav.org/Ups/Pdf/SETA_Policy_Brief_A_Raid_from_the_Sea_Ufuk_Ulutas.pdf.
19 Russell Buchan, "The International Law of Naval Blockade and Israel's Interception of the Mavi Marmara," *Netherlands International Law Review* 58 (2011): 209–241.
20 UN Human Rights Council, *Report of the International Fact-Finding Mission to Investigate Violations of International Law*.
21 Diana Allan and Curtis Brown, "Media's Messengers: The *Mavi Marmara* at the Frontlines of Web 2.0," *Journal of Palestine Studies* 40, no. 1 (2010): 63–77.
22 Herb Keinon, "Netanyahu Apologizes to Turkey Over Gaza Flotilla," *The Jerusalem Post*, last modified March 22, 2013, www.jpost.com/International/Obama-Netanyahu-Erdogan-speak-by-phone-307423.
23 Haroon Siddique, "Gaza Flotilla Attack: UN Report Condemns Israeli 'Brutality,'" *Guardian*, last modified September 22, 2010, www.theguardian.com/world/2010/sep/22/gaza-flotilla-un-condemns-israeli-brutality.
24 Ibid., paragraphs 2–3.
25 Max Blumenthal, *Israelis Celebrate IDF Flotilla Attack*, YouTube, last modified June 6, 2010, www.youtube.com/user/mblumenthal#p/u/18/ZWha0aMGIlQ.

Domestic and international critiques

26 Fahmy and Eakin, "High Drama on the High Seas," 88.
27 Ben-Solomon, "Turkish Organization Behind," paragraph 4.
28 Benjamin Netanyahu, quoted in Keinon, "Netanyahu Apologizes," paragraph 14. Compensation talks were also apparently underway as officials tried to smooth Turkish–Israeli relations after the incident. See Herb Keinon, "Jerusalem Plays Down Turkish Report that '*Mavi Marmara*' Compensation Deal 'Almost' Complete," *The Jerusalem Post*, last modified December 25, 2013, www.jpost.com/Middle-East/Jerusalem-plays-down-Turkish-report-that-Mavi-Marmara-compensation-deal-almost-complete-336126.
29 Gideon Levy, "The Curse of the *Mavi Marmara*," *Ha'aretz*, last modified June 17, 2012, www.haaretz.com/opinion/the-curse-of-the-mavi-marmara.premium-1.436818.
30 Ibid., paragraphs 3, 10.
31 Itamar Ben-Gvir, quoted in Yonah Jeremy Bob, "Court Rejects Petition to Criminally Charge MK Zoabi for Mavi Marmara Involvement," *The Jerusalem Post*, December 23, 2013, paragraph 6, www.jpost.com/National-News/Court-rejects-petition-to-criminally-charge-MK-Zoabi-for-Mavi-Marmara-involvement-335880.
32 See, for example, Shlomo Hasson, "Gaza Enclave: Victim, Enemy, Rival," *Geopolitics* 15, no. 2 (2010): 385–405, DOI: 10.1080/14650040903486983.
33 *CNN News*, "Sharon Announces New Israeli Buffer Zones," *CNN*, last modified February 21, 2002, http://edition.cnn.com/2002/WORLD/meast/02/21/mideast/index.html?related.
34 Darryl Li, "The Gaza Strip as Laboratory: Notes in the Wake of Disengagement," *Journal of Palestine Studies* 35, no. 2 (2006): 38–55, 45.
35 Ibid., 45.
36 Human Rights Watch, *Razing Rafah: Mass Home Demolitions in the Gaza Strip* (New York: Human Rights Watch, 2004), 2, www.hrw.org/reports/2004/rafah1004/rafah1004text.pdf.
37 B'Tselem, *Policy of Destruction: House Demolitions and Destruction of Agricultural Land in the Gaza Strip*, B'Tselem, February 2002, 3, www.btselem.org/download/200202_policy_of_destruction_eng.pdf.
38 B'Tselem, "Demolition for Alleged Military Purposes," last modified January 1, 2011, www.btselem.org/razing/rafah_egyptian_border.
39 Ibid., 1.
40 GOC Southern Command, *Transcript of GOC Southern Command Regarding the Finds of the Investigation of the Demotion of the Buildings in Rafah (10–11.Jan.02)*, IMRA, January 28, 2002, www.imra.org.il/story.php3?id=9932.
41 Ibid., paragraphs 4–6.
42 Ibid., paragraph 9.
43 Ibid., paragraphs 11–12.
44 Lazaro Gamio, Richard Johnson, and Adam Taylor, "The Crisis in Gaza," *Washington Post*, last modified August 1, 2014, www.washingtonpost.com/wp-srv/special/world/the-gaza-crisis.
45 Ibid., paragraph 2.
46 Sara Roy, "Where's Our Humanity for Gaza?" *Boston Globe*, last modified November 23, 2012, www.bostonglobe.com/opinion/2012/11/23/roy/sctFniw6Wn2n9nTdxZ91RJ/story.html.
47 Dennis Kucinich, "Crimes Against Humanity in Gaza: Is It Really a 'Buffer Zone'— Or a Bigger Plan?" *Guardian*, last modified August 5, 2014, paragraph 3, www.theguardian.com/commentisfree/2014/aug/05/gaza-buffer-zone-dennis-kucinich.
48 Ibid., paragraph 12.
49 For a typical binary way of illustrating how some NGOs get caught up in critiques of the Israeli armed forces, see Pascal Vennesson and Nikoas M. Rajkovic, "The Transnational Politics of Warfare Accountability: Human Rights Watch Versus the Israel Defense Forces," *International Relations* 26, no. 4 (2012): 409–429, DOI: 10.1177/0047117812445450.

50 Human Rights Watch, *"I Lost Everything": Israel's Unlawful Destruction of Property During Operation Cast Lead* (New York: Human Rights Watch, 2010), www.hrw.org/sites/default/files/reports/iopt0510webwcover_1.pdf.
51 Richard Goldstone, Christine Chinkin, Hina Jilani, and Desmond Travers, *Report of the United Nations Fact-Finding Mission on the Gaza Conflict, United Nations General Assembly* (New York: United Nations General Assembly, 2009), 13.
52 Ibid., 16.
53 Ibid., 21.
54 Goldstone, who led this mission, would later back off from the comments that circulated in the Goldstone Report regarding "intentional" targeting of civilians by Israelis. See Richard Goldstone, "Reconsidering the Goldstone Report on Israel and War Crimes," *Washington Post*, last modified April 1, 2011, www.washingtonpost.com/opinions/reconsidering-the-goldstone-report-on-israel-and-war-crimes/2011/04/01/AFg111JC_story.html.
55 Goldstone et al., *Report of the United Nations Fact-Finding Mission*, paragraphs 1032–1085.
56 Ibid., 15.
57 Michael Foucault, "Technologies of the Self," in *Technologies of the Self: A Seminar with Michel Foucault*, eds. L.H. Martin, H. Gutman, and P.H. Hutton (London: Tavistock, 1988), 16–49.
58 Goldstone et al., *Report of the United Nations Fact-Finding Mission*, paragraph 1680.
59 Ibid., 17.
60 Ibid., 18.
61 Ibid., 23.
62 Ibid., 18.
63 Ibid., 20.
64 Ibid., 20.
65 Several years later, other observers would claim that the Israelis were once again firing flechette shells into Gaza. Harriet Sherwood, "Israel Using Flechette Shells in Gaza," *Guardian*, last modified July 20, 2014, www.theguardian.com/world/2014/jul/20/israel-using-flechette-shells-in-gaza.
66 Ibid., 21.
67 Tom Farer, "The Goldstone Report on the Gaza Conflict: An Agora," *Global Governance* 16 (2010): 139–143.
68 Goldstone et al., *Report of the United Nations Fact-Finding Mission*, 24.
69 *Reuters News*, "Israel Warns Hezbollah War Would Invite Destruction," *Reuters*, last modified October 3, 2008, paragraph 3, http://uk.reuters.com/article/2008/10/03/uk-israel-lebanon-hezbollah-idUKTRE49231020081003.
70 Goldstone et al., *Report of the United Nations Fact-Finding Mission*, 24.
71 Ibid., 253.
72 Ibid., 253.
73 Gadi Eisenkot, quoted in *Reuters News*, "Israel Warns Hezbollah," paragraph 2.
74 Ibid., paragraphs 4–5.
75 Amos Harel, "Analysis/IDF Plans to Use Disproportionate Force in Next War," *Ha'aretz*, last modified October 5, 2008, www.haaretz.com/print-edition/news/analysis-idf-plans-to-use-disproportionate-force-in-next-war-1.254954.
76 Giora Eiland, "The Third Lebanon War: Target Lebanon," *Strategic Assessment* 11, no. 2 (2008): 16.
77 Eiland, quoted in Harel, "Analysis/IDF Plans to Use," paragraph 15.
78 Eiland, "The Third Lebanon War," 16–17.
79 Gabriel Siboni, quoted in Goldstone et al., *Report of the United Nations Fact-Finding Mission*, 254.
80 Gabriel Siboni, quoted in Harel, "Analysis/IDF Plans," paragraph 5.

Domestic and international critiques

81 Ibid., paragraph 6.
82 Eli Yishai, quoted in Raanan Ben-Zur, "Yishai: Destroy 100 Houses for Each Rocket Fired," *Ynet News*, last modified February 2, 2009, www.ynetnews.com/articles/0,7340,L-3665517,00.html.
83 Adam Horowitz, "Goldstone Headed to Israel in July, hosted by Israeli Minister Criticized in Gaza Report for Advocating Collective Punishment," *Mondoweiss*, last modified April 5, 2011, http://mondoweiss.net/2011/04/goldstone-headed-to-israel-in-july-hosted-by-israeli-minister-criticized-in-gaza-report-for-advocating-collective-punishment.html.
84 Human Rights Watch, "Israel: Soldiers' Punishment for Using Boy as 'Human Shield' Inadequate," *Human Rights Watch*, November 26, 2010, www.hrw.org/news/2010/11/26/israel-soldiers-punishment-using-boy-human-shield-inadequate.
85 Stephanie Nebehay, "Palestinian Children Tortured, Used as Shields by Israel: U.N.," *Reuters*, last modified June 20, 2013, www.reuters.com/article/2013/06/20/us-palestinian-israel-children-idUSBRE95J0UJ20130620.
86 Barak, "International Humanitarian Law," 186.
87 For a typical example of how Moreh himself thinks about his own intentionality and the impact of circulating *The Gatekeepers*, see Dror Moreh, Interview with Richard Peña, NYFF Select Committee Chairman, found in Film Society of Lincoln Center, "NYFF Press Conference: *The Gatekeepers*," YouTube, published October 17, 2012, www.youtube.com/watch?v=jczwdsmIvNo.
88 Elizabeth Sydor, "*The Gatekeepers*," *Oral History Review* 41, no. 1 (2014): 139–141. DOI: 10.1093/ohr/ohu001.
89 Ibid., 139.
90 Gil Troy, "'*The Gatekeepers*': Speaking Spooks' Coup d'etat," *The Jerusalem Post*, last modified April 30, 2013, www.jpost.com/Opinion/Columnists/The-Gatekeepers-Speaking-spooks-coup-detat-311628.
91 Ami Ayalon, quoted in Troy, "'Gatekeepers,'" para. 8.
92 Paul Byrnes, "*The Gatekeepers* Review: The Power Within," *Sydney Morning Herald*, last modified August 31, 3013, paragraph 5, www.smh.com.au/entertainment/movies/the-gatekeepers-review-the-power-within-20130829-2srhf.html. See also, Don Futterman, "*The Gatekeepers*' Two-state Message Continues to Vex Israel's Right," *Ha'aretz*, last modified June 18, 2013, www.haaretz.com/opinion/.premium-1.530580.
93 Troy, "*The Gatekeepers*," paragraph 1.
94 Barak Ravid, "In a Flurry of Telegrams, Israeli Diplomats Respond to *The Gatekeepers*," *Ha'aretz*, last modified March 20, 2013, paragraph 12, www.haaretz.com/news/diplomacy-defense/in-a-flurry-of-telegrams-israeli-diplomats-respond-to-the-gatekeepers.premium-1.510699.
95 Hadas Wittenberg Silberstein, quoted in Ravid, "In a Flurry of Telegrams," 17.
96 Michael Oren, quoted in Ravid, "In a Flurry of Telegrams," 26. For examples of some of Avraham Shalom's commentary, see Valerie Elverton-Dixon, "We've Become Cruel," *Tikkun.com*, last modified July 30, 2014, www.tikkun.org/tikkundaily/2014/07/30/weve-become-cruel.
97 Dror Moreh, quoted in Alan Johnson, "*The Gatekeepers* is an Important Film," *Telegraph*, last modified April 24, 2014, paragraph 1, http://blogs.telegraph.co.uk/news/alanjohnson/100213410/the-gatekeepers-is-an-important-film-friends-of-israel-must-not-dismiss-it.
98 On the continued importance of the Bus 300 affair in Israeli geopolitical imaginations, see Gideon Levy, "The Shin Bet Scandal That Never Died," *Ha'aretz*, last modified October 2, 2011, www.haaretz.com/print-edition/opinion/the-shin-bet-scandal-that-never-died-1.387594. For fine academic contextualizations of this incident, see Shlomo Shapiro, "No Place to Hide: Intelligence and Civil Liberties in Israel," *Cambridge Review of International Affairs* 19, no. 4 (2006): 629–648, DOI: 10.1080/09557570601003361; Gil Merom, "Israel's National Security and

the Myth of Exceptionalism," *Political Science Quarterly*, 114, no. 3 (1999): 409–434.
99 Gid Weitz, "Newly Released Papers Reveal How Shin Bet Tried to Hide 'Bus 300' Killings," *Ha'aretz*, last modified September 27, 2011, www.haaretz.com/print-edition/news/newly-released-papers-reveal-how-shin-bet-tried-to-hide-bus-300-killings-1.386889.
100 Gill Cohen, "Former Shin Bet Chief Avraham Shalom Dies at 86," *Ha'aretz*, last modified June 19, 2014, www.haaretz.com/news/national/1.599830.
101 Tarah Judah, "Tower of Babble: Shin Bet *Gatekeepers* Talk," *Overland*, last modified August 27, 2013, https://overland.org.au/2013/08/tower-of-babble-shin-bet-gatekeepers-talk.
102 Roz Rothstein and Roberta Seid, "The Dishonesty of '*The Gatekeepers*,'" *The Jerusalem Post*, last modified February 13, 2013, www.jpost.com/Opinion/Op-Ed-Contributors/The-dishonesty-of-The-Gatekeepers.
103 Ibid., paragraph. 6.
104 Ibid., paragraph 8.
105 Ibid., paragraph 9–10.
106 Sydor, "*The Gatekeepers*," 140.
107 Rothstein and Seid, "The Dishonesty," paragraph 11–14.
108 Ibid., paragraph 22.
109 Ibid., paragraph 23.
110 Ibid., paragraph 26–29.

3 Occupational hazards and the evolutionary, rhetorical development of Israeli targeted killing rationales

In the first two chapters I provided readers with an overview of the rhetorical nature of some of the contentious and contradictory stories that have been circulated by Israelis and Palestinians as they have debated about the control of territories, bodies, and even ideologies over the years. In this particular chapter I extend that work by highlighting the post-2000 conversations that have taken place regarding what Israelis often call the "liquidation" of key Palestinian leaders who plan, fund, or carry out terrorist campaigns. In spite of international detractors who regard many of these strikes as illegal "assassinations" that are carried out against both militants and Palestinian political dissenters,[1] most Israelis adamantly defend these "liquidations" as an essential part of the securitized weaponry that is needed in fighting what Israelis call a "new" struggle that is either an "armed conflict" or "almost" an armed conflict.[2]

In the interdisciplinary literatures these are called Israeli "targeted killing" (TK) policies that were geared toward liquidating some of the threatening leadership of Fatah, Hezbollah, Hamas, and other enemies of the Israeli State.[3] According to Michael Gross, between the fall of 2000 and January of 2006, Israelis "successfully" targeted some 204 named combatants while killing 115 civilians.[4] After 2006 many skeptics would observe that the Israeli High Court (IHC) was taking the position that "a continuous state of armed conflict" had existed between Israel and "various terrorist organizations active in Judea, Samaria, and the Gaza Strip" since "the first Intifada."[5]

Note how this can be used to militarize or securitize any type of Palestinian opposition that might be deemed an existential threat by empowered Israeli military or judicial social actors.

Critics of these TK programs often argue that the second Intifada should have been treated as civilian disputation that involved legitimate grievances about occupation conditions, but several generations of Israelis have honed their argumentative skills as they respond that this has nothing to do with territorial expansionism or settlement policies. Outsiders might insist that controlling angered Palestinian populations living in Gaza or the West Bank required policing—not militarized—solutions to these problems, but the Israelis argue that this naively ignores the growing threats that have been posed when thousands of AK-47s and other weapons were placed in the hands of the fledgling Palestinian Authority.

Fatah leaders who should have been grateful for the easing of restrictions after the first Intifada were configured as dangerous neighbors who looked the other way as more radical terrorists threatened Israeli lives.

As I noted in Chapter 1, in theory some of the Palestinian people, by following Hamas in Gaza, were contributing to their own humiliation and to their own discomfort by their obstinate refusal to follow the lead of beneficent Israeli neighbors. The crafting of these types of Israeli narratives are not just the discursive productions that come from a few Israeli settlers who were kicked out of Gaza after the 2005 disengagement, nor are these the narratives that are the exclusive property of a few high-ranking leaders of the Likud party who might be interviewed by newspapers. Polling data, anecdotal evidence, and other materials highlight the suasory impact of these narratives in public circles, and heterogeneous Israeli audiences follow their leaders in rationalizing the existence of targeting lists. For example, in July 2001, a poll that was published by *Ma'ariv* found that some 90 percent of those polled supported the official Israeli TK policy.[6] In other words, defenses of TK are a *cultural* phenomenon, a way of showing the world that Israeli populations were willing to militarize and to retaliate against those who allegedly were trying to destroy the Israeli state.

Some of this populist support for TK policies has to do with the way Israeli storytellers tell their tales of violence perpetrated by "the other," and they often underscore the phantasmagoric nature of existential terrorism. Note, for example, how the former president of the IHC talked about the second Intifada on the very first page of a 2006 decision that would ratify the criteria that would have to be used by military and security forces that wanted to carry out liquidations:

> They [terrorist attacks] are directed against civilian centers, shopping centers and markets, coffee houses and restaurants. Over the last five years, thousands of acts of terrorism have been committed against Israel. In the attacks, more than one thousand Israeli citizens have been killed. Thousands of Israeli citizens have been wounded. Thousands of Palestinians have been killed and wounded during this period as well.[7]

This allows the author of the text to focus on much more than an assertion about what a potential individual terrorist may actual have done or plotted to do during any single incident, and it lumps together all of the deaths from several of the conflicts that are all configured as acts of terrorism. This sleight-of-hand creates the impression that Intifadas are performative activities that threaten Israelis' very existence.

When the IHC reviews TK petitions it does not focus on all of the material, structural, or institutional causes of terrorism. Instead, it selectively uses nationalistic and securitized metanarratives that highlight the collective suffering of Israeli victims while it rubber stamps the decisions of the IDF or Shin Bet as they characterize the dangers posed by individual militants. Secrecy shrouds the process of determining who gets targeted, what behavior led to their designation, and how anyone can use any process to object to these characterizations. All of

68 *Hazards and development of TK rationales*

this decisionism stays within the Israeli command structure, and the judiciary becomes a key player in all of this Israeli lawfare. One might even go so far as to argue that the IHC provides a unique form of hasbara that fends off attempts to get the ICC or other organizations involved in Israeli or Palestinian affairs.

If we use a critical rhetorical lens to recontextualize the 2006 Barak fragment referenced above, we would notice that he does not quantify the numbers of Palestinian dead, and he avoids mentioning the tens of thousands who were killed or wounded between 2000 and 2005. His last sentence is almost a throw-away line in this judicial text, where the Palestinian civilians who have suffered under decades of occupation make cameo appearances in a jurisprudential Israeli story that focuses almost exclusive attention on Israeli worries that assume the ontological existence of continued, and deadly, terrorist threats. Like Netanyahu, when former Judge Barak mentions Palestinian dead, he can always claim that terrorists were the responsible social agents. This allows the IHC to act as if killing Palestinian or other terrorists helps the cause of Arab moderation.

Several scholars have written about the "cosmopolitan" or liberal nature of the opinions of the IHC that tries to emphasize the importance of customary international humanitarian law (IHL),[8] but make no mistake, these laws are not going to be interpreted in ways that dramatically alter Israeli military decision-making. Aharon Barak may talk about how the law still exists and operates when the "cannons speak" and the "Muses are silent,"[9] but this hides the ways the laws themselves dispense and sanction violence. In this case, the specific petition that reaches this IHC might come from "left-wingers" who were demanding some guidance on the parameters or legality of TK (*Ynetnews*),[10] but all this was situated in a nationalistic metanarrative that took for granted the special, unique, or extreme dangers that confronted Israelis on a daily basis. This has to be the way that Israelis argue, otherwise they will lose the debates with those who will say they did not discriminate between civilians and combatants during peacetime, that they used excessive force that violated the laws of proportionality, and that their cavalier treatment of Gazans or West Bank civilians violated other human rights laws.

As I note below, in this situation the IHC was able to use the TK case as an activist vehicle for intervening in domestic and international disputation that would have both short-term and long-term consequences. TK cases allowed the IHC to provide pedagogical lessons for those who needed "balancing" tests and "prongs" that would help legitimate the liquidations. It also showed the world that the Israeli judiciary *was constraining the IDF*, so that nations like Belgium would quit going after Ariel Sharon for the Sabra and Shatila massacre.[11] These nationalistic legal arguments could also be used to tell New Zealand that it needed to stop proceedings in that country that were filed against former Chief of General Staff Moshe Ya'alon. Doron Almog and Avi Dichter, and former IDF Chief of General Staff Lt. Dan Halutz. These were some of the Israelis who have to watch their step as they travel abroad,[12] part of what Matthew Cohen and Charles Freilich call the attempted "delegitimation of Israel."[13]

Regardless of the specific rules and the decisionism that might be pronounced by the IHC in TK cases, the three members of this Israeli court were not about to deconstruct the dominant terrorist narratives that circulated in elite and vernacular Israeli circles, and they were not about to totally ban liquidations. If they had banned TK, it would have meant that hundreds (if not thousands) of Israelis who were involved in liquidation programs since 2000 would have violated the laws of armed conflict, or IHL, and they would have been scrambling to find lawyers who would have had to represent them in even more civil and criminal proceedings. Yet the political power, and the legal impunity of the empowered, protected them from having to appear in international courtroom docks.

Earlier chapters pointed out that when Israelis craft their causal narratives and chronicle the "factual" beginning of the second Intifada they don't often focus attention on the activities of Ariel Sharon as he moved with his hundreds of guards toward the Al Asqa mosque. Nor will they give much credence to the texts that come from Amnesty International, Human Rights Watch, the UN, or B'Tselem. Instead, elite and public chronicles of these events are filled with subplots of countless Palestinians who are now armed with more than rocks.

This is not to say that all Israelis agreed with the government's liquidation policies or the unleashing of arbitrary military force. The advent of the second Intifada brought what Laura Blumenfeld has called a "divisive struggle" in Israel over TK, and those who favored unleashing the military, or Shin Bet, often reconfigured occupational disputes as dogmatic, nationalistic, counterterrorist struggles. After all, if Palestine does not exist as a nation, and if Zionists lawyers see them as "present-absentees,"[14] then any opposition that appears outside of the Israeli governmental apparatus can be criminalized and this in turn swells the ranks of potential drone or aircraft targets.

As noted in earlier chapters, a popular tale that circulated during this period explained how Yasser Arafat and the other Palestinian leaders could have prevented all of this at Oslo or in Cairo, but the Palestinians made major mistakes when misplaced confidence in their own military wings pushed them away from the negotiating table. The outside world may have fallen for the Palestinian stories of legitimate grievances, but as far as most Israelis were concerned, the Al Asqa uprising had been a carefully orchestrated affair by those who refused to accept political, economic, and military realities. Israelis liked to argue that their hands were now tied by "lost opportunities," and that military necessity demanded that they follow their Basic Laws and defend their own people.

Cultural and military constraints often created situations where Israelis had to adopt contradictory positions as they argued with their detractors. For example, when their critics complained about the collateral damage that came from these liquidation attacks Israelis focused on their own *good intentions*, but when they wanted to highlight the terrorist harms that came from militant Palestinian terrorist attacks they adopted different argumentative strategies and focused instead on the *consequences, and not the motives*, of the attackers.

A convergence of vectors, including technological talk of Israeli know-how and "precision" warfare, as well as Israeli political willingness to leave behind police framing of Intifada affairs, made for a perfect storm as Israelis geared up for what they regarded as an armed conflict "short" of war. Ehud Barak, the former Israeli prime minister, was asked to reactivate TKs in the wake of the Al Asqa uprising. Moshe Ya'alon, the military chief of staff, came to Barak with the idea of carrying out "surgical operations" against terrorists in place of imposing restrictions against all Palestinians. As the story goes, Barak was willing to consider using this tactic, but he had an aide exhume four typed pages that had been archived in an old dusty plastic sleeve so that they could look over the old rules of engagement that had once guided the hand of the "avengers of the 1972 Munich massacre."[15]

Note the way this hagiographic framing of spying affairs tapped into the heroic Zionist narratives of stealth, guile, revenge, perhaps even perfidy, that have been a part of the heroic tales that have circulated in Israeli elite and public circles since at least the time of the War of Independence. This helped assuage the guilt of those who might have thought that "post-heroic" TK was some new practice that deviated from Israeli heroic traditions or collective memories.

This story of Barak's careful weighting of factors as he contemplating reactivating liquidations is a fascinating, coherent, logical, and persuasive framing of TK rationales, because it makes it appear as though caring Israeli civilian and military decision-makers are looking out for the welfare of both Israeli and Palestinian populations by searching for alternatives to the horrors that would follow in the wake of more heavy-handed military *re-occupation* of *all* of the West Bank and Gaza. The TK proposal that is so despised by NGOs and other Israeli detractors can be (re)characterized as the lesser evil, where the killing of dozens or hundreds of Fatah or Hamas terrorists can serve as decapitations that damage the terrorist network that are configured as obstacles to peace.[16]

This Kafkaesque or Orwellian language, where thanatopolitical killing of select terrorist suspects helps preserve the life of several biopolitical bodies, can become one more permutation of the nationalistic metanarratives that are told by Israelis who want to underscore the point that when it comes to fighting terrorism they are the progressive, democratic voices who are trail blazers in the global war against terrorism. Why get into messy debates about resource wars, the responsibilities of neo-colonial occupiers, negotiating two-state solutions, or the hyper-threat inflation that is needed for massive Israeli arm sales when attention can be lavished on the "successes" that come from the liquidation of those who were allegedly plotting to blow up Israeli buses, pizza parlors, malls, or settler buildings? Any US or Israeli reader who is interested in stopping terror finance can then use these stories to rationalize the efficacy of Israeli TK.

Again, as I noted in Chapter 1, there are many social agents who have a hand in constituting these nationalistic myths and Israeli fables, when Palestinian uprisings morphed into violent "insurgencies" in new narratives that were used to explain why so many thousands of Israelis had lost their lives in some of these Palestinian–Israeli conflicts. In these social dramas, the protagonists are the members of the IDF, the Israel Security Agency (ISA), the Israel National Police (INP) or the Israeli Parliament (Knesset) who have the acumen and fortitude that is needed to deploy harsh, Israeli counterterrorism (CT) strategies.

Hazards and development of TK rationales 71

The coverage of the 2000 sniper attack on Thabet Thabet would be a harbinger of things to come, and Israelis incrementally moved away from having to defend individuated, "furtive" assassinations to more complex and public defenses, of openly acknowledged killings by helicopters, drones, poisoning, rigged phone-booths, etc. As I argue below, it would be a mistake to leave out *the cultural dimensions* of these liquidations as we note the legal or military framings of these affairs, because many of these rhetorics would migrate and become reified as Israelis sought to rationalize the targeting of civilian populations during Operation Cast Lead and Operation Protective Edge.

If one is confident that the liquidations that were carried out after 2000 were righteous killings, then why not marshal together the moral, legal, and military arguments that might help Israeli leftist dissenters, and the rest of the world, understand the efficacious nature of "deterrence" policies that protected Israelis from all types of terrorist threats?[17] Unlike American CIA operatives—who usually refused to confirm or deny their role in Central Asian drone attacks–the Israelis underscored their open defense of this type of lawfare.

All of this would become a part of what Rebecca Stein has called the "purity of arms mythology," where textual and visual images of humane and moral fighters are used to create structures of feeling that become pillars "of the nation state's military project."[18] These discourses—that often highlighted the importance of *peh'u' lat men'a* (preventative action)—circulate in many Israeli circles, and given the fact that it is estimated that somewhere around 338 Palestinians died during TK strikes that were carried out between September 29, 2000 and February 28, 2007, it needed to be convincing.[19]

I begin my critical genealogical review of how all of this unfolded by taking an evolutionary, ideological look at how various Israeli generations have historically debated about the efficacy, the morality, and the legality of assassinations. The first section reviews some of the antecedent genres that were circulating in Israeli rhetorical cultures between the time of the War of Independence and the second Intifada, while the second portion highlights how military experts were asking for the reactivation of "new" liquidations. After that I present a segment that critiques the 2006 Israeli Supreme Court decision on targeted assassination (*Public Committee Against Torture in Israel* v. *Government of Israel, or PCATI*), and this is followed by a subsection that explains how all of this helped revive interest in debates about lawfare and counterlawfare. Finally, in the fifth and concluding section, I explain what all of this has to tell us about the twenty-first-century targeting of Gazan populations.

Understanding the rhetorical importance of "liquidation" in Israeli historiographic contexts

Members of each generation may have their own unique ways of conceptualizing what are generally regarded as existential terrorist threats, but some of this is new wine in old bottles as twenty-first-century arguers have no trouble finding cultural, legal, or military precedents for today's actions. As Adam Stahl has insightfully observed, some of the Israeli views on "assassination" or "liquidation" can be traced at least as far back as the time of the Yishuv in the 1920s.[20]

Other academics who study the origins of Israel's policy of TKs are willing to punctuate time a little differently, noting that the Bible offers examples of murders that were undertaken in order to advance political interests. Steven David, in his essay "Fatal Choices," notes that King David once ordered the killing of the head of his own army because he worried about ambitious rivals.[21] Steven David also wrote about the Zealots of Masada who killed opponents as they fought Roman occupiers, and he was aware of the ways that the Haganah,[22] Irgun, and Lehi referenced some of these biblical and ancient historical examples as they sought to justify their own TKs of British and Palestinians in the years before the Nakba.[23]

Post-World War II struggles were also carried out in ways that underscored the acceptance of assassination as a viable military option. During the 1950s, Israelis assassinated Fedayeen attackers from Egypt, and they later used the threat of mail bombs to put an end to German scientists' plans for helping Nasser's Egypt develop missile systems that would have reached Israel. A general by the name of Ariel Sharon would command an Israeli anti-group that operated in Gaza, and his units during the early 1970s captured or killed hundreds of Palestinians.[24]

Talk of secret service intrigue and the taking out of Israeli enemies has always been a part of military, security, and popular Israeli folklore.[25] Note, for example, how Menachem Begin and Yitzhak Shamir were able to become leaders of modern Israel, and how their sanctioning of TKs during the early years of the British mandate system did not hinder their rise to power. "From its independence in 1948," noted Steven David, "to the present, Israel has used the policy of targeted killings to advance its interests."[26]

Former Labor Party leader Ehud Barak has been involved in multiple stories that have been told by several generations that have reminisced about the need for selective assassination. Israeli youngsters and adults grow up hearing tales about how Barak, in 1973, wore high heels and a woman's wig in Beirut so that he could help gun down three of the terrorists who had been involved in the murder of almost a dozen Israeli athletes at the Munich Olympics.[27] The deaths of the 11 Israeli athletes at the Munich games "galvanized the policy of targeted killing as no previous event had done," and a "Committee X" was chaired by Prime Minister Golda Meir and Defense Minister Moshe Dayan as they studied how Mossad could systemically track down the thirteen Black September members who were held responsible for the Munich massacres.[28] Steven Spielberg's film *Munich* (2005) only brought to Western audiences what Israelis had known about for years.[29]

During the 1990s Barak helped organize undercover units, called "Cherry" and "Sampson," that had Israeli soldiers dress as Arabs so they could kill Palestinian terrorist suspects.[30] Israelis were regaled with tales of the effectiveness of major assassinations that were said to have disrupted fundamentalist Islamic terrorist efforts, and they got to hear about the 1996 killing of Yahya Ayyash, the "engineer," in Gaza, who was killed while talking on a mobile phone that had been booby-trapped by Shin Bet.[31] Stories like Ayyash's assassination could be used symbolically to make the point that the TK of prolific bomb-makers saved countless lives, in spite of the unleashing of retaliatory suicide bombers by the Palestinians.[32] This is just one way of conceptualizing the Israeli way of *arguing about causes of suicides and terrorism*, as evidenced by the work of Assaf Moghadam[33] and others who focus on many other possible motivations and incentives.

A critical genealogical analysis of these Israeli histories and select historiographies reveals how many Jews living in the Yishuv and in Israel understood the political importance of using assassination as a weapon, and it was not so much the modality but rather the "scale" of the targeted killings after the second Intifada that made them newsworthy. Many Palestinian "militants" would be killed in a relatively short span of time, and this included the head of the Palestinian Front of the Liberation of Palestine (PFLP), Abu Al Mustafa, the secretary-general of the PFLP, Mustafi Zibri, and one of the key leaders of the Tanzim movement, Ra'ed al-Karmi. What made all of this even more controversial was the fact that many of these "targets" knew they were being pursued, and that "collaborators" working with the Israeli intelligence apparatus were involved in the taking out of these suspected Palestinian threats.[34]

As I note in the next section, this "reactivation" of old assassination activities also revived the rhetorical narratives that would help organize the arguments that would be used to legitimate and legalize the "liquidation" of those during the early twenty-first century who threatened Israeli soldiers and civilians.

Deliberating about the morality, legality, and legitimacy of "liquidations," 2000–2005

Israeli talk about the legality or morality of their liquidation of terrorists involved more than just a review of some single technology or tactic in a nation-state's counterterrorist arsenal. How one felt about their particular targeting of political or military enemy figures, and the rationales that Israelis gave for their killings of these individuals, often served as a litmus test for how one felt about their post-2000 framing of what much of the rest of the world still called an "occupation." The formation of the "autonomous" PA, and the disengagement from Gaza, meant that many of those who were targeted were no longer insiders living under Israeli occupation but outsiders who threatened the Israeli body politic.

When Israelis today take a retrospective look back to the time of the second Intifada they often highlight the *exceptional* nature of these dangers and the fact that they only targeted those who were "on their way to a terrorist attack" or were "planning one."[35] Whether this actually was a time of exceptional danger will always be a point of contention, but the Israelis were convinced that their lethal decapitations of Palestinian terrorist networks were preventative actions that were "degrading" enemy capabilities, and the usage of these clinical, thanatopolitical grammars could highlight the assumed professionalism of those who carried out these liquidations. As long as one could argue that this was not done in the name of revenge, or that this was not done with any animus toward any particular ethnic group, it could be justified as the type of action that any democracy would condone in the war against terrorism.

In 2004 Amos Guiora, who would pen one of the most famous early essays defending Israeli TK as "active self-defense," wrote eloquently about how the "years 1967–1987 were characterized by the Palestinian population's acceptance of the post-1967 Six-Day occupation,"[36] but this is fanciful. I've talked to countless Palestinians over the last 40 years who suffered through those periods and they were not about to accept Israeli tutelage. Many may have wanted to accept some negotiated, two-state solution that would have pushed the borders back to the famous "Green line," but they were never going to accept second-class citizenship, the humiliation, and the creative destruction that came with Israeli control of east Jerusalem or many parts of the West Bank. Palestinians were willing to accept the realities of Israel "proper," but not the permanent establishment of settlements in what the Israelis called "Judea" and "Samaria."

Although Israeli historiographies of their TK program usually include origination tales that begin with the second Intifada, there are some academics who are convinced that this began much earlier. Lisa Hajjar, writing in 2012, averred:

> Israel instituted a policy of "targeted killing" against Palestinians in the occupied territories during the first *intifada* in the late 1980s. Initially, undercover units of soldiers and secret agents undertook these operations by perfidiously disguising themselves as Arabs (*mista'aravim*) to approach and execute their targets, or snipers killed them from a distance. When Islamists introduced the tactic of suicide bombings in the mid-1990s, these operations increased, spurring a cycle of violence.[37]

Perhaps it was the move toward more "aerial" attacks, spurred on by technological developments in drone and "precision" warfare that accounts for some of these different punctuations of time as academics study the origins of these liquidation policies.

When Israelis tell their tales of how their nation moved toward the reactivation of TKs they contextualize the post-Intifada years as a period of time when knowledgeable politicians got together with the best and brightest military officers as they brainstormed together about how to selectively choose their targets. Eyal Weizman has argued that by 2003 government authorization was given "to kill the entire *political* leadership of Hamas without further notice" (emphasis mine).[38] Outsiders complained that all of this amounted to "extra-judicial" murdering of Palestinian political figures who didn't pose actual military threats, but that was not the way that Israelis characterized their liquidation program.[39]

Oftentimes the stories that were crafted about Israeli TKs were narrated in ways that underscored the supposed unity of Israeli civilian and military decision-makers who understood that liquidations were a "necessary evil" or the

Hazards and development of TK rationales 75

"lesser" of evils. One popular tale chronicled how Ehud Barak and Ariel Sharon were engaged in lengthy deliberations with figures like Lt. General Dan Halutz, who was the chief of the Air Force, Major General Amos Yadlin, the chief of military intelligence, Avi Dichter, the head of Shin Bet, and Major General Yoav Gallant, the military secretary. These individuals were portrayed as patriots who held strong opinions, individuals who sometimes disagreed about the propriety of taking out certain targets when terrorists were surrounded by families and neighbors. However, they were said to be working together to defend the TK program in spite of some of their misgivings, and it was argued that the majority of these Israeli decision-makers accepted the legitimacy of using assassination tactics. They, like the Americans who followed them, also searched for the legal shields that would help immunize those who were involved in carrying out these TKs.

Ehud Barak was one of the decision-makers who sought this type of jurisprudential protection for those who were going to assassinate Palestinian terrorists and one writer remarked that he would secretly ask Daniel Reisner to find out if TKs were legal. Notice how this telling makes it appear that inductive reasoning was being deployed instead of *post-hoc* rationalizations of policies that were already in place.

Reisner would later recall that he agonized over this for more than a month, and then he thought: "Instead of two states living amicably side by side, I have to write opinions on how and when we kill each other."[40] Again, this was highly symbolic from a diplomatic standpoint, because Reisner had been a legal adviser who represented the Israelis at the Arab–Israeli peace talks. All these conversations about TK were also leaving rhetorical traces of evidence that more and more Israeli decision-makers, especially after the violence of the second Intifada, were less inclined to continue talking about "two-state" solutions. The killing of hundreds of Palestinian leaders, however, did not help the cause of the Israeli leftists who still petitioned the IHC and who still held out hope for peaceful solutions to Palestinian–Israeli conflicts.

Long before Aharon Barak's three-person Supreme Court handed down their 2006 TK opinion, Reisner and those around him were debating about the conditions that should be met before Israeli F-16s or drones took out terrorist suspects.

Military praxis merged with legal theorizing as Reisner came up with these six conditions:

1   The arrest of the terrorist suspect had to be impossible.
2   The targets had to be identified as combatants.
3   Approval for these TKs had to come from senior Israeli Cabinet members.
4   The attacks had to be carried out in ways that minimized civilian casualties.
5   The operations had to be limited to areas that were NOT under Israel control.
6   The targets had to be identified as a future threat, and could not be targeted for any past transgressions.[41]

In the abstract all of this looks very much like some of the typical, formalistic commentary that comes from military experts who write about the "international" law of armed conflict, but when all of this was put into practice it looked as though the IDF was often killing those it could have detained, captured, and questioned.

Perhaps it is human nature that those who justify the taking of life like to find clinical matrices that might help them with their moral calculations; Gary Solis has written about how the Israeli chief of military intelligence, who was haunted by the civilian deaths that occurred during some of these strikes, asked a mathematician to write out a formula to "determine the number of acceptable civilian casualties per dead terrorist."[42] Solis claims that all of these conversations about exact numbers went nowhere because of the ad hoc nature of the military's crafting of rules of engagement (ROE), but there is some anecdotal evidence that at least one Israeli committee considered a standard of 3.14 civilian deaths per terrorist to be an acceptable ratio. This same committee intoned that it might be a smaller acceptable ratio if the dead were children, but no agreement on this calculus was ever reached. Avi Dichter, however, was willing to cite Shin Bet studies that showed that every time the Israelis killed a suicide bomber this prevented the loss of 16–20 lives.[43]

These multiplier effect claims circulate in all types of Israeli military, legal, and even social media venues (see Chapter 6), and all of this shows the gradual move away from Israeli deliberations regarding the propriety of using assassinations in the first place and toward talk of how to carry them out. Military mission creep takes the place of civilian and diplomatic solutions to Israeli–Palestinian relational problems.

Oftentimes it would be the General Security Service (GSS) that developed some of the early lists of targets that might be handed over to the Israeli Air Force, and each of the planned assassinations involved a large-scale operation. Between 2000 and 2005 these types of operations depended on the integration of hundreds of specialists from several security and military branches, and they used the diverse materials that they collected from Palestinian collaborators who were detained or stopped at checkpoints. "After a Palestinian is placed on the death list," argued Eyal Weizman, "he [sic] is followed, sometimes for days, by a 'swarm' of different kinds of unmanned aerial vehicles."[44] As soon as one of the terrorist targets moved away from any major population center or civilian intersection, they could be killed by sniper fire, Apache helicopter missiles, an F-16 attack, or a drone attack.

All of this commentary about calculating life and death can be viewed as familiar biopolitical or necropolitical generalized rationalizations for TK, and yet particular geopolitical events have influenced who ends up in the Israeli scopic visions that are used to frame who will be liquidated. For example, those who study the history of Israeli intelligence services write about the time when Arafat, during his time in Lebanon, was once in the crosshairs of an Israeli sniper, but the sniper was not given the go-ahead to shoot because of the presence of foreign diplomats at a farewell ceremony. Steven David argues that in

February 2002 then-Prime Minister Ariel Sharon bemoaned the fact that the Israelis hadn't killed Arafat when they had their chances.[45] This would be one of those "lost opportunities" that I mentioned above.

Some former members of the Israeli secret service joined the chorus of those who stoutly defended the efficacy of Israeli TK policies. Avi Dichter, who retired in 2005, had once been the chief of the Shin Bet domestic security service, and while speaking at a conference on aerial moves against terrorism in Herzliya he remarked that senior Hamas leaders had decided that they "were tired of seeing the sun only in pictures." Dichter concluded that the adoption of Israeli targeting polices led to a period of "calm."[46] The message was clear: Accept Israeli domination, hegemony, and occupation, and the TK will slow down. Reject Israeli occupation and you face the drones, jets, or snipers who went after terrorists.

Oftentimes Israeli warriors who are asked to carry out these TKs are so convinced of the rectitude of their CT efforts that they don't mind openly lampooning the efforts of those they believe might be mollycoddling terrorists. One of the most famous of these types of remarks came from Israeli Air Force commander Major General Dan Halutz, an individual who participated in the 2004 debates in which military leaders and Israeli lawyers mulled over the rhetoric that should be used by the State before the High Court of Justice. Segal was fascinated by the fact that retired Halutz was still in a position to participate in those kinds of conversations, because two years earlier, when he had been asked about his feelings regarding the potential killing of innocent people as a result of the bombing of densely populated areas, Halutz got into hot water. "I feel a slight blow to the plane as a result of the release of the bomb," explained Halutz, and "after a second it passes. And that's it."[47] Many Israeli leftists were horrified when they heard this flippant remark, and Halutz later found himself having to serve as a respondent in a petitioned case that came from left-wing activists and members of the Yesh-G'vul movement.

All of this demonstrates the care that had to be taken in the framing of some of the lawfare that I referenced in Chapter 2. Halutz's frankness was jarring to hear if you believed that universal, ethical norms precluded any political assassinations or other problematic usages of TKs. In contrast, the Israelis who supported liquidations thought that Halutz's glibness was the proper way to handle the inappropriate questioning of Israeli military decision-making.

Halutz's commentary also provided cultural clues regarding the perceptual views of those who lived and operated in military cultures that condoned or accepted the de facto practices of targeted assassinations that were being tolerated long before Aharon Barak or other members of the IHC set up "balancing" tests for their *de jure* usage.[48]

The arguments of these military lawyers and Israeli jurists are often couched in idioms that reflected the taken-for-granted cultural assumptions of most Israelis, and all of this talk of "deterring" terrorism resonated in broader rhetorical cultures. As Neve Gordon notes, the post-2000 Israeli rationalizations for TK, that were formed from both Talmudic templates and legalistic templates, usually vacillated between "blood on their hands" and "ticking time bomb" narrations of terrorist events.[49] Both of these templates were anchored in the vilification of Palestinian politicians who were thought to be hiding their militant operations or supporting their militant brothers and sisters.

Defenses of liquidations often became a national signifier as Israelis pushed back against their detractors. Between 2000 and the handing down of Barak's opinion in PCATI in 2006, the IDF and security leaders would be joined by Israeli and American academics, journalists, and others who stoutly defended the propriety of Israel's liquidation policy. "Israelis dislike the term 'assassination policy,'" Gal Luft would write in 2003. Luft was a former lieutenant colonel in the IDF, and he elaborated by writing about some of the preferred, alternative terms that might profitably be used to describe these activities—"extrajudicial punishment," "selective targeting," or "long-range hot pursuit."[50] This mirrored the American commentary on "lethal" strikes during "armed conflict."

Again, all of those key ideographs helped Israelis position themselves as realists who were using the least problematic ways of engaging in CT pursuits. Steven David provided a nice summary of this perspective when he remarked:

> Until a settlement (or victory) is achieved, however, targeted killing stands out as a measured response to a horrific threat. It is distinctly attractive because it focuses on the actual perpetrators of terror, while largely sparing the innocent. For a dangerous region in an imperfect world, the policy of targeted killing must remain a necessary evil.[51]

David, like many other defenders of these attacks, assumed that the Israelis had reliable intelligence about the activities of would-be terrorists, that these were not just political dissenters, and that their "thwarting" would mean that Israelis could ride buses or go to malls without fearing for their lives.[52]

Defenders of Israel's liquidations policies were fully aware that some outsiders viewed many of these assassinations as ineffectual and illegal. Gal Luft, for example, admitted that there were foreign and domestic observers who thought that this mode of operation was "senseless and illegal," in that assassination of "Palestinian militants only brings harsh retaliation" and infringes on the "sovereignty of foreign political entities."[53] He also knew that they thought that Israeli security services had too much discretion in deciding who needed to be liquidated, and detractors were arguing that there was still no compelling evidence that these decapitations did anything to stem the tide of what Luft called "the terror menace." Yet he rebutted this by noting that what the critics were missing were the "cumulative" effects "of targeted killings on terrorist organizations," and how the taking out of priceless leadership was leaving some of these networks in chaotic conditions. Luft had his own graphic way of suggesting how his readers needed to reevaluate the logic of Israel's TK program:

> Fighting terror is like fighting car accidents: one can count the casualties but not those whose lives are spared by prevention. Hundreds, if not thousands,

Hazards and development of TK rationales 79

of Israelis go about their lives without knowing that they are unhurt because their murderers met their fate before they got the chance to carry out their diabolical missions. This silent multitude is the testament to the policy's success.[54]

Later in his essay, Luft provided a fairly typical explanation of just who he thought the Israeli security services were targeting when he wrote about the "intermediate" level of command that included those who planned, recruited, trained, armed, and dispatched the militant terrorists. In language that was redolent with both colloquial and expert meanings, that would have been understood by just about any American or Israeli who had been reading or talking about terrorist cells, he explained how these "intermediate" members were not that well-known in public circles, and thus their liquidation raised unnecessary worries regarding Israeli intentions. The targeting of these various levels of terrorism made perfect sense to the Israelis living in the twenty-first century because "Israel has always believed that draining the swamp is more important than fighting the mosquitoes."[55]

This type of necropolitical or thanatopolitical commentary turned terrorism into a biopolitical public health issue, where Israeli TKs of select Palestinians were configured as necessitous and remedial medical measures.

All of this figurative talk was assuming that terrorism was some ill that could be cured through decapitations. Note here the assiduous avoidance of any commentary on any Palestinian grievances, and the absence of any discussion of the root causes of disaffection or disagreement. These securitizing and militarized frames of terrorism assumed that each and every one of those who died after the second Intifada had something to do with what Luft and many others called "martyrdom" operations. This, as W.J.T. Mitchell explained in his essay on Jacques Derrida's ideas about autoimmunity, turned them into something like spectral, engineered, cybernetic organisms. "Small wonder that images of Palestinian suicide bombers circulated on the Internet" argued Mitchell, because they "are almost indistinguishable from the faceless 'clone army' of the second episode of the Star Wars Saga, *Attack of the Clones*."[56]

At the same time, note how the very absence of any massive catastrophe coming from lulls in terrorist attacks is not configured as something that has anything to do with diplomatic efforts, ceasefire, or the cessation of attacks by Palestinians. Instead, this lull is treated as demonstrable evidence of the invisible effectiveness of the Israeli TK policies.

These types of reductionist causality stories, that I referenced in Chapter 1, resonate with many former security leaders and military officers because they magnify their own social agency, and these put on display their heroism and their role in taking out the terrorist cells. These nationalist fables also create social bonds as Israeli men, women, and children who share in these global imaginaries get to sleep well at night because the liquidators have manned the ramparts.

From a critical genealogical perspective, all this talk of deterrence and liquidation is a permutation of the old military typologies that were represented in the movie *A Few Good Men* (1992), in which the character of Nathan Jessup (played by Jack Nicholson) explains to Lieutenant Daniel Kaffee (Tom Cruise) that he eats "breakfast 300 yards from 4,000 Cubans who are trained to kill me" and that "he can deal with the bullets and the bombs and the blood." During the penultimate scene in the movie, when Kaffee is questioning Jessup during cross-examination, Jessup seems to become a cipher for all global military hardliners when he admits that his "existence, while grotesque and incomprehensible" to some, "saves lives."[57] To carry this analogy to its logical conclusion, Jessup seems to represent the Israeli views of some who respond to outside criticism when he says that he has "neither the time nor the inclination to explain [himself]" to someone "who rises and sleeps" under the "blanket" that is provided by those who have to take drastic steps in the name of military necessity. Post-structuralists and others may view some of this as examples of what Jacques Derrida called "hauntology,"[58] but for those who believe in the massive dangers posed by Palestinian militants it makes perfect sense to target those who may, some time in the future, plan or carry out devastating raids.

Readers should not think that writers like Luft are the only players in these complex social dramas about TK. Note, for example, how there are times when "the rule of law" can be anthropomorphized in ways that make it appear as though jurisprudential principles can become dynamic or organic weapons in the hands of jurists who also want to take the fight to these Palestinian militants. Aharon Barak, in a portion of his opinion on TKs that usually gets skipped over by formalists, used this division of labor to explain his own appointed task as president of the IHC: "The State's fight against terrorism is the fight of the state against its enemies. It is also the law's fight against those who rise up against it."[59] This fragment, as Markus Gunneflo opines, features "two modalities of legal violence," where the "judiciary and the law appeared in full bellicose partisanship with the state."[60]

This may be one of the reasons why the Israel Security Agency, Israeli academics, and Israeli military experts realized they could wait patiently on the 2006 *PCATI* decision. By the time the targeting case reached the IHC, most Israeli elites and members of the public *were already convinced* that their military and security knew about, and kept track of, the networks of bomb-makers, young recruits, trained spies,[61] Palestinian collaborators, and others who were a part of this complex, network-centric warfare in this "new" irregular conflict. Few were willing to doubt that the secret services were providing them with accurate mosaics that helped with the preparation of precise technological targeting of those who deserved extermination, but they also realized that it never hurt when elite Israeli jurists changed their minds on the issue of jurisdiction and decided to hear this case.

Now the IHC could provide its own imprimatur to decisions that had been made long ago. Most were on the same page as cadres of military lawyers, and academics realized that they needed to be proactive in circulating rhetorics about their *peh'u' lat men'a*. The publication of material from Barak's *Public Committee Against Torture in Israel* v. *Government of Israel* would provide more protective layers of argumentation for those who wanted to stay out of European docks.

The 2006 Israel Supreme Court Case of *Public Committee Against Torture in Israel* v. *Government of Israel*

On January 24, 2002 a petition was filed by the Public Committee Against Torture in Israel (PCATI) and the Palestinian Society for the Protection of Human Rights and the Environment; these organizations were trying to abolish Israeli's open usage of TKs. It took many years for this case to reach Israel's highest court because at various times ceasefires had led to the temporary suspension of TKs, and for a time the PCATI petition was considered to be "frozen."[62]

The petitioners in this case were represented by Avigdor Feldman and Michael Sfard, and they argued in this case that Article 51 of the UN Charter, which referenced national defense rights, did not apply in a situation where Israel was involved in a conflict with individuals from "the occupied territories." Moreover, the petitioners averred that targeted assassinations denied those targeted the right to due process and violated provisions of international human rights laws and IHL. Feldman and Sfard qualified some of these arguments by arguing that even if Israel was involved in an "international armed conflict" the would-be targets had to be characterized as civilians who were protected from Israeli military attacks.[63]

Shai Nitzan, the state attorney, responded that Israelis needed to use TKs because their nation was involved in a "new kind of conflict," as evidenced by that fact that since September 2000 Israelis had to confront all sorts of acts of "combat and terrorism." This meant that the IHC ought to recognize that the laws of armed conflict should guide their deliberation, and that the terrorists who were targeted were neither civilians nor soldiers but members of a third legal category, "unlawful combatants." Nitzan asked the Israeli Supreme Court to recognize the fact that the planning, launching, and commanding of terrorist acts constituted evidence that they were involved in the direct participation in hostilities. The state's attorney also noted that the Israeli TK policy satisfied the IHL requirements of proportionality because these liquidations were rare events that were only performed in exceptional circumstances when there was no viable alternative.[64]

PCATI v. *Government of Israel* was decided after three Israeli jurists heard the arguments from Feldman, Sfard, and Nitzan, and the opinion would be delivered by former President Aharon Barak around the time of his retirement. He would be joined by President Dorit Beinisch and Vice-President Eliezer Rivlin, who supported Barak but wrote their own concurring opinions.

Although Barak's opinion dealt with formalistic and technical legal questions that had little to do with the initial formation of assassination guidelines, this rhetorical fragment could also be read as a didactic text that was filled with Zionist subtexts and narratives that reinforced the notion that major parts of

"Judea, Samaria" were Israeli territories and that the Gaza Strip was populated by "terrorist organizations." In order to secure jurisdiction to hear the case, Barak, Beinisch, and Rivlin had to accept the baseline argument that the violence that was taking place in Israel's battle against terrorism was not just a matter of law enforcement, and they treated this conflict as one that had a "mixed" character.

The Israeli jurists who participated in the *PCATI* v. *Government of Israel* case signaled their acceptance of militarized ways of framing occupation policies when they opined that Palestinians terrorists were *both* "unlawful combatants" and particular types of civilians. This, as Keller and Forowicz explain, created a situation where Barak was treating Palestinian terrorists as if they had civilian *status* but were carrying out combat *functions*, which in turn meant that their alleged transgressions took away any potential privileges or civilian protections.[65] This discursively placed the targets of liquidations into liminal subject positions that militated against their treatment as prisoners of war. Like the fanatical suicide bombers and other despicable characters in Israeli morality plays, those targeted became examples of Giorgio Agamben's *homines sacri*, "the accursed," those who could be killed with impunity.[66]

It is hard to see how this differentiated them from the "outlaws" that Barak mentioned elsewhere in his decision. Barak, Beinisch, and Rivlin were going to admit that the IHL principle of "distinction" was meant to provide civilians with protections, but they were unwilling to treat members of terrorist organizations as traditional, privileged "combatants." This set the contextual stage that led them to conclude that in many cases Israeli military forces could legally assassinate unprotected, terrorist targets.

One of the most creative parts of the *PCATI* v. *Government of Israel* judgment had to do with the ways that the IHC used this decision as a vehicle for responding to foreign pundits who refused to discriminate between different types of civilian populations. Barak could explain how some Palestinian civilians had to refrain from directly participating in hostilities against Israelis if they wanted to keep their privileged and protected status,[67] and he could quote from a number of Geneva Convention texts or international court rulings that proved his point. For example, Barak referenced Article 51 (3) of the 1977 Additional Protocol to the Geneva Convention that stated: "Civilians enjoy the protection afforded by this section, unless, and for some time as they take a direct part in hostilities." While international detractors remarked that some of those targeted had left Hamas, were elected political officials, or were even involved in maneuverings that tried to stem the tide of violence, Barak refused to second guess the decisions of Israeli military commanders or the security officials who put together their targeting lists.

All legal texts are inherently indeterminate, but they become even more so during times of alleged "war," when empowered state actors are allowed to craft their own definitions of what it means to be a "civilian," a "combatant," and an individual who has taken "a direct part in hostilities." Interesting enough, if we compare the "old" rules for covert assassination of victims to the supposedly

Hazards and development of TK rationales 83

"new" criteria that Chief Justice Barak's lays out in *PCATI*, we can understand just why some legal commentators thought he was handing Israeli soldiers "a license to kill." In one key portion of his decision Barak contends that those who bear arms, open or concealed, or those who use them against the army, or civilians who collect intelligence on the army, or civilians who transport unlawful combatants, or those who operate, supervise, or service weapons that are used by unlawful combatants, or those who drive trucks carrying ammunition, are all individuals who have given up their civilian status. He also comments on the status of those who intentionally serve as human shields, those who plan attacks, and others deemed by Israelis to have taken "a direct part in hostilities."[68] The Israelis, of course, are the ones who get to make those designations.

Barak's defenders claim that this helped set out rules that constrained the Israeli military, but it could be argued that while he set out "rules" for TKs, Barak spends just as much time *helping magnify the nature and scope of alleged Palestinian threatens* when he broadens the range of individuals who can now be legally targeted by the Israelis. Many of those who read this portion of Barak's decision realized that, in many ways, he was simply providing jurisprudential rationalizations that were ratifying the actions of Israeli soldiers who already took it as a given that they could target suspects who supposedly exhibited an assortment of terrorist behaviors. In Barak's narrations terrorism was treated in reductionist ways, where there was little commentary on the possibility that the assassinations might be "contributing to the actual emergence of the threat" that liquidations were trying "to preempt."[69]

The avoidance of any discussion of occupation grievances in this case raised as many questions as it answered. Does Barak's opinion mean that the Hamas leader who calls for boycotts or strikes, or the person who tries to organize rallies, or the individual who critiques the partitioning of the West Bank's A, B, and C sectors is someone who is directly participating in hostilities? What would be an example of "indirect" participation? Can that person be targeted? How does one prevent the GSS, the Israeli courts, or the IDF from acting as judge, jury, and executioner when they decide that some Palestinian civilian has engaged in risky behavior that has nothing to do with the rights of combatants who would otherwise be treated as prisoners of war?

What many legal formalists have missed are the rhetorical, cultural arguments that Barak is making about the legitimacy of the armed conflict paradigms that are being used by those who want to expand the list of targeting categories. This, as I argue below, *is enabling*—not constraining—Israeli warhawks.

To be fair, parts of what Barak wrote in *PCATI* make it appear as though there might be some civilians who need to be protected and should not be assassinated. For example, Barak does note that if Palestinian civilians disengaged from battle they need to be left alone. However, those who join terrorist organizations are said to have provided indications that they can be treated as if they were targetable civilians.

Barak and the others may have sincerely believed that they were using "balancing" tests that took into account the rights of the petitioners as well as the security interests of the state, but the way they defended TKs left little room to contest one's placement on the list in the first place. Moreover, it could be argued that former President Barak, by quoting this passage from Michael Schmitt, may have helped open the door for many more abuses of the law down the road:

> Grey areas should be interpreted liberally, i.e. in favor of finding direct participation. One of the seminal purposes of the law is to make possible a clear distinction between civilians and combatants. Suggesting that civilians retain their immunity even when they are intricately involved in a conflict is to engender disrespect for the law by combatants endangered by their activities. Moreover, a liberal approach creates an incentive for civilians to remain as distant from the conflict as possible—in doing so they can better avoid being charged with participation in the conflict and are less liable to being directly targeted.[70]

Note some of the ideological features and potential political motivations behind this formalistic textual fragment that was produced by an American military expert on the "law of armed conflict" (LOAC). At first glance one could argue that Schmitt is simply asserting that there are gray areas that can be cleared away if we presume that some civilians, who are "intricately involved" need to be deterred from being around conflict zones. Schmitt is assuming that civilians have a choice, and he is probably referencing all of the "human shield" scenarios that bother those who want to unshackle IDF forces fighting in urban settings. At the same time, Schmitt is making an argument about an "incentive" that would resonate with Israeli audiences who care deeply about "deterrence."

This type of militaristic, formalistic commentary hides the consequential, *realpolitik* impact of adopting this type of posturing for those who live in Lebanon, the West Bank, or Gaza. What Schmitt's analysis obscures are the ways that his analysis transform thousands of innocent civilians into *presumptively* unprotected "direct participants" in conflict zones. The danger here, as Professor Cassere has pointed out, is that this type of latitude creates situations where "belligerents would be authorized to shoot at any civilian *on the mere suspicion* of their being a potential or actual unlawful combatant."[71] All of this inverts the traditional IHL laws that were meant to presume that civilians were not combatants. Opinions like Barak's help legitimate that transvaluation of values that opens the door for abuses. As Michael Gross explains, if we follow this type of logic then "Palestinian militiamen are now combatants and not criminal terrorists."[72] Military frames replace domestic policing frames of representation.

What is fascinating to note here are the veiled ways that Barak uses a legal text that is supposed to be about TK to provide hints of how "good" and docile Palestinian populations can show their allegiance to Israel or the PA so that they can avoid being targeted. Note, for example, how some of his characterizations of who is not participating in armed conflict or terrorism reads like a story of

Gazans who are peacefully living off of humanitarian aid and avoiding contact with Hamas. Barak, for example, argues that if Palestinian civilians want to retain their protected status they can offer support by selling drugs, food, or providing general aid, but they cannot do much else. This narrowing of civilian status is exactly what pleases aggressive warfighters who despise population-centric counterinsurgency paradigms.

PCATI v. *Government of Israel* is thus a text that has been authored by Israelis who try to create the impression that they are enlightened, twenty-first-century Zionist progressives who are helping with the evolutionary advancement of terrorism law. Barak and his colleagues comment on how they are helping close some international law loopholes when he writes about how terrorist civilians can no longer hide behind the "revolving door" phenomenon, and this in turn allows the liquidation of terrorists who in the past might have rested between acts of hostilities in order to try to get some immunity.[73]

Barak was explicitly refuting the position of organizations like Amnesty International, which had been arguing for years that Palestinian militants were transformed into protected or privileged civilians when their armed engagements ended, or when they no longer posed an "immediate threat" to Israeli troops or civilians.[74] Amnesty International was trying to treat all unlawful combatants as if they were equals, including terrorists who disengaged, but Barak and the rest of the Israeli jurists were not going to accept those types of foreign interpretations. Accepting the Amnesty International frameworks would have resulted in the drastic curtailment of Israeli TKs, and it would have reduced the number of supposed "militants" that could have been legitimately and legally targeted by the Israelis. Utilizing the Amnesty International framework would have also paved the way for more trials of Israeli decision-makers.

Barak needed to find a way of humanizing what many regarded as an Orwellian, inhumane process.[75] Barak certainly did not want to give the impression that he was simply rubber-stamping military procedures or that the Israelis had already decided the legal parameters of these attacks, so he tried to argue that his court was placing a high burden of proof on the Israeli authorities who sought authorization for TKs. For example, he wrote about how even Palestinian civilians who directly participate in hostilities were not to be treated as "outlaws" in ways that might extinguish their "human rights":

> Needless to say, unlawful combatants are not beyond the law. They are not "outlaws." God created them as well in his image; their human dignity as well is to be honoured; they as well enjoy and are entitled to protection, even if most minimal, by customary international law.[76]

If this was taken seriously if would have meant that future critics of Israeli policies could argue that the military was constrained by both IHL and "human rights" law. Of course, it would be the Israelis who would interpret those laws, and Barak's eulogistic invocation of theology did not lead him to ban TKs as ungodly.

86 *Hazards and development of TK rationales*

This blending of the secular and the sacred deftly deflected attention away from any talk of total bans on liquidations. Barak's tales of Israeli exceptionalism focused on Israeli, and not ICRC, UN, EU, or ICC definitions of who engages in unprotected hostile activities.

Barak, like many Israeli security leaders or military experts, was convinced that those who carried out liquidations had exhausted all of their other potential remedies as they confronted the realities of counterterrorist warfare. He reiterated the point that if terrorists could be arrested, interrogated, and tried, then the military is in a situation that obviates the need for assassination.[77] Yet Barak defers to the military interpretations when he qualifies this by saying that in many situations the possibility of capture "does not exist whatsoever" to perform those other activities and that the Israel military need not get itself in situations that involve a "risk so great to the lives" of the Israeli soldiers. This highlights the biopolitical value of Israeli lives, and it reminds readers of the morality of Israeli fighting forces who understand the importance of force protection.

Again, these are not arguments that appear *ex nihilo*, and the above commentary on not risking the lives of IDF soldiers is an example of President Barak simply echoing the prefigurative arguments that had been circulating for years before the handing down of this 2006 decision. Note, for example, how Asa Kasher and Amos Yadlin, two influential Israeli writers, were commenting on the difficulty of arresting those who might have to become a part of the process of "preventive killing":

> If there is a way to capture and arrest a person who is crucially participating in carrying out an act of terror, without jeopardizing the life of combatants, he or she ought to be captured rather than killed. This norm follows from our Principle of Military Necessity and the present principle [distinction]. However, when there is no effective way to capture the terrorist in time, killing him [*sic*] is morally justified as a military act of self-defense and as a last resort. The demand that under such conditions a military force treat the terrorist in the same way that a police squad treats an armed criminal rests on a grave confusion. The moral, ethical and legal ingredients of the normative framework of police activity do not apply to territories that are not under the effective control of the state.[78]

All of this talk of "police" rules is a coded way of avoiding any discussion of who decides when there is "effective control of the state," and it mutes any talk of overwhelming Israeli power or the relevance of occupation law. Supporters of militaristic framings of these Palestinian–Israeli affairs want to constantly reiterate the point that it is the law of armed conflict, and not international interpretations of IHL, that governs Israeli judicial decisionism.

This simply rehearses, and buttresses, the public and elite claims that have been made in other venues about the minimalistic responsibilities of Israelis who allowed for "autonomy" in the West Bank and "disengagement" in Gaza. Those who were supposedly confused about the logic of this reasoning, of course, were the Israeli leftists, the NGOs, the members of the international Red Cross, and others who did not have the acumen and experiences of individuals like Asa Kasher and Amos Yadlin.

Barak's commentary on the principles of military necessity and humanity in *PCATI* follow fairly traditional formalistic patterns of reasoning, but he was able to add a twist to this decision when he mentioned that after each "attack" there had to be a thorough investigation regarding the "precision of the identification of the target."[79] At the same time, where warranted, there would be compensation paid to those innocent civilians who might have been harmed by Israeli attacks.

When Barak was trying to come up with examples of Israeli military actions that he thought clearly *violated* the principle of proportionality he mentioned a case that involved bombing from the air that might lead to scores of residents and passersby being harmed. This was no hypothetical concocted out of thin air that might help Barak put on display the pragmatism of his new proportionality test. What he was referring to was the killing of Sheikh Salah Shehadeh, who was one of the leaders of Hamas' Izzedine al-Qassem Brigades. On July 22, 2002 some 17 people were killed, and more than 100 injured, when an Israeli F-16 jet dropped a one-ton bomb right on top of Shehadeh's house. This killed 15 civilians, including Shehadeh's wife and nine children. In 2008 Helen Keller and Magdalena Forowicz would contend that following "Barak's reasoning, it appears that the Israel Defense Forces will no longer be able to carry out this type of targeted killing, as it will now constitute a war crime."[80] This, however, was overly optimistic, and was written before several other operations, including Operation Cast Lead and Operation Protective Edge.

The dominant reading of Barak's decision in *PCATI* v. *Government of Israel* will probably be that it shields many Israeli security officials and IDF leaders, but the polysemic and polyvalent nature of texts always allows for some alternative readings of this case by other interpretive communities. One might argue that Barak's opinion could serve as a precedent for Palestinian petitioners to argue that Israeli attacks on civilian "infrastructure" during Operation Protective Edge violated the guidelines and tests for targeting that were outlined by the High Court in 2006. Even though the attacks on Hamas tunnels or rockets were not going through the same vetting processes, or the same identification processes that were used by Israeli security services in assassination contexts, they were nevertheless raising similar issues regarding both *jus ad bellum* and *jus in bello* matters.

Given the fact that Israelis take for granted that they are in an "armed conflict" they will not want to revisit some of these *jus ad bellum* issues, but this does not mean that Palestinians can't try to raise those issues—especially if any of this ever gets to the ICC.

In other words, Israelis, over the long run, may find themselves trapped by their own rhetoric. At the same time Barak was trying to put on display Israel's willingness to abide by the laws of humanity and the IHL, he was helping lay the scaffolding and the counterlawfare that could potential turn into the lawfare of the Palestinians.

If we follow both the letter and the spirit of the *PCATI* decision, then each and every time anyone was involved in what might be called indiscriminate "area" bombing of hospitals, schools, or mosques then this would trigger the need for a thorough investigation. Why? Because this did not follow the rules of proportionality and other doctrines regarding "precise" targeting that were part of Barak's "targeting" test in *PCATI*. Those future investigations of what happened in Gaza in 2014, in turn, might result in possible war crimes allegations or the espousal of other IHL transgressions.

In order to stave off those types of accusations, pragmatic Israelis may need more than just Barak's 2006 opinion if they want to shield the heroes who had inherited the duties that were once carried out by Dayan, Sharon, and others. Today's post-human Israeli fighters, who carry out liquidations or attack civilian "infrastructures" that supposedly house tunnels and rockets, may need the help of teams of Israeli advocates who may have to deconstruct some of the very same arguments that Barak so eloquently made in 2006.

However, there is little question that between 2006 and 2013, many defenders of Israel's TK policies hailed Barak's *PCATI* decision as an exemplar of the type of "balancing" that was needed to protect both the rights of petitioners and the interests of the state.

Post-*PCATI* lawfare and the shielding of those Israelis who "liquidate" terrorists

After the circulation of Barak's opinion in *PCATI*, defenders of Israeli policies who lived on many continents praised it as an example of a measured jurisprudential way of reasoning that supposedly was avoiding the extremes of either totally banning all assassinations or foregoing the use of a tactic that many believed saved thousands of lives. Helen Keller and Magdalena Forowicz averred that Chief Barak's decision provided a needed "safety net."[81]

The notion that Barak had not provided the Israeli military with *carte blanche* authority resonated with many reviewers of his decision. Eric Berlin argued that Barak's opinion was important, "not because it ensures that targeted killing will never occur, but because it solidifies the rule of law in situations where the laws are often ignored."[82] Yuval Yoaz, who summarized the holding in *PCATI* for *Ha'aretz* readers, used the headline "International Law Does not Forbid Targeted Killings" to explain the dominant conclusion in the opinion.[83] Then-Minister Gideon Ezra, a former top Shabak figure, told the press that Barak's ruling "basically reflects how the army already works."[84] Hillel Fendel, writing for *Arutz Sheva*, remarked that this ruling had been postponed for some five years, and that the ruling had been translated into English, which was an unprecedented move that showed its international importance.

Barak's opinion would be attacked by representatives of Israel's left and right wings of the political spectrum. Gideon Levy, an Israeli journalist known for his harsh criticism of his government's occupation politics, caricatured Barak as the "enlightened occupier," someone who had produced a text that was a farce because the "executioners" were the ones who were being allowed to judge how to apply vague and ambiguous requirements.[85]

The right-wing Shurat Hadin organization was willing to applaud the part of Barak's opinion that upheld the legality of liquidations, but it complained about the fact that the IDF and the security services had to make their decisions on a case-by-case basis. "This is clearly a case of the High Court, once again, dangerously showing mercy to the cruel, argued Nitzana Darshan-Leiner for Sharat Hadin.[86] "Carl in Jerusalem," who produced the *Israel Matzav* blog, argued that Barak's opinion would open the door for hundreds of compensation cases in which plaintiffs would be suing the Israeli state. He specifically referenced Gazan contexts when he argued that "terrorist leaders," in order to avoid being legally targeted in the aftermath of the case, simply had to be "surrounded by human shields." Carl argued that in places like Gaza this was not that "hard to do," and he worried that Barak's decision would have a chilling effect on the IDF. As a result, the security of Israelis would suffer.[87] Carl pointed out that Barak and the other two members of this court were using a vague term like "former terror operative" that had temporal contextualization, which meant that readers had no way of knowing how long a "target" has to be out of the "terror business" before they avoid being targeted. This seemed to imply that courts were going to have the jurisdiction to examine each and every single targeted killing in order to assess after the fact whether the IDF should have been allowed to go after that particular individual.

This underscores the point that more than a few Israelis were willing to allow the IDF and the security services to have *total authority and absolute discretion* to go after anyone they suspected of having any ties to any terrorist organization, regardless of whether they belonged to the "political" or "military" wings of Fatah or Hamas.

American commentators often framed *PCATI* as a case where the IHC was "backing" the Israeli military.[88] Scott Wilson of the *Washington Post* remarked that the "unanimous decision departs little from the guidelines" of the Israeli military, and he provided a nice encapsulation of the usual vetting processes that were used by the Israelis before each liquidation:

> Under current practice, Israel's military works with Shin Bet, the domestic security service, to compile lists of Palestinians who are influential or active figures in armed groups. Using eavesdropping equipment, aerial surveillance and informants, air force pilots or drone operators receive detailed information about a target's movements, most commonly in the Gaza Strip, where the army no longer operates regularly on the ground.[89]

Wilson then gets melodramatic as he notes how the military officers sometimes have to make decisions to strike in a matter of minutes, and this means they have to work at "balancing the threat posed by the target against the potential for injuring bystanders."[90] Wilson also mentions in passing that many of these strikes have killed civilians in addition to targeted killings, but this sanitized way of talking about these programs turns this process into some abstract killing machine, an apparatus that looks like what Joseph Pugliese has called "a biopolitical matrix of power, bodies, life and death."[91]

Yet Americans were willing to see the Israeli policies as measured targeting processes that needed to be *emulated by the US government*. Scott Wilson, for example, explains that Barak's decision will help provide more guidance for Americans who are carrying out drone strikes, and he was sure it represented "a disappointed defeat for Israeli and Palestinian human rights organizations that have called the tactic, pioneered during the most recent Palestinian uprising, a war crime."[92] Readers are left thinking that these NGO complaints were just another example of lawfare, frivolous complaining that could do little to help guide those who have already decided that these constituted moral and legitimate activities. Americans could now read about and watch as their own military experts traveled to Israel so they could learn about the latest "targeted killing" strategies and tactics.

Some American pundits liked the ultimate outcome of the *PCATI* decision, but they quibbled with some of the specific wording or the guidance in the case. Michael Schmitt, for example, explained that Barak's advocacy of ad hoc decision-makers still left open the door for disputation, in that interpretations regarding "direct participation" varied widely, even among experts. Some were arguing that the "intent" of the terrorists mattered, while others opined that you could not always determine the "*mens rea*" during the heat of battle. Others mentioned that maybe it was the proximity to the frontlines of the battle that made a difference, but this might mean having to chase down terrorists in massive "battlespaces," stood in the way of "the adoption of a geographical criterion."[93]

In spite of this quibbling many of those who reviewed Barak's TK opinion considered it to be measured, and even those who would have liked to have seen a total ban on liquidations often tried to look on the bright side and accept the wisdom of having "precise" Israeli targeting replace indiscriminate "area" bombings. For many Americans, the worries about localized Hezbollah attacks from Lebanon or Hamas raids from Gaza made perfect sense. This fit with what they were hearing and reading in the broader rhetorical cultures about the dangers of Jihadism in places like Somalia, Yemen, Mali, Iraq, or Pakistan.

Barak's supporters followed the lead of those who discriminated between the "good" Palestinians who collaborated with the Israelis and passed along information about potential targets at checkpoints, and the "bad" Palestinians who were either anti-Semitic or simply did not understand the benign nature of Israeli decision-making. Orientalism and paternalism aside, the occupation and the conflicts with the Palestinian ranks had to be framed in militarizing *dispositifs*, in ways that included the adoption of what Eyal Weizman has called "thanotactics."[94] From a post-structural standpoint, those who worried about the spread of "militant" Palestinian terrorism may have had their qualms regarding the efficacy of some of these efforts, and they may have expressed skepticism about the amount of intelligence the Israeli Security Agency actual had, but they did not doubt the metanarratives that were told about existential terrorist threats. This meant that Barak's *PCATI* opinion became the perfect example of counterlawfare.

Bright Israeli lawyers who now advised members of the Israeli Air Force and the IDF can now follow Aharon Barak and produce the counterlawfare that will became a part of what Derek Gregory called the "modern 're-enchantment of war,'" where fighting terrorism can be portrayed as "surgical, sensitive, and scrupulous."[95] As noted above, some of the most popular Israeli assassination narratives were the ones that could evidence just how many dozens or hundreds of Israelis or Palestinians were saved when individual terrorists were liquidated by snipers, helicopters, airstrikes, or raids in places like Dubai or Lebanon. I would hazard a guess that from now on most defenders of Israeli military policies will spent their time writing and talking about the most "efficacious" way of taking out floors on buildings, or using the right munitions that would cause the least amount of collateral damage.

These historical, contemporary and future narrations of conditions in Gaza or the West Bank assume that if Palestinians want to make sure they are not hit by Israeli helicopters or snipers, then they will have to provide irrefutable proof that they are not terrorists. If they live on the West Bank they can provide this proof by joining those in the diaspora. If they live in Gaza they can stop voting for Hamas and they can try to support those who wanted to work with Israelis. Again, these are fanciful ways of thinking about human conditions and choices, but they fit within the Zionist and secular master narratives that were crafted by Israelis who treat liquidations in clinical ways.

Conclusion

In this chapter I provided readers with a critical genealogical explanation of why Israeli TK rationales veered in particular directions, and I've outlined the paths not taken. I've shown readers some of the historiography behind the "liquidations" that were "reactivated" by Barak and other Israelis in the aftermath of the beginning of the second Intifada. At the same time, I've illustrated how some of the key baseline questions that are often asked by Israelis about assassinations were often answered in cultural as well as military ways, as communities thought back to biblical times, or reminisced about more modern incidents like the 1972 attack on the Munich Olympic athletes. It could be argued that in comparison with other generations who fought in 1947–1948, 1967, 1973, etc., this Israeli generation is relatively secure and has little to fear from any form of terrorism, but this has little to do with Israeli *perceptions*.

Outside critics like to comment on the need for totalizing bans on all assassinations, but Israelis conversations are more about the nature and scope of these targeted killings. While a few vocal Israeli leftists have tried to draw lines between "political" and "militant" members of Fatah, Hezbollah, or Hamas, this does not appeal to many Israelis who believe that membership in these organizations signals that one wants to violently attack the State of Israel. As far as most

92 *Hazards and development of TK rationales*

Israelis are concerned, it is naive to think that exchanging "territory for security" is going to stop the propagandizing efforts of jihadists, and when Israelis debate among themselves about their liquidation polices they are more likely to ask the question of who will, or will not, be held responsible for terrorist behavior. Israelis have no use for those who don't understand that Israelis have to go after the bomb-maker who was at the center of stories about "ticking" time-bombs, or the individual who fired rockets at Israelis during declared wars.[96]

Readers, in the future, will have to deal with the question of where this slippery slope ends, whether Israelis can go after any Palestinian who supports Hamas, or whether it is legal or moral to target anyone associated with "infrastructures." These questions also have to be asked: Did the advent of asymmetrical conflicts change the moral or legal equations to the point that military legal advisers or jurists were willing to ratify the decisions that were made by those who wanted to go after financiers, taxi drivers, politicians, or the unwitting transporters of goods who traveled through Gaza ports? Were snipers going to be allowed to kill Fatah politicians, as well as Hamas terrorists? What about the "human shields" who showed their steadfastness by refusing to leave their homes—even after receiving warnings from the Israeli military? Were these individuals now going to be included in the statistics that were collected of those "terrorists" who were killed in TK strikes?

There are no easy answers to these types of questions, but if one is going to try to help immunize those who carried out targeted killings then one needs to see the ideological and cultural nature of the formulas that are dreamed up to help with the establishment of jurisprudential norms and balancing tests.[97] These may be trumpeted as edicts that only help constrain targeted killing and guide tactical and operational practices, but it is possible that they also *embolden* those who know that they can carry out these attacks with relative impunity.

Widening the circumference of the matrices that are used by the Israeli Security Agency (ISA) to designate "militant" activists involves art and science, and all sorts of rhetorical factors seem to have influenced the gradual acceptance of almost unfettered targeting decisions. The Israeli assassination lawfare may look as though it moves toward support for a type of "precision" warfare that obviates the need for more collective punishment, but this ignores the ways that most of the rhetorical fragments circulating in decisions like Barak's in *PCATI* continue to instantiate the patriotic metanarratives that are told about the existence of massive existential threats. Opinions regarding the potential causes of terrorism are turned into irrefutable facts, and this in turn allows the targeted killing decision to join the growing list of Israeli cases that Nimer Sultany critiqued in his commentary on bifurcated Israeli court systems that employed differential rules for the treatment of Palestinian and Israeli settlers.[98]

Note, for example, how Barak failed to mention something that will be discussed in one of my other chapters—the "terrorist" threats that Shin Bet believed were posed by *settler extremists* and others who plotted to attack Palestinians. Barak's entire *PCATI* opinion is written in ways that allow readers to structurally configure dogmatic Palestinians as the only terrorists that matter. This, I am convinced, helped pave the way for taking seriously the possibility that Gazan populations might be terrorists.

The elite and public acceptance of expansive targeting of many Palestinians did not happen overnight. Lisa Hajjar has shown us that during the first Intifada Israelis did carry out assassinations, but cultural expectations and prying international eyes may have stayed the hands of hardliners who wanted to go after not dozens, but hundreds of Palestinian "militants." Some of these hardliners, before the second Intifada, had a hard time trying to convince members of the Labor Party that political dissenters should be targeted along with the "military" members of Fatah. This changed with the magnification of the role of suicide bombers. The building of the massive "separation barrier," as well as the work on the Iron Dome, provided even more evidence that Israelis were seeking unilateral, military solutions to what the rest of the world viewed as peacekeeping matters that might require multinational intervention.

The *perceived* "qualitative" difference in the violence of the second Intifada convinced many Israeli politicians, military experts, and legal advisers that none of this was spontaneous. A rhetorical analysis of hundreds of articles written during and after the beginning of the second Intifada underscores this point, as rhetor after rhetor talked about the men and women who turned into suicide bombers.[99]

David Kretzmer has pointed out the real dangers that confront all of us when we witness the "over-reaction of states" that are acting "outside accepted standards of human rights" and international law. Kretzmer recognizes that the problem here is that readers cannot think that this danger will be "contained only by pious words and proposals" that do not take into account the "unrealistic perception" that so many civilians are engaged in acts that render them "suspected transnational terrorists."[100] Kretzmer joined those commentators who believed that even if the IDF was targeting persons who might be legitimate targets, the results of their targeting appeared to show that these attacks did not meet the proportionality tests of the IHL.[101]

While many Israeli decision-makers and pundits would have liked to change the minds of critics like Kretzmer, and persuade cosmopolitan thinkers of the wisdom of Aharon Barak's words, some of their primary audiences have always been the *domestic* Israeli Labor or Likud Party members and citizens who no longer have to worry about the legality or legitimacy of Israel's liquidation policies. The IHC, after all, had spoken, and it sanctioned "balanced" targeted policies.

Targeted killings do have ripple effects, but all of this decapitation may or may not degrade terrorist cells. What often gets left out of the equation is the possibility that some of these practices are making many more enemies than anticipated. Donald Rumsfeld, former US defense secretary of war, once famously asked in a memo to General Dick Myers, Paul Wolfowitz, General Pet Pace, and Doug Feigh: "Are we capturing, killing or deterring and dissuading more terrorists every day than the madrassas and the radical clerics are recruiting, training and deploying against us?"[102] What these warhawks would perhaps not acknowledge is that their own invasion of Iraq may have contributed to the swelling of the ranks of those who would willingly give their lives for a host of insurgent causes. The TKs may have swelled the ranks of the terrorist organizations that can now find disaffected youths who witnessed the attacks in both Gaza and the West Bank.

The IDF planners who eyed their targets should also have been thinking about the long-term relationship impacts of their decision-making. Political geographer Derek Gregory once explained:

> by fastening on a single killing—through a "surgical strike"—all the other people affected by it are removed from view. Any death causes ripple effects far beyond the immediate victim, but to those that plan and execute a targeted killing the only effects that concern them are the degradation of the terrorism or insurgent network in which the target is supposed to be implicated. Yet these strikes also, again incidentally but not accidentally, cause immense damage to the social fabric of which s/he was a part—the extended family, the local community and beyond—and the sense of loss continues to haunt countless (and uncounted) others.[103]

Eyal Weizman, in "Thanato-tactics," similarly argues that instead of helping Abbas and the moderates on the Palestinian streets, these targeted strikes have "fed the conflict by seeding terror, uncertainty, and rage and by promoting social chaos" they create "further motivations for violent retaliations and dramatically increasing Palestinian popular support for the acts of terror."[104]

Israelis may believe that President Barak's opinion provided a counterlawfare shield for soldiers and pilots who might end up in foreign courtrooms, but the open defense of these same strikes most likely contributed to the rise of Hamas in Gaza. Those who carried out the targeted killings, or those who may have enjoyed reading about phone-booth gadgetry and the liquidation of those who attacked malls, pizza parlors, and military targets, may find that, over the long run, the Iron Dome can only keep out some kinds of terrorist threats.

Notes

1 *BBC News*, "Israel's Assassination Policy," *BBC News*, last modified August 1, 2001. http://news.bbc.co.uk/2/hi/middle_east/1258187.stm. For some representative samples of the harsh criticism of these policies that was circulating before 2006, see Amnesty International, "Israel and the Occupied Territories: Israel Must End Its Policy of Assassination," last modified July 4, 2003, www.amnesty.org/en/library/asset/MDE15/056/2003/en/0f527cb4-d6bd-11dd-ab95-a13b602c0642/mde150562003en.pd; Yael Stein, "By Any Name Illegal and Immoral," *Ethics & International Affairs* 17 (2003): 127. For more on Israeli law and the relevance of occupation law, see David Kretzmer, *The Occupation of Justice: The Supreme Court of Israel and the Occupied Territories* (Albany, NY: State University of New York University Press, 2002).
2 For an analysis of the Israeli press coverage of these liquidation policies, see Alina Korn, "Israeli Press and the War against Terrorism: The Construction of the 'Liquidation Policy,'" *Crime, Law and Social Change* 41, no. 3 (2004): 209–234.

3 Unfortunately, far too many of these critiques of TK rationales are written in abstract, arhetorical ways that assiduously avoid grappling with the cultural, social, and political dynamics of Israeli and Palestinian historiographies. Some lawyers who are used to writing in styles that treat the "rule of law" as some detached sets of rules and principles can offer guidance without taking any normative or ideological positions in these debates. These types of critiques not only miss *the power* dynamics of these historical and contemporary usages of TK—they also gloss over and obfuscate the ways that debates about TK have everything to do with the ways that Israelis argue about the occupation in general, or the role of Fatah, or the future of "Judea" and "Samaria." For an example of a work that tries to get at some of the pragmatic issues that are involved, without getting committed to overly formalistic legal discussions of IHL principles, see Avery Plaw, *Targeting Terrorists: A Licence to Kill?* (Hampshire: Ashgate Publishing Limited, 2008).

4 Michael Gross, "Assassination and Targeted Killing: Law Enforcement, Execution or Self-Defence," *Journal of Applied Philosophy* 23, no. 3, (2006), 323–325, 332–333, see also Or Honig, "Explaining Israel's Misuse of Strategic Assassinations," *Studies in Conflict & Terrorism* 30, no. 6 (2007): 563–577. DOI: 10.1080/10576100701329584.

5 Marko Milanovic, "Lessons for Human Rights and Humanitarian Law in the War on Terror: Comparing *Hamdan* and the Israeli *Targeted Killings* Case," *International Review of the Red Cross* 89, no. 866 (2007): 373–393, 382. For more on the challenges that came with the two Intifadas, see Sergio Catignani, *Israeli Counter-Insurgency and the Intifadas: Dilemmas of a Conventional Army* (New York: Routledge, 2008).

6 Steve R. David, "Fatal Choices: Israel's Policy of Targeted Killings," *Mideast Security and Policy Studies* 51 (2002): 7.

7 President Barak, *The Public Committee Against Torture in Israel* v. *The Government of Israel*, HCJ 769/02 (2006) (herein called *PCATI*), paragraph 1. For helpful overviews of this case, see Orna Ben-Naftali and Keren R. Michaeli, "'We Must Not Make a Scarecrow of the Law': A Legal Analysis of the Israeli Policy of Targeted Killings," *Cornell International Law Journal* 36 (2003): 233–292; Orna Ben-Naftali, "A Judgment in the Shadow of International Law," *Journal of International Criminal Justice* 5, no. 2 (2007): 322–331.

8 See, for example, Amichai Cohen and Stuart A. Cohen, "Israel and International Humanitarian Law: Between the Neo-Realism of State Security and the 'Soft Power' of Legal Acceptability," *Israel Studies* 16, no. 2 (2011): 1–23.

9 Israeli Supreme Court, [Aharon Barak], *Ajuri* v. *IDF Commander*, HCJ 7015/02, paragraph 41 (2002).

10 Aviram Zino, "Left-Wingers Demand Ruling on Targeted Killings," *Ynetnews*, last modified November 13, 2006, www.google.com/webhp?rct=j#q=left-wingersdemand+ruling+on+targeted+killing.

11 See Seth Anziska, "A Preventable Massacre," *New York Times*, last modified September 16, 2012, www.nytimes.com/2012/09/17/opinion/a-preventable-massacre.html?_r=0.

12 Ben-Naftali, "A Judgment in the Shadow," 325.

13 Matthew S. Cohen and Charles D. Freilich, "The Delegitimation of Israel: Diplomatic Warfare, Sanctions, and Lawfare," *Israel Journal of Foreign Affairs* 9, no. 1 (2015): 29–48.

14 See Professor Shalhou-Kevorkian's excellent analysis on this point. Nadera Shalhoub-Kevorkian, "Human Suffering in Colonial Contexts," *Settler Colonial Studies* 4, no. 3 (2014): 277–290.

15 Laura Blumenfeld, "In Israel, a Divisive Struggle Over Targeted Killings," *Washington Post*, last modified August 27, 2006, paragraph 28, www.washingtonpost.com/wp-dyn/content/article/2006/08/26/AR2006082600917.html.

96 *Hazards and development of TK rationales*

16 On decapitation, see Jenna Jordan, "When Heads Roll: Assessing the Effectiveness of Leadership Decapitation," *Security Studies* 18 (2009): 719–755.
17 Adam Stahl, "The Evolution of Israeli Targeted Operations: Consequences of the Thabet Thabet Operation," *Studies in Conflict & Terrorism* 33 (2010): 111–133. Stahl himself was convinced that TK could be defended as a legitimate military tactic (see p. 121).
18 Rebecca Stein, "Impossible Witness: Israeli Visuality – Palestinian Testimony and the Gaza War," *Journal of Cultural Research* 16, no. 2/3 (2012): 135–153, 150.
19 These statistics came from the B'Tselem Israeli organization and were cited in Helen Keller and Magdalena Forowicz, "A Tightrope Walk between Legality and Legitimacy: An Analysis of the Israeli Supreme Court's Judgment on Targeted Killing," *Leiden Journal of International Law* 21 (2008): 185–221, 186.
20 Stahl, "The Evolution of Israeli Targeted," 111–133.
21 Steve R. David, "Fatal Choices: Israel's Policy of Targeted Killings," *Mideast Security and Policy Studies* 51 (2002): 2, DOI: 10.4324/9780203485422.ch9. For more on the use of biblical references by those who carried out political assassinations, see Franklin L. Ford, *Political Murder: From Tyrannicide to Terrorism* (Cambridge, MA: Harvard University Press, 1985), 7–22.
22 For an excellent history of the role the Haganah played in the evolutionary development of Israeli CT, see Daniel Byman, *A High Price: The Triumphs and Failures of Israeli Counterterrorism* (London: Oxford University Press, 2011).
23 David, "Fatal Choices," 2. For more on the battles with the British see Nachman Ben-Yehuda, *Political Assassination by Jews: A Rhetorical Device for Justice* (Albany, NY: SUNY Press, 1992).
24 Ibid., 3.
25 Note, for example, Dan Raviv and Yossi Melman, *Every Spy a Prince: The Complete History of Israel's Intelligence Community* (Boston, MA: Houghton Mifflin, 1990); Ian Black and Benny Morris, *Israel's Secret Wars: A History of Israel's Intelligence Services* (New York: Grove Weidenfeld, 1991); Ami Pedahzur, *The Israeli Secret Services and the Struggle Against Terrorism* (New York: Columbia University Press, 2009).
26 David, "Fatal Choices," 3.
27 See Aaron J. Klein, *Striking Back: The 1972 Munich Olympics Massacre and Israel's Deadly Response* (New York: Random House, 2005).
28 David, "Fatal Choices," 4.
29 Alex von Tunzelmann, "Spielberg's *Munich*: Earnestly Searching for Truths that Refuse to be Found," *Guardian*, last modified March 15, 2012, www.theguardian.com/film/2012/mar/15/reel-history-spielberg-munich.
30 Blumenfeld, "In Israel, A Divisive Struggle," paragraphs 26–27.
31 The very topic of TK's effectiveness has almost become an obligatory way of answering the lamentations of foreign critics. See, for example, Avi Kober, "Targeted Killing during the Second Intifada: The Quest for Effectiveness," *Journal of Conflict Studies* 27, no. 1 (2007), http://journals.hil.unb.ca/index.php/JCS/article/viewArticle/8292/9353.
32 David, "Fatal Choices," 4.
33 Assaf Moghadam, "Palestinian Suicide Terrorism in the Second Intifada: Motivations and Organizational Aspects," *Studies in Conflict & Terrorism* 26 (2003): 65–92: Scott Atran, "Genesis of Suicide Terrorism," *Science* 299 (2003): 1534–1539; Eyad El-Sarraj, "Suicide Bombers: Dignity, Despair, and the Need for Hope," *Journal of Palestine Studies* 31, no. 4 (2002): 71–76.
34 David, "Fatal Choices," 5.
35 Ibid., 5.
36 Amos Guiora, "Targeted Killing as Active Self-Defense," *Case Western Journal of International Law* 36 (2004): 319–334, 320.

Hazards and development of TK rationales 97

37 Lisa Hajjar, "Lawfare and Targeted Killing: Developments in the Israeli and US Contexts," *Jadaliyya*, last modified January 15, 2012, paragraph 10, www.jadaliyya.com/pages/index/4049/lawfare-and-targeted-killing_developments-in-the-i.
38 Eyal Weizman, "Thanato-tactics," in *The Power of Inclusive Exclusion: Anatomy of Israeli Rule in the Occupied Palestinian Territories*, eds. Adi Ophir, Michal Givoni, and Sari Hanifi (New York: Zone Books, 2009), 555.
39 For an example of domestic criticism in Israel, see Yael Stein, *Israel's Assassination Policy: Extra-judicial Killings* (B'Tselem, 2001), www.btselem.org/download/200101_extrajudicial_killings_eng.doc.
40 Daniel Reisner, quoted in Blumenfeld, "In Israel, A Divisive Struggle," paragraph 29.
41 Ibid., paragraph 30.
42 Gary D. Solis, *The Law of Armed Conflict: International Humanitarian Law in War* (New York: Cambridge University Press, 2010), 543.
43 Daniel Byman, *A High Price: The Triumphs and Failures of Israeli Counterterrorism* (New York: Oxford University Press, 2011), 313.
44 Weizman, "Thanato-tactics," 544.
45 David, "Fatal Choices," 4.
46 Amos Harel and Ha'aretz Correspondence, "Ex-Shin Bet Chief: Israeli Assassination Policy Led to Period of Calm," *Ha'aretz*, last modified May 31, 2005, paragraph 4, www.haaretz.com/news/ex-shin-bet-chief-israeli-assassination-policy-led-toperiod-of-calm-1.160054.
47 Ze' ev Segal, "Morality vs. Security," *Ha'aretz*, last modified December 6, 2004, paragraphs 1–4, www.haaretz.com/print-edition/opinion/morality-vs-security-1.142629.
48 The "balancing" that was supposed to be taking place was between "human rights" and "military needs." Barak, *PCATI*, paragraph 22. This was not supposed to involve absolutist positions, but rather case-by-case assessments. Yuval Yoaz provided readers of *Ha'aretz* with a nice summary of the four major elements in Barak's "test" for targeted killings in Yuval Yoaz, "High Court: International Law Does not Forbid Targeted Killings," *Ha'aretz*, last modified December 14, 2006, www.haaretz.com/news/high-court-international-law-does-not-forbid-targeted-killings-1.207185.
49 Gordon, "Rationalising Extra-Judicial," 318.
50 Gal Luft, "The Logic of Israel's Targeted Killing," *Middle East Quarterly* 10, no. 1 (2003): 3–13.
51 David, "Fatal Choices."
52 This commentary on "thwarting" made its way into the titles of early academic critiques of the Israeli targeting policy. Emanual Gross, "Thwarting Terrorists' Acts by Attacking the Perpetrators or Their Commanders as an Act of Self-Defense: Human Rights Versus the State's Duty to Protect Its Citizens," *Temple International & Comparative Law Journal* 15 (2001): 195–246.
53 Luft, "The Logic of Israel's Targeted Killing," paragraph 2.
54 Ibid., paragraph 4.
55 Ibid., paragraph 31–32.
56 W.J.T. Mitchell, "Picturing Terror: Derrida's Autoimmunity," *Cardozo Law Review* 27 (2005): 913–925, 914.
57 Rob Reiner, *A Few Good Men*, 1992.
58 Jacques Derrida, "Autoimmunity: Real and Symbolic Suicides," in *Philosophy in a Time of Terror: Dialogues with Jürgen Habermas and Jacques Derrida*, interviewed by G. Borradori (Chicago, IL and London: University of Chicago Press, 2003), 85–136.
59 Barak, *PCATI*, paragraph 62.
60 Markus Gunneflo, "The Targeted Killing Judgment of the Israeli Supreme Court and the Critique of Legal Violence," Lund University Faculty of Law, *Selected Works of*

Markus Gunneflow, last modified January 2012, 16, http://works.bepress.com/markus_gunneflo/4.
61 For a 2004 discussion on how the IDF expanded the scope of targeted killing to include those who were training for an attack, see Amos Guiora "Targeted Killing as Active Self-Defense," *Case Western Reserve Journal of International Law* 36 (2004): 291–334, 322.
62 Keller and Forowicz, "A Tightrope Walk," 186. For other commentaries that thought the Barak result was an improvement over the status quo, see William J. Fenrick, "The *Targeted Killings* Judgment and the Scope of Direct Participation in Hostilities," *Journal of International Criminal Justice* 5, no. 2 (2007): 332–328, DOI: 10.1093/jicj/mqm007.
63 Michelle Lesh, "Case Note: *The Public Committee Against Torture in Israel* v. *The Government of Israel*—The Israel High Court of Justice Targeted Killing Decision," *Melbourne Journal of International Law* 8(2) (2007): 4, www.law.unimelb.edu.au/files/dmfile/download51921.pdf.
64 Ibid., 5.
65 Keller and Forowicz, "A Tightrope Walk," 200.
66 Gorgio Agamben, *Homo Sacer: Sovereign Power and Bare Life*, trans. Daniel Heller-Roazen (Stanford, CA: Stanford University Press, 1998).
67 Barak, *PCATI*, paragraph 23.
68 Ibid., 34–36.
69 Weizman, "Thanato-tactics," 557.
70 Michael Schmitt, quoted by Chief Justice Barak, cited in Keller and Forowicz, "A Tightrope Walk," 206.
71 Professor Cassese, quoted in Keller and Forowicz, "A Tightrope Walk," 200.
72 Michael L. Gross, "Fighting by Other Means in the Mideast: A Critical Analysis of Israel's Assassination Policy," *Political Studies* 51, no. 2 (2003): 350–368, 354.
73 Barak, *PCATI*, paragraph 40.
74 Amnesty International, *Israel and the Occupied Territories: State Assassinations and Other Unlawful Killings* (London: Amnesty International, 2001), 29.
75 For Orwellian references, see the texts and comments that appear in Richard Falk, "The Latest Gaza Catastrophe," *Al Jazeera*, last modified November 18, 2012, www.aljazeera.com/indepth/opinion/2012/11/2012111874429224963.html; Hisham Melham, "Palestine and Israel: Arsenals of Swords and Words," *Al Arabiya News*, last modified July 26, 2014, http://english.alarabiya.net/en/views/news/middle-east/2014/07/26/Palestine-and-Israel-arsenals-of-swords-and-words-.html.
76 Barak, *PCATI*, paragraph 40.
77 Ibid., 40.
78 Asa Kasher and Amos Yadlin, "Assassination and Preventive Killing," *SAIS Review of International Affairs*, 25, no. 1 (2005): 41–57, 51, DOI: 10.1353/sais.2005.0011.
79 Barak, *PCATI*, paragraph 40.
80 Keller and Forowicz, "A Tightrope Walk," 215.
81 Ibid., 213.
82 Eric Berlin, "The Israeli Supreme Court's Targeted Killing Judgment: A Reaffirmation of the Rule of Law During War," *Michigan State International Law Review* 21 (2013): 517–546, 540.
83 Yoaz, "High Court: International Law Does Not Forbid."
84 Gideon Ezra, quoted in Hillel Fendel, "High Court Essentially Upholds Current Targeted Killing Policy," *Israel National News*, last modified December 14, 2006, paragraph 2, www.israelnationalnews.com/News/News.aspx/117451#.VAHzvfldXTo.
85 Gideon Levy, "An Enlightened Occupier," *Ha'aretz*, last modified December 17, 2006, www.haaretz.com/print-edition/opinion/an-enlightened-occupier-1.207387.
86 Nitzana Darshan-Leitner, quoted in Dan Izenberg, "High Court Allows Conditional

Targeted Killings," *The Jerusalem Post*, last modified December 14, 2006, www.jpost.com/Israel/High-Court-allows-conditional-targeted-killings.

87 Carl in Jerusalem, "Supreme Court Restricts Targeted Killings," *Israel Matzav*, last modified December 14, 2006, http://israelmatzav.blogspot.com/2006/12/supreme-court-restricts-targeted.html.
88 Scott Wilson, "Israeli High Court Backs Military on Its Policy of 'Targeted Killings,'" *Washington Post*, last modified December 15, 2006, www.washingtonpost.com/wp-dyn/content/article/2006/12/14/AR2006121400430.html.
89 Ibid., paragraph 3.
90 Ibid., paragraph 4.
91 Joseph Pugliese, *State Violence and the Execution of the Law: Biopolitical Caesurae of Torture, Black Sites, Drones* (New York: Routledge, 2013), 2.
92 Wilson, "Israel High Court Backs Military," paragraph 9.
93 Michael N. Schmitt, "Deconstructing Direct Participation in Hostilities: The Constitutive Elements," *International Law and Politics* 42 (2010): 697–739, 711.
94 Eyal Weizman, "Thanato-tactics."
95 Derek Gregory, "War and Peace," *Transactions of the Institute of British Geographers* 35, no. 2 (2010): 154–186.
96 The firing of rockets from Gaza has once again triggered the call for the reactivation of liquidation policies. Associated Press, "Israel Considers Resuming Targeted Killings of Gaza Military Leaders to Stop Rocket Fire," *Fox News*, last modified November 13, 2012, www.foxnews.com/world/2012/11/13/israel-considers-resuming-targeted-killings-gaza-militant-leaders-to-stop.
97 Amos Guiora has written one of the most popular examples of this type of guidance. Amos Guiora, *Legitimate Target: A Criteria-Based Approach to Targeted Killing* (New York: Oxford University Press, 2013).
98 Nimer Sultany, "The Legacy of Justice Aharon Barak: A Critical Overview," *Harvard International Law Journal Online* 48 (2007): 83–92.
99 See Dorit Naaman, "Brides of Palestine/Angels of Death: Media, Gender, and Performance in the Case of Palestinian Female Suicide Bombers," *Signs* 32, no. 4 (2007): 933–955; Gadi Wolfsfed, Paul Frosh, & Maurice T. Awabdy, "Covering Death in Conflicts: Coverage of the Second Intifada on Israeli and Palestinian Television," *Journal of Peace Research* 45, no. 3 (2008): 401–417.
100 David Kretzmer, "Targeted Killing of Suspected Terrorists: Extra-Judicial Executions or Legitimate Means of Defence?" *The European Journal of International Law* 16, no. 2 (2012): 171–212, 212.
101 Ibid., 211.
102 Donald Rumsfeld, quoted in *USA Today*, "Rumsfeld's War-On-Terror Memo," *USA Today*, last modified October 16, 2003, http://usatoday30.usatoday.com/news/washington/executive/rumsfeld-memo.htm.
103 Derek Gregory, "Darkness Descending," *Geographical Imaginations*, July 29, 2014, http://geographicalimaginations.com/2014/07/29/darkness-descending.
104 Weizman, "Thanato-tactics," 557.

4 Disengagement from Gaza, "institutionalized impoverishment," and the biopolitics of Israeli pressuring of Gazans, 2005–2013

It is notoriously difficult in some Gazan contexts to ascribe motives, and it is no easy task for observers to determine when empowered Israeli civil or military leaders are really trying to target small numbers of Hamas terrorist fighters and when they are trying to terrorize entire Gaza populations. In some situations they may be trying to carry out both tasks in the name of defending Israel. Regardless, the stubborn refusal to bow to the overwhelming material power of the Israelis puzzles those who can only configure Hamas as a terrorist organization.

The election of Hamas officials, and the relative disempowerment of more "moderate" Arabs from the Palestinian Authority (PA), infuriated many Israelis who were already convinced they were surrounded by extremists who wanted to drive them into the sea. While members of Likud, Labor, or other parties in Israel often disagreed about the nature, scope, and magnitude of terrorists threats in general, they often set aside their political bickering and agreed that the Gaza Strip provided complex challenges that went beyond the ones that confronted the Israelis in the West Bank.

Before the first Intifada, it could be argued that many Israelis genuinely believed in land for security arrangements and the importance of developing regulatory practices that allowed for the flow of Palestinians in and out of Israel. These earlier debates were about the pros and cons of one- or two-state solutions, and the valence of these conversations changed with the advent of the Intifadas. As noted in earlier chapters, the Israelis began to deploy more segregationist policies that controlled the mobility of Palestinians while protecting the settlers, the occupants of Jerusalem, and others who lived in the "disputed territories" or Israel "proper."[1]

While many academic, military, and legal defenders of these policies have cited applicable laws of "belligerency," domestic Israeli law, or international law that seemed to undergird the Israelis' pragmatic decision-making since that first Intifada, detractors have argued that shifting political, economic, and military needs have created a situation where Gazans are faced with "deliberately nonrational bureaucracies" that allow unpredictable, often arbitrary, control over travel, economic trade, demographic registration, permits, privileges, and even dietary needs.[2] Trude Strand, writing in 2014, similarly remarked that "the Gaza Strip became the object of a deliberate and sustained policy of institutionalized impoverishment."[3] Shenhar Yehouda and Yael Berda, who sought out some of the historical origins of these regulatory schemes, argued that a study of some of these Israeli bureaucratic rules illustrated how they seemed to have uncanny parallels with some of the older British colonial regulations that were deployed in mandate and informal imperial systems.[4]

Regardless of how one feels about the relevance of those historical parallels, there is little doubt that the Israeli permutations of these rules and regulations are intended to meet the presentist needs of contemporary Israeli decision-makers and publics. Rami Zurayk, Anne Gough, Ahmad Sourani, and Mariam Al Jaajaa have tried to get readers to attend to some of the food security challenges that confront Gazans who live under "a systematic policy of control."[5] As I note in more detail below, this biopolitics of control became more visible with the rise of Hamas in Gaza.

At the heart of much of this disputation over Gazan territorial sovereignty and the control of human mobility is the question of how one conceptualizes the nature, scope, and causes of terrorism, as well as how one tries to distance themselves from this terrorism. By the mid-1980s it could be argued that an increasing number of Americans and Israelis started to configure militant critics of Israeli occupation policies as terrorists who were spreading insecurity, traumas, and feelings of dread. Paul Johnson, in an essay that was published in a book edited by Benjamin Netanyahu in 1986, provided a typical summary of Israeli perceptions in this commentary on the "threat of terrorism":

Terrorism is the cancer of the modern world. No State is immune to it. It is a dynamic organism which attacks the healthy flesh of the surrounding society. It has the essential hallmark of malignant cancer: unless treated, and treated drastically, its growth is inexorable, until it poisons and engulfs the society on which it feeds and drags it down to destruction.[6]

As long as terrorism in the Middle East was viewed as an activity that had nothing to do with legitimate grievances, freedom-fighting, or political anti-occupational motivations it could be characterized as a fanatical, irrational, quasi-religious force that allowed jihadists to indiscriminately target Israelis or Americans. This made it easy to vilify, and to annihilate, those who are considered to be existential and irredeemable terrorist threats.[7]

All sorts of rhetorical centripetal and centrifugal forces can be used to formulate strategic ways of deciding who should be characterized as a terrorist, a supporter of terrorism, or an individual who needs to be "pressured" into not voting for a terrorist. If one wants to go to the extreme, they can use necropolitical lexicons that configure human beings, or networks of human beings, as cancerous growths that need to be operated on by military doctors.

Hamas, for example, has become the condensation symbol for all of the evils that Israelis have faced, and some Israelis—especially members of the Israeli Air Force, the IDF, or personnel working for the Israeli Security Agency (SIA)— write and talk as if Hamas is some metastasizing cancerous growth. The patient, in Gazan contexts, is the impoverished Gazan population, and while leftists in Israel think that medicine, education or peaceful co-existence for that cancer patient may provide a cure, more skeptical Israelis will argue that some religious extremist carriers of cancers only understand the language of coercive force.

Talk of cancers, national (in)securities, and the problems with Hamas since the second Intifada have made it difficult to conduct any meaningful peace talks, because many Israelis will only bargain with those Arabs that they consider to be "moderate." Even those readers who might disagree with my critiques of these medical metaphors may nevertheless agree that it is fair to argue that an increased number of Israelis are willing to unleash those who control the high-tech weaponry that promises to rid Israel of the cancerous, terrorist threats posed by Hamas.[8]

Poll after poll shows that few Israelis view Hamas as a legitimate political entity, and this has meant that Gazans' political elections are often described as shams or not in the best interests of the Gazans. In the future, in the wake of Operation Protective Edge, will Gazans be treated as illiterate and misguided neighbors who will only change their tune after the PA replaces Hamas, or will they be configured as the voters who put Hamas in power in 2006 and rendered visible the fact that those who physically fired rockets aimed at Gaza were not the main, or only, existential security threat facing Israel? In other words, has the "Hamas regime"—along with Gazan citizenry—metastasized to the point where massive surgical strikes are the only answer?

Granted, there are times when these cancerous metaphoric clusters can be re-deployed in other perspectival ways as we debate about what to do about Gazan problems. Some of these same rhetorical figurations can be re-appropriated in other ways, as Israelis, fairly united about the dangers posed by rockets, may disagree about specific tactics, strategies, and operational methods that are used during incursions into Gaza. Haggai Matar, for example, an Israeli journalist and activist, laments what he views as the incremental move away from more peaceful times:

> We have seen politicians passing bills against human rights NGOs ... and very high-ranking politicians saying that the NGOs and leftists are a cancer and are traitors and trying to destroy our society—these are not words of regular democratic or political conflict.... Our parents would remember having gone to Palestinian cities for shopping or seen more Palestinian workers coming into Israel. It was never an equal relationship but it was a chance to meet, and that you haven't had for 20 years or more.[9]

Matar was expressing his views during the early weeks of Operation Protective Edge, and his dissenting opinions were being drowned out by more angry voices. Gal Tuttnauer, who was interviewed in Jerusalem while some Israeli soldiers were being buried, perhaps expressed a more widely held view when he remarked: "Palestinians don't care about human life, whereas we appreciate life. We want to live, they want to die."[10] In the name of Israeli security, and love, biopolitical discourses travel right along with thanatopolitical rationalizations.

Given the evocative power of these types of metaphors, how far are Israeli military and civil administrators willing to go in Gaza as they deal with disaffected Palestinian civilian populations? Does the Israeli usage of military, civic, and legal argumentation about the differences between the regulation of "humanitarian" aid and threatening Hamas' "trade" mean that they are willing to starve Gazans in order to destroy Hamas? What types of arguments do they use about "disengagement" that allegedly relieves them of responsibility for civil administration in Gaza, and how has this impacted the daily lives of the civilians who live there? Is it really true, as Sari Bashi argues, that the Israelis have never really relinquished control of Gaza and are simply using "hyper-categorization" as a way of reifying the borders of "Judea and Samaria" while they micromanage the social, economic, and cultural life of Gazans?[11]

In many popular Israeli materials that circulate in the blogosphere, it is the Israelis, and not Hamas that have been dispensing humanitarian aid to the Gazans since the time of the 2005 disengagement. Note, for example, how authors for the Jerusalem Center for Public affairs, writing in 2015, would describe Israeli military and governmental efforts:

> The State of Israel has a government agency exclusively dedicated to the welfare of the civilian population in the Gaza Strip. Staffed by military and civilian personnel, the Coordinator of Government Activities in the Territories (COGAT) in the Israel Defense Ministry was the official body responsible for civil affairs in the Gaza Strip before Israel's disengagement from the area in 2005. Due to its expertise and experience, the Israeli government decided that COGAT would continue to coordinate interaction with the Gaza Strip with respect to civil affairs despite Israel's no longer having a presence in the area. Most of the coordination effort is concentrated in COGAT's Coordination and Liaison Administration (CLA) located on the Israeli side of the Erez crossing point.... Throughout Operation Protective Edge, Israel, through the IDF and COGAT, conducted an intensive and wide-ranging humanitarian campaign aimed at alleviating the suffering and hardship of civilians in the Gaza Strip.[12]

Does all of this bureaucratic commentary on that "coordinated interaction" and talk of humanitarian aid sound like Israelis actually think they gave up control over the Gaza Strip? Was Eyal Weizman on to something when he asked, in 2009, whether it was true that "after the evacuation of the ground surface of Gaza," bodies, "rather than territories," or "death, rather than space" turned "into the raw material of Israeli sovereignty?"[13]

If one simply reads the general formalistic commentaries about Israeli humanitarianism like the ones produced by The Jerusalem Center for Public Affairs, or if we study the arguments about securitization and the treatment of the Gazans that circulate in many of the Israeli legal cases, foreign ministry pronouncements, military texts, or diplomatic communiques on these topics, everything seems non-discriminatory and non-racial. The melding of humanitarian and securitizing discourses makes it appear as if Israeli military and political decisionism are all about the protection of not only the Israelis, but the protection of the "moderate" Palestinians in the West Bank who support Fatah and not Hamas. If one does not focus on the actual implementation of these lofty ideals, or if one does not review the material consequences of the micro-decisions that are made in the application of some of these general principles, then it makes sense that Israelis can argue that they not only follow IHL, but help with the development of human rights principles as well. This hides all sorts of vague rules and exceptions that are used to make life miserable for Palestinians who continue to feel as if they still live under "belligerent occupation."[14] The COGAT and the IDF carry out their ideological functions.

As usual, the devil is in the details, and the Gazans who manage to survive occasional military incursions must also deal with thousands of Israeli micro-management decisions because of Israeli efforts to legitimate economic blockades of Gaza. Talk of the efficacy of control of the sea to prevent "terrorist" shipments is almost always linked by Israelis to commentaries about Qassam rockets. After the 2005 disengagement, the Israeli Security Cabinet, deliberating in September 2007, assumed that Gaza had been turned into a "Hamas regime" that constituted "hostile territory." This was just one other reminder that the Israelis often viewed themselves as living in a state of perpetual warfare. From a Foucauldian perspective, the exact geopolitical region that brought these threats might discursively change, but the securitizing *dispositif* of constant threats remained the same.

Popular academic theorizing about necropolitics or thanatopolitics is certainly apropos as we note the claims of Lisa Bhungalia, who has argued that after this period of time the control of Gazan mobility, and the regulation of their dietary habits, was entangled in all of this talk of trying to control Hamas. This, she contends, was not an articulation of the usual "pure" politics of life and death, but one where we saw "the modulation of crucial life-sustaining and life-eliminating flows into and out of the territory."[15] This all goes beyond simply making things uncomfortable or unpleasant for Gazans.

As I argue in more detail below, in many ways the economic and social features of Gazan geopolitical terrains that I will be covering in this chapter contain narratives and arguments that are remarkably similar to the securitization and militarization rhetorics that circulate in other contexts, including the targeted killing rationales that I discuss in other chapters. What I will put on display in this chapter are the maze of Kafkaesque Gazan rules about blockades, closures, and mobility that are justified on the basis that they are helping with the dismantling the "Hamas regime." Note, for example, how one researcher contextualizes some of the motivations for these rules:

> Many of the restrictions on the movement of people and goods appear to be motivated by genuine concerns for security.... A precondition for any travel—whether of persons or goods—is the absence of any individualized security objection. For travel in and out of Gaza via Erez Crossing or in the

rare cases in which Israel permits a Palestinian resident ... to travel to or from the West Bank ... the ISA (also known as the Shin Bet) must approve the request after running a background check of the would-be traveler.[16]

This is just one of countless reminders that physical abandonment of territorial land has not meant the relinquishment of power or control over bodies and spaces.

In fact, it could be argued that as long as land was physically occupied one could go to Israeli magistrates, or one could appeal to international communities and talk to them about occupational grievances, and these conversations might provide you with some fragile, yet visible, textual record of some administrative response. But after the 2005 disengagement, as the forms and contours of control became more virtual and more invisible, this made it more difficult for Gazans and outside parties to decide who was supposed to be accountable and who actually made the Israeli micro-decisions. Like Josef K in Kafka's *Trial*, the Gazans have to make educated guesses about what will be considered a transgressive act and where they can try to take their appeal.[17]

The advent of the 2005 disengagement did not put an end to the attempts to seek some forms of social justice in difficult times. For example, some Palestinian advocates and supporters took the unusual step of trying to appeal to members of the Israeli Supreme Court in 2007 and 2008 so there could be some public debates about the cutting off of electricity or water to the Gaza Strip. Not all of these complaints fell on deaf ears, and there were pragmatic disputes, both before and after the "disengagement," regarding the Israelis' continued legal and moral responsibilities as their military and humanitarian organizations dealt with Gazans.

Foreign critics may think that the post-2000 Israeli rules for Gaza are oppressive, arbitrary, multi-layered, convoluted, and often sophistic, but these same rules can always be defended as necessitous security measures that had to be passed because Israelis were forced to respond to Gazans' election of Hamas "terrorists." For many Israelis, if detractors would simply read the texts that are produced by jurists, military officials at weekly meetings, or by the Coordinator for Government Activities in the Gaza, then they would learn something about the substantive differences that existed between the older jurisprudential rules for "belligerent" occupation and the newer legal responsibilities after "disengagement." In theory, after reading these texts, detractors could see how all of this Israeli micro-management of defense and humanitarian initiatives is not only advancing securitization interests but is serving other causes. As far as Israelis are concerned, disengagement was a process that helped all of the parties involved—or at least this was the dominant metanarrative that circulated before the rise of Hamas in the Gaza Strip.

Israelis are often very open about some of their motives and their intentions regarding Hamas terrorists who fire rockets, but things get murky, strategic, and ambiguous when international law experts are parsing their words regarding the treatment of Gazan refugees or other civilians, especially during the interim periods between Israeli military incursions. Unlike the Americans, who altered some of their wartime strategizing in Iraq by moving from "shock and awe" counterterrorism (CT) techniques to softer counterinsurgency (COIN)—rhetorics that were aimed toward drinking tea with locals and winning "hearts and minds"—the Israelis have opted for open defenses of more aggressive forms of economic and political lawfare that complements the warfare that is used during physical battles. I leave it up to readers to decide if they want to agree with some of the more radical critics who call this "ecocide" or "cultural ecocide."[18]

What some traditional, non-rhetorical legalistic or militaristic ways of thinking about "belligerent" or "occupation" rules often leave out are the more micro- and macro-ideologies that hover over all of the Israeli bureaucracies that plague Gazans. Israelis, after all, may or may not be interested in taking over all of the water rights or controlling all of the mineral wealth that might be found on the Gaza Strip, but critics do not hesitate to write about the motivations that might be tied to population pressures, resource scarcity, and rising standards of living. Does any of this have to do with the decisions that are made about the setting up of the lengthy Gazan fences, the formation of expansive buffer zones, or the maintenance of port blockades, that are allegedly needed for Israeli security?

As noted above, one of the avowed purposes of strict economic regulation of Gaza has to do with the linkages that can be made between money flows and the "Gaza regime,"[19] but many of these regulatory schemes were put in place *long before* Hamas politicians won some of the Palestinian elections. Moreover, there is plenty of empirical evidence that indicates that Gazans do feel pressured. In 2010, UN studies revealed that food security is a major issue when most of the Gaza Strip depends on the help that is afforded by organizations like the United Nations National Relief and Works Agency for Palestine Refugees in the Near East (UNRWA), and the World Food Program (WFP). These two large UN agencies provide direct food assistance to more than one million Gazans.[20] They are often viewed by Israelis as threats to Israeli hegemony in Gaza.

In this Kafkaesque world that blurs together military planning with humanitarian aid, Israelis who view themselves as in a state of perpetual war with Hamas do not want to provide more than the basic humanitarian aid to Gazans. However, they do not want to be viewed as neocolonial imperialists who continue to control the Gaza Strip, so they have to find creative arguments that explain why their defense postures require the continued imposition of blockades, sanctions, and other barriers that stand in the way of Palestinian economic independence. In the name of promoting security for Israelis, they create food insecurities in Gaza. One of the major issues, of course, is whether allowing Gazans to live near what humanitarians call the "red line" is helping or hurting the causes of those who want to destroy Hamas.

This chapter invites readers to understand the intertextual and dynamic nature of all of the various discourses that are used to rationalize what might be thought of as the creative destruction of Gaza. While I will often be focusing on the economic, humanitarian, and diplomatic arguments that go into this mix of rationalizations, I will constantly be reminding readers that all of this has to be tethered to the militarization and securitization grammars that will be critiqued in other chapters. Here, I intend to show how Gazans, before and after Operation Protective Edge, have been caught in more than just the crossfires and crosshairs of sniper fire or drone screens. As Gazans listen to patronizing Israeli lectures on military necessity, "preconditions" for peace, moves away from "belligerent" occupational frames, and the need for political "pressure" on Hamas, they have had to endure many other privations.

Unfortunately, Israelis are not the only parties involved in the constitutive production of a devastated Gaza. All sorts of Israeli, Egyptian, and PA anxieties about alleged dangers posed by "Islamic" military terrorism have contributed to the effective destruction of small farms and Gazan corporate ventures. Military incursions are bad enough, but Gazans also suffer during peacetime from massive unemployment, and outside worries about the "Hamas regime" impact the decisions that are made by Israelis who control everything from chickens to chocolate, flowers to cement, gasoline to fishing, medical supplies to tunnels.

A critical, argumentative study of the evolutionary nature of some of the Israeli discourse that covers these topics reveals how all of this micromanagement of economic life is just one more part of "mowing the grass" for the Israeli Foreign Ministry and the civil authorities who help the General Security Service (GSS), the IDF, the Air Force, and others as they securitize Gaza. All of the legal disengagement discourse that is linked to this micromanagement, I argue, continues to deflect attention away from potential peace processes and two-state solutions. Talk of disengagement also fends off talk that Israelis in any way contributed to a Gazan "humanitarian crisis."

By the time readers get to the end of this chapter I hope they will see that Israeli attempts to "punish" Hamas—or the Gazan populations that live alongside Hamas—have been counterproductive, and that they have contributed to the formation of humanitarian crises that only add to Israel's security dilemmas. Hamas has also contributed to these privations, but they are not the only culpable parties in these rhetorical situations.

I will begin with an analysis of the economic and diplomatic rhetorics about Gazans that circulated during the decades of "belligerent occupation," and then I will explain how some of these interpretations changed with the coming of the second Intifada.

The biopolitics of Gazan life during the years of "belligerent occupation," 1967–2005

Cultural amnesia, and attempts to write presentist stories about Greater Israel, have a way of making us forget where the people Gaza came from. As Lorenzo Kamel explains, those who live in the Gaza Strip are populations composed of families of Palestinian refugees. Many were expelled in 1948 during the Nakba from places like Najd, Al-Jura, and Al-Madal, that have been renamed Haner, Sderot, and Ashkelon. Oftentimes these refugees can remember times when their villages were razed to the ground by the IDF, which did everything it could to prevent them seeking any right of return.[21] In some cases the refugees were taken by bus to the camps and to the cities, and some parts of these traumatizing genealogies have become a part of Palestinian histories and public memories.

For more than four decades Israelis have had control over all travel by sea in and out of Gaza, but that is just the beginning of the tales that could be told regarding what Israelis in their legal texts call the "belligerent occupation" of this region. In 1967 the Israeli Ministry of Justice, like many other bureaucracies, needed to be able to rationalize why they legally and legitimately had military governmental powers, and cases like *Ajuri* v. *IDF Commander in the West Bank* (2002) could summarize the historical events in ways that explained why the Israelis did what they did in both the West Bank and Gaza.[22] Detlev Vagts, writing in the *American Journal of International Law*, provided a fairly typical explanation of some of this historicizing when he averred in 2003:

> The increasingly desperate struggle of the Israeli government to provide its citizens with a minimal level of security against suicide bombings and other acts of violence by Palestinians has driven it to take actions that test the frontiers of international humanitarian law. These actions have included the demolition of houses of families of suicide bombers, the imposition of curfews, the targeting of suspected planners of bombings, and the preventive detention of suspects. In *Ajuri* v. *IDF Commander* the Supreme Court of Israel sitting as the High Court of Justice had to consider the legality of orders by the Israel Defense Force (IDF) commander in Judea and Samaria requiring three residents of that region—the West Bank—to live for the next two years in the Gaza Strip.[23]

Judge Barak, after arguing that international conventions speak of "imperative reasons of security," went on to argue that the IDF should only be worried about family members who reasonably present real danger of harm to the security of the territory.

In this particular case Ambassador Muhammed Ahmed Ajuri had a brother who allegedly sent suicide bombers into Israel, and it was said that they had been responsible for an attack at the Central Bus Station in Tel Aviv. The board that looked into this incident found that five had been killed and many injured, and they accused Ambassador Ajuri of knowing about these activities, and one of those aggrieved parties was said to have sewed explosive belts for her brother before he went on his suicide missions. The court in the *Ajuri* case ultimately concluded that the available evidence did not establish that the petitioner knew about her brother's terrorist errands, and it distinguished between appropriate and inappropriate uses of Israeli security power.[24] While reviewers of the case, like Detlev Vagts, believed that this showed how the Israeli Supreme Court was far ahead of the United States in providing heightened scrutiny tests in violent contexts, the case has also been viewed as one that set in jurisprudential stone the idea that Israel had been consistently applying the law of belligerent occupation since 1967. This was another example of what I mentioned in Chapter

Disengagement from Gaza 109

3—the tendency to make tiny concessions in order to legitimate much larger Israeli decisionism.

In the West Bank this decisionism included the establishing of the legal and military rules that would govern both East and West Jerusalem, as well as the jurisprudential guidance that would be provided for the hundreds of thousands of Jewish settlers who lived among the more than two million Arab Palestinians. Few Israelis questioned the fact that it was the Israeli courts, and the Israeli military, that needed to be making these decisions. Yet, as Sari Bashi explains, during the "first decades of the occupation, it was not entirely clear what the fate of the West Bank and Gaza would be," whether other sections would be annexed and whether Israel would have to take responsibility for many Palestinian residents.[25]

This meant that during these earlier years the biopolitics of this region were often guided by the presumption that there would be some eventual "two-state" solution to the problems in this region, and that Israeli security needs would have to be balanced with Palestinian pursuit of autonomy and independence.[26] Questions about any Palestinian right of return were deferred over and over again as Israelis fretted over the potential demographic imbalances, and the ethnic and religious quandaries, that might be posed by allowing too many into the region from the diaspora.

During this period of time Gaza workers traveled into Israel, and Palestinians could travel between the West Bank and Gaza, but all of this started to change in the aftermath of the shuttling of the Oslo Accords.

When the PA was created, Israelis found they had the power to delegate many civic responsibilities while maintaining military and securitization powers over both the West Bank and Gaza. The Israeli position would be that in Gaza the law of belligerent occupation would continue to provide the legal scaffolding for Israeli–Gazan relations as long as the military occupied Gaza and protected some 6,000 settlers who lived in the Gaza Strip. By 2003, the Israelis were even arguing that any disputes regarding population registry needed to be taken up with the PA and not with the Israeli military.[27] The belligerency laws could also be used to explain the carving up of the West Bank into areas A, B, and C, where the PA would be responsible for civil efforts such as education and health in areas A and B, but Palestinian police did not have authorization to enter Area B and C. Area C, which ended up constituting about 60 percent of the West Bank, included many of the Jewish settlements.[28]

Growing worries about the spread of terrorism, especially after the second Intifada, brought new regulations and a tightening up of the older laws as every year brought new rhetorical evidence that Israelis had become convinced that separation from Palestinians was to be preferred over integration. Many physical and symbolic changes were signaled when the Israelis decided to construct the 2003 "separation wall" in the West Bank, which was ostensibly built to keep out suicide bombers. This impacted Palestinian villages, Jerusalem neighborhoods, agricultural lands, and Israeli settlements.

As early as 1993 the Israelis put up a fence that separated them topographically from the Gaza Strip, but this only set the stage for the more complex separationist types of activities that would later lead to the 2005 "disengagement" from Gaza.

The post-2005 "disengagement" and the advent of the "Hamas regime"

Although the Israel movement of settlements and soldiers out of Gaza began in 2005, disengagement policies were actually announced a year earlier. The official legal stance that Israel was taking regarding the "Disengagement Plan" was characterized by General Avichai Mandelblit, Israel's chief military advocate, as one where Israel was "no longer" involved in the "belligerent occupation of the Gaza Strip." Instead, given the state of affairs at the time, Israelis would view themselves as remaining in a "state of armed conflict."[29] Years later, Elizabeth Samson did a fine job of summarizing some of the Israel lawfare on this topic when she remarked:

> In recognizing the need for a political solution to the conflict with the Palestinians while balancing that recognition with Israel's security considerations, the Israeli government withdrew all military and civilian personnel from Gaza in September 2005 in the hope that their initiative would end the occupation of the territory and be a positive step towards a resolution of the conflict. By applying the standards laid out in the Hague Regulations, the Fourth Geneva Convention and the precedent derived from the *Hostages* case to the situation in Gaza after Israel's disengagement, Gaza can no longer be considered occupied and "effective control," as the term of art is understood in the context of the laws of occupation.[30]

This played well in front of Israeli audiences who were tired of having to take care of Gazans, but many international communities noted how the Israelis continued to have de facto control of many supplies, access to the sea, etc. These same Israeli discourses also treated Palestinian political dissent and anti-occupation campaigns as matters that required military—not police—responses.

Optimists might argue that this talk of disengagement should have been viewed as a unique, if different, way of thinking about putting Gaza populations onto the road to freedom, peace and prosperity. However, after more than three decades of belligerent rule, the Israelis still controlled the five major land crossings, including Karni and Kerem Shalom. Gaza had no major seaport or airport, so Gazans were still dependent on Israeli willingness to open up land crossings. At the same time, after the disengagement, whenever Israelis wanted to put "pressure" on Gazan populations in the aftermath of Hamas rocket attacks they closed the major land crossings. With UN intervention relegated to aiding refugees, the Israelis could come and go as they pleased, with no outside pressure to protect the sovereignty of any Palestinians.

At the same time, the Israelis started to appropriate "humanitarian" rhetorics that made it appear as if the control of population mobility, the cutting off of trade with Gazans, and the naval blockades were all intended to help control the military wing of Hamas. In theory, stifling trade, maintaining aerial surveillance, etc. would constrict Hamas to the point where civilian support would dry up. This all assumed that the sooner Hamas was gone, the quicker the Gazan populations would learn from their PA brothers and sisters who joined the Israeli security establishment.

Again, these types of logics or arguments may have resonated with Israelis, but this ignored the role of Palestinian nationalism, and it hid the structural and functional dynamics that linked Israeli control of the Gaza Strip to the very empowerment of Hamas. From a Foucauldian vantage point, it could be argued that the Israelis were seeking disengagement from civilian Palestinians while their securitization strategies and visual surveillance re-engaged with Hamas enemies.

Ironically, the more the Israelis vilified and attacked Hamas, and the more they refused to lift the sea blockades, the more attractive Hamas appeared in the eyes of the dispossessed. Given the fact that no outside state power or NGO would do anything substantive about Israeli control of the West Bank or Gaza, Hamas appeared to be the only alternative for those who refused to accept Israeli expansionism.

Academics were not always sure why Israel decided to begin the process of disengagement in 2005. Trude Strand recently argued that while the Israeli government used rhetoric that indicated that the disengagement plan was designed to break political stalemates in the region, she believed that "the exact opposite" was the case, because Israel "sought to neutralize the peace process" and the "road map" that the Middle East Quartet (United States, EU, Russia, and the UN) had set up a year earlier.[31] This would be yet another variant of the "lost opportunities" genre.

In October 2004, Dov Weissglass, Ariel Sharon's senior adviser, told *Ha'aretz* the significance of the disengagement plan had everything to do with the way it would allow for the "freezing of the peace process." Weissglass elaborated by arguing that if you freeze the process, then you "prevent the establishment of a Palestinian State," and this in turn would prevent a "discussion of the refugees, the borders, and Jerusalem."[32] For anyone who had any doubts about what he meant by these statements, he allegedly used his own ghastly grammars as he explained: "The disengagement is actually formaldehyde. It supplies the amount of formaldehyde that is necessary so that there will not be a political process with the Palestinians."[33] For empowered Israelis who were having their own way on the West Bank, this all made sense, because the freezing of the peace process meant that Israelis could continue on the road to expanding settlements in "Samaria" and "Judea." Only a few thousand settlers had to be moved out of Gaza, but all of this could be telegenically communicated to make it appear as if the Israelis were making huge sacrifices when they carried out their disengagement practices.

Dov Weissglass was surprisingly forthcoming about some of the social, political, and economic factors that had gone into Israeli planning, and all of this could be traced back to 2003. At that time, everything looked "stuck." There was "international erosion" of support for Israeli plans, there was economic stagnation, and the "Geneva Initiative" was getting too much support. As if that wasn't bad enough, Prime Minister Ariel Sharon and Dov Weissglass were getting bombarded with letters from Israeli officers, pilots, and commandos who said they were going to refuse to serve in the disputed territories. "These were not weird kids with green ponytails and a ring in their noise with a strong odor of grass," but were some of Israel's finest.[34] Something had to be done to unite Israelis, and that something was the negotiated and pragmatic rhetoric of disengagement.

From a perceptual standpoint, the adoption of the disengagement plan, that had the advantage of killing more problematic, foreign initiatives, was deemed a security matter. Sharon and Weissglass thought that when the Middle East Quartet and others started pressuring Israel, then Israelis needed to realize that the "bundle of concepts" that were a part of what others were calling the "peace process" meant the possible evacuation of settlements from the West Bank, the return of refugees, and the partition of Jerusalem. This, for some, was intolerable as well as unnecessary.

For those who believed that this was a delusional way to think about the responsibilities of those in charge of Eretz Israel, freezing the peace talks was essential.

Thankfully, argued Weissglass, the support for the disengagement would freeze all of this, so that the Americans would learn that all of those "bundle of concepts" would not be dealt with until "Palestinians turned into Finns."[35] This colorful—if ethnically insensitive—way of characterizing the situation made it clear that the thanatopolitical death of others' plans for peace processes was going to bring to life the disengagement plan.

All of the American rhetoric about some two-state solution—that would include "an independent, democratic, and viable Palestinian state living side by side in peace and security with Israel and its neighbors"[36]—must have looked incredibly utopian and naive to those who pressed for disengagement. Israelis, after all, were dealing with Hamas rockets, and they could always argue that the settlements provided buffer zones, and were an essential part of the natural growth of their nation-state. Unilateral movement out of Gaza would mean that most settlers on the West Bank could stay put, and Israelis would be the ones who would determine their own future obligations.

The Americans who gave their blessings to the disengagement plans could not help intervening in the debates regarding the "disputed" West Bank territories.

President George W. Bush's letter to Ariel Sharon explained that the United States understood that Israel had the right to "take actions against terrorist organizations," and that after the withdrawal, pending agreements on other arrangements, "existing arrangements regarding control of airspace, territorial waters, and land passages of the West Bank and Gaza will continue."[37] With the benefit of hindsight, we now know that American support for Ariel Sharon's plans would mean that Israel had "full control and *carte blanche* on military action," two key elements in Israel's blueprint for dealing with Gaza conundrums.[38] The United States had also provided the green light that was needed for settlement expansion and for greater Israeli control of all parts of Jerusalem.

Some hopeful international observers hailed the disengagement as a positive step that might lead to the reconstruction of the Gaza Strip. Then-US Secretary of State Condoleezza Rice, for example, told some Israelis that she sincerely believed that after disengagement the PA would become empowered to the point where they could eventually disarm Hamas. Mahmoud Abbas' appointment as chairman of the PA was taken as a sign that Palestinian demilitarization was on the way. "It is not possible to maintain a political option, as well as an option of violence," Rice intoned, and she explained that the mixing of the two would not be allowed by the international community.[39] The next day, Prime Minister Ariel Sharon added that the PA had been told that the ball was in their court, and that they had been warned they needed to fulfill Israeli expectations that changes would be made in the fields of security, law, and the economy that would help with deterrence of Hamas' rocket attacks.[40] Again, all of this talk of Israeli expectations only unscored the empirical fact that they had de facto control of the Gaza Strip, as well as hegemonic control over disengagement rhetorics.

Interestingly enough, while some of Sharon's domestic and international critics complained about his own cabinet's motivations and their sophistry, his defense minister, Shaul Mofaz, accused Hamas of perfidious behavior:

> The significance of our operation [participation in resumption of the peace process] is also [to] harm the Hamas image on the Palestinian street. For a long time now, Hamas has been resorting to "doublespeak." On the one hand, the organization is interested in calm in order to gain legitimacy for parliamentary elections, but on the other hand its extensive terror activity continues all the time.[41]

Israelis could always claim that they were the ones who were negotiating in good faith by pointing to the removal of the few settlements in Gaza and their disengagement from the region *before* the political empowerment of Hamas. One of the key difficulties, of course, arose when the Israelis wanted to leave behind some responsibilities associated with occupation while at the same time expressing an unwillingness to view Hamas as anything other than a terrorist entity.

Ariel Sharon was able to muster enough domestic and international support for his plans to make disengagement a reality, but it could be argued that Gazan populations would have to feel the wrath of other Israelis who resented having to leave those areas. Many Israelis shared the collective perception that Hamas was the primary culprit in Gaza, but their leaders and parties had vehement disagreements when it came to the question of whether leaving Gaza's territories was the answer to their conundrums. While the Labor Party in Israel struggled to convince Israeli voters that they did not consider Hamas to be a partner in peace, Likud leader Benjamin Netanyuhu came up with his own ideagraphic moniker for the land that was created in the aftermath of disengagement: "Hamastan." In January 2006, for example, he had this to say in front of the Knesset:

Before our very eyes, Hamastan has been established, the step-children of Iran and the Taliban. It's in firing range of our airport, our highways and cities. This has to be a day of soul searching because the writing was on the wall. The policy of giving land for free gave a prize to terror and a winning card for Hamas. How are Olmert and Peres getting ready for this challenge? They are moving the fence 500 meters closer to the Jerusalem–Tel Aviv highway (Beit Iksa). They gave more land to the Hamas state.[42]

More conservative Israelis were thus able to complain to moderates about the efforts of more liberal Israelis who were presented as delusional social agents who actually believed the Palestinians could be reasoned with. The election of Hamas delegates to Palestinian parliaments only served as more evidence that the conservatives were the realists in these situations.

As noted above, even after disengagement the Israelis still found no shortage of ways of controlling the movement of Gazans as well as the biopolitics of their daily lives. For example, Dov Weissglass, never at a loss for words, allegedly explained just how Israel might dispense just enough humanitarian aid without having to help Hamas: "It's like an appointment with a dietician," he noted metaphorically as he commented on the caloric measurements that were used to calibrate what most dependent Gazans needed, and it was alleged (and later denied), that he continued on and said "Palestinians will get a lot thinner, but won't die."

Not all Israelis appreciated this type of levity. The determined Gideon Levy was one of the few Israelis who openly did more than laugh when they heard about what Dov Weissglass was saying about calories and diets in Gaza. "The proposal to put hungry people on a diet is accepted here without shock," Levy observed, "without public criticism." Even if these types of remarks were made in jest, argued Levy, this was not the way to talk about the consequences of Israel's "economic siege on the Palestinian Authority."[43]

All of this talk of calibrated, Israeli aid to needy Gazans simply underscored the tensions that existed when Israelis viewed with alarm the growing power of Hamas in the region. The Dov Weissglass remark had been presented during a high-level meeting that had been convened in order to decide what to do in the aftermath of the Hamas electoral victory in Gaza. That high-level meeting included the IDF chief of staff, the director of Shin Bet, civil officials, and senior generals in the military. Gideon Levy spoke for many on the left in Israel when he contextualized matters this way in February 2006:

Like the thunder of laughter it elicited, it again revealed the extent to which Israel's intoxication with power drives it crazy and completely distorts its morality. With a single joke, the successful attorney and hedonist from Lilenblum Street, Tel Aviv demonstrated the chilling heartlessness that has spread throughout the top echelon of Israel's society and politics. While masses of Palestinians are living in inhumane conditions, with horrifying levels of unemployment and poverty that are unknown in Israel, humiliated and incarcerated under our responsibility and culpability, the top military and political brass share a hearty laugh a moment before deciding to impose an economic siege that will be even more brutal than the one until now.[44]

In September 2007 Israel declared Gaza a hostility entity, and life became even more precarious for Gazans as the Israelis imposed a full-blown blockade of Gazan seaports.

Israelis now controlled the major checkpoints for land travel, and they argued that they had to control Gazan access to the sea in order to keep out military shipments to Hamas.

By early January 2008 many Israeli officials were circulating incredibly vague and convoluted messages about Israeli intentions in Gaza. Israeli Prime Minister Ehud Olmert, who was already feeling the heat from opposition leaders like "Bibi" Netanyahu, told members of the press: "We won't allow for a humanitarian crisis, but have no intention of making their lives easier ... excluding humanitarian damage, we will not allow them to lead a pleasant life."[45] Olmert elaborated by explaining that as long as the militants kept firing their rockets across the border, then the Palestinians in the Gaza Strip needed to worry about Israeli-supplied petrol for their cars. "As far as I am concerned," remarked Olmert, "all of the residents of Gaza can walk [because] they have a murderous terrorist regime that doesn't allow people in the south of Israel to live in peace."[46] In a not-so-veiled attempt to respond to international NGOs complaints about Israel's treatment of Gazans, Olmert referenced social scientific data that showed that some 75 percent of the children living near the Gazan communities were suffering from anxiety, and he argued "the Palestinians" were attacking the Rothberg Power Station in Ashkelon.[47]

The constant discursive co-mingling of "Hamas" and "Palestinian" attacks—intentionally or unintentionally—meant that all of this strategic ambiguity could be used by members of Kadima factions to infer that perhaps Olmert really did understand what "focused obstruction" was all about. Once again, it was the Gazan populations, and not just the leaders of Hamas, who were configured as the social agents who threatened Israel.

While many cosmopolitans and other members of the international communities continued to argue that the Gazans were suffering economically and socially because of the blockade and the Israeli control over Gazan mobility, the Israelis argued that their detractors had little situational awareness of what was actually happening in Gaza. "There is no humanitarian crisis in Gaza," Israel's foreign affairs minister would tell reporters in Paris on January 1, 2009.[48] The Israeli foreign minister who played a major role in overseeing some of the Israeli humanitarian aid that flowed into Gaza, Tzipi Livni, explained in October 2010 that Israel never had any intention of harming the Palestinian population living in Gaza.[49]

With the passage of time many Israeli critics started to articulate their belief that the Israelis had merely disengaged from Gaza so they could concentrate their attention on legitimating their hold on the West Bank. Moreover, those

Palestinians living in the West Bank who showed their allegiance to Fatah, or to the PA, were now configured differently from the more "militant" Palestinians living in Gaza. As Yehouda Shenhav and Yael Berda have explained, many of the rules that the Israelis have used over the years to control Gazan populations construct different categories of people that are based on the assumption that many Palestinians, because of their ethnic background, constitute threats.[50] This in turn means that some of the flexible, undisclosed, and discretionary rules that are used to give or take away permits or other benefits are not always predictable, nor are they merely "flaws" in a system that has a bureaucracy set up to wear down Palestinians. As long as the Gazans, after disengagement, continued to support Hamas, then this in turn allowed Israelis to argue that they had no reason to expect that Israelis should provide electricity, water, or supplies to those who kept empowering terrorism.

This, I argue, set the stage for treating most Gazan civilians as if they were terrorists, or at least aiders and abettors who did not realize what they missed as they distanced themselves from the modern, and democratic, state of Israel.

Conclusion

What this chapter explains are the myriad ways Israeli foreign ministers, defense ministers, and other Israelis have rationalized the continued economic strangulation and attempted isolation of populations in the Gaza Strip after the "disengagement." It is no coincidence that from a critical, argumentative vantage point some of the same rationales and operative logics that are used to justify military incursions into the region can be used to justify the continued control of everything from travel to the amount of spices that are allowed into Gaza. Israeli military and security authorities keep track of everything from cellphones to the amount of value-added tax that enters Gaza, and as long as some empowered official can come up with any plausible argument that links goods to any type of "dual" purpose, then there are an inexhaustible number of ways that cutting off aid to needy Gazans can be justified. Cement, building materials, and anything else Israelis want to argue can be used by Hamas can be regulated and prevented from entering Gaza if empowered decision-makers deem that this threatens Israeli security interests. This is why so many outside critics argue that Israelis may have made a convincing case for *de jure* "disengagement" but they have a more difficult time arguing against their de facto control over the lives of Gazans. The generations who survived Operation Pillar of Defense or Operation Protective Edge realize the precariousness of their daily existence, and they obviously do not always appreciate the Israeli humanitarian aid that comes their way.

While we may never know if Ariel Sharon and others who talked about the benefits of disengagement sincerely believed that over time there would be fewer incursion into this land and more Palestinian autonomy, what we do know is that obsessions with Hamas and their rockets were used to rationalize all sorts of destabilizing and dehumanizing activities—blockading of the sea, the closing of the five major checkpoints in Israel, and the pauperization of more and more Palestinians. If Israelis thought that their collaboration with the PA—that extended to spying, information-sharing, and preferential treatment—would help with the dismantling of Hamas, they were sadly mistaken. As Eyal Weizman once insightfully observed, all of the incarcerations, the interrogations, the issuance of work permits that might divide Palestinian communities, was all a part of "surveillance assemblages" that were considered to be a help for "focused preemption."[51] These "thanato-tactics" that became a part of a "humanitarian" war ended up being dystopic elements of a problematic "necroeconomy."[52] Reacting to these Israeli moves united Gazans behind Hamas, the only community in the region that appeared to stand up to Israeli might.

Perhaps, during earlier times, in the aftermath of the 1967 or 1973 conflicts, some members of other Israeli generations may have planned for the possible annexation of these lands, but today Gaza must appear as little more than an isolated, terror-infested land that provides a (temporary?) home for populations that have to be relentlessly pressured. This is why disengagement policies were so controversial, and this is part of the reason why the rise of Hamas can be chalked up to the loss of control following the Israeli exit.

As long as international communities continue to accept at least some of the Israeli arguments regarding their limited responsibilities under international law provisions, then the Israelis will continue to define the major paradigmatic frameworks that are used to demonize Hamas and those who do not bow to the will of the Israelis. Voices like Gideon Levy's are silenced as Israeli resources shift away from Gaza and toward the coveted lands of the West Bank.

Notes

1 Sari Bashi, "Controlling Perimeters, Controlling Lives: Israel and Gaza," *Law and Ethics of Human Rights* 7, no. 2 (2013): 243–282.
2 Ibid., 243–265.
3 Trude Strand, "Tightening the Noose: The Institutionalized Impoverishment of Gaza, 2005–2010," *Journal of Palestine Studies* 43, no. 2 (2014): 6–23, 6. Trude Strand credits Aidan O'Leary, the former director of UNRW operations in Gaza, for coming up with the phrase "institutionalized impoverishment" (p. 18).
4 Yehouda Shenhav and Yael Berda, "The Colonial Foundations of the State of Exception: Juxtaposing the Israeli Occupation of the Palestinian Territories with Colonial Bureaucracy History," in *The Power of Inclusive Exclusion: Anatomy of Israeli Rule in the Occupied Palestinian Territories*, eds., Adi Ophir, Michael Givoni, and Sari Hanafi (New York: Zone Books, 2009), 337–374.
5 Rami Zurayk, Anne Gough, Ahmad Souran, and Mariam Al Jaajaa, *Food Security Challenges and Innovation: The Case of Gaza, Food Insecurity in Protected Crises* (Rome: FAO, 2012), 1.
6 Paul Johnson, "The Cancer of Terrorism," in *Terrorism: How the West Can Win*, ed. Benjamin Netanyahu (New York: Farrar, Straus and Giroux, 1986), 31–49, 21, quoted in Emanual Gross, "Democracy in the War Against Terrorism: The Israeli Experience," *Loyola of Los Angeles Law Review* 35, no. 11 (2002): 1161–1216, 1161–1162.
7 For an overview of how various views regarding terrorism impact violent reactions to that terrorism, see David C. Rapoport, *Inside Terrorist Organizations* (London: Frank Cass, 2001).

8 Israelis, of course, are not the only ones who circulate these types of metaphors during times of war. See Colleen Bell, "Hybrid Warfare and Its Metaphors," *Humanity* 3, no. 2 (2012): 225–247. DOI: 10.1353/hum.2012.0014.
9 Harriet Sherwood and Orland Crowcroft, "Gaza Crisis: 'Hamas Killed My Friend; We Need to Kill Them,'" *Guardian*, last modified July 21, 2014, paragraphs 21–22, www.theguardian.com/world/2014/jul/21/gaza-crisis-hamas-killed-friend-need-kill.
10 Tuttnauer, quoted in Sherwood and Crowcroft, "Gaza Crisis," paragraph 12.
11 Bashi, "Controlling Perimeters," 243–282.
12 Hirsh Goodman and Dore Gold, *The Gaza War 2014: The War Israel Did not Want and the Disaster It Averted* (Jerusalem: Jerusalem Center for Public Affairs, 2015), 56, http://jcpa.org/pdf/The-Gaza-War-2014-Site.pdf.
13 Eyal Weizman, "Thanato-tactics," in *The Power of Inclusive Exclusion: Anatomy of Israeli Rule in the Occupied Palestinian Territories*, eds. Adi Ophir, Michal Givoni, and Sari Hanifi (New York: Zone Books, 2009), 544.
14 For representative formalistic overviews that touch on the legal and military aspects of this "belligerent occupation," see Yoram Dinstein, *The International Law of Belligerent Occupation* (Cambridge: Cambridge University Press, 2009); Eyal Benvenisti, *The International Law of Occupation* (Oxford: Oxford University Press, 2012). For former President Aharon Barak's take on these issues, see Aharon Barak, "International Humanitarian Law and the Israeli Supreme Court," *Israel Law Review* 47, no. 2 (2014): 181–189, DOI: 10.1017/S0021223714000041.
15 Lisa Bhungalia, "Im/Mobilities in a 'Hostile Territory': Managing the Red Line," *Geopolitics* 17 (2012): 256–275, 256.
16 Bashi, "Controlling Perimeters," 269.
17 For an excellent overview of some of Kafka's legal insights and his analyses of bureaucracies, see Douglas E. Litowitz, "Kafka's Outsider Jurisprudence," *Law & Social Inquiry* 27, no. 1 (2002): 103–137, DOI: 10.1111/j.1747-4469.2002.tb01109.x.
18 See, for example, Ecocide Alert, "Gaza and Israel Crisis: Open Letter to Foreign Minister John Baird on International Humanitarian Law Violations," last modified July 24, 2014, http://ecocidealert.com/?p=6199.
19 See, for example, the use of American courts for the control of "terrorist financing" that allegedly goes to Hamas. Glenn R. Simpson, "Arab Bank's Link to Terrorism Poses Dilemma For U.S. Policy," *Wall Street Journal*, April 20, 2005, www.wsj.com/articles/SB111396116907311600.
20 Strand, "Tightening the Noose," 17. See The World Food Programme (WFP), The Food and Agriculture Organization (FAO), and the Palestinian Central Bureau for Statistics (PCBS), *Socio-Economic and Food Security Survey: West Bank and Gaza Strip, Occupied Palestinian Territory* (London: UK Department for International Development, 2010).
21 Lorenzo Kamel, "Why Do Palestinians in Gaza Support Hamas?" *Ha'aretz*, last modified August 5, 2014, paragraph 2, www.haaretz.com/opinion/.premium-1.608906.
22 *Ajuri v. IDF Commander in the West Bank*, 56, no. 6 PD 352, HCJ 7015/02, (2002) [Israel].
23 Detlev F. Vagts, "*Ajuri v. IDF Commander in West Bank*," *The American Journal of International Law* 97, no. 1 (2003): 173–175, 173.
24 Vagts, "*Ajuri v. IDF Commander*," 174–175.
25 Bashi, "Controlling Perimeters," 245.
26 For an intriguing discussion that extends Foucault's work on statistics and explains how some of these data impact the ways we think about demographics and social science in biopolitical contexts in the Gaza and West Bank, see Jan Busse, "The Biopolitics of Statistics and Census in Palestine," *International Political Sociology* 9 (2015): 70–89.
27 See *Abu Baker v. Defense Ministry*, September 23, 2003, HCJ 6133/03.
28 Bashi, "Controlling Perimeters," 245–246.

Disengagement from Gaza   119

29 General Avihail Mandelbilt, quoted in Strand, "Tightening the Noose," 8.
30 Elizabeth Samson, "Is Gaza Occupied? Redefining the Legal Status of Gaza," *Mideast Security and Policy Studies* 83 (2010): 38–39, www.biu.ac.il/Besa/MSPS83.pdf.
31 Strand, "Tightening the Noose," 7.
32 Dov Weissglass, quoted in Ari Shavit, "Top PM Aide: Gaza Plan Aims to Free the Peace Process," *Ha'aretz.com*, last modified October 6, 2004, www.haaretz.com/print-edition/news/top-pm-aide-gaza-plan-aims-to-freeze-the-peace-process-1.136686.
33 Ibid., paragraph 4.
34 Ibid., paragraph 5.
35 Ibid., paragraph 7.
36 US State Department, "A Performance-Based Road Map to a Permanent Two-State Solution to the Israeli–Palestinian Conflict," *US Department of State Archive*, April 30, 2003, http://2001-2009.state.gov/r/pa/prs/ps/2003/20062.htm.
37 "Ariel Sharon and George W. Bush's Letters in Full," *Ha'aretz*, last modified June 6, 2009, www.haaretz.com/news/ariel-sharon-and-george-w-bush-s-letters-in-full-1.277418.
38 Strand, "Tightening the Noose," 8.
39 Yitzhak Benhorin, "RICE: PA Will Eventually Disarm Hamas," *Ynetnews*, last modified October 1, 2005, paragraphs 3–4, www.ynetnews.com/articles/0,7340,L-3149831,00.html.
40 Diana Bahur-Nir, "Sharon: Ball in Palestinian Court," *Ynetnews*, last modified October 2, 2005, www.ynetnews.com/articles/0,7340,L-3150234,00.html.
41 Shaul Mofaz, quoted in Bahur-Nir, "Sharon: Ball in Palestinian Court," paragraph 6.
42 Benjamin Netanyahu, quoted in Sheera Claire Frenkel, "Netanyahu Warns of Birth of Hamastan," *The Jerusalem Post*, last modified January 26, 2006, www.jpost.com/Israel/Netanyahu-warns-of-birth-of-Hamastan.
43 Gideon Levy, "As the Hamas Team Laughs," *Ha'aretz*, last modified February 19, 2006, www.haaretz.com/print-edition/opinion/as-the-hamas-team-laughs-1.180500.
44 Ibid., paragraph 2.
45 Ehud Olmert, quoted in Amnon Meranda, "Olmert: No Fuel? Gazans Can Walk," *Ynetnews*, last modified January 21, 2008, www.ynetnews.com/articles/0,7340,L-3496947,00.html.
46 Ehud Olmert, quoted in *Reuters*, "Olmert Says Fuel-Starved Gazans Can Walk," *Reuters*, last modified January 21, 2008, www.reuters.com/article/2008/01/21/us-palestinians-israel-olmert-idUSL2156250620080121.
47 Meranda, "Olmert: No Fuel," paragraphs 9–10.
48 Tzipi Livni, quoted in Bhungalia, "Im/Mobilities in a 'Hostile Territory,'" 265.
49 Tzipi Livni, *Testimony by Former Foreign Minister Tzipi Livni to the Public Commission to Examine the Maritime Incident of 31 May 2010* [herein Turkel Commission], Session 14, (October 25, 2010), 12, www.turkel-committee.gov.il/files/wordocs/8808report-eng.pdf.
50 Shenhave Yehouda and Yal Berda, "The Colonial Foundations."
51 Weizman, "Thanato-tactics," 545.
52 Ibid., 561.

5 Arguing about the legality and legitimacy of Operation Protective Edge, 2014

In previous chapters I have explained to readers some of the genealogical origins of the textual and visual arguments that have circulated in Israeli–Palestinian debates about Gaza before 2014, and in this chapter I want build on that work by highlighting the claims that have been used by Israelis and their supporters during Operation Protective Edge (OPE). Here I will be arguing that what began as a dispute over Israel's alleged "disproportionate" responses to Hamas missile attacks quickly morphed into larger disputation about the existence of "terror tunnels" and the rationales that were used to justify Israeli incursions into many parts of Gaza. While it may be years before we actually know what the Israel military and diplomatic game plans were for this particular campaign, we can get a glimpse of the perceptual views of those who debated about the morality, the legality, and the legitimacy of OPE.

In May 2015 the State of Israel put its own spin on how to frame OPE when it came out with an official document entitled *The 2014 Gaza Conflict: Factual and Legal Aspects* that focused on providing the rest of the world with Israeli interpretations of the Israeli bombings and incursions into Gaza.[1] The executive summary of this document claimed that this would be a manuscript that would outline the overall objectives for Israel as well as the rationales behind Israel's strategic decision. The authors of *The 2014 Gaza Conflict* argued that OPE was the culmination of a decade-long conflict that had been waged by "terrorist organisations operating from the Gaza" Strip, and that the report was going to detail the "costs borne by Israel's civilian populations as a result of the 2014 Gaza Conflict."[2]

The Israeli authors of *The 2014 Gaza Conflict* elaborated by noting that many Palestinians lost their lives during OPE because Hamas was said to have used "combat manuals and training materials" that encouraged their fighters to "deliberately draw the hostilities into the urban terrain." At the same time, the authors of this official text claimed that professional Israeli soldiers and pilots were dealing with "non-state actors who defy international law."[3] One portion of *The 2014 Gaza Conflict* noted that:

> IDF airborne and ground forces faced militants disguised as civilians and as IDF soldiers, residential homes converted to military command centres,

multi-story buildings used as pre-prepared surveillance positions, mosque minarets employed as sniping posts, schools utilized as weapons caches, civilian structures extensively booby-trapped, and tunnel openings and infrastructure hidden in and under civilian areas.[4]

Conveniently left out of the discussion was the massive air, sea, and land power of the Israelis, and the fact that so many members of the international communities refused to frame this as a military engagement. Moreover, the authors of this text were assuming that their Israeli researchers had the ability to discern when Hamas supporters were disguising themselves as militants. A host of assertions about empirical conditions were tangled up with normative claims about operational conditions in Gaza as well as the motives of Hamas supporters.

Given the massive loss of Palestinian lives during OPE, the Israelis needed to come up with a credible narrative that explained all of this death and destruction, and they argued that "many alleged 'civilian' casualties were in fact militants."[5] In a carefully worded portion of this summary the Israeli government argued that those civilians who died suffered as the "result of unfortunate—yet lawful— incident effects of legitimate military action in the vicinity of civilians and their surrounds."[6] Pages later, the same authors argued that "an analysis by IDF experts found that as of April 2015, at least 44 percent of the total Palestinian fatalities had been positively identified as Hamas militants or militants of other organisations in the Gaza Strip," and they guessed that this figure may, over time, prove "to be higher."[7]

Like many Israeli texts that are written about OPE, *The 2014 Gaza Conflict* summary is a rhetorical document that can also be used to delegitimate Palestinian resistance and Intifadas. Instead of simply listing the numbers of civilians who actually died in OPE the Israelis used this official summary as a way of highlighting the dangers that Israelis had supposedly faced since 2000. For example, according to Israeli estimates, since the time of the second Intifada "terrorist attacks by Hamas and other terrorist organizations have killed at least 1,265 Israelis, wounded thousands more, and terrorized millions."[8] Conspicuously absent is any discussion of the total number of Palestinian women, children, and male civilians who died in the West Bank or Gaza during this same period, and the authors of this text paint a picture of restrained Israeli military forces that were only unleashed when "diplomatic efforts or limited military action was insufficient to protect Israel's civilian population."[9]

In many ways *The 2014 Gaza Conflict* served as a rebuttal document that anticipated and refuted the arguments that were advanced by domestic and international critics of Israel's warfighting strategies and tactics. The timing of the release of this text seemed to be aimed at domesticating and containing the allegations that were being circulated by an Israeli dissident organization, called Breaking the Silence. Dozens of dissident Israeli soldiers provided witness statements that appeared in *This is How We Fought in Gaza*,[10] which contradicted the notion that the IDF had restrained its soldiers during OPE. Released during the spring of 2015, *This is How We Fought in Gaza* contained the testimonies that came from more than 60 Israeli soldiers who wrote, anonymously, about alleged Israeli breaches of Israeli state obligations under international law.[11] Theirs was a tale of martial aggression and ethnic hostility, where the civilians of Gaza were treated presumptively as legal and hostile targets.

A quarter of the Israeli soldiers who provided testimony for *This Is How We Fought* were officers up to the rank of major, and they, and the soldiers who served, made a series of allegations about the hostile atmosphere created by key Israeli leaders who seemed intent on taking the fight to the enemy. For example, those who contributed to Breaking the Silence's *This Is How We Fought* averred that Israeli ground troops were briefed before engagements to regard everything in Gaza as a "threat." At the same time, Israeli soldiers who accompanied the tanks into Gaza used non-existent or "lax" rules of engagement and it was alleged that they were supposed to treat anyone seen looking at them as if they were "scouts." This would be just one of the ways Gazan civilians could be recharacterized as militant threats.

Some of the claims that circulated in *This is How We Fought* were apparently aimed at those who violated both Israeli codes as well as international humanitarian laws. Allegations were made that some Israeli tanks fired randomly, or for revenge, at Gazan buildings without taking the time to discern whether those inside the buildings were legitimate military targets or civilians.[12] One Israeli sergeant, who served in a mechanized infantry unit in Deir al-Balah, recalled that they were supposed to make sure that parts of the Gaza Strip were "sterilized," empty of people, and if you did not see civilians waving a white flag, or screaming that they wanted to give up, then you presumed they were a threat because the saying among the Israeli troops was that there was no such thing as a "person who is uninvolved."[13] Is it possible that these types of presumptive assumptions that were being made by the Israeli military are the reason they could claim that so many civilians were disguised as militants?

How do critics, who read these contrasting reports, analyze the empirical evidence that is presented by the sides, and how do they study the motives of those who offered these very different contextualizations of what happened during OPE? At the same time, what do we do when the UN has a Commission that was appointed by the UN Human Rights Council that determined that *both* Israel and Hamas may have committed possible war crimes during Operation Protective Edge?[14]

In this particular chapter I will be advancing one of my most controversial claims—that both the military wing of Hamas and the Israeli military consistently exaggerated the existential threats they supposedly confronted, and in the process are oftentimes trapped by their own rhetoric. Each side claims to be innocent as it threatens the "other" with various forms of annihilation, but as the UN Special Commission recently pointed, the leaders on both sides were potentially culpable under international law. The UN Commission of Inquiry, which was dismissed by the Israelis as a group that did not know the "profound difference" between "Israel's moral behavior" and the "terror organisations" it confronts, argued that the leaders on both sides should have been aware as OPE progressed that the failures to change course were contributing to the reporting of mounting civilian casualties.[15] This type of dichotomizing would lead to some critics commenting on the pro-Israeli bias of this particular UN Commission of Inquiry, but that was not how the IDF or many Israelis felt about the investigation.

Moreover, in this chapter I will be defending the position that each of these military communities, during and after OPE, promised much more than they could deliver, and both Israeli and Palestinian populations suffered as a result of threat inflation and exaggerated promises.

This chapter will also show that the textual arguments that appear in diplomatic, military, UN, or NGO reports are just some of the fragments in these ideological contests, and Israel's latest incursion is also framed in ways that use distance and popular visual registers to erase competing, alternative visualizations of OPE.[16] The Israelis work hard to try to convince foreign governments and populations that if we would only "see" the war through Israeli eyes then we would truly understand why there are few innocent civilians in Gaza.

A detailed, rhetorical analysis of the discourse and visualities that circulated during and after OPE illustrates how both Hamas and the IDF acted in performative ways that often undermined the possibility of finding the security they each claim they desire. The Israelis exaggerate the dangers that are posed by Hamas rockets as well as the technical capabilities of the Iron Dome, and part of the reason they do this is to rationalize their collective punishment of Palestinian communities. At the same time, when Israelis talk and write about the existential threats that are posed by so-called "terror tunnels," Hamas refuses to admit the impotent nature of their responses. Instead, Hamas officials *accept* the ominous characterizations of the terror tunnels and they try to craft their own deterrent narratives that appear to be aimed at terrifying Israelis.

Ironically, as some Palestinians and Israelis argued in 2014 about the alleged war crimes of the "other," they made arguments, or engaged in practices, that put on display their own disrespect for vaunted IHL principles. These problems are exacerbated during times of actual conflict, where growing numbers of Israelis and Palestinians become disenchanted with the possibility of ever seeing any two-state solutions, and jurisprudential disputation is seen as a mask that hides the existential dangers that are allegedly posed by "the Other."

In some of my earlier chapters I noted how Israelis view themselves as some of the experts on state–actor interpretations of universal jurisdiction, counterinsurgency, asymmetrical warfare, and terrorist studies, and this in turn has meant that many hardliners have circulated arguments about force protection and casualty aversion that have now drifted into the Israeli mainstream. By 2014, many Israeli readers or viewers were rarely shocked when they heard the constant iteration of claims about the existence of "human shields" and the "regret" that came when journalists announced the loss of thousands of Palestinian lives. Even those who contributed to liberal outlets like *Ha'aretz* were willing to argue that Hamas was primarily responsible for the reluctant targeting of civilian "infrastructure," and those Gazans who refused to listen to Israeli warnings were believed to be accountable for their own actions.

Permutations of some of the same arguments that had been crafted during Operation Cast Lead were now recycled and modified as Israelis began to circulate more sophisticated explanations for why they were not violating either international humanitarian laws (IHL) or human rights laws during OPE.

Let me begin with a brief genealogy that explains how Israeli nationalistic mythologies have contributed to the constitutive formation of these hegemonic wartime explanations, and after that I will critique some of the rhetoric surrounding the vaunted Iron Dome.

Israeli visuality, Operation Cast Lead, and the picture of "uncivilized and fundamentalist Gaza"

As Rebecca Stein has explained, since at least the time of the Nakba, the Israeli archives have contained a plethora of violent photographs and other images that have been framed in triumphalist, instead of dispossession narratives.[17] She follows Ariella Azoulay and argues that "seeing" and comprehension depends not on paying attention to how faithfully a visual image accurately mirrors what is happening during times of war, but rather on how national gazes and prisms are inextricably tied to the interplay between visualization and national ideologies.[18] This nationalistic gaze, for example, can allow Israeli audiences to see graphic pictures of the violence that might be inflicted on Palestinian enemies, but those images can also be filtered through a patriotic gaze that might be triumphalist, dismissive, deflective, or accusatory. That nationalistic gaze, Azoulay argues elsewhere, can take visualities that might provide evidence of destruction, injury, potential criminality, misery, and injustice, and "processes" them through a dominant patriotic gaze that refuses to see the "substratum of visual facts" that are being compiled.[19] Stein contends that in spite of bans on journalistic access to Gaza during the early days of Operation Cast Lead in 2008 and 2009, the images of Palestinian suffering—where some 1,400 individuals lost their lives—were filtered through binary frames that contrasted "uncivilized and fundamentalist Gaza" with the humanity of the Israeli soldiers and populations.[20]

Here I would extend the analysis of Azoulay and Stein and argue that the hegemonic fields of perception they are writing about are dense and influential rhetorical figurations that can always be framed in ways that either blame Hamas, the Gaza populations, the images themselves, leftist Israelis, NGOs, or foreign critics for alleged misrepresentation. In theory, these are misrepresentations of the picture of wartime violence that might be circulated by Israel's critics as well as the (mis)reads of Israeli "intentions" during OPE.

From a biopolitical perspective, Israeli framings of incursions into the West Bank or Gaza can be deployed to explain Israeli suffering, and the attempt of Israelis to lead normal lives, even in situations where Hamas or other enemies have forced the IDF to fire on Palestinian civilians.[21] Israelis can counter the allegations of their cosmopolitan critics by taking advantage of the emotive impact of pictures that show the palpable fear of Sderot residents.

During the supposed "failed" Israeli military campaign in Lebanon in 2006, many international communities were arguing that the IHL of proportionality and distinction were violated when pictures supposedly showed the indiscriminate killing of Lebanese civilians, and the Israelis tried to respond to some of this negative publicity by engaging in traditional psychological warfare that took the form of jamming broadcasts or dropping leaflets in Arabic.[22] As I will explain in more detail in Chapter 6, this helped with the formation of new Israeli strategic organization communities and it generated immense interest in the persuasive power of the blogosphere.

Over the years Israeli elites have learned how to package and represent their wars and incursions, as evidenced by the Israeli population's support of both Operation Cast Lead and Operation Protective Edge. At the same time many Israelis deploy their own hermeneutics of suspicion when they confront foreign frames of their incursions into Gaza that do not put on display what they believe to be the latent truths of the matter: That Hamas perfidy is said to be responsible for both Israeli and Palestinian civilian deaths. Netanyahu and his supporters may want to articulate their positions on the power of the telegenically Palestinian dead that circulate in international media outlets, but what he does not point out are the ways that Israelis use their own visualities and their own recontextualizations as they try to correct the misimpressions and misrepresentations of those who refuse to see Israel's good intentions.

None of this iconophobia can be separated from the hegemony that is achieved when a national consensus of some sort is reached that brings together television anchors, Israeli journalists, and IDF soldiers who can all talk and write about Israeli self-restraint in the face of provocations. As Stein so eloquently argued during Operation Cast Lead, the Israelis became adept at fabricating a "narrative that posited Israeli citizens as the war's penultimate victims and Hamas as chief aggressor."[23] Again, readers will have to decide if this is, or is not, a part of the Masada complex I referenced earlier.

Optical metaphors become intertwined with national ideologies as Israelis can show their patriotism by writing to newspapers or calling up television stations and complaining when they see reporters who don't parrot back the official nationalist narration of events in Gaza. All of this also involves contests over epistemic authority, because Israelis view themselves as realists who can see through the telegenic Palestinian imaging during times when foreign framers seem to have lost their moral clarity. In theory, foreigners do not have the acumen of the Israelis, whose everyday life is consumed with terrorism.

No wonder Israel's transatlantic supporters write essay after essay that argues that international critics are using anti-Semitic or "anti-Zionist" lenses as they review what transpires during Israeli military incursions. Within some of these binary nationalist narrations the "propaganda" of Hamas is contrasted with the "truth" of Israeli accounts, where the world's most moral army, often fighting with one hand tied behind its back, does the best it can.

All of this iconophobia, when it converges with actual military practices and Israeli doctrines, has tragic consequences because it leads to a plethora of intended and unintended consequences. For example, in order to get "proof" that goes beyond "hearsay" that Hamas really poses existential dangers, and in order to show the world the justness of Israeli causes, those who get into their tanks and move into Gaza after the 2005 "disengagement" participate in a performative transvaluation of values where they note the transformation of "smuggling" tunnels into "terror" tunnels. In the same way that the Lebanese civilians were turned into Hezbollah aiders and abettors, now Gazan populations are blamed for the formation of the "Hamas regime." What the Israeli security forces, foreign minister, IDF, Air Force, and public want to "see" and what they want to "understand" converges, as violence is acknowledged, but repackaged for domestic consumption. If bystanders in the United States or elsewhere learn from this so much the better, but that would simply be added value.

The "discovery" of the Hamas tunnels—that can only come from more incursions into Gaza—thus helps to add some key pillars to the Israeli national mythology, and the images of brave soldiers destroying the "terror" tunnels can be shown countless times and recycled in mainstream outlets and in the Israeli blogosphere. What, of course, adds to the mystique of all of this warfighting, and destruction of the tunnels, is the technical prowess of the Israeli military–industrial complex that helps with these efforts.

It does not hurt the Israeli cause that the Iron Dome provides aerial protection at the same time that Israeli detection equipment helps with the discovery and destruction of the "terror" tunnels.

The mythic Iron Dome and Israeli elite and public views of Israel's missile defense capabilities

The Iron Dome is the name that has been given to Israel's missile defense system. Designed and built by Rafael Advanced Defense Systems in 2011, this system is made up of seven major missile batteries that are placed around Israel, and they fire projectiles that are about ten feet long so that they can intercept the rockets from Hamas that are fired on Israel territories.[24] The Iron Dome is the smallest of Israel's antimissile defense systems, and it relies on miniature sensors to help make sure it can take-out short-range rockets.

Israel has invested more than $1 billion so it can build this Iron Dome system, and during OPE US Congressional leaders pledged hundreds of millions of dollars for future support of these Israeli efforts. By 2015 it is expected that Americans will have contributed more than half a billion dollars to this vaunted missile defense system.[25]

In many ways, both the national and the diplomatic symbolic features of Israel's Iron Dome are as important, if not more important, than the technical capabilities of this missile defense system. When President Obama traveled to Israel in March 2013, one of his first stops involved an inspection of one of the main Iron Dome installations. "The photo op," argued William Broad, "celebrated a technological wonder built with the help of American dollars, came with considerable symbolism," because this showed that Obama was showcasing his support for Israel after years of tensions over the Jewish settlements and disputes over how to curb Iran's nuclear ambitions.[26]

There is little question that most mainstream Israeli journalists, and many members of the Israeli public, sincerely believe that the Iron Dome system took out thousands of deadly Hamas rockets during the summer of 2014. The IDF publicly claims that this defensive network now has somewhere around a 90 percent success rate in taking out incoming missiles. After the first nine days of missile attacks during OPE, the IDF claimed to have an 86 percent interception rate.[27] This is disputed by various engineers and others, both inside and outside Israel, who claim that it would be more accurate to say that it really has somewhere between a 5 and 40 percent success rate. For example, Thomas Postol, an MIT physicist, argues that there is evidence that the Iron Dome is not working, and that detailed review of a large number of photographs from the earlier, November 2012, conflict showed that Israel's rocket-defense system interception rate was very low—perhaps as low as 5 percent or less. Postol attributed the low casualty rates from the artillery rocket attacks to the *warning systems* of the Israeli civil defense efforts, and the data that he was collecting during the early days of OPE indicated that the performance of Iron Dome had not markedly improved.[28] When the Israeli defense minister heard these types of criticisms, he responded that these were "baseless claims" that relied on "amateur YouTube videos."[29]

Criticisms like Postol's are fairly mild in comparison with some other analyses, because Postol at least holds out the possibility that the Israeli missile defense system might be taking-out some incoming missiles. Not everyone shares this assessment. Dr. Moti Shefer, an Israeli aerospace engineer, caused considerable consternation among the true believers in the Iron Dome system when he argued that there was no missile in the world today that was able to intercept rockets or missiles, and that the "Iron Dome" was nothing but a "sound and light show that was intercepting only Israel public opinion."[30] Shefer elaborated by explaining:

> Actually, all the explosions you see in the sky are self-explosions. No Iron Dome missile has ever collided with a single rocket. Open spaces are a myth invented in order to up Iron Dome's current interception percentages. The rockets announced as intercepted by Iron Dome either never reach the ground, or are virtual rockets invented and destroyed on the Iron Dome control computer. To this day, no one has ever seen an intercepted rocket fall to the ground.... What lands here is what's launched. The parts we see on the ground are from Iron Dome itself. We're shooting at ourselves, mainly virtually. The virtual rocket was invented in order to increase the vagueness surrounding Iron Dome.[31]

As far as Shefer was concerned, what the Israeli command and control system was doing was creating nine more "virtual" rockets each time a real rocket was arriving, and then the computers with their computer graphics were keeping track of all ten of these. Then what happens is the "launch operators" see "10 rockets and launch 10 Iron Dome inceptors" and people then hear ten booms, one rocket enters, and "you get a 90% success rate."[32] This was embarrassing for Shefer because he thought that two of the interested parties who were afraid of peace were the defense industries and Prime Minister Netanyahu. Reserve Brigadier General Daniel Gold, who is often given credit for launching plans for the Iron Dome, responded to this by arguing that somewhere between 300 and 400 very talented people had been working on this, and that all of the "interceptions to date" were recorded and documented. "We're the startup nation because of things like this," argued Gold, and this was much bigger than a startup.[33]

All of this disputation is obviously about more than just the technical capabilities of the Iron Dome. This technical discourse becomes entangled in military, legal, and diplomatic debates about real or perceived threats from Hamas, the need for peace or war, or threat inflation. This, in turn, impacts the national identities of those want to believe that Gaza and Israel are in a perpetual state of war as long as the "Hamas Regime" is in power.

The Iron Dome is supposed to be part of a sustained, evolutionary and progressive effort by the Israeli military to counter the perceived threats that have been posed by terrorist rockets since at least the time of the al-Aqsa Intifada. Beginning in 2001, some Palestinians began firing the short-range Qassam rockets, named after Sheikh izz ad-Din al-Qassam, a 1930s Syrian preacher who had warned the Arabs of the need to rebel against the European invaders. Israelis responded to these threats by attacking some of the launching sites of these missiles in Gaza.[34]

Between 2001 and 2014, a series of violent clashes between Israel and Hamas created situations in which both sides were working on trying to improve their technical missiles and counter-missile capabilities, but they did so in very different ways. Hamas worked on the production of unguided, locally produced rockets that carried small payloads that would have relatively short ranges, while the IDF worked on complex defense systems that could protect places like Ashkelon and Sderot. Again, neither side would gain from focusing on the asymmetrical nature of the military power disparities in these cases.

Reports from organizations like the Israeli Center for Victims of Terror and War report that a significant percentage of children of adults living in places like Sderot have post-traumatic stress disorder, and these disorders have been linked to the worries of those who live in fear of the rockets. For many Israelis rockets thus pose a host of real psychological, social, and military threats, and over the years various warning systems have been developed that allow Israelis to know just how much time they have before they have to get to their bunkers. All of these drills, scenarios, and conversations about the rockets work to make an asymmetrical conflict look as though the threats are symmetrical.

One of the key issues, of course, is whether the Hamas rockets really posed a threat, or whether the Israeli publics who believe in the Iron Dome are really warding off existential threats. One blogger, Nafich, who was responding to the

July 20, 2014 IDF release of data on the effectiveness of the missile defense system, argued that this was the "8th wonder," because it was undeniable that only a few rockets had hit populated areas. This was in spite of the fact that by the third week of that month some 2,000 missiles had been fired, and Nafich noted that the system was set up so precisely that every Tamir that was launched could take out a threatening incoming missile. "Had it not been amazingly successful," argued Nafich, then hundreds of hits inside the populated areas would have been recorded.[35]

From an argumentative standpoint, what needs to be recognized here is the rhetorical nature of the Iron Dome, and its symbolic value for Israeli populations that feel threatened by Hamas or Hezbollah. Donald MacKenzie, in *Invented Accuracy*, has explained how perceptions of missile accuracy and precision are tethered to a host of social interests, goals, traditions, and experiences, including the need for "relative prestige and credibility of different links in the network of knowledge."[36] In this particular case, the Israeli populations who rushed to bomb shelters when they were told about the firing of Hamas rockets needed to take solace from the fact that the Iron Dome would protect them. One might be forgiven for wondering, however, whether these fighting faiths *emboldened* those who supported incursions into Gaza.

The first ten days of Operation Protective Edge

Given all of the conflicting rhetoric and alternative framing of events, it is always difficult to pinpoint all the major factors that contribute to the beginning of a major conflict. However, with the benefit of hindsight, it is fair to argue that for the first week to ten days of OPE, it was the firing of Hamas rockets that often took center stage in the self-defense narratives that were told by many Israeli journalists, military experts, and lay persons.

Nathan Thrall has made the interesting observation that when OPE began on July 8, 2014, neither Hamas nor Israel really sought this current war, although they each realized that some new confrontation was going to be inevitable. After all, Thrall argues, the November 21, 2012 ceasefire that technically ended the eight-day-long Operation Pillar of Defense was never actually implemented.[37] During the lull between these violent engagements the ceasefire had stipulated that Hamas and the other Palestinian factions in Gaza would stop their hostilities in Gaza; Israel, in turn, would end the land, sea, and air attacks against the Palestinians. In theory, this would also mean the suspension of the targeted killing of Hamas leaders as well as the ending of the closure of Gaza.

During more hopeful times, the written plans for a ceasefire included Israel's potential opening of the crossings into Gaza that would have facilitated the movement of people as well as the transfer of goods. A more controversial additional clause in the 2012 ceasefire referred to the help that Egypt and the United States would give to those who were trying to stop arms smuggling into Gaza.[38]

During the rest of 2012 and 2013 both the Israelis and Hamas sent ambivalent signals to each other as they talked about trying to maintain a ceasefire while they each acted in ways that undermined any chances of having peaceful reconciliation of their differences. Shin Bet kept on eye on the number of mortar shells that came their way, and Israeli military officials made regular incursions into Gaza at the same time that they fired away at some of the Palestinian fishing boats. Fewer and fewer Gazans were given any exit permits so that they could travel to either Israel or the West Bank, and the blocking of exports added to the misery of the Gazans.[39] Hamas, however, tried to set up a police force that was tasked with arresting Palestinians who tried to launch rockets, and wary Israelis interpreted this as a hopeful sign.

Hamas' reconciliation with Fatah and the formation of a PA government during the spring of 2014 also provided more hopeful signs, but the earlier coup in Egypt, led by General al-Sisi, created a host of other problems as Egyptians started to blame the Muslim Brotherhood and Hamas for all of Egypt's lingering problems. Travel bans were imposed on Hamas officials, and some of the hundreds of tunnels that were used for smuggling and trading with Egyptians were closed. This, as Thrall explains, created problems for Hamas because it adversely impacted the lives of tens of thousands of civil servants who were usually paid by Hamas through the taxation that was levied on the goods that had gone through the tunnels.[40]

The formation of the new government in Gaza, that tried to bring together Palestinians from the West Bank with Gazans, split the ranks of Hamas because it seemed as though PA personnel, who had the lion's share of control in the new government, were acting in ways that reminded Hamas of the collaborations with the Israelis that had been such a big part of the bloody in-fighting that took place between Fatah and Hamas in 2006 and 2007. Hamas leaders, who had hoped that formation of the new government might swell the ranks of those who sought military solutions to the Israeli–Palestinian conflicts, now appeared to be worried that they might be losing the hearts and minds of the Gazan populations.

Many journalists and observers are convinced that what actually triggered the beginning of OPE was the June 12, 2014 disappearance of three young Israelis. Mouin Rabbani has argued that despite "clear evidence presented to him by the Israeli security forces that the three teenagers were already dead," and the difficulty of proving that Hamas was responsible for these three deaths, Israeli Prime Minister Benjamin Netanyahu launched a "hostage rescue operation" throughout the West Bank.[41] This resulted in mass arrests, and at least six Palestinians were killed. The abduction of a Palestinian teenager in Jerusalem only added rhetorical gasoline to a growing fire. On the night of July 6, an Israeli air raid resulted in the deaths of more than a half-dozen Hamas militants, and Hamas retaliated by sending missiles into Israel.[42]

On July 8, 2014 the Israelis officially launched what they called Operation Protective Edge, or *Mivtza Tzuk Eitan* (Operation Strong Cliff),[43] and during the next several days Israeli newspapers carried photographs of gray smoke rising up from Gaza's buildings. Oftentimes these were captioned with texts that explained that the Israeli missiles were targeting the "smuggling" tunnels in places like Rafah. *Ha'aretz*, for example, would report that the IDF had hit hundreds of targets in

Gaza during the second day of the war, and Hamas by this time had fired some 180 rockets "at the Israeli home front."[44] Readers were told that while a few Israelis had suffered light injuries as they were running for shelter, dozens were treated by emergency units for shock.

Many of these early Israeli reports also commented on the efficacy of the Iron Dome system, and they often recycled the IDF argument that the Israeli interceptor missiles had a "near-90 percent success rate." Israeli readers were told about the mounting civilian casualty rates in Gaza, but unlike many international outlets they rarely carried any of the thanatopolitical pictures of the dead or dying Gazans. One author remarked during the first two days of OPE that the Israelis had attacked "more Hamas targets" than it did during all of the eight days of Operation Pillar of Defense.[45]

While polls and anecdotal evidence showed that the vast majority of Israelis supported this latest attack on Hamas forces in Gaza, there were a few vocal dissidents who argued that the Israeli military was committing war crimes. Knesset member Ahmed Tibi, for example, argued that the IDF was "purposely wiping out entire families."[46]

During this same period of time Israeli officials realized that they needed to explain why they were not just going after clearly identifiable Hamas fighters who were caught in the act of firing rockets. As noted in previous chapters, since at least the time of the second Intifada an increased number of members of think-tanks, Israeli military strategists, and even American legal observers had been writing about how civilians in urban areas might be serving as "voluntary" human shields and losing their non-combatant status, and now these arguments were starting to become mainstream. Euphemisms like "Hamas infrastructure" or "government buildings" were used to signal to audiences that an increased number of civilian locales were going to be considered by the military as viable targets. Defense Minister Moshe Ya'alon, for example, admitted that Israeli strikes in Gaza had destroyed weapons, terrorists infrastructures, command centers, Hamas institutions, government buildings, and terrorist homes. Here there was no detailed explanation of how one decided whether a home belonged to terrorists or not, but instead Israeli leaders were told: "We are killing terrorists at different ranks, and this operation will persist and intensify."[47]

Some of the Israeli military leaders provided reading publics with more details that explained how they were going to interpret the law of armed conflict during OPE. One unnamed Israeli Air Force officer said that when a residential building in Gaza was targeted because of the suspicion that militants were living there, some residents reacted to the warnings by trying to ward off the airstrikes by going to the top of the roofs en masse. That same Air Force officer indicated that this was merely a "ploy" that was not going to be effective in staving off air attacks.[48]

We may never know all of the motivations of some of the Gazans who stayed in their homes during OPE, but what we do know is that there is evidence that many civilians were traumatized, dazed, and confused by the fog of war. One unnamed Gazan resident, simply identified as a "social and feminist activist," told *Ha'aretz* that everyone "in Gaza, without distinction, is a bomb target now." "Most of the casualties are innocent civilians," she asserted, and the women, children, and the elderly were dying because they "naively thought that staying home would keep them safe."[49]

After one week of war, visitors to *Ha'aretz*'s *Facebook* page were told that many families in central Israel were struggling to make their children feel safe, and photographs were posted that showed families in shelters discussing how to respond to siren drills.[50] Other images, like personal selfies, were used to put on display the resolve of the Israelis who wanted to carry on with their daily lives, in spite of the firing of Hamas rockets.

Some pundits contend that no amount of Israel spin could make up for the ontological realities on the ground, where thousands of citizens were dying, infrastructures were being dismantled, and UN schools were being bombed. Some, like Colin Daileda, were positive that Israel might be losing the social media portions of the conflict. In order to provide some proof to back up this assertion, Daileda talked about one of the most iconic images that had gone viral, the picture that was taken by *New York Times* photographer Tyler Hicks, of a lifeless arm of a Palestinian boy who was being carried by an adult running along the beach. What adds to the poignancy of the picture is the fact that the adult is having to walk past a small child who is lying face down in the sand, seemingly dead.[51] Readers of the *New York Times* would later learn from the photographer who took the picture that four young Palestinians, all cousins, had been killed during an Israeli air strike.[52]

Hicks, who had survived encounters with government soldiers in Libya in 2011, explained that he was putting on body armor and a helmet when he heard several blasts and saw the boys lying motionless. He was about to run toward the boys when he realized that in this war of perceptions he himself might be in danger:

> By the time I reached the beach, I was winded from running with my heavy armor. I paused; it was too risky to go onto the exposed sand. Imagine what my silhouette, captured by an Israeli drone, might look like as a grainy image on a laptop somewhere in Israel: wearing body armor and a helmet, carrying cameras that could be mistaken for weapons. If children are being killed, what is there to protect me, or anyone else?[53]

Hicks' essay included infograms and aerial maps with red circles that pinpointed where the first boy had been killed, and where the three other boys were killed 30 second later. His summary of events, however, was not going to be a dispassionate or neutral-sounding account, for he ended the essay by saying that no place was safe in Gaza at the time he took the picture, because bombs could land at anytime, anywhere. The IDF's intended targets, Hicks concluded, seemed to have been a small metal shack with no electricity or running water, on a jetty. This, he argued, did not seem "like the kind of place frequented by Hamas militants," and the children, "maybe four feet tall, dressed in summer clothes, running, from an explosion, don't fit the description of Hamas fighters."[54]

It would be commentaries like this that triggered the type of visuals that Nicholas Mirzoeff was writing about, and this may have been one of the images that Netanyahu alluded to when he talked about the telegenically dead Palestinians. Hicks, like so many others in these conflicts, was no objective observer, and we need to keep in mind that the very framing of these image events during these emotive social media wars becomes an inevitable part of these ideological media campaigns.

The power of telegenic images like Hicks' should not deflect attention away from the fact that the Israelis were becoming increasingly comfortable using a host of social media outlets as they tried to tell their stories about the heroism of their soldiers in the face of adversity. Those who supported the Israeli wars with Hamas often contend that the Israeli military, the IDF, is the most "moral" fighting force on earth, an organization that constantly monitors itself and has a democratic judiciary watching its every move. As Bill Van Esveld of Human Rights Watch explained in July 2014:

> The Israeli argument goes like this: The IDF does its best to avoid civilian casualties. It employs state-of-the-art intelligence to find targets and then uses precision-guided weapons to hit them. And it even calls nearby civilians on the phone and warns them to leave before firing at the target. Hamas, on the other hand, unlawfully hides among civilians. So Hamas is responsible whenever the IDF unintentionally kills civilians – like the inevitable, not culpable, killing of these four boys [Ismail, Ahed, Zakariya, and Mohammad].[55]

When Israeli spokesperson Mark Regev had to explain why these accidental killings happened, he said: "The story with these four boys is a tragedy. Let's be clear: the Israeli military does not target civilians."[56]

In permutations of arguments that had been around since the time of Golda Meir, Israelis argued that Hamas was responsible for both the deaths of Gazans as well as the traumas of Israelis worried about Palestinian rockets. Oftentimes the threat of these rockets, as well as the dangers that came from "terror" tunnels, were used as rationalizations for the possible (re)occupation of Gaza. Even before the ground offensive began, many Israeli citizens were writing in newspapers and explaining why ceasefires would not suffice. For example, on July 14, 2014, David Malkiel would write to *The Jerusalem Post* and explain that if the Israeli government was really determined to "eliminate Hamas's arsenal and human and technical infrastructure, a ground invasion is necessary." For those who had any moral qualms about this, Malkiel went on to explain that while the IDF was up to the task of turning the area upside-down, street by street, and house by house, this would endanger the lives of thousands of Palestinian "non-combatants." He suggested that the Israelis might want to consider opening up a temporary refuge for these civilian non-combatants on the Israeli side of the border.[57] Writing on the same day, Jack Cohen of Netanya argued that it was really impossible to get any reliable casualty figures from Gaza because terrorist operatives did not wear uniforms and this made it impossible to tell civilians from combatants.[58]

Many civilians clearly realized that the second phase of OPE was about to begin, where the IDF and the other Israeli forces were going to go in and go after those tunnels, and they provided all types of indications that they backed these efforts. Albert Jacob, of Beersheba, argued that Sigmund Freud would have had something pertinent to say about the "Gazans' love affair with their rockets," while Michael Plaskow's entire missive was about the Palestinian civilian involvement in the building of tunnels.[59] Plaskow, in his letter to *The Jerusalem Post*, parroted back what many military officials had been talking about for months when he explained:

> In civilian areas the people of Gaza have built tunnels to infiltrate into Israel. They have built underground storerooms for missiles. They have built underground bunkers for their top brass. They have built underground missile-launching pads. They have become the most prodigious underground builders since the Viet Cong. But they have not managed to build a public underground shelter.[60]

There are several argumentative reasons why this passage is noteworthy. First of all, notice that the enemy is no longer just the Hamas leadership, but rather the civilians who are accused of building the tunnels. Second, notice the claim that all of this threatens Israel, a claim that is meant to create a sense of moral equivalence so that Western readers no longer obsess over Palestinian telegenics. Third, all of this used to magnify these dangers, and Israeli citizens are trying to equate the three dozen or so tunnels that were found with the thousands of Vietnamese tunnels that were used during the Vietnam War. At the same time, this focus on building tunnels instead of shelters made it appear as if the Palestinian victims of attacks had contributed to their own trials and tribulations. The Israeli building of shelters was viewed as the pragmatic norm, while the Gazans' failure to build their own shelters was taken as proof of their deviance and complicity with twenty-first-century terrorists.

The second phase of Operation Protective Edge, and the beginning of the ground offensive

When the Israelis began their ground offensive they took their video equipment with them, and the IDF posted on Twitter and other social media platforms pictures of the infantry soldiers who unearthed some 22 tunnels by the second day of the incursion.[61] I will have more to say about this in Chapter 6, but for now notice how talk of the tunnels is being used to legitimate Israeli land incursions.

This second phase of the war, that followed in the wake of Israeli aerial attacks on Hamas targets, was now being described by Yaakov Lappin of *The Jerusalem Post* as "the IDF's ground incursion into the Hamas-ruled enclave." Lappin noted that the military was releasing pictures of the tunnels that were being unearthed, and he sutured into his article several pictures of these tunnels. One IDF commentary invited Twitter visitors to follow along with the soldiers as the IDF asked: "What do you think this tunnel was used for?" Lappin helped to answer that question by noting that the 22 tunnels were used to "smuggle weapons and explosives."[62]

For my purposes here it is important to comment on some of the possible ideological motivations of the Israelis who dwelled on these tunnels. By focusing on the militarizing features of these tunnels those who were trying to counter enemy lawfare could accomplish several tasks. First of all, the very existence of the tunnels could be used by Prime Minister Netanyahu as evidence that Israel was not violating the *jus in bello* principles of IHL. After all, even Amnesty International, during this same period, was writing about how it was "not unlawful to directly attack soldiers, those who are directly participating in hostilities, and military objects (such as army bases, weapons and munitions caches)."[63] This was all fairly traditional, formalistic commentary on the law of armed conflict.

The discovery of these "Hamas" tunnels did more than just help Israelis magnify the existential dangers posed by terrorists—it also allowed the IDF to argue that they were uncovering evidence of Palestinian war crimes. Legal scholars and experts back in Israel could now argue that the *very digging* of the tunnels violated both the letter and the spirit of the law of war. Daphné Richemond-Barak, for example, writing for *The Times of Israel*, remarked that OPE had brought "unprecedented attention to tunnel warfare."[64] She explained to visitors of her blog site that although tunnels had been used by the British Army during World War I, the Vietcong in Vietnam, and Al Qaeda in Afghanistan, those older tunnels had not been viewed as a key "strategic threat" in decades—until the tunnels "formed the Israeli government's main justification" for OPE.[65] She was convinced that the Hamas tunnels presented "novel" issues for international law because they were designed to burrow under "an international recognized border."[66]

What is rhetorically intriguing about these types of framings of the tunnels is that they once again provide another way of blaming the victims, the Gazans, for the suffering that they brought on themselves by being complicit in these alleged war crimes. Richemond-Barak explained that none of this differed significantly from waging war in urban areas:

> [the tunnels] traverse civilian areas, and their primary objective and effect – contrary to international law – is to harm and endanger civilians, both Israeli and Palestinian. While being constructed, Gaza's tunnels pose a substantial risk to those building them – often children – and to the civilian structures under which they are dug. The last few weeks have shown us that most tunnel digging begins within homes, hospitals, mosques and other "protected objects." Filled with explosives and weapons, tunnels can detonate at any time, risking not only the lives of the diggers and operatives who use them, but also the civilians living above them. And this is only on the Palestinian side of the border.[67]

She was sure that the unfortunate, regrettable, and "unforeseen consequences caused by the destruction of a tunnel complex cannot be avoided," and that those who placed these "combat tunnels" under civilian populated areas and infrastructures were violating international law.[68]

Daphné Richemond-Barak seemed to at least care about the innocent civilians who were living in Gaza, but as the transatlantic debates about relative culpability of Israel or Hamas heated up, there were no shortage of Americans and Israelis who were now willing to frame international law debates in ways that enabled, rather than constrained, aggressive warfighting. Thane Rosenbaum, writing for audiences of the *Wall Street Journal* in July 2014, argued that the only communities who seemed to want to see dead children were the members of Hamas, who were outmatched by Israel's military but could play the "long game of moral revulsion."[69] Rosenbaum's defense of Israel's military incursions included an interesting attack on both the militants who shot rockets as well as the millions of civilians in Gaza who voted for Hamas. In a fascinating example of how far some participants in these emotional debates are willing to go, Rosenbaum, like many of the hardline Israeli officers who had been writing in wake of the second Intifada, refused to even countenance the possibility that populations in Gaza were even "civilians":

> To make matters worse, Gazans sheltered terrorists and their weapons in their homes, right beside Ottoman sofas and dirty diapers. When Israel warned them of impending attacks, the inhabitants defiantly refused to leave. On some basic level, you forfeit your right to be called civilians when you freely elect members of a terrorist organization as statesmen, invite them to dinner with blood on their hands and allow them to set up shop in your living room as their base of operations. At that point you begin to look a lot more like conscripted soldiers than innocent civilians. And you have wittingly made yourself targets.[70]

Rosenbaum is thus assuming that the elderly, the young, and the terrified of Gaza had the volition and the power to flee to some safe haven.

Mikko Joronen has recently explained that Israeli warnings of impending attacks does not mean they have complied with the IHL. Article 57(2) of Protocol I of the Geneva Convention does indicate that civilian populations need to be given "effective advance warning," but Article 57 of the ICRC (1977) does not suggest that the provision of those advanced warnings somehow removes the other legal obligations of the attacking party. Nor does it necessarily obligate residents to leave after the issuance of that advanced warning.[71]

Yet those who wish to vilify Hamas, and who want to valorize the efforts of the IDF or the Israeli Air Force, can always cherry-pick through IHL commentaries so they can rationalize the killing of innocent men, women, and children. Intentionally or unintentionally, by using Israeli interpretations of the law of armed conflict to strip away civilian protections, this ends up reinforcing the notion that I have talked about in other chapters, the *presumption* that hidden civilians must all be terrorists, or aiders and abettors. The circulation of this type of militaristic *dispositif* evidences sedimented mentalities that help turn densely populated urban regions into battlefields where the Geneva Convention protections are inverted or thrown out the window.

It may be years before we know just how many Israelis and Americans share these sentiments. Rosenbaum may be articulating the positions of many other Americans who wanted to blame both Hamas and Gazan populations for all the mounting deaths in the Gaza Strip. Representative Ileana Ros-Lehtinen, a Republican from Florida, introduced a symbolic measure, House Congressional Resolution 107, that denounced the "use of civilians as human shields by Hamas and other terrorist organizations in violation of international humanitarian law." The resolution went on to claim that Hamas had been urging the residents of Gaza to "ignore the Israeli warnings and remain in their houses and has encouraged Palestinians to gather on the roofs of their homes to act as human shields." When Phyllis Bennis, a senior fellow for the Institute of Policy Studies heard about this resolution, she argued that this showed that the "elected representations of the American people are standing for the slaughter of children" and are paying "Israel's bills."[72]

Not all of those living miles away from Gaza argued in this manner. One critic insightful observed: "Nobody is looking at the crisis in terms of origins in the context of the existing crisis of the occupied Gaza day-to-day when there are no bombs falling. This is a besieged territory where people have no ability to run for safety."[73] Wartime dangers only exacerbated the situation.

This, as one might imagine, was not the way that most Israelis thought about their latest round of fighting with Hamas. In July 2014, Professor Avi Bell sent a legal opinion to the Knesset, arguing that Israel could stop supplying water and electricity to Gaza under both Israeli and international law.[74] Bell noted that some nine years ago, during the disengagement, Israel had relinquished all control over the Gaza Strip. Yet after that move Israel still continued to provide megawatts of electricity to Gaza that amounted to somewhere between 25 and 50 percent of the Gaza Strip's normal needs. Citing the work of Yoram Dinstein and others, Bell argued that there was no record of any international practice that indicated that nation-states were required to provide electricity and other goods to territories they do "not control absent specific agreements requiring supply."[75] While he admitted that international law did bar "collective punishment," he argued that withholding water and electricity did not constitute collective punishment. While he was at it, Professor Bell also argued that there had never been any prosecution for the war crime of collective punishment on the basis of economic sanctions.[76] After noting that the Israeli Supreme Court in *Bassiouni* v. *Prime Minister* (2008) had ruled that reductions in electricity and other supplies did not constitute collective punishment, he went on to explain that any nation can engage in something called "retorsion" as a way of "disciplining" the "misbehavior" of some other international actors. Professor Avi went so far as to argue that Israel could withhold all of these commercial items, and seal its borders at the discretion of the Israelis, "even if it adopts these measures" as "punishment" for "Palestinian terrorism."[77]

A few days later Eric Posner, a faculty member of the University of Chicago Law School, defended Avi Bell's position and argued this was just a "hypothetical question because Israel has expressed no intention of shutting down the flow of electricity into Gaza."[78] However, within a matter of days, Israeli attacks were taking out Gaza's electrical grids and other infrastructures. "In the context of the ill wind that is being borne of waves of anger, hatred and fear," noted Eitan Diamond on July 30, 2014 in *Ha'aretz*, "there is a demand to disconnect Gaza from electricity and water" supplied by Israel.[79]

Diamond, the director general of Gisha, a legal center in Israel, was an expert on humanitarian and international law, and he accused Bell and others who were trying to ignore obligations of engaging in "dubious sophistry" as they parsed the meanings of applicable international law. Diamond admitted that Gaza was not like the "classic occupation" on the West Bank—that he identified as "Occupation 1.0"—but he went on to dispute Bell's claims that Gaza was some independent entity separate from Israel. Eitan Diamond averred that Gaza was an "updated" version of strategic occupation, something that he called "Occupation 2.0." This type of occupation was a "long distance occupation by means of control of the external boundaries of the territory," which enables Israel to dictate what leaves and what enters, thereby leaving the Strip dependent on its good will.[80]

In some cases, Israeli critics denounced some of the ethnic or racial commentaries that were coming from Israeli leaders who were very vocal about what needed to happen in Gaza. One of the most thanatopolitical and inflammatory remarks that circulated during OPE came from Ayelet Shaked, a member of the ultra-religious Home Party while she was serving in the Knesset. Shaked allegedly would have this to say on one of her Facebook pages:

> The Palestinian people has [*sic*] declared war on us, and we must respond with war. Not an operation, not a slow-moving one, not low-intensity, not controlled escalation, no destruction of terror infrastructure, no targeted killings. Enough with the oblique references. This is a war. Words have meanings. This is a war. It is not a war against terror, and not a war against extremists, and not even a war against the Palestinian Authority. These too are forms of avoiding reality. This is a war between two people. Who is the enemy? The Palestinian people. Why? Ask them, they started [it].[81]

Shaked, like many, appeared to be trying to sift through the rhetoric so she could get to the underlying reality.

To be sure, we may never know how many Israelis or international supporters of IDF policies were willing to adopt the positions that were said to have been articulated by Ayelet Shaked. Journalists and others have argued that in her lengthy Facebook story Shaked tried to spell out in more detail why she simply did not understand why so many thought it was horrifying to see the "entire Palestinian people" as the enemy. Her Facebook missive supposedly explained that every war was really between two peoples, and that the "whole people" were really the enemy. Given the fact that a declaration of war was not a war crime, and that responding with war was certainly not a war crime, why not have a "clear definition" of who the enemy was instead of making up new names for every war every other week? Visitors to her Facebook site needed to realize that in war the "enemy is usually an entire people, including its elderly and its women, its cities and its villages, its property and infrastructure."[82]

Ayelet Shaked, regarded by many in Israel as a very educated woman (a computer engineer), allegedly proceeded to defend a policy that looked like a combination of messianic violence, Malthusian thinking, and aggressive counterterrorist planning. "Behind every terrorist," Shaked intoned, "stand dozens of men and women, without whom he [sic] could not engage in terrorism," so this means "they are all enemy combatants." This included the delusional "mothers of the martyrs," who sent the terrorists "to hell with flowers and kisses." Given their social agency they "should follow their sons" she argued and "should go, as should the physical homes in which they raised the snakes."[83] Otherwise, Shaked warned, "more little snakes will be raised there."[84]

The international circulation of these alleged comments caused a firestorm of protest. In the United Kingdom Mira Bar Hillel said that reading Ayelet Shaked's remarks put her on the brink of burning her Israeli passport. Hillel argued that hearing Shaked's words made her think about her aunt Klara and her three small children who were living in Krakow in 1939 when the Germans invaded. The Germans decided that all Jews were the enemy and had to be eliminated. "Why? Ask them, they started" would have been the response to aunt Klara from "every Nazi she came across." Coming out near the time of the murder of 17-year-old Muhammad Abu Khudair, these types of statements were probably indicative of the vitriol that was coming from all sides in this tragic affair.

Yet when all was said and done, there was little question that most Israelis viewed OPE as a major success. In theory the "terror" tunnels had been identified, the Hamas' infrastructures had been dismantled, and all of this had been accomplished with relatively minimal loss of Israeli lives.

Conclusion

At the heart of this book is the question of whether there is such a thing as what Raji Sourani calls the "Gaza Doctrine," an updated label that deliberately relies on what some are calling "disproportionate force" in any encounter with Arab enemies in Gaza. Richard Falk, for example, contends:

> The Gaza Doctrine is a renewal of what was originally known as the "Dahiya Doctrine" after the destruction of the Dahiya resident neighborhood in South Beirut, where many of Hezbollah's faithful were living, during the 2006 Lebanon War. The inability of Hamas to mount any sort of defense or even provide protection via shelters and the like, epitomizes the criminal nature of Protective Edge, and more generally, of totally one-sided warfare.[85]

Yet Israelis viewed this asymmetrical power as a blessing, and they were grateful that the Iron Dome had protected their populations while they waged war in Gaza.

As we review these arguments, military paradigms, and legal figurations that swirled around OPE, we need to keep in mind that the Israeli populations were not the only parties that had something to say regarding who did or did not deserve protection. In spite of the countless essays that appeared in foreign law reviews, or the web commentaries on alleged Israeli violations of international humanitarian law, very few states, NGOs, or UN officials *did anything to stem the violence in Gaza*. They became bystanders. When the Israelis convinced themselves that they ended the tunnel threats, and that they had empirical evidence of Palestinian violations of the law of armed conflict, they simply left, convinced of the rectitude of the most moral army in the world.

Notes

1 State of Israel, *The 2014 Gaza Conflict, 7 July–26 August 2014: Factual and Legal Aspects* (Tel Aviv: State of Israel, 2015).
2 Ibid., vii.
3 Ibid., viii.
4 Ibid., viii.
5 Ibid., viii.
6 Ibid., viii.
7 Ibid., ix.
8 Ibid., ix.
9 Ibid., ix.
10 Breaking the Silence, *This Is How We Fought in Gaza: Soldiers' Testimonies and Photographs from Operation "Protective Edge" 2014*, www.breakingthesilence.org.il/pdf/ProtectiveEdge.pdf.
11 Peter Beaumont, "Israeli Soldiers Cast Doubt on Legality of Gaza Military Tactics," *Guardian*, last modified May 4, 2015, www.theguardian.com/world/2015/may/04/israeli-soldiers-cast-doubt-on-legality-of-gaza-military-operation.
12 Beaumont, "Israeli Soldiers Cast Doubt on Legality," paragraphs 1–5.
13 Ibid., paragraphs 15–17.
14 See Independent Commission of Inquiry on the 2014 Gaza Conflict, *Report of the 2014 Gaza Conflict*, (New York: Office of the Commission for Human Rights, 2015); Peter Beaumont, "U.N. Accuses Israel and Hamas of Possible War Crimes During 2014 Gaza Conflict," *Guardian*, last modified June 22, 2015, www.theguardian.com/world/2015/jun/22/un-accuses-israel-and-hamas-of-possible-war-crimes-during-2014-gaza-war.
15 Beaumont, "U.N. Accuses Israel and Hamas," paragraphs 1–5.
16 A growing number of scholars are studying the complex ideological features of these wartime or occupational erasures. See, for example, Eyal Weizman, *Hollow Land: Israel's Architecture of Occupation* (London: Verso, 2007). Saree Makdisi, "The Architecture of Erasure," *Critical Inquiry*, 36, no. 3 (2010): 519–559.
17 For more on Israeli representations of the Nakba, see Ariella Azoulay, "Declaring the State of Israel: Declaring a State of War," *Critical Inquiry* 37, no. 2 (2011): 265–285, DOI: 10.1086/657293.
18 Rebecca L. Stein, "Impossible Witness: Israeli Visuality, Palestinian Testimony, and the Gaza War," *Journal for Cultural Research*, 16, nos. 2/3 (2012): 135–153, 135. DOI: 10.1080/14797585.2012.647749. For more critical critiques of mediated

coverage of Operation Cast Lead, see Menaham Blondhem and Limor Shifman, "What Officials Say, What Media Show, and What Public Get: Gaza, January 2009," *Communication Review* 12, no. 3 (2009): 205–214; Peter Lagerquist, "Shooting Gaza: Photographers, Photographs, and the Unbearable Lightness of War," *Journal of Palestine Studies*, 28, no. 3 (2009): 86–92, Shani Orgad, "Watching How Others Watch: The Israeli Media's Treatment of International Coverage of the Gaza War," *Communication Review*, 12, no. 3 (2009): 250–261.
19 Ariella Azoulay, *The Civil Contract of Photography* (New York: Zone Books, 2008), 195–196. For other helpful critical and cultural critiques of these representations, see Didier Fassin, "The Humanitarian Politics of Testimony: Subjectification Through Trauma in the Israeli–Palestinian Conflict," *Cultural Anthropology*, 23, no. 3 (2008): 531–558, DOI: 10.1111/j.1548-1360.2008.00017.x.
20 Stein, "Impossible Witness," 147–148.
21 Ibid., 150.
22 See M. Kalb and C. Saivetz, "The Israel–Hezbollah War of 2006: The Media as Weapon in Asymmetric Conflict," *Press/Politics* 12, no. 3 (2007): 43–66, W.B., Caldwell, IV, D.M. Murphy, and A. Menning "Learning to Leverage New Media: The Israel Defense Forces in Recent Conflicts," *Military Review* 89, no. 3 (2009): 2–10.
23 Stein, "Impossible Witness," 139.
24 Olivia Bolton, "Israel's Iron Dome in 60 Seconds," *Telegraph*, last modified July 21, 2014, www.telegraph.co.uk/news/worldnews/middleeast/israel/10960593/Israels-Iron-Dome-in-60-seconds.html.
25 William J. Broad, "Weapons Experts Raise Doubts About Israel's Antimissile System," *New York Times*, March 20, 2013, www.nytimes.com/2013/03/21/world/middleeast/israels-iron-dome-system-is-at-center-of-debate.html.
26 Ibid., paragraph 1.
27 Jenny Binni, "ISD Releases Iron Dome Interception Rate," *Jane's Defence Weekly*, www.janes.com/article/40943/idf-releases-iron-dome-interception-rate.
28 Theodore A. Postol, "The Evidence that Shows Iron Dome is Not Working," *The Bulletin of Atomic Scientists*, July 19, 2014, http://thebulletin.org/evidence-shows-iron-dome-not-working7318.
29 Broad, "Weapons Experts Raise Doubts," paragraph 10.
30 Moti Shefer, "Defense Prize Winner Moti Shefer: Iron Dome is a Bluff," *Globes.com*, last modified July 13, 2014, www.globes.co.il/en/article-defense-prize-winner-shefer-iron-dome-is-a-bluff-1000954085.
31 Ibid., paragraph 2.
32 Ibid., paragraph 2.
33 Daniel Gold, quoted in ibid., paragraph 4.
34 For an example of how seriously some researchers take the threat of Qassam rockets, see Lian Zuker and Edward H. Kaplan, "Mass Casualty Potential of Qassam Rockets," *Studies in Conflict & Terrorism* 37, no. 3 (2014): 258–266. DOI: 10.1080/1057610 X.2014.872024.
35 Comment by Nafich, after Jenny Binni, "ISD Releases Iron Dome Interception Rate," *Jane's Defence Weekly*, last modified July 20, 2014, www.janes.com/article/40943/idf-releases-iron-dome-interception-rate.
36 Donald MacKenzie, *Inventing Accuracy: A Historical Sociology of Nuclear Missile Guidance* (Cambridge, MA.: MIT Press, 2001), 10–11.
37 Nathan Thrall, "Hamas's Chances," *London Review of Books*, August 21, 2014. www.lrb.co.uk/v36/n16/nathan-thrall/hamass-chances.
38 Ibid., paragraph 1.
39 Ibid., paragraphs 2–3.
40 Ibid., paragraphs 5–7.
41 Mouin Rabbani, "Israel Mows the Lawn," *London Review of Books*, last modified July 31, 2014, www.lrb.co.uk/v36/n15/mouin-rabbani/israel-mows-the-lawn.

42 Ibid., paragraphs 12–13.
43 Shalom Bear, "IDF's Operation 'Protective Edge' Begins Against Gaza," *The Jewish Press*, last modified July 8, 2014, www.jewishpress.com/news/breaking-news/idfs-operation-protective-edge-begins-against-gaza/2014/07/08.
44 *Ha'aretz*, Jack Khoury and news agencies, "ID Expands Attacks on Day 2 of Operation Protective Edge," *Ha'aretz*, July 10, 2014, paragraph 1, www.haaretz.com/news/diplomacy-defense/1.604159.
45 Ibid., paragraphs 2–7.
46 Ahmed Tibi, quoted in ibid., paragraph 13.
47 Moshe Ya'alon, quoted in ibid., paragraphs 11–12.
48 Ibid., paragraph 19.
49 Ibid., paragraphs 15–16.
50 *Ha'aretz*, "Five-Year Olds Know the Siren Drill, While Tel Aviv Parents Try to Keep Calm," Facebook.com, July 14, www.facebook.com/haaretzcom/posts/10152573360406341.
51 Colin Daileda, "Israel is Losing Control of the Gaza Media War," *Mashable*, last modified July 22, 2014, http://mashable.com/2014/07/22/israel-losing-media-war-gaza.
52 Tyler Hicks, "Through the Lens, 4 Boys Dead By Gaza Shore," *New York Times*, last modified July 16, 2014, www.nytimes.com/2014/07/17/world/middleeast/through-lens-4-boys-dead-by-gaza-shore.html.
53 Ibid., paragraph 7.
54 Ibid., paragraphs 10–11.
55 Bill Van Esveld, "Dispatches: Explaining Four Boys Dead on a Gaza Beach," *Human Rights Watch*, July 17, 2014, paragraph 4, www.hrw.org/news/2014/07/17/dispatches-explaining-four-dead-boys-gaza-beach.
56 Mark Regev, quoted in ibid., paragraph 4.
57 David Malkiel, "July 14, Readers React to Operation Protective Edge," *The Jerusalem Post*, last modified July 13, 2014, paragraph 4, www.jpost.com/Opinion/Letters/July-14-Readers-react-to-Operation-Protective-Edge-362634.
58 Jack Cohen, "July 14, Readers React to Operation Protective Edge," paragraph 6.
59 Michael Plaskow, July 14, "Readers React to Operation Protective Edge," paragraphs 13–14.
60 Ibid., paragraphs 13–14.
61 Yaakove Lappin, "IDF Unearths 22 Tunnels, Kills 40 Terrorists as Ground Offensive Enters Second Day," *The Jerusalem Post*, last modified July 19, 2014, www.jpost.com/Operation-Protective-Edge/First-soldier-killed-in-Gaza-ground-offensive-363343. The IDF spokesperson posted many representations of what the IDF was finding in Gaza. See, for example, IDF@IDFSpokesperson, "MPA: Opening of a Hamas Tunnel Inside Israel Territory," Twitter.com, last modified July 17, 2014, https://twitter.com/idfspokesperson/status/489618873610616832; IDF@IDFSpokesperson, "Found This in Gaza House. UNRWA Bags Once Had Wheat," Twitter.com, last modified July 23, 2014, https://twitter.com/idfspokesperson/status/491952391055355905. For examples of YouTube coverage, see Israel Defense Forces, "IDF Targets Terror Tunnels in Gaza," YouTube, last modified July 19, 2014, www.youtube.com/watch?v=xvb-8V0XCxY.
62 Lappin, "IDF Unearths 22 Tunnels," paragraph 6.
63 Amnesty International, "Document: Israel and the Occupied Palestinian Territories – Israel/Gaza Conflict," last modified July 25, 2014, paragraph 13, www.amnesty.org/en/library/asset/MDE15/017/2014/en/5b79b682-8d41-4751-9cbc-a0465f6433c3/mde150172014en.html.
64 Daphné Richemond-Barak, "Tunnels as War Crime," *The Times of Israel*, last modified August 12, 2014, http://blogs.timesofisrael.com/tunnels-as-war-crime/#.
65 Ibid., paragraph 2.

66 Ibid., paragraph 3.
67 Ibid., paragraphs 4–6.
68 Ibid., paragraphs 8–9.
69 Thane Rosenbaum, "Hamas's Civilian Death Strategy," *Wall Street Journal*, July 21, 2014, paragraph 1, http://online.wsj.com/articles/thane-rosenbaum-civilian-casualties-in-gaza-1405970362.
70 Ibid., paragraphs 10–11.
71 Mikko Joronen, "'Death Comes Knocking on the Roof': Thanatopolitics of Ethical Killing During Operation Protective Edge in Gaza," *Antipode* (2015), DOI: 10.1111/anti.12178.
72 Phyllis Bennis, quoted in Sarah Lazare, "In 'Ugly' Resolution, U.S. Politicians Back Israel's Assault on Gaza," *Common Dreams*, July 29, 2014, www.commondreams.org/news/2014/07/28/ugly-resolution-us-politicians-back-israels-assault-gaza.
73 Ibid., paragraph 12.
74 Professor Avi Bell, "Israel May Stop Supplying Water and Electricity to Gaza," *KJohelet.org*, July 2014, http://kohelet.org.il/uploads/file/israel%20may%20stop%20supplying%20water%20and%20electricity%20to%20Gaza%20updated.pdf.
75 Bell, "Israel May Stop," 1.
76 Ibid., 2.
77 Ibid.," 2–3.
78 Eric Posner, "Would It be Unlawful for Israel to Shut Off Electricity to Gaza," EricPosner.com, last modified July 24, 2014, http://ericposner.com/would-it-be-lawful-for-israel-to-shut-off-electricity-to-gaza. For more on this particular sub-issue, see Kevin Jon Heller, "Can Israel Cut Off Water and Power to Gaza," *Opinio Juris*, last modified July 27, 2014, http://opiniojuris.org/2014/07/26/can-israel-cut-water-power-gaza.
79 Eitan Diamond, "Israel and Gaza: Occupation 2.0," *Ha'aretz*, last modified July 30, 2014, www.haaretz.com/opinion/.premium-1.607958.
80 Ibid., paragraph 3.
81 Ayelet Shaked, quoted in William McGowan, "The Member of Knesset Who Called For Genocide: Against the Mothers of the Snakes," *Mondoweiss*, last modified August 2, 2014, paragraph 4, http://mondoweiss.net/2014/08/knesset-genocide-against.html.
82 Ibid., paragraph 5.
83 Ibid., paragraph 6.
84 Ayelet Shaked, quoted in Mira Bar Hillel, "Why I'm On the Brink of Burning My Israeli Passport," *Independent*, last modified July 11, 2014, paragraph 3, www.independent.co.uk/voices/why-im-on-the-brink-of-burning-my-israeli-passport-9600165.html.
85 Richard Falk, "No Exit From Gaza," Richard Falk Word Press, last modified July 16, 2014, paragraph 8, https://richardfalk.wordpress.com/2014/07/16/no-exit-from-gaza-a-new-war-crime.

6 Public diplomacy and the post-disengagement social media wars, 2005–2014

For more than a decade many military experts, academics writing on strategic communication, journalists, bloggers, and many others have realized the potential power of visualities and the World Wide Web, and much of this was happening before Prime Minister Benjamin Netanyahu was making his infamous remarks about Hamas' usage of the telegenically dead during Operation Protective Edge. For example, before Operation Pillar of Defense Danny Danon, a Likud Party member, insisted that Israel needed to go from "defense to offense" in the public diplomacy wars that had to be waged by those who were dealing with the Palestinian "Nakba narrative."[1] Danon was urging that the Israeli Foreign Ministry get with the program and spend more money on social media, because public diplomacy had become the "central front," where "lectures at overseas universities, Facebook pages and interviews in Arabic are worth as much and have as much impact as a tank—and sometimes more."[2]

This was a brave new world of "*memes*," and those who participated in war also had to deal with images, video, or phrases that circulated virally in all types of novel generic forms, including mashup, parody, pastiche, and other creative works.[3] The "will engraved in the hearts and minds of the men [*sic*] of resistance," argued Abu Ubaida, a spokesperson for Hamas' armed wing in 2013, "is much more important than the tunnels dug in mud. The former will create thousands of the latter."[4] As Rebecca Stein astutely observed, Israelis who were used to expressing their patriotic pride as they celebrated traditional nationalist tales of a "monolithic" state entity, or "a" state with omnipotent power were going to have to get used to learning some of the artistry of what she called "digital vernacularism" if they hoped to compete with the young and savvy Palestinians who were spreading their anti-occupation messages.[5]

While Rebecca Stein studied how the IDF, the Israeli Prime Minister's Office, and the Israeli Foreign Ministry were learning how to cope with "digital diplomacy," what this chapter will show is that many other citizens, Israeli soldiers, former soldiers, and supporters of Israeli policies overseas also wanted to get onboard and help. They wanted to aid what they considered to be beleaguered Israeli communities who are trying to fight off all sorts of social media threats.

In earlier chapters I focused most of my attention on the textual claims, the written evidence, and the logical warrants that have circulated in key Israeli critiques of the actions of Hamas and Israeli detractors, and in this chapter what I invite readers to do is shift gears and pay attention to the role that virtuality, visuality, and technology play in the so-called social media wars or the "Twitter battles." I've occasionally referenced some of this visual argumentation in earlier chapters, but this is where I want to home in on how social media materials and platforms have developed as Israelis have reacted to the perceived "loss" of the media war with Hezbollah in Lebanon in 2006. Since that time, the IDF and other Israeli organizations have recognized the importance of social media outlets for spreading the word about the threats that are posed by Hamas. Part of the reason that Prime Minister Netanyahu's comment on the telegenically dead is so telling is that it is coming from a man whose own ministry has been heavily involved in related propagandizing efforts, especially after 2011.

My critical genealogies in this chapter will trace how Israelis have approached various social media issues as they contemplated what to do after the second Intifada, the second War in Lebanon, Operation Cast Lead,[6] Operation Pillar of Defense (2012), and Operation Protective Edge. By extending the work of Rebecca Stein and other scholars who have been interested in the study of wartime rhetorical usage of some of these media platforms, I hope to show that the IDF and the Israeli Foreign Ministry are not the only social agents who co-produce persuasive visualities in these Palestinian–Israeli conflicts.

Oftentimes it is the technologically savvy, younger generations who know best how to deploy some of these social media weapons, and they join their elders as they take the fight to the enemy and defend Gazan incursions or particular treatment of Palestinian populations. They are a part of the same generation that brought us the Arab Spring, as well as the network-centric technologies and relationships that have impacted so many lives.

Some of those who have supervised these efforts are not always sure how best to talk about these social media wars. For example, in February 2011, when IDF spokesperson Avi Benayahu waxed eloquently about the army recruitment efforts that were aimed at enlisting "new media fighters," he told a panel that had gathered to discuss the topic of "the digital medium as strategic weapon" that the IDF was searching for "the little hackers who were born and raised online." This made these youngsters sound like some of the cyborgs that Donna Haraway has written about, working away in some post-human universe, and it did not help matters when Benayahu went on to say that the Israelis "screen" these applications "with special care and train them to serve the state."[7] Talking about these young Israelis as if they were eugenically fit and programmed cyberwarriors was probably not Benayhu's intention, but he may have been caught up in the excitement that came with the recognition of the persuasive power of weaponized social media platforms.

This is a world fraught with contradictory feelings regarding the limits of aesthetics, the usage of hashtags,[8] graphic sexual image, and "war porn," where military "selfies" are taken by citizen-journalists or soldiers who want to communicate with folks back home. Social media thus becomes a particular type of vernacular "hasbara,"[9] where anyone armed with a new cellphone can take pictures and upload them in the name of helping either the Israeli or Palestinian causes.

Sadly, a few pictures of the violence that circulate during some of these media wars are filled with some misleading information, and those who wish to call attention to the mainstream media's supposedly blind eye sometimes recycle pictures of images from previous conflicts. Reporters for the UK's *Independent*, for example, found that some of the pictures of violence that circulated on the #gazunderattack thread during Operation Protective Edge *were actually taken in 2007*, during a previous bombardment. Ian Burrell complained that some of these images were not even from Gaza and were actually depictions that showed what was going on *in Syria*. Many of these problematic images were widely distributed as the subjects of thousands of retweets, and they were one manifestation of a "propaganda war" that is "open to everybody and sources of information are increasingly difficult to determine."[10]

Sometimes the messages that are circulated through these social media outlets recycle, supplement, reinforce, or extend the arguments that might be made by someone like Netanyahu or the IDF commanders in the field, but at other times soldiers or civilians may be circulating materials that appear to undercut the coherence and persuasiveness of other nationalistic or diplomatic arguments.

Some optimists are convinced that social media outlets can play a constructive role in the ways that we think about the enforcement of international humanitarian laws and the ways that we try to regulate the way that armed conflict is conducted. Anne Herzberg and Gerald Steinberg, for example, argue that there are enforcement and monitoring roles that can be played by citizens who are involved in what they call "IHL 2.0," where social media materials can be used to educate the public about the law of armed conflict rules and regulations. While they are aware of all of the manipulation of images that goes on in the blogosphere, Herzberg and Steinberg nevertheless argue that social media sites can be used to "protect the civilian population by providing a direct link between those experiencing the events on the ground and humanitarian and military assistance."[11]

In the abstract this sounds very defensible and pragmatic, but this all depends on the political will of the observers, as well as their situational awareness and their positionality. Note, for example, the differential ways that American audiences talk about the "rescue" of Kurds and others minorities from the power of ISIS, while few US diplomats have the temerity to talk about immediate intervention in Gaza.

It is extremely difficulty for contentious national and ethnic communities to listen to the horror stories circulated by the "other." During the middle of July 2014 Palestinians who went to West Bank cafés had little interest in watching the programs that were controlled by the television station that was loyal to Mahmoud Abbas. Instead, they simply switched over to other media so they could tune in to one of Hamas' two satellite channels. This switching meant they could watch footage of Palestinian commandos storming the enemy lines as "cowardly Israeli soldiers collapse in tears."[12] This would have seemed bizarre to Americans or Israelis, who characterized Hamas as an organization that was filled with terrorists who hid behind women and children in schools, homes, or other infrastructures during Operation Protective Edge.

There is no doubt that the advent of the internet has complicated the ways we depict what has happened in Gaza during the first decades of the twenty-first century, and this in turn has raised some major issues regarding the representation of Gazan deaths and the depiction of distant suffering. This is especially the case where states like Israel engage in both the macro- and micro-dimensions of social media surveillance, where keyboards and computers are the new weapons that are used to wage war on Facebook and Twitter mediascapes.[13] Twenty-first-century wars no longer end when territories are acquired and held. Instead, these conflicts are interpreted as having been won or lost depending on how one's social media campaigns resonate with domestic or international audiences.

The very existence of the World Wide Web has also created situations where mainstream press outlets now have to compete for attention with alternative outlets, personal blog sites, and critics of their coverage, and this has not escaped the attention of empowered governmental communities. At the same time that the IDF has spent countless shekels putting up and maintaining elaborate materials for their own website, Facebook, YouTube, Twitter, etc., the "Hamas regime" has to constantly fight censorship in the West, and they work to find creative ways of producing their own visualities.

Orthodox views regarding the coverage of Israeli histories and the heroic warfighting, that often link past biblical heroism and battles against anti-Semitism to today's sacrifices, are now juxtaposed with outlandish cartoons, enemy videos put to music, and haunting video stills. All of this becomes so complex that during and after conflicts pundits all over the world argue about who "won" or "lost" social media battles in the same way that post-Westphalian communities once wrote books about the successes or failures of those who fought pitched land battles, established city-states, or controlled territory.

The social media outlets have become so important for the Israelis that they have at times used these alternative media platforms to announce the targeted killing of major Hamas figures or the beginning of the latest Gaza conflict. No wonder that so many of those who work for *Reuters* and other organizations now contextualize the Israeli–Palestinian conflicts in ways that emphasize the importance of what is now called "weaponized" social media.[14]

Observers like Gerry Shih contend that some of this "public relations tug-of-war has long been understood as a central element of the Israeli–Palestinian conflict," and he credits Yasser Arafat for skillfully "courting international media during the first Intifada" in order to sway public opinion and put on display Palestinian struggles.[15]

This may be so, but this is no longer the age where any single "great" leader has any monopoly on mass-media representations. Sixteen-year-old Farah Baker, for example, has now been credited with live-tweeting of a Gaza bomb attack, and her messages have gone viral as she shares these events with audiences around the world "in real time."[16] Self-identifying as "Farah Gazan," she was at home with her family when the Israeli bombardments of Gaza began, and she decided to tweet through the night. One of her tweets explained that the bombs were hitting her area and that she could not stop crying and that she might "die tonight"; this admission was shared more than 10,000 times.[17] *Reuters* explained that as the bombs were exploding all over Gaza, Baker was picking up her smartphone or laptop before "ducking for cover" and then she tapped "out tweets that capture the drama of the tumult and fear around her."[18] Her tweets were described as a "social media sensation," and the followers of her website jumped from 800 to more than 166,000.

Farah Baker's father was a surgeon who worked at Gaza City's al-Shifa Hospital, and this geographical proximity added a personal touch to the layers of geopolitical debates that would later take place about this particular area when she sent out live feeds of blaring ambulance sirens as well as the blasts that came from air strikes and Israeli artillery shells. Baker explained to *Reuters*' reporters that in the beginning she only intended to write for a small audience, and that one day she would like to become a lawyer who could become an advocate for what Nidal Al-Mughrabi called "crowded and impoverished Gaza."[19]

Farah Baker's anxieties, as well as the mass-mediated framing of both the bombings that she covered and her own tweets, became entangled in layers upon layers of polysemic personal and social messages that were flowing through various platforms. Baker did not mind sharing with readers some of her own motivations for sending out her tweets:

> I noticed that most of the Western media supports Israel, so also some people abroad believe that we Palestinians are the murderers and that it is us who started the attacks on Israel. This is not right. I felt I had to do something to help Gaza. I used *Twitter* as a weapon to share what exactly happen in Gaza by posting links of recorded clips of bombs, photos of the smoke to make people who follow me feel as if they are living in Gaza. [T]o let them know we are the victims.[20]

Baker may, or may not, have been right about the valences and the *epistemes* of the dominant portrayals of Operation Protective Edge that were circulating in Western outlets, but she let everyone know that this was her third war and that she was a survivor.

What Farah Baker's tweeting shows is that "Bibi" Netanyahu and his supporters have to worry about many different facets of the telegenic coverage of the incidents that captured the attention of Gazans, other Palestinians, and their supporters. Yousef al-Helou notes that Baker was just one of the Palestinians who turned to social media platforms such as Facebook and Twitter, and that when the electric power was out in Gaza citizen journalists still found inventive ways of posting pictures of dead bodies, and destroyed neighborhoods and villages that reached the outside world. "The Gaza conflict," noted al-Helou, "was one of the first wars to be photographed mainly by amateurs and social media platforms, allowing those images to spread far and wide at the click of a

Public diplomacy and social media wars 149

button."[21] This allowed even more outsiders to become involved in consciousness-raising because the photos sent by Gazans could then be enlarged and carried by demonstrators who were demanding that their own governments intervene.

One of the issues that needs to be addressed in this chapter is the question of whether the social agency of a citizen like Farah Baker has any hope of competing with the materials that are put out by the IDF and Israeli supporters who have their own weaponized versions of social media. For example, does a critical genealogical analysis of the development of Israel's public diplomacy, that was produced between 2000 and 2014, lend credence to Evgeny Morozov's famous claim in *The Net Delusion* that too many are focusing on the emancipatory potential of digital technology and not enough are paying attention to the "dark side" of the internet?[22] Does all of this attention on what is circulating in social media platforms during Israeli–Palestinian conflicts really have an impact on the social, political, legal, or economic aspects of Gazan life, or are Baker's followers just more of Morozov's "cyberutopians" who don't pay attention to the ways their activism can be *depoliticized* by more powerful states?

Omar al-Ghazzi is probably right when he explains that unlike some of the Arab Spring stories of social mediation that involved "romantic stories of private people becoming political activists," some of the Palestinian–Israeli campaigns—especially after 2012—were government- or institution-sponsored affairs that felt "very different."[23] Given the ambiguous positioning of Hamas after 2006, and the fact that so many Arab communities have to worry about Western perceptions regarding the spread of militant radicalism, we can readily appreciate why so many communication strategists keep track of the rhetorical effectivity of all of this social media weaponry.

Regardless of actual causal impact, what are the *perceptual* features of these social mediated conflicts, and what are supporters of both the Israelis and the Palestinians doing to impact the rhetorical lenses that are used to configure the bombs, rockets, tunnels, and other artifacts that now populate so many of today's mediascapes?

In order to help answer those types of questions I want to focus primary attention in this chapter on the Israeli visualities that are circulating in these social-mediated wars, and I will be tracing how various factions argue that they are "winning" or "losing" particular battles in this war.[24] By the end of the chapter what I hope to show readers are the ways that Israelis have become adept at domesticating, answering, and containing many of the Palestinian claims. At the same time, I will show that both elite and vernacular Israel visualities are often produced for domestic consumption, and that some of the messages that circulate in these social media platforms don't always resonate with foreign critics.

I share the views of many observers who have argued that both sides in this disputation often take liberties and use their creative license as they artfully put on display the depravities of "the other," and that neither the Israelis nor the supporters of Hamas have any monopoly on moral virtue. If anything, this chapter will demonstrate that there are times when the citizens of Gaza, who are just trying to survive, are caught up in the maelstroms of representational media wars that can be almost as chaotic as the warfare itself.

While I do believe that Farah Baker's work represents more than clicktivism or slacktivism, I am convinced that a study of Israeli government blogs, Israeli soldiers' social media, and journalist reactions to those efforts shows us that the Iron Dome is not Israel's only technical wonder. Even those who may not agree with the content of the messages that are being circulated by Israeli supporters need to be cognizant of the persuasive power of social media outlets that are complementing the work of elite military lawyers and others who try to show the rectitude of the "most moral" army in the world.

The Palestinians who try to use social media may appear to outsiders as the parties that have a distinct advantage in this type of "irregular" weaponized conflict, but the reality is that they face Sisyphean tasks when they try to counter the power of the Israeli visualities. For example, as I noted in several other chapters, the Israelis can reiterate over and over again the alleged dangers that are posed by "Gazan" tunnels and rockets. Moreover, we should not underestimate the ability of Israeli soldiers who can circulate messages that look nothing like traditional diplomatic arguments about IHL or human rights.

The question has to be asked: Does the increased involvement of social media platforms help raise consciousness regarding what needs to be done in Gaza, or does it hinder these efforts and lead to some banal moral equivalence? While I lean toward agreeing with Morozov regarding the power of counterinsurgency forces to domesticate and contain the arguments of weaker advocates in situations like this,[25] I also realize that the protean, vernacular, and diffuse nature of some social-mediated events sometimes has unintended and unanticipated consequences. Yet from a *realpolitik* standpoint, even if one assumes that the use of Twitter,[26] YouTube, and other platforms have some impact on the flow of arguments and outcomes of lawfare and warfare policy debates, there is still the question of who "wins" these types of mass media wars and what this has to do with stopping the cycles of violence in Gaza.[27] I argue that as long as the ICC or other organizations don't intervene in Gazan contexts, then the Israelis need to be viewed as the winners in this mediated disputation.

The Israelis once again realize that time is on their side, and that they don't need to be declared the outright victors in any major media battles. They need to fight their mediated wars in more incremental ways, so that their social media battles of attrition help stave off international interventionism in this region. If they can effectively use social media to counter the claims that they are violating IHL principles during Gazan conflicts, then they can continue business as usual and militarize the borders of Greater Israel.

In order to defend these claims, I will begin with a study of how social media battlers were arguing during the second Lebanese conflict, and then I will move on to a review of how Israelis used various platforms during Operation Cast Lead, Operation Pillar of Defense, and Operation Protective Edge. These are obviously not the only media events that one could study, but these selections do provide key rhetorical nodal points for the study of how both elites and citizens,

Public diplomacy and social media wars 151

between 2005 and 2014, tried to use visual representations in defenses of Israeli military and foreign policies.[28]

As I noted in Chapter 1, there will be times when I provide readers with a few examples of Palestinian social activism and international visualizations of Israeli activities in Gaza,[29] but my primary gaze will always be on how Israelis are using social media to justify to viewers why they treat Gazan civilians in particular ways. These are some of the performers who become involved in what Nicholas Mirzoeff calls the "crises of visuality." Mirzoeff, like many of those writing during the post-9/11 years, sutures together wartime commentary with talk of the importance of visualities, and it is no coincidence that he uses the ideas of military theorists like Carl von Clausewitz when he avers that "today's counterinsurgency doctrine" indirectly "relies on strategies of local and remote visualization."[30] In Israeli contexts, this has meant that everything from selfies to IDF websites are deployed by those who wish to visually demonstrate the need to continually combat "Gazan" terrorism.

Each particular counterinsurgency situation has its own unique challenges and features, and journalists and scholars who might disagree about who has been "winning" the social media wars since the "belligerent occupation" ended in 2005 can still agree that both the Israelis and the Palestinians are obsessed with getting out their messages. They have all started to use more sophisticated platforms and more intricate textual and visual arguments as they try to garner the attention of many different generations in the blogosphere.

This increased sophistication may mean that each side will try to control the dominant frame that is used to explain wartime causes and effects, but even the most thanatopolitical of images do not speak for themselves and require captioning. In spite of Krauthammer's claims about "moral clarity" that I mentioned earlier in this book,[31] messages and ideological flows are not that easily contained. The meanings of images depends on both the referential value of a depiction as well as the motivations, interests, and prejudices of those who see telegenic images. As Susan Sontag so eloquently argued before her untimely death:

> To those who are sure that right is on one side, oppression and injustice on the other, and that the fighting must go on, what matters is precisely who is killed and by whom. To an Israeli Jew, a photograph of a child torn apart in the attack on the Sbarro pizzeria in downtown Jerusalem is first of all a photograph of a Jewish child killed by a Palestinian suicide-bomber. To a Palestinian, a photograph of a child torn apart by a tank round in Gaza is first of all a photograph of a Palestinian child killed by Israeli ordinance. To the militant, identity is everything. And all photographs wait to be explained or falsified by their captions.... Alter the caption, and the children's deaths could be used and reused.[32]

If anything, these insights have even more resonance if readers consider the ways photographs are now just one of many diverse forms of imaging that are now deployed in diverse mediascapes that cover events in Gaza.

152 *Public diplomacy and social media wars*

Let me begin my critical genealogy of Israeli interest in social media weaponry by looking back at one of the media wars that they supposedly "lost," the coverage of the second war in Lebanon with Hezbollah.

Visualizing the "losses" of the second Lebanese War

Daniel Ben Simon has argued that the loss of every soldier killed in war is a tragic loss for that family, but it is also the case that in Israel the "casualties quickly become part of the national *mythos* of the fallen soldier."[33] This is in spite of the notorious "Hannibal Directive," that supposedly tries to ensure that injured Israeli soldiers do not fall into the hands of the enemy.[34]

Israel's second war in Lebanon, that would be fought against Hezbollah and other forces in 2006, was a bloody affair that underscored the human tragedies of warring Lebanese and Israeli factions that tried to survive this latest round of irregular and urban warfare.[35] When the Israeli president at the time, Shimon Peres, responded to a news anchor's question regarding whether Israel worried about its national standing in international circles, he indicated that he was more concerned with security and safety concerns and that he was less worried about whether Israelis were popular.[36]

When media experts and journalists looked back at the 2006 War in Lebanon the general consensus seemed to be that defenders of Israeli policies were not taking advantage of all of the available means of persuasion that were at their disposal. The fighters for Hezbollah had supporters who did a fine job of blogging during this particular media campaign, and some of the pictures that came out of Qana in Southern Lebanon showed a rescue worker holding up a dead child for the camera. This looked staged, and members of the mainstream presses worried about publishing it,[37] but emotive images like this were used to depict the general suffering of Lebanese populations who were caught between Israeli and Hezbollah fighters. This would not be the first, nor the last, time that Israeli forces would be accused of having violated the international humanitarian law (IHL) principles of humanity, proportionality, and distinction.

Supporters of Israelis during this conflict often wondered why the journalists spend so little time taking pictures of the Hezbollah guerrillas who were threatening the Israelis, but journalists who had been in Lebanon for four or five weeks explained that these fighters—young, bearded, and walking around with walkie-talkies—often made sure they were not armed when they were mingling with foreign photographers.[38]

During the social media phases of this war Hezbollah used strategic repetition by posting the same images and footage of damaged Lebanese homes, and these could be sent across several different media platforms. For example, Rob Gehl has explained how some of the same images could be used on satellite TV and then migrate to other regional media, including billboards and YouTube. This not only helped Hezbollah amplify the "perception of Israel aggression"—it also gave them the chance to show that Israelis were using disproportionate force in responding to the kidnapping of some Israeli soldiers by Hezbollah.[39] Lieutenant

General William B. Caldwell, Dennis Murphy, and Anton Menning have argued that all of this allowed Hezbollah to "create 'a perception of failure' for the Israelis, with consequences more important than the actual kinetic outcome."[40]

Hezbollah was actually losing most encounters with the Israelis during the fighting on the ground, but this was not the way things were always represented in the mainstream media or in the blogosphere. During the 2006 campaign Hezbollah used its own satellite station, Al-Manar, to try to reach hundreds of millions of reviewers. For example, when missiles hit the Israeli naval destroyer, *Hanit*, Hezbollah's general secretary, Hassan Nasrallah, called in live to the Al-Manar station so that he could help orchestrate the coverage, and suddenly footage of the missile launch appeared on YouTube.[41] This allowed Hezbollah to create the impression that they were doing more than just hold their own in a major asymmetrical conflict.

All of this was going on as the mainstream presses were debating about the authenticity or manipulation of some of the photos that were sent from Lebanon to international presses. Some of these photos, for example, that showed massive numbers of civilian casualties following Israeli attacks, were said to have been doctored to make the smoke look darker and the planes look more menacing by adding flares to the images. Some skeptics tried to argue that *Reuters* had no business circulating these images, but all that this did was create opportunities for other journalists to talk about the horrors of the fighting and the representation of that violence. *Washington Post* photographer Michael Robinson-Chavez, who was asked to talk about the possibility that all of this doctoring was impacting coverage of the war, responded by noting: "Everyone was dead, many of them children. Nothing was set up. There was no way photographs could have been altered with a dozen photographers around."[42]

The image wars with Hezbollah leaked over into the mediations of the Gaza conflicts, and this in turn added more layers to the coverage of Israel's army activities. Some Israeli leftists seemed to second the opinions of those who were arguing that the Israelis may have been technically winning the war on the ground against Hezbollah but were losing the perceptual battles that were taking place in mainstream and alternative press outlets. As Gideon Levy would note in March 2006, since "the abduction of Gilad Shalit, and more so since the outbreak of the Lebanon War, the Israel Defense Forces has been rampaging through Gaza—there's no other word to describe it—killing and demolishing, bombing, and shelling indiscriminately."[43] In one of the most acerbic parts of his September 3, 2006 essay, Levy alleged:

> Nobody thinks about setting up a commission of inquiry; the issue isn't even on the agenda. Nobody asks why it is being done and who decided to do it. But under the cover of the darkness of the Lebanon war, the IDF returned to its old practices in Gaza as if there had been no disengagement. So it must be said forthrightly, the disengagement is dead. Aside from the settlements that remain piles of rubble, nothing is left of the disengagement and its promises. How contemptible all the sublime and nonsensical talk

about "the end of the occupation" and "partitioning the land" now appears. Gaza is occupied, and with greater brutality than before. The fact that it is more convenient for the occupier to control it from outside has nothing to do with the intolerable living conditions of the occupied.[44]

Levy's commentary on the occupation of Gaza was something that many Israelis assiduously avoided, and this included the messages that they prepared for social media dissemination.[45] However, they soon learned that the formation of their own commissions of inquiry could provide one more tactic in the arsenal of those who fought these media battles.

Israeli governmental ministries have also been some of the communities who have traced the "history" of their gradual, if grudging, adoption of social media to Israel's "failed" 34-day offensive in Lebanon in 2006.[46] Lawrence Pintak summed up the feeling during that time as soul-searching over official media manipulation, lack of balance in the selection of "expert" interviews, concern about public reactions to graphic images, and "misguided moral equivalence."[47] This catalyzed the appointment of many new sets of directors who were supposed to help with the coordination of media efforts in future campaigns.[48] Eventually the Israelis would form a new "National Information Directorate" that would oversee some of this social media traffic.[49]

What the Israelis learned from the war in Lebanon is that the new media platforms had become a combustible mix of 24/7 news cables, call-in radio, television programming, cell phoning, and internet blogging, and this had "injected an equation-altering sense of scale and speed into the traditional calculus."[50] The Israelis started to adapt to this new mediated environment, and by the summer of 2006, as the IDF battled Hezbollah in Lebanon, the Israelis started to use cameras, computers, video phones, and portable satellite dishes. "Israel soldiers," noted Caldwell, Murphy, and Menning, sent "cell phone text messages home," and both sides used videos of the fighting.[51]

For the next several years Israelis invested more and more in their social media programs, and they prepared during times of peace for what they needed to do during times of war.

Social media coverage of Operation Cast Lead, 2008–2009

On December 27, 2008 the Israelis launched a major offensive in Gaza, and at the same time the Israeli Air Force started to bombard Gaza, their stated objectives including the stopping of Hamas rocket fire attacks on southern Israel as well as the destruction of the "arms smuggling routes" into the region. By January of the following year the IDF began a ground invasion and several weeks later the Israelis unilaterally declared a ceasefire and withdrew on January 21. Mainstream media outlets and academic journals would characterize this three-week performance as a conflict that followed a typical asymmetric pattern, where Hamas would fire inaccurate rockets while the Israelis responded with their overwhelming air and land forces. The disproportionate power of the Israelis was reflected in the number of reported casualties, where the Palestinian losses ranged somewhere between 1,150 and 1,400 dead while the Israelis reported 13 deaths.[52]

These statistical disparities provided challenges to Israeli bloggers and those who wrote for the "IDF VLOG," because they needed to simultaneously magnify the existential dangers that were posed by Hamas rocket fire while producing narratives that explained why Israelis were not violating their own laws that had incorporated the customary IHL. This is why, near the beginning of Operation Cast Lead, Major Avital Leibovich gave lectures that appeared on YouTube that outlined exactly how the Israel Air Force was "forced to" fire on mosques that were storing "Grads and other rockets."[53]

As I've mentioned elsewhere in this book, when Operation Cast Lead began in December 2008 the Israelis also prevented foreign journalists from entering and reporting from Gaza, and this in turn limited the scope of some of the reporting and influenced some of the early narratives that would be told about what was happening during this incursion.[54] The Israelis also managed to block cellphone bandwidth.[55] One headline in Australia read "Officials Afraid of Getting Blogged Down in Gaza," and it was reported that after Israel "launched its offensive against Gaza, lobbyists, spin doctors and public relations experts were mobilized to head off critical reaction around the globe."[56] The operational logic seemed to be that access to IDF information was key, as well as the ability to at least hinder enemy propagandizing efforts, but censorship may have only created more headaches in venues where "no voice could refute Palestinian claims of atrocities and civilian targeting."[57]

During Operation Cast Lead the IDF embedded camera crews in its combat units, and they told foreign reporters that they were doing all of this to defend their troops against accusations of war crimes. This, obviously, was an intriguing way of heading off some types of lawfare, especially if you believed in the rectitude of your own soldiers and shared the "digital suspicion" of those who believed the enemy was using selective truth claims, hoaxes, and cyberactivism in ways that potentially threatened the dominant Israeli narration of the war.[58] For example, when the Israelis wanted to provide visual, evidentiary proof that they were trying to use precision warfare in order to cut down on Gazan civilian casualties, they could circulate some of the drone strike footage that was collected in late 2008 and early 2009.[59]

Hamas, on the other hand, sought to counter this type of visualization by telegraphing how easily they could bring together the materials they needed to make inexpensive rockets as they displayed their own craftiness. For example, some Hamas fighters allowed an Algerian journalist by the name of Zouheir Al-Najjar to videotape the inside of their homemade rocket factory. One of the clips that Al-Najjar circulated showed a masked Hamas operative casually igniting a test spoonful of homemade rocket fuel.[60]

IDF's newly minted YouTube channel included materials for English-speaking audiences, and social critics noted how the Israelis seemed to be interesting in using these platforms to answers questions and participate in conversations that were such an important part of Twitter practices.[61]

156 *Public diplomacy and social media wars*

The Palestinians countered all of this by arguing that their very survival was at stake, and they claimed that the portrayal of their resoluteness following the loss of some 1,400 people put on display the unity of the Palestinians. This all showed their unwillingness to bow down to the will of the Israelis. For Khaled Hroub, writing in January 2009, the Israelis seemed to be trying to use their military might to force Gazans to internalize the belief that they were a defeated people. Hroub argued that after weeks of vicious pointing by one of the largest armies in the world the opposite had happened:

> After three weeks of intense and round-the-clock attacks by air, land and sea, Israel is far from achieving either its immediate aim of halting rocket-attacks from Gaza or the larger "psychological" aim enunciated by Moshe Ya'alon. It has become apparent that the war itself will instead convince many more Palestinians that their ability again to withstand an assault by the fourth most powerful army in the world is a source of their power rather than their weakness. In this, the 1.5 million Palestinians under siege in Gaza are writing a new chapter in their own uncompleted modern history. They are also demonstrating a more general lesson of warfare: that wars and armed conflicts have unexpected consequences, including often the creation of a new reality quite different from what it was launched to achieve. In this case, the outcome of the Gaza war of 2008–2009 is likely to leave Hamas stronger and with an enhanced legitimacy among the Palestinians and within the region.[62]

The Israelis, however, were convinced that both their military victories during Operation Cast Lead, and their adroit usage of social media, was helping convince outside communities that the IDF was doing all it could to avoid excessive civilian casualties.

The IDF launched its interactive media branch near the end of 2009, but overtime the IDF's strategic communication staffs ballooned, and both sides "jostled to control the conflict's social narrative."[63] The advent of Operation Pillar of Defense, in 2012, would provide Israelis with a testing ground to determine where they stood in these protracted media wars.

Social media coverage of Operation Pillar of Defense, 2012

For some Israel's Operation Pillar of Defense (2012) would become what some called the first "Twitter" or "first 'social-media' war."[64] This particular war began in an incredibly strange and ghastly way when the IDF did not just kill a Hamas military leader by the name of Ahmed al-Jabari—they also posted a short YouTube video of the attack that took place while he was driving his car down the street in Gaza.[65] The Israelis followed this up by tweeting a warning to the other members of Hamas: "We recommend that no Hamas operative, whether low level or senior leaders, show their faces above ground in the days ahead."[66] The al-Jabari targeted attack would be a part of one of the biggest assaults the

Israelis had launched in Gaza in more than three years, and it was "accompanied by one of the most aggressive social media offenses ever launched by any military."[67] By the beginning of the next major operation, the IDF YouTube video on the Ahmed al-Jabari strike had been visited some five million times.

The killing of Ahmed al-Jabari made absolutely no sense to some political scientists, international relations experts, diplomats, and others who thought he was a major peacekeeping broker between Hamas and the Israelis, but the Israeli rap sheet that was posted on the IDF blog alleged that he had committed numerous transgressions, including playing some role in the kidnapping of Gilad Shalit.

The constant, reiterated message that the IDF wanted to send was that their two main goals in Operation Pillar of Defense involved the protection of Israeli civilians and the crippling of "the terrorist infrastructure in the Gaza Strip."[68] This sounded like a deceptively simple message because it could be interpreted to mean that the main targets of the Israelis would be the rockets of Hamas or the launchers that were used to help with the firing of missiles. Overtime, however, it became clear that the term "terrorist infrastructure" was a mobile and protean signifier, that could be used to describe just about any civilian structure that was destroyed in Gaza.

The Israeli grand narrative that circulated during this period contrasted the indiscriminate firing of Hamas missiles with the "precise" taking out of some 20 Hamas leaders. The IDF also started to liveblog the rockets that were directed at southern Israel, and some texts and images migrated between Facebook, Flickr, and Twitter platforms. One of the most iconic images of all of these conflicts would be produced when "IDFSpokesperson" posted a large red and white image entitled "Ahmed Jabari: Eliminated."[69]

This would retweeted more than 1,000 times during the coming years. Israel's Shin Bet security service argued that Jabari had been responsible in the decade before Operation Pillar of Defense for "all terrorist activities against Israel from Gaza."[70] Many of the IDF tweets that followed in the coming hours after the attack talked of how Hamas was an organization fighting a proxy war for Iran, and that the Iron Dome was intercepting incoming rockets heading toward major Israeli cities. When the Israeli Navy joined the fray there were tweets on this as well, and IDFSpokesperson tried to head off the inevitable necropolitical or thanatopolitical conversations by arguing: "Number of casualties is irrelevant. It doesn't make rocket fire on Israeli citizens any more acceptable" (November 14, 2012).[71] Another clever IDF tweet argued that some 12,000 rockets had been fired at Israel over the last 12 years, so visitors were asked to retweet if they thought that Israel had a right to defend itself. More than 5,000 retweeted in a matter of hours.

The attack on Ahmed al-Jabari would become the signature media event that many journalists and academics would characterize as the demonstrative evidence of the power of "weaponized social media." Dara Kerr, for example, recalled how Jabari probably never saw the missiles that hit him, and he did not have a chance to evade the drones who tracked his movements. Unlike American

CIA operatives or Joint Special Operations Command (JSOC) officials, the IDF was willing to openly publicize their attack, and within hours, noted Kerr, hundreds of thousands of people had learned about al-Jabari's death. Just after the IDF uploaded their tweet on "Ahmed Jabri: Eliminated" their Facebook account invited followers to stay tuned for updates.[72] The Al Qassam Brigades responded that the IDF had "Opened Hell Gates On Yourselves," and that "our blessed hands will reach your leaders and soldiers wherever you go."[73]

Yet by the time Israel had launched the "Twitter" campaign phase of Operation Pillar of Defense it seemed as though Hamas was having to fight an uphill battle. John Timpane explains that while the IDF had almost 300,000 followers who were being tweeted the times and places of rocket strikes against Israel, a "rag-tag" bunch of pro-Hamas Twitter feeds were constantly being shut down.[74] Timpane may not be taking into account the persuasive power of Palestinian civilian activities, but he was pointing out the disparate power relations of those who also influence the closing of Hamas accounts on major Western social media platforms.

The 2012 reportage of Jabari's death was just one of the creative ways the IDF was harnessing the power of social media platforms during this conflict. For example, there was a time when the IDF uploaded the surveillance footage to YouTube of what they thought was a long-range Fajr-5 rocket, and at the same time they tweeted a Google Maps-style picture of the launcher's alleged location in Zeitoun.[75]

During Operation Pillar of Defense former Israeli military leaders were often invited by mainstream presses to talk about the significance of Ahmed al-Jabari's death and this latest round of fighting. Gabi Siboni, a colonel in the Israeli reserves who lead the military and strategic affairs program at the Institute for National Security in Tel Aviv, explained that "deterrence has to be maintained." As noted elsewhere Siboni's name is often linked to the Dahiya doctrine, but on this particular occasion he simply argued that it was only a question of time before Israel had to step in again to stop what the Israelis perceived as the advanced weaponry build-up in Gaza.[76]

By 2012 the sophistication of the technologies that were used in these social media wars allowed for instantaneous forms of visual argumentation that blurred the event that was being represented with the media that was used to do that mirroring.

Each side, while they fired the weapons in real time, simultaneously narrated "its side of things and attacked the other side in real time."[77] Lawrence Husick, the co-chairman of the Center on the Study of Terrorism at the Foreign Policy Research Institute, argued that while the IDF had more resources, Hamas was trying to play a "kind of brinkmanship" to keep the Israelis from striking back with devastating force.[78]

In order to help the IDF carry out this Twitter warfare, Israelis in 2012 paid for the formation of a new Interactive Media Branch, which included almost three dozen people. Headed by Lieutenant Colonel Avital Leibovich[79] this organization did their best to show that Israel military efforts in Gaza had nothing to do with war crimes.

Public diplomacy and social media wars 159

In countless ways, Leibovich came to symbolize "IDFSpokesperson" and she was viewed as an expert on vernacular rhetoric and strategic communication. One essayist called her the "IDF's social media czar," and the some three dozen Israelis who worked in her division were often photographed as they produced tweets, built apps, edited views, snapped Instagrams, and kept updating all the relevant Google+ posts for the Israeli military.[80]

Leibovich is someone who is interviewed often to talk about this particular version of Israel's "shock and awe" or "cyber-social battles," and she often explains to readers some of the contradictory features of this type of campaigning that are often missed by other observers. She notes how the Israeli military is a relatively closed organization, that is secretive and doesn't enjoy sharing, while her Interactive Media Branch can only succeed if it is directly the opposite— open, interactive, sharing, and creative.[81]

By 2012 that creativity and openness was helping Israelis counter some of the bad publicity they faced during their incursions into Gaza. Gabriella Blum, a professor of international law and international conflict management at Harvard Law School, argued that this time around the Israel social media used during Operation Pillar of Defense had several intended audiences:

> I believe the video is aimed to deliver three different messages to three different audiences. A warning to militants in Gaza (we can get you anywhere, anytime); an appeasing message to the Israeli public (we will not remain helpless in the face of repeated rocket attacks), and a reassuring message to those concerned about the use of targeted killings, especially for its potential collateral damage (we can do this with utmost precision).[82]

These intended audiences, in turn, responded to all of this attention, and I would argue that the weaponization of Israeli social media aided in the unification of Israeli communities who now moved toward the right side of the political spectrum. By 2012 Israelis felt they were becoming proficient in the use of Twitter, YouTube, and other social media platforms, but it was not always clear whether it was domestic or international communities who visited IDF websites.

In the interim between Operation Cast Lead and Operation Pillar of Defense the Israelis had learned how to use the visual media to communicate the arguments they wanted to make about the legality and legitimacy of their attacks in Gaza. For example, the Interactive Media Branch's strategizing included the circulation of aerial videos that showed pinpoint bombing, which in turn provided graphic evidence that the Israelis were scrupulously following the international humanitarian law principles of distinction and proportionality.

One of the Israelis' most intriguing strategies involved what rhetoricians call an attempt at establishing *identification*, where international visitors to Israeli blog sites were asked to put themselves in the shoes of the residents of the settlements or other places that were targeted by Hamas missiles. For example, on one typical tweet an IDF spokesperson posts "What Would you Do?," a tweet that then shows missiles raining down on London and Paris.[83] This obviously is meant to counter the allegations that were often made by cosmopolitans in cities like Madrid, Rome, or London that threatened to put in the dock those Israeli military leaders who stepped off Israeli airplanes in those major cities.

Many Israelis realized that one of the most difficult challenges they faced came from the ways Palestinians could show the world the horrors that were experienced by Gazans who faced heavy bombardment after the death of Ahmed al-Jabari. One of the most emotive images that circulated during the beginning of Operation Pillar of Defense involved the awful footage of a burnt, dead baby who was handed in the direction of reporters at a press conference.[84] This very traumatizing material was posted online with Arabic captioning that provided very explicit arguments that the Israelis were not the only ones who were ignoring the plight of the Gazans. The warning that was posted along with the video of the dead baby read:

> Watching this is not recommended for the faint-hearted. Zionist missiles of hate aim at the children of Gaza and pour their hatred upon them. Are you not ashamed of your humanity, which has become meaningless and illegitimate? Have you no shame Arabs?[85]

Some of the *New York Times* reporters who covered this incident believed the video was uploaded without any description of where it was recorded, which might have raised the suspicions of some viewers, but those familiar with the scene thought the video had to have been taken in the lobby of the al-Shifa Hospital in Gaza. Other videos of the same scene had been posted by the Palestinian al-Aqsa TV station, and the man who holds out the body of the dead child speaks in crisp, very formal Arabic as he chastises those Arabs and the members of the UN who have not contributed to the "defense of Palestine." The dead girl is characterized as a "martyr" who has gone to God, and the speaker asks who is going to protect "your country and mine"? The man, who continues to hold the corpse, explains that this is what the true meaning of burning signifies in 2012, and it is "not the burning of the Holocaust."[86] This not only makes the implicit argument that one victimized people should not be tormenting another, but shows that Israelis were not the only people in the world that the Gazans blamed for their predicament.

The display of the dead girl at the al-Shifa Hospital was not the only performative act of witnessing that was used to garner sympathy for the Palestinian cause. Another related tweet showed the *BBC*'s Arabic journalist, Omar Jihad, mourning the death of his 11-month-old son after the Israeli air strikes; the death of this innocent child was heart-rending.

By the time Operation Pillar of Defense had ended, many Israelis could congratulate themselves and tell their ministers that they were at the cutting edge of nationalistic usage of social media during wartime. Israelis could now forget about the "lost" Lebanese social media wars as they honed their messages and prepared for the next time they had to "mow the lawn" in Gaza.

Operation Protective Edge, the IDF, and the perfecting of weaponized social media

Is it possible that there are times when the weaponized usage of social media may help *provoke* a war, instead of simply announcing the beginning of a conflict? In 2014 it is possible that another round of fighting in Gaza was triggered by the coverage of the treatment of three Israeli teens—Eyal Yifrach, 16, Gil-ad Shaar, 19, and Naftali Frankel, 16—who were allegedly "snatched by Hamas" while they were hitchhiking home from their religious schools in Gush Etzion. Debra Kamin contends that the motivation for the kidnapping had to do with a "toxic combination of terror and a desire for leverage in the nation's increasingly lopsided prisoner exchanges."[87] The discourse about the kidnapping of these three teens circulated at a time of heightened tensions as Israelis were already worried that Hamas was stockpiling some sophisticated weaponry that endangered more Israeli lives.

In June 2014 the bodies of three Israeli teenagers had been found, and within two days, a Facebook group named "The people of Israel Demand Revenge" raked in over 35,000 members in two days, many of whom were soldiers.[88] One selfie sent in to Facebook came from a uniformed soldier that showed him saluting, while the inscription under the selfie repeated the name of the group. This Facebook group's managers, who did not identify themselves by name, invited surfers to send in photographs of themselves, and they explained that the inscription "the nation of Israel demands revenge" could be written down on a piece of paper, sent by cellphone, inscribed on their bodies, or even put on walls. The goal was to simply share and put all of these in an album that could not be ignored. This type of vernacular performance was intended to send a message to Prime Minister Netanyahu and the Knesset that Israeli people wanted revenge, and they were willing to back those who went after Palestinians who did this to the three Israeli teenagers.

Revenge is one of those motives that is not something that can justify controversial actions in debates about the applicability of the law of armed conflict, but this was a different context in which Israeli publics simply wanted to express their outrage and need for retribution. The Facebook pages of "The People of Israel Demand Revenge Group" started filling up with messages advocating the avenging of the kidnapping by killing Arabs. One photograph that was sent in showed two teenage girls embracing each other while they hold up a piece of paper that read: "Hating Arabs is not racism, its values." Another image sent in showed an army beret and a gun with a sign written on paper that was addressed to Bibi (Benjamin Netanyahu) letting him know that people wanted revenge.

The Israeli governmental representatives appreciated the fact that so many Israeli patriots were willing to support efforts at finding those responsible for the deaths of the three teenagers, but at the same time they realized the harm that could come when foreigners noticed the racialized nature of some of these public responses. An official press statement from the IDF indicated:

> If soldiers are involved in sending racist photographs and in calling on harming the innocent, then this is a serious incident that does not accord

with what is expected of IDF soldiers, and every case made known to the commanders will be handled with utmost severity.[89]

The Israelis wanted their hasbara and their social media weaponry, but this needed to be done in ways that put on display the measured restraint of a democratic nation that was already trying to show that their control of "disputed" territory had nothing to do with what outsiders called "apartheid" policies.

By 2014 the Israeli government had many personnel who recognized the importance of social media wars, and their confidence was tempered by the recognition that outsiders were still having a difficult time understanding why Israelis did what they had to do in Gaza. Not all patriotic revenge narratives had to be presented in overtly racialized rhetorics. Caroline Glick, writing in *The Jerusalem Post* in August 2014, provided what I believe to be one of the best narratives that explained what Israelis were trying to get across in what she called the "information war":

> For most Israelis, the international discourse on Gaza is unintelligible. Here we were going along, minding our own business. Then on a clear night in June, apropos of nothing, Palestinian terrorists stole, murdered and hid the bodies of three of our children as they made their way home from school. Before we could catch our breath from that atrocity, they began shelling our major population centers with thousands of rockets, missiles and mortars, and infiltrated our communities along the border with Gaza through underground tunnels to kidnap and murder us. And as the Palestinians did all of these things, they used their civilian population and the foreign press corps as human sandbags. They ordered their own people not to evacuate their homes from which Hamas, Fatah and Islamic Jihad terrorists launched their missiles, rockets and mortars at Israel.[90]

This type of narrative underscored the point that the Israelis cared about the loss of even one of their loved ones, while the Palestinian leaders seemed to be willing to risk the lives of their own civilians in order to gain the sympathy of foreign journalists. This all looked so obviously immoral that Israelis did not understand why anyone was willing to debate about any of this.

The passage of some eight years since the time of the second War in Lebanon meant that Israelis no longer doubted their ability to wage successful media campaigns. Glick, for example, argued it was wrong to make the knee-jerk assumption that "our hasbara (public diplomacy) is a catastrophe," or that our "defenders are incompetent idiots."[91] She was convinced that the Israeli hasbara had to start forcing an unwilling media and international community to discuss the truth, because the media, the US State Department, and the UN are all "wedded to a narrative in which Israel is to blame for its enemies' desire to destroy it."[92]

The dominant narrative that appeared in Israel visualities was one of Israeli victimhood and controlled aggression that responded to that victimization. The social media wings of the IDF were doing what they could during Operation

Protective Edge, and by this time the Israelis were managing 30 different social media platforms that allowed listeners to follow along as the IDF disseminated messages in Arabic, English, French, Hebrew, and Russian.

To give readers an example of some of the growing complexity of many of the IDF's usage of social media, notice some of the features of the massive IDF webpage, entitled "Special Report: Operation Protective Edge."[93] This website contains information that is said to be "free to be used and distributed," and some of its links contain materials on such topics as "tunnel threat," "rocket threat," "human shields," "Shuja'iya," "Hamas violations international law," "IDF Minimizing Civilian Casualties," and "IDF Humanitarian Aid to Gaza." The dominant front page of the Special Report on Operation Protective Edge explains that on July 8, 2014, "following incessant rocket fire from Gaza at Israel," the IDF initiated Operation Protective Edge. Those who uploaded this website then explained that on the tenth day of the operation, after continued terrorists assaults, the IDF commenced the ground phase of the operation. Just below this textual commentary is a photographic image of a tank firing artillery shells. Both the dominant narrative of the website, as well as the selected topics, allow any visitor to see that any questions regarding counterlawfare will focus on Palestinian violations of the law of armed conflict. This report is linked to a Twitter account that as of August 17, 2014 had almost 400,000 followers.[94]

The official Twitter account (@IDFSpokesperson) appears in English, and had at least 292,000 followers by the second week of the war. Graphics, photographs, and "infographics" were used to show how Hamas was using Palestinian civilian homes as human shield for Hamas command centers and storage facilities.[95]

Hamas tried to keep up with the Israeli efforts, but some of their accounts were cancelled and they often depended on the private citizens or journalists who sent in gruesome images of those who died during Israeli bombings. This did not mean that Hamas didn't try to invest more in these platforms, and al-Qassam had increased its Twitter activity as it posted messages in Arabic, English, and Hebrew.[96] However, the Israelis, who kept track of their "likes" and other *memes*, were now noting the volume of traffic that flowed in as hundreds of thousands of bloggers sent Twitter messages that were supportive of Israeli efforts during Operative Protective Edge. All of this was taking place during a time when the Hamas Twitter account had fewer than 12,000 followers.

In some instances supporters of Hamas tried to counter some of this imbalance in traffic by noting some of the alleged prejudices of mainstream reporters who seemed to be emulating the Israelis as they tried to magnify the dangers that were posed by the Palestinians. One of the clearest examples of how prior prefigurations and media frames can influence perceptions came during the early days of Operation Protective Edge, when Diane Sawyer of *ABC News* was trying to show pictures of those suffering from the war. As Adam Horowitz has pointed out, Sawyer began a segment on the Israeli attack on Gaza by showing two photographs in the aftermath of some of the Israel bombings, and then she proceeded to say: "Overseas now to the rockets raining down on Israel today....

164 *Public diplomacy and social media wars*

All part of a tinder box Israelis and Palestinians and here, an Israeli family trying to salvage what they can. One woman standing speechless among the ruins."[97] While Sawyer was giving her voiceover, a photographic image was presented to television viewers. The photograph was in reality taken from Gaza city, and Horowitz charitably argued the mix-up probably occurred because Sawyer was trying to show some of the horrors of the war by showing losses by both sides.[98] This, however, was not how bloggers who supported Palestinians framed Diane Sawyer's contextualization of this incident, and they were convinced that this showed how confused Americans were when it came to covering Gazan affairs.

Hamas clearly could not outspend the Israelis in these social media wars, but what they could do is appreciate the help that came from some Israeli NGOs that served as witnesses during Operation Protective Edge. It may be too soon to tell if these images will become iconic, but the image and the word came together in the assemblages that appeared on B'Tselem's webpages. One of B'Tselem's photographers, Muhummad Sabah, has left us some of the most memorable, and haunting collection of images that were taking during some of the ceasefires (see Figures 6.1 and 6.2).[99]

Sabah's haunting visual representations of the town of Beit Hanoun, in the northern part of the Gaza Strip, appeared to have been taken from all types of angles as he looked down from devastated buildings in that town. B'Tselem reported that during these early offensives Beit Hanoun had been one of the

Figure 6.1 Beit Hanoun (photo credit: Muhummad Sabah and B'Tselem).

Public diplomacy and social media wars 165

Figure 6.2 Beit Hanoun rubble (photo credit: Muhummad Sabah and B'Tselem).

hardest hit communities, along with Beit Lahiya, Gaza City, Khuza-ah, and Rafah.

In order to help contextualize some of Muhammad Sabah's images, B'Tselem collected testimony from individuals like Suhair Shabat, Shadi Taleb, and Muhammad Hamad. Suhair Shabat's testimony appears on B'Tselem's website, and she is allowed to describe the dangers that she, her husband, and their five children faced as they tried to keep their family together during the early days of this war. Shabat noted in July 2014:

> Since the war began, we've been hearing terrible reports of bombings and families and children killed. At first, my husband and his relatives decided that we all stay together at home for the war, and that we face together the difficult times when there are bombings. We decided not to leave our home and not go anywhere else. In the previous war, we had to leave home and we suffered a lot. Ultimately, my husband ended up working round the clock, photographing what was going on, so he wasn't home at all. We stayed at home until today, 19 July 2014, despite the ongoing bombings. Things are getting progressively worse. There are air strikes as well as shelling from land and sea. Several houses in our area were bombed and people were injured and killed. I can no longer keep up with the names of all the casualties. I feel like my memory isn't working properly. Since the war began, I haven't really been able to sleep. Last night, I didn't manage to sleep at all, not even for a moment.[100]

Note the absence of any commentary on Hamas, the lack of any referencing of any tunnels or rockets. Suhair Shabat's husband was a journalist, who was trying to keep the family together. B'Tselem captioned this type of testimony by noting that they had only been able to verify some of this by using the telephone, and circumstances prevented them from publishing this type of testimony with supplemental information. Visitors to their blog site are told that the information would be provided as soon as the military campaign ended.

After the Egypt-brokered ceasefire, members of the Al-Qassam Brigades would return to Beit Hanoun, and Ismail Haniya, the top Hamas leader in Gaza, worked his way through crowds as he kissed the cheeks of elders and some of his masked fighters,[101] but Figure 6.2 shows the extent of the devastation in this locale.

Journalists who visited this region in September 2014 reported that electricity was still scarce, that residents had to line up for clean water, and that the militant faction of Hamas was handing out $2,000 to each of the families whose home was hit. In theory, the deal that had been brokered with the PA government in the West Bank meant that official control of Gaza ministries was being handed over to a new parliamentary government, but in the meantime it was Hamas that "paradoxically" seemed to be "politically in its strongest position in years."[102] Hamas, after all, seemed to be the community that stood steadfast and lived among the ruins of places like Beit Hanoun.

The Palestinian depictions of places like Beit Hanoun look nothing like the mass-mediated representations of the Gazan towns that circulated in Israeli webpages. As noted earlier, one of the major facets of the Palestinian–Israeli social media wars involves the conflicting accounts of what Israelis and Americans refer to as the "attack tunnels"[103] or "terror tunnels"[104] of Hamas or the Palestinians.

The geopolitical impact of all of this talk of "terror tunnels" is that it can be used as a securitizing rationalization for why Israel, after the 2005 disengagement, needed to avoid sending construction supplies that might aid in the economic rebuilding of "Hamas." For example, Israeli Defense Minister Moshe Y'aalon, in October 2013, halted the transfer of construction supplies to the Gaza Strip, alleging that some 500 tons of cement had been diverted to construct underground passages.[105] Security forces had discovered that a tunnel ended up in "Israel proper," near the Kibbutz Ein Hashlosha in the western Negev. Major General Shlomo Turgeman, the Southern Command head, argued that the tunnel constituted a "violation of our sovereignty, and he warned that if Hamas used this type of tunnel to carry out any terror attacks against Israel then the Israeli response would look "very different."[106]

Many Israelis turned the tunnels into potent symbols that allegedly illustrated the "moral" divide that existed between Hamas and Israel. James Conway, for example, argued that while he understood why so many Americans might be concerned when they heard about the massive loss of Palestinian civilian life during the fighting between Hamas and Israel, the US publics needed to remember that all of these "images of houses in Gaza reduced to rubble and women wailing" did not put on display the alleged "moral chasm" that existed between Israel and Hamas. What Conway wanted readers to worry about was the three-mile-long tunnel that that was designed for the explicit purpose of launching murderous attacks on Israelis.[107] The IDF could provide visitors to their website with illustrations of how the IDF operated with "precision" in order to remove these types of threats.[108]

Although many of those outside Israel have been characterizing these tunnels as "smuggling" tunnels that have been around for years in order to try to circumvent Israeli blockades and Egyptian closures,[109] the Israeli Ministry of Foreign Affairs used webpages to argue during Operation Protective Edge that these tunnels were constructed by the military wing of Hamas so they could carry out terrorist attacks against Israeli towns and settlements.[110] Visitors to the official website of the Israeli Ministry of Foreign Affairs can see infographics that are used to complement the written word as the Israelis use this website to argue that "Hamas' priorities" include the targeting of hospitals, schools, towers, and halls.

In a fascinating illustration of argumentative dexterity the Israeli Ministry of Foreign Affairs anticipates, and then answers, the usual Palestinian or critics' contentions that these were just used to get around Israel's tightening of Gazan mobility by land or sea. What the Israeli Ministry of Foreign Affairs argues is that the "Hamas Tunnel Industry" "*used*" to be "a well-known conduit" for smuggling goods, funds, weapons, etc., but now that Egypt had cut down on the smuggling it had been transformed by Hamas "for a far more sinister purpose: terrorist attacks on Israel territory" [my emphasis]. This particular essay, uploaded on July 22, 2014, argued that by that time Hamas had already built an extensive network of tunnels that ran into "Israeli territory," and it was said that they were used to murder and kidnap Israeli citizens. The Foreign Affairs Ministry remarked that since the beginning of Operation Protective Edge, the IDF had discovered 23 tunnels, and some of those tunnels had exit points inside Israel's territory. The rest of the tunnels, argued those who uploaded this essay, were used for "other terrorist purposes."[111]

Some of the visuals that were produced by the Israeli minister of foreign affairs were used in ways that reiterated and buttressed the claims that by this time were circulating in countless Israeli and American journalistic, military, and legal circles—that Hamas was using the civilians of Gaza as human shields. In their "Behind the Headlines" essay, the minister of foreign affairs argued that the "attack tunnels" were dug "starting" at sites hidden deep within the Gaza Strip, and they contended that "most" of these were dug under private homes, greenhouses, or public buildings. In order to add to their ethos and credibility, those who produced this website claimed that the tunnels made their way underground for up to a mile, until they reached their destination "deep inside Israeli territory."[112] Blurry photographs from the IDF, filled with red arrows, were used to show where some of the tunnels were hidden, and this image makes it appear as though one of the major tunnels was near a medical center, a school, and many civilian homes.

Another infogram used by the Israeli minister of foreign affairs, that came from the IDF, painted a graphic picture of some of the cumulative dangers that were posed by Hamas rockets that were fired from above, while terrorists threatened Israeli populations from below. Israeli fighters who responded to some of these dangers were characterized as soldiers who used precision warfare, while the members of Hamas were configured as terrorists who indiscriminately fired at civilians.

For any of those who might argue that there was little proof that anyone had been hurt by these supposed terror tunnels, the Ministry of Foreign Affairs provided four of what might be called "melodramatic terrorist narratives" that were crafted about the tunnels, including a story of how, on July 17, the IDF had foiled a potentially dangerous raid by Hamas raiders. This particular story explained that on that day some 13 Hamas terrorists emerged from a tunnel that was less than a mile from Sufa, a kibbutz, and "fortunately they were discovered by the IDF before they could invade the village."[113]

Several days later, another group of Hamas terrorists traveled some 765 yards from the Kibbutz of Ein HaShlosha, and again the IDF soldiers are described as having prevented them from attacking the farming village. On July 20, "a massive terror tunnel" was discovered near Kibbutz Native HaAsara, and residents of the village were told to stay indoors and lock their doors and windows until it was confirmed that terrorists were not a threat. The next day, "more than 10 heavily-armed terrorists infiltrated Israel" through another tunnel, but this time they split into two groups, one that went after those living in Kibbutz Erez and the other that went after Kibbutz Nir-Am. The Israeli Ministry of Foreign Affairs reported that the terrorists were wearing IDF uniforms so they could deceive civilians and Israeli security forces. Again, the narrative closure turns out well for the Israelis, because all ten of the terrorists were killed, while the IDF only lost four IDF soldiers during the battle.[114] An infogram is then used to show the path of the terrorist attacks and how close the tunnels were to Israeli agricultural communities.[115]

These types of visuals—that rarely if ever are accompanied by text that mention the specific names of Gazan communities or comment on the numbers killed during Israeli attacks—are used to make it appear as if peaceful Israeli pastoral settings are constantly under attack from perfidious Hamas forces.

The rhetorical beauty of these type of messages is that they convey massive amounts of contested, partial, and contingent material on Operational Protective Edge in relatively short spaces. The captions and images look as though they are meant to appeal to many different types of audiences, regardless of nationality or age, as evidenced by the captions that explain to potential viewers that a kibbutz is an Israeli agricultural community.

Moreover, these types of vernacular, populist, and patriotic combinations of word and image subtly provide some of the same Israeli arguments about Israel's *jus ad bellum* right to go to war without having to use a great deal of the type of legalese that might appear in law reviews that mention Gazan populations serving as human shields or losing their status as non-combatants protected by the Geneva Convention. Anyone who visits the sites—especially young Israelis or those who identify with those threatened by the rockets—could treat all of these infograms, captioning, and textual material as proof that the Israelis had irrefutable evidence they had to defend themselves against both aerial and underground threats. This served several rhetorical functions, including underscoring the nefarious nature of the activities of the Palestinian civilians who might have helped build the tunnels or allow missiles to be fired from their homes, schools, or medical centers. At the same time, this helped counter some of the telegenic persuasion that Prime Minister Netanyahu was complaining about, because the images of the tunnels both underscored the existential dangers that confronted innocent Israelis while implicitly vilifying the not-so-innocent Palestinian civilians in Gaza. One could even conclude that Israel's critics could talk all they wanted to about the Israeli use of "disproportionate force," but didn't the existence of the "terrorist tunnels" show just why artillery attacks, drone strikes, and tank incursions were needed?

The Israeli Ministry of Foreign Affairs could even use essays like the one on Hamas tunnels as a way of explaining for web visitors just why Israelis, after the 2005 disengagement, could not reason or negotiate with Hamas. Visitors who read this "Behind the Headlines" are told that Hamas has been "utilizing this method as early as 2006," which implied that the end of the old belligerent occupation spelled the end of adequate policing of terrorism in Gaza. For example, in that year terrorist organizations were said to have used a cross-border tunnel to kill two IDF soldiers, and kidnapped a third, Gilad Shalit, who was held by Hamas for five years.

The minister of foreign affairs' decision to mention Gilad Shalit is fraught with significance—he was abducted in 2006 when Hamas-affiliated militants went into Israel near a border-crossing.[116] Verini explains that "Shalit became the embodiment of a ceaseless war, his face staring out from roadside billboards much like the faces on martyrdom posters that adorn the walls in Jabalia and the other camps."[117] Shalit was finally released during a prisoner exchange in the fall of 2011, but his abduction traumatized those who could identify with his predicament.[118] He became the Israeli everyman, the invaluable biopolitical Israeli soldier who was worth rescuing, even if that meant releasing hundreds of would-be Palestinian terrorists.

The minister of affairs' essay on "terror" tunnels also argued that Hamas was said to be using massive amounts of manpower and supplies to create tunnels that were transformed into "giant landmines." One could easily conjure pictures of the deaths in Iraq caused by IEDs as one read this type of commentary. This Ministry of Foreign Affairs report concluded by complaining that even more twisted were the ways that Hamas, instead of providing for the needs of the population of Gaza, was investing huge amounts of money in the construction of underground networks and bunkers. These were characterized as "literal money pits," a "malevolent underground city built for the sole purpose of terrorism, emptying the already depleted coffers of the people of Gaza."[119] The wastefulness of the Gazans is thus juxtaposed with the frugality and practicality of the Israelis.

This type of nationalistic, militarized storytelling—that helps critics see the picture that the Israeli Ministry of Foreign Affairs wants to get across—makes it appear as if Israel is the friend of the people of Gaza and that it is Hamas that is to be blamed for all of the Gazans' trials and tribulations. This point is driven home with hyperlinks to select excerpts from the infamous "Hamas Covenant" that called for the destruction of Israel through jihad.[120] From beginning to end, this entire Ministry of Foreign Affairs narration reads like an IDF success story.

Like all ideological configurations, the Israeli Ministry of Foreign Affairs telling of the terror tunnel is selective and partial, and this was not the only way to conceptualize the material and the symbolic value of these tunnels and their representations in mainstream and alternative outlets. For example, two days after the uploading of the essay that I've critiqued above, *Ha'aretz* carried a story by Anshel Pfeffer that was entitled: "Hamas is Losing on the Battlefield but Hitting Israel Where It Hurts."[121] Pfeffer's essay contains a photograph of an IDF soldier peering into the darkness of a small tunnel entrance, and viewers might surmise that he is in no rush to go into the tunnel. Pfeffer tells readers about some of the same events that were chronicled by the Israeli Ministry of Foreign Affairs in their coverage of the terror tunnels, but the *Ha'aretz* essay lets readers know that "destroying these tunnels is a dangerous job, as seen in the deaths of three IDF paratroopers who were blown up by a Hamas booby trap when they entered a tunnel entrance."[122] Pfeffer saw some of the strategic and tactical advantages of the Hamas usage of these tunnels when he averred that they were just some of the weapons that could be used to "challenge and undermine Israel's close knit, Westernized and relatively affluent society."[123] He used evidence of the IDF's astonishment at the extent of the tunnel usage as a way of critiquing the intelligence "blindspot" that had allowed Hamas to take advance of the proximity of Gaza's urban sprawl and "Israeli kibbutzim." Pfeffer asserted that some of the Hamas tunnels were not built by their leaders but by members of families from Rafah who made their living using the smuggling tunnels that went into Egypt.[124] Pfeffer expressed worries about the lack of detection technology, the dangers to Ben Gurion Airport, and the terrorist leveraging that might come from the capture of even one Israeli soldier. In this complex, biopolitical calculus that has been a part of these Israeli–Palestinian conflicts for decades, Pfeffer knew that numbers mattered:

> Hamas of course is much more aware of the Israeli sensitivity to its soldiers being taken captive. The organization does not hold a live Israeli soldier now, though it is trying very hard, but they have tried very hard to exploit the fact that missing Golani Sergeant Oron Shaul's body has yet to be fully recovered and identified. The moment they managed to scavenge part of his uniform, or a dog-tag, from the battlefield and had his name and number, they immediately acted to sow confusion and despair in Israel with false claims of having taken him prisoner. At least 150 Hamas fighters have so far been taken prisoner by the IDF and are currently undergoing questioning, but for Hamas this will all be worthwhile if they can take even one prisoner of their own. They know this is probably Israel's softest spot.[125]

By "softest spot" this writer did not mean that Israeli soldiers were weak or easily defeated. This softness referred to Israeli casualty aversion, which in turn prioritized the importance of the Israeli body. The kidnapping and murder of three teens, after all, underscored the point that some were willing to go to war in the name of vengeance.

The search and "discovery" of the tunnels involved key performance acts on the part of Israelis during the incursion that ratified and authenticated what the Israelis had already been commenting on during the circulation of their social media weaponry. Both mainstream and alternative presses circulated some of the same pictures of "terror" tunnels over and over again, and visitors to Israeli YouTube videos could see all sorts of images of brave IDF infantry discovering caches of weapons that were hidden in tunnels.[126]

The discovery of the tunnels could then be linked to a much larger militarized narrative: The existence of "terror" tunnels showed that there were few, if any, innocent civilians in Gaza. Israeli economic minister Naftali Bennett, a former company commander of Israeli special forces, argued that in Gaza there was a "world of weapons tunnels penetrating into Israel, creating the possibility of a mega-attack."[127] Bennett, a hardliner, would not rule out the possibility that Israel might have to topple the Hamas regime.

The Israelis, having spent years crafting constitutive narratives that explained why they were not occupiers, told the world that as soon as they destroyed the tunnels they would leave Gaza. Captain Eytan Buchman, a spokesperson for the Israel military, denied that the IDF had any intention of reoccupying Gaza. He argued that the main objective of the Israel ground offensive had been, and remained, the destruction of the tunnel network and the rocket launchers that Hamas militants were using to attack Israel. Yet Buchman had to admit that the IDF had expanded the numbers of forces on the ground because they found that all "of Gaza is an underground city, and the amount of infrastructure Hamas built up over the years is immense."[128] Again, the term "infrastructure" serves as a mobile, ambivalent, and protean signifier, a word that could mean they were referencing a rocket launcher, a home housing those rockets, hospitals near the rockets, or anything else that had been destroyed in Gaza.

This candid summary of the IDF goals—that appeared in a *Washington Post* essay that also had hyperlinks to a video showing some of the burials in the aftermath of Gaza's shelling—helps explain how the Israelis were using talk of tunnels and infrastructure as a way of countering some of the lawfare and the bad press that was coming their way from the telegenically dead that Netanyahu and others were worried about. If the Israelis could just convince their readers *that ALL of Gaza* was this massive network of tunnels—and not just a few dozen tunnels that were just 500 yards or so away from the Israeli fence—then this would alter both the topographical and the thanatopolitical landscapes so that just about any Israeli air strike could be deemed to have been directed at some terrorist "infrastructure." No matter where a bomb or artillery shell landed in Gaza, it could be linked to some supposed "terror" tunnel.

This helps explain the Israeli obsession with documenting the existence of "terror" tunnels, and why Israel authorities and members of the public—who knew about the existence of the tunnels that were used for smuggling and other purposes—*waited until the third week of July* to carry out a media blitz that portrayed the tunnels as some novel and deadly addition to the Hamas arsenal. The firing of rockets was the reason Israelis felt they needed to begin Operation Protective Edge, but it would be the discovery and demolition of the "terror" tunnels that paved the way for the end of OPE and their departure from this "disengaged" land.

Hamas officials could have responded to all of this use of the image and word by focusing on the overwhelming power of the Israelis, but this was not the way they responded to all of the Israeli and American coverage of the tunnels. Former Hamas Prime Minister Ismail Haniya argued that the tunnels were just one of the "surprises" they had in store for the Israelis. The tunnels, argued Haniya, were a "new strategy in confronting the occupation and in the conflict with the enemy from underground and from above the ground."[129]

The visual afterimages in the wake of OPE put on display the lasting rhetorical force of these terror tunnel conversations. For example, Michael B. Mukasey argued that during the middle stages of Operation Protective Edge it seemed as though tunnels mattered more than rockets to Hamas, because they wanted to infiltrate Israel so they could stage attacks like the one that received so much press attention in Mumbai in 2008.[130] In July 2014 millions of American viewers watched as *CNN*'s Wolf Blitzer bent down and climbed inside one of the 30 or more "Palestinian" tunnels that were described as going from "Gaza to southern Israel."[131]

After seeing this type of ideological coverage, countless visitors around the world could reasonably ask: If Gazans didn't want to get bombed, then why did they dig, or put up with, the existence of these "terror" tunnels? Not how all of this deflected attention away from the horrors of the blockades that led to the usage of tunnels in the first place.

Conclusion

This chapter has provided readers with a critical genealogical explanation of the Israeli usage of social media during wartime, that began with perceived "losses" during the 2006 campaign in Lebanon and ended with the ceasefire following Operation Protective Edge. Although Israelis often seemed to indicate that both the content of their messages and their usage of these social media outlets was providing with them with some advantages in these wars of words and images, critics are just beginning to assess their efficacy. Dara Kerr has argued that while militaries and militias have "skirmished virtually" in Bahrain, Egypt, Kenya, Libya, Somalia, and Syria, the Israeli–Palestinian conflicts were somehow qualitatively different, in that these were some of the first times when "actual physical hostilities were mirrored by cyber-social battles for hearts and minds."[132] This was certainly the case as one reviews their deployment during Operation Cast Lead, Operation Pillar of Defense, and Operation Protective Edge.

While several observers are convinced that the Israelis are winning some of these social media wars, at least in Anglo-American public venues, other media experts believe that it is not always easy to tell who is winning or losing these conflicts. For example, Professor James Der Derian, who gained fame by writing on the advent of "virtuous" and "virtual" wars, provided what looked like a "fog of war" type of analysis as he employed Clausewitzian militaristic frameworks as he assessed the latest confrontation. Der Derian opined that it was too difficult to tell at this stage who might be winning:

> I think it's difficult to say who's winning the "war." In a conventional war you seize the centre of gravity which might be a capital city or a strategic battlefield – but in a media war the centre of gravity is diffused. Obviously people are fighting for the moral high-ground; they're fighting for public opinion and measuring who's winning that part of the war is exceptionally difficult.[133]

While Der Derian did think it was important that researchers kept track of the participatory nature of some of these social media affairs, he was not all that interested in simply counting the number of hash tags or "likes" that appeared on various social media platforms.

Der Derian, and writers like Rebecca Stein, have reminded us that there are social as well as military dimensions to many of these socially mediated campaigns, and Sherwood was perhaps being kind and charitable when she explained that both the Palestinians and Israelis were posting narrative accounts that were "at best partial and often blatantly distorted."[134] Her assessment was that although they had been clashing in the blogosphere for years, this latest variant of the social media wars in 2014 was a ferocious fight, one without precedent, and she wrote that the asymmetry on the battlefield was matched by the "strengths and resources" of what she called the Israeli "social media troops."[135]

While it may take some time before academics are able to assess the long-term suasory impact of some of these messages as they circulate in foreign and international spheres, it could be argued that there is a plethora of evidence that the vast majority of Israelis not only condoned, but supported the fighting in Gaza. Many twenty-first-century Israelis echoed the words of Golda Meir when they blamed Hamas for forcing Israelis to kill Palestinian men, women, and children.

Future researchers may also find that citizen-soldiers, and citizen-journalists, played key roles in some of these mediated conflicts, and these younger generations had their own ways of participating in the social media wars that were fought during OPE. For example, Gavriel Bio assembled together a Facebook campaign called "Girls Keeping the Cliff Strong" in response to the Israeli name for Operation Protective Edge, known in Israel as Operation Strong Cliff. Gavriel Bio's Facebook campaign invited young Jewish women from Israel and around the world to send in anonymous selfies, and many of these images appeared on Facebook with "I love IDF" written "on their scantily clad or sometimes naked bodies."[136] This Facebook campaign was taken down after four days because of objections from feminists and others, but before that time "Girls Keeping the Cliff Strong" had managed to draw tens of thousands of clicks while the fighting in

Gaza was going on. Gon Ben-Ari contends that the project went viral within a matter of minutes, and that even after it was taken down dozens of spin-offs took its place, including "Standing with the IDF," "Russian Girls for the IDF," etc. Anti-Israeli users flooded Facebook with hateful remarks, while soldiers fighting in the Gaza Strip were sharing the photos by the thousands.[137]

In Ben-Ari's critique of what was called Israel's atmosphere of "political misogyny" Ben-Ari contrasted the Israeli publics harsh treatment of female celebrities who spoke openly about the cost of the war in Palestinian and Israeli lives—Gila Almagor, Orna Banai, and Rona Kenan—with the cheering on of the "faceless women" who sent their photographs to "Keeping the Cliff Strong." This "Israeli military-erotica," Ben-Ari argued, was allowing the circulation of a type of "selfless selfies" where the current war in Gaza was being "stimulated by a crowd of virtual, faceless women."[138]

In sum, the IDF, the Israeli Foreign Ministry, and individuals like Gavriel Bio were just a few of the social agents who are willing to expend a great deal of time and energy on the defense of Israel in the blogosphere. As Harriet Sherwood of the *Guardian* would write in July 2014, the Israeli military's Twitter account provided only one example of the growing sophistication of Israeli usages of social media. By this period the IDF had become a media player that could not be ignored, where dozens of specialists in strategic communication were producing and disseminating dozens of updates each day on the latest military clashes in Gaza. As Sherwood explained, this provided what looked like "real time" reportage, and it meant that the IDF—instead of just feeding bland information to reporters—could now put their own spin on Hamas' motives and actions.[139]

One of the key questions that must be asked is whether all of this social media warfare, like the lawfare I studied in other chapters, emboldens those who sincerely believe that they were "forced" into going to war. Given the protracted and evolutionary nature of these battles, it does not take a crystal ball to reasonably conclude that within a few months or years, after Gazans have rebuilt some of their towns, we will once again be reading about the Dahiya doctrine, the "mowing of lawns," and dangers associated with more "terror" tunnels and rockets. "It cannot be that the citizens of the state of Israel will live under the deadly threats of missiles and infiltration through tunnels," Netanyahu remarked, a state of affairs where his nation faced "death from above and death from below."[140]

Gazan pasts, unfortunately, will become prologue without international interventionism, and unless things change this will not be the last time we hear about "real time" coverage of Gazan–Israeli conflicts.

Notes

1 Danny Danon, quoted in Rebecca Anna Stoil, "Danon Calls For Israeli Satellite TV in English, Arabic," *The Jerusalem Post*, last modified May 18, 2011, www.jpost.com/Diplomacy-and-Politics/Danon-calls-for-Israeli-satellite-TV-in-English-Arabic.
2 Ibid., paragraph 4.

3 Limor Sifman, "An Anatomy of a YouTube Meme," *New Media And Society* 12, no. 2 (2011): 187–203; Rebecca L. Stein, "StateTube: Anthropological Reflections on Social Media and the Israel State," *Anthropological Quarterly* 85, no. 3 (2012): 893–916, 893.
4 Abu Ubaida, quoted in Gavriele Fiske and Mitch Ginsburg, "IDF Blames Hamas for 'Terror Tunnel' from Gaza to Israel," *Times of Israel*, last modified October 13, 2013, paragraph 10, www.timesofisrael.com/hamas-terror-tunnel-found-running-from-gaza-to-israel/#.
5 Stein, "StateTube," 893–916.
6 Many have characterized Operation Cast Lead as the first of the "Twitter wars." See Nathalie Rothschild, "The First Twitter War," *Spiked*, last modified January 5, 2009, www.spiked-online.com/newsite/article/6076#.VAXkxfldXTo.
7 Avi Benayahu, quoted in Boaz Fyler, "IDF Says Enlisting Hackers," Yediot Aharonot, last modified February 8, 2011, paragraphs 1–3, www.ynetnews.com/articles/0,7340,L-4025751,00.html.
8 Robert Mackey, "Young Israelis Fight Hashtag Battle to Defend #IsraelUnderFire," *New York Times*, last modified July 15, 2014, www.nytimes.com/2014/07/16/world/middleeast/young-israelis-fight-hashtag-battle-to-defend-israelunderfire.html.
9 Another interpretation of the word might be simply "explaining." Israel's detractors, as one might expect, use a different nomenclature when they comment on this "hasbara." Jamil Khader, a professor of English at Bethlehem University, indicated that this was another word of Israeli "propaganda," and argues that in the face of "global solidarity with Palestinians" Israeli social media efforts have failed. Jamil Khader, "The Grand Failure of Israeli Hasbara," *Al Jazeera*, last modified August 22, 2014, www.aljazeera.com/indepth/opinion/2014/08/grand-failure-israeli-hasbara-20148221228220202.html.
10 Ian Burrell, "Israel–Gaza Conflict: Social Media Becomes the Latest Background in Middle East Aggression: But Be Beware of Propaganda and misinformation," *Independent*, last modified July 14, 2014, paragraphs 4, 7, www.independent.co.uk/news/world/middle-east/israelgaza-conflict-social-media-becomes-the-latest-battleground-in-middle-east-aggression-but-beware-of-propaganda-and-misinformation-9605952.html.
11 Anne Herzberg and Gerald M. Steinberg, "IHL 2.0: Is There a Role for Social Media in Monitoring and Enforcement?" *Israel Law Review* 45, no. 3 (2012): 493–536, 535.
12 *The Economist*, "Both Sides Consume Fantasy News" last modified August 16, 2014, paragraph 4, www.economist.com/news/middle-east-and-africa/21612240-both-sides-consume-fantasy-news-propaganda-war.
13 IDF spokesperson, quoted in Stein, "StateTube," 893.
14 See, Gerry Shih, "In Gaza, New Arsenals Include 'Weaponized' Social Media," *Reuters*, last modified November 16, 2012, www.reuters.com/article/2012/11/16/us-palestinians-israel-socialmedia-idUSBRE8AF0A020121116.
15 Ibid., paragraph 4.
16 Radhika Sanghani, "Teen Girl 'Live Tweets Gaza Bomb Attack,'" *Telegraph*, last modified July 29, 2914, www.telegraph.co.uk/women/womens-politics/10997610/Teen-Palestinian-girl-on-Twitter-live-tweets-Gaza-bomb-attack.html.
17 Sanghani, "Teen Girl Live Tweets," paragraph 4.
18 Nidal Al-Mugharabi, "Gaza Teen's War Tweets Make Her a Social Media Sensation," *Reuters*, last modified August 11, 2014, http://in.reuters.com/article/2014/08/11/mideast-gaza-twitter-idINKBN0GB0K220140811.
19 Ibid., paragraph 9.
20 Farah Baker, quoted in Yousef al-Helou, "Social Media: The Weapon of Choice in the Gaza–Israel Conflict," *Middle East Eye*, last modified August 21, 2014, www.middleeasteye.net/news/social-media-weapon-choice-gaza-israel-conflict-1807202428.

176 *Public diplomacy and social media wars*

21 Al-Helou, "Social Media," paragraph 2.
22 Evgeny Morozov, *The Net Delusion: The Dark Side of Internet Freedom* (New York: PublicAffairs, 2011).
23 Omar al-Ghazzi, quoted in John Timpane, "Israeli–Hamas Hostilities Play Out in Real Time on Social Media," *Philly.com*, last modified November 18, 2012, paragraph 20, http://articles.philly.com/2012-11-18/news/35172911_1_hamas-tweets-alqassambrigade.
24 For one of the examples of where observers think that Israeli *hasbara* is improving and that purveyors of social media in favor of Israel are moving in the right direction, see Dmitry Shapiro and Alexa Laz, "Counterattack: Israel's Information PR Blitz is Finding Its Mark," *The Jewish Chronicle*, last modified August 8, 2014, http://thejewishchronicle.net/view/full_story/25573405/article-Counterattack–Israel-s-information-PR-blitz-is-finding-its-mark?instance=news_style.
25 Morozov is a popular and prolific writer on the powers of the state to control and contain the liberatory potential of social media during events such as the Arab Spring. See, for example, Evgeny Morozov, "Tunisia, Social Media and the Politics of Attention," *Foreign Policy*, last modified January 14, 2011, http://neteffect.foreignpolicy.com/posts/2011/01/14/tunisia_social_media_and_the_politics_of_attention.
26 Eugenia Siapera, "Tweeting #Palestine: Twitter and the Mediation of Palestine," *International Journal of Cultural Studies* 17, no. 6 (2014): 539–555, DOI: 10.1177/1367877913503865.
27 Sylvia Varnham O'Regan, "A Battle for Hearts and Minds: Who's Winning Gaza's Social Media War?" *SBS*, last modified July 17, 2014, www.sbs.com.au/news/article/2014/07/17/battle-hearts-and-minds-whos-winning-gazas-social-media-war.
28 As I have noted elsewhere, Rebecca Stein has provided one of the best overviews of some of these communicative challenges. See Rebecca L. Stein, "Impossible Witness: Israeli Visuality, Palestinian Testimony and the Gaza War," *Journal for Cultural Research* 16, no. 2/3 (2012): 135–153, DOI: 10.1080/14797585.2012.647749.
29 For those who wish to study how Palestinians are using the power of social media, see Abeer Najjar, *Othering the Self: Palestinians Narrating the War on Gaza in the Social* Media (Sarjah: United Arab Emirates, n.d.).
30 Nicholas Mirzoeff, "The Right to Look," *Critical Inquiry* 37, no. 3 (2011): 475. For some of Mirzoeff's own application of some of his ideas, and those of Eyal Weisman's, to the Gaza situation, see Nicholas Mirzoeff, "The Crisis of Visuality/Visualizing the Crisis," *Hemispheric Institute e-Misférica*, n.d., http://hemisphericinstitute.org/hemi/en/e-misferica-71/mirzoeff.
31 Charles Krauthammer, "Moral Clarity in Gaza," *Washington Post*, July 17, 2014, www.washingtonpost.com/opinions/charles-krauthammer-moral-clarity-in-gaza/2014/07/17/0adabe0c-0de4-11e4-8c9a-923ecc0c7d23_story.html.
32 Susan Sontag, *Regarding the Pain of Others* (New York: Farrar, Straus & Giroux, 2003), 10.
33 Daniel Ben Simon, "In Israel, Social Media Threatens Sacred Duty," *Al-Monitor*, last modified July, 2014, www.al-monitor.com/pulse/ru/originals/2014/07/gaza-protective-edge-idf-social-media-ramon.html#.
34 The "Hannibal Directive" is a controversial military doctrine that encourages Israeli forces to do everything that they can to make sure their soldiers do not get captured or provide enemies with precious information regarding Israeli military strategizing. For more on the directive, see Max Blumenthal, "Politicide in Gaza: How Israel's Far Right Won the War," *Journal of Palestine Studies* 44, no. 1 (2014): 14–28.
35 For a fine overview of the media coverage of this particular asymmetrical war, see Marvin A. Kalb, "The Israeli–Hezbollah War of 2006: The Media as a Weapon in the Asymmetrical Conflict," *The Harvard International Journal of Press/Politics* 12, no. 3 (2007): 43–66.

36 Simon Peres, quoted in Rothschild, "The First Twitter War," paragraph 1.
37 Deborah Howell, "A War of Image and Perceptions," *Washington Post*, last modified August 13, 2006, www.washingtonpost.com/wp-dyn/content/article/2006/08/11/AR2006081101549.html.
38 Ibid., paragraph 8.
39 Robert Gehl, "What's On Your Mind? Social Media Monopolities and Noopower," *First Monday* 18, no. 3 (2013), www.firstmonday.dk/ojs/index.php/fm/article/view/4618/3421.
40 Lieutenant General William B. Caldwell IV, Dennis M. Murphy, and Anton Menning, "Learning to Leverage New Media: The Israel Defense Forces in Recent Conflicts," *Military Review* 89, no. 3 (2009): 2–10, 6. http://usacac.army.mil/CAC2/MilitaryReview/Archives/English/MilitaryReview_20090630_art004.pdf.
41 Ibid., 5.
42 Howell, "A War of Images."
43 Gideon Levy, "Gaza's Darkness," *Ha'aretz*, last modified September 3, 2006, www.haaretz.com/print-edition/opinion/gaza-s-darkness-1.196390.
44 Ibid., paragraph 2.
45 Stein, "StateTube," 908.
46 For other examples of how international journalists also viewed the 2006 Israeli campaign in Lebanon as a "public relations disaster," see Lucy Bannerman, "Officials Afraid to Get Blogged Down in Gaza," *The Australian*, last modified January 1, 2009, www.theaustralian.com.au/archive/news/afraid-of-getting-blogged-do/story-e6frg6tx-1111118448255.
47 Larence Pintak, "Gaza: Of Media World and Borderless Journalism," *Arab Media & Society* 7 (2009), paragraph 6, www.arabmediasociety.com/?article=698.
48 Stein, "StateTube," 901.
49 For studies of how this battle is taking place between various times of conflict, see Laurie Copans, "Israelis, Palestinians Battle on *Facebook*: Historic Conflict Strains and Tensions on Social Networking Site," last modified March 18, 2008, *NBCNews.com*, *MSNBC*. www.msnbc.msn.com/id/23692745; Miriyam Aouragh, "Everyday Resistance on the Internet: The Palestinian context," *Journal of Arab and Muslim Media Research* 1, no. 2 (2008): 109–130.
50 Caldwell *et al.*, "Learning to Leverage," 3.
51 Ibid., 5.
52 Naila Hamdi, "Arab Media Adopt Citizen Journalism to Change the Dynamics of Conflict Coverage," *Global Medial Journal* 1, no. 1 (2010): 3–15, 3.
53 Major Avital Leibovich, "IDF Vlog: Weapons in Mosques," *YouTube*, last modified January 3, 2009, www.youtube.com/watch?v=rfTr609whl8&feature=related. By September of 2014 this one vlog alone had been visited more than 110,000 times.
54 For an example of one international press reaction to these containment practices, see *Der Spiegel*, "Covering Gaza: Israel Shuts Out World Press," last modified January 14, 2009, www.spiegel.de/international/world/covering-gaza-israel-shuts-out-world-press-a-601217-2.html.
55 Daileda, "Israel is Losing Control," paragraph 14.
56 Bannerman, "Officials Afraid of Getting Blogged Down," paragraphs 1–2.
57 Caldwell *et al.*, "Learning to Leverage," p. 9.
58 Adi Kuntsman and Rebecca L. Stein, "Digital Suspicion, Politics, and the Middle East," *Critical Inquiry* (2011): 1–10.
59 Schactman, "Israel Kills Hamas Leader," paragraph 5.
60 Will Ward, "Social Media in the Gaza Conflict," *Arab Media & Society*, 7 (2009), paragraph 2, www.arabmediasociety.com/?article=701.
61 Kristen Nicole, "Social Media Takes Center Stage in Gaza War," *Social Times*, last modified December 31, 2008, paragraph 6, www.socialtimes.com/2008/12/social-media-gaza-war.

178 *Public diplomacy and social media wars*

62 Khaled Hroub, "Hamas After the Gaza War," *Open Democracy*, last modified January 16, 2009, www.opendemocracy.net/article/hamas-after-the-gaza-war. Hroub quotes Moshe Ya'alon as saying in 2002, when he was Israeli military chief-of-staff, that "the Palestinians must be made to understand in the deepest recesses of their consciousness that they are a defeated people" (paragraph 1).
63 Orr Hirschauge, Nicholas Case, and Lisa Fleisher, "Videos from Gaza Front Lines Going to Facebook and Twitter Streams," *Wall Street Journal*, last modified July 23, 2014, paragraph 1, http://online.wsj.com/articles/israel-and-hamas-take-fight-to-social-media-1406130179.
64 John Timpane, "Israeli–Hamas Hostilities Play Out in Real Time on Social Media," *Philly.com*, last modified November 18, 2012, http://articles.philly.com/2012-11-18/news/35172911_1_hamas-tweets-alqassambrigade.
65 Idfnadesk, "IDF Pinpoint Strike on Ahmed Jabir, Head of the Hamas Military Wing," YouTube, published on November 14, 2012, www.youtube.com/watch?v=P6U2ZQ0EhN4.
66 IDF tweet, quoted in Noah Shachtman, "Israel Kills Hamas Leader, Instantly Posts It to YouTube," *Wired*, last modified November 14, 2012, paragraph 1, www.wired.com/2012/11/idf-hamas-youtube.
67 Shachtman, "Israel Kills Hamas Leader," paragraph 2.
68 Nick Bilton, "In Israeli Attack on Hamas: Shock, Awe and Social Media," *New York Times*, last modified November 14, 2012, http://bits.blogs.nytimes.com/2012/11/14/in-israeli-attack-on-hammas-shock-awe-and-social-media.
69 IDF@IDFSpokesperson, "Ahmed Jabari: Eliminated," Twitter.com, last modified November 14, 2014, https://twitter.com/idfspokesperson/status/268795866784075776.
70 David Gritten, "Obituary: Ahmed Jabari, Hamas Commander," *BBC News*, last updated November 14, 2012, www.bbc.com/news/world-middle-east-20328270.
71 Rappler, "Israel Defense Force Live-Tweets Attack Against Hamas," *Storify*, last modified November 14, 2012, https://storify.com/rappler/israel-defense-force-live-tweets-attack-against-ha. See Robert Mackey, "Israel's Military Begins Social Media Offensive as Bombs Fall on Gaza," *New York Times*, last modified November 14, 2012, http://thelede.blogs.nytimes.com/2012/11/14/israels-military-launches-social-media-offensive-as-bombs-fall-on-gaza.
72 Dara Kerr, "How Israel and Hamas Weaponized Social Media," *Cnet.com*, last modified January 13, 2014, paragraphs 1–4, www.cnet.com/news/how-israel-and-hamas-weaponized-social-media.
73 Al Qassam Brigades, quoted in ibid., paragraph 5.
74 John Timpane, "The Social-Media Side of War," *Philly.com*, last modified July 20, 2014, paragraph 5, http://articles.philly.com/2014-07-20/news/51749894_1_social-media-war-ahmed-al-jabari-social-media.
75 Shachtman, "Israel Kills Hamas Leader," paragraph 7.
76 Isabel Kershner and Fares Akram, "Ferocious Israel Assault on Gaza Kills a Leader of Hamas," *New York Times*, last modified November 15, 2012, paragraph 7. www.nytimes.com/2012/11/15/world/middleeast/israeli-strike-in-gaza-kills-the-military-leader-of-hamas.html.
77 Timpane, "Israeli–Hamas Hostilities Play Out," paragraph 6.
78 Husick, quoted in Timpane, "Israeli–Hamas Hostilities," paragraph 15.
79 For more on Avital Lebovich, see John Herman, "Israel Defense Forces Social Media Head Defends Tweets," *BuzzFeedNews*, last modified November 16, 2012, www.buzzfeed.com/jwherrman/israel-defense-forces-social-media-head-defends-tw#165qrfn.
80 Kerr, "How Israel and Hamas Weaponized," paragraph 9.
81 Ibid., paragraph 10.
82 Gabriella Blum, quoted in Schactman, "Israel Kills Hamas Leader," paragraph 5.
83 Timpane, "Israeli–Hamas Hostilities," paragraph 17.

84 Andy Carvin, "Graphic, Awful Footage of Burnt, Dead Baby in Gaza," Twitter, last modified November 14, 2012, https://twitter.com/acarvin/status/268787402154328064.
85 Mackey, "Israel's Military Begins Social Media Offensive," paragraph 9.
86 Ibid., paragraphs 10–11.
87 Debra Kamin, "The 5 Most Lopsided Prisoner Swaps In Israeli History," *Times of Israel*, last modified June 19, 2014, www.timesofisrael.com/the-5-most-lopsided-prisoner-swaps-in-israeli-history.
88 Ruth Perl Baharir, "Israelis Launch Facebook Campaign Calling For 'Revenge' of Teens' Murders," *Ha'aretz*, last modified July 2, 2014, www.haaretz.com/news/national/1.602661.
89 Ibid., paragraphs 1–10.
90 Caroline B. Glick, "Column One: Why Israel is Losing the Information War," *The Jerusalem Post*, August 20, 2014, paragraphs 1–5, www.jpost.com/Opinion/Columnists/Column-One-Why-Israel-is-losing-the-information-war-371615.
91 Ibid., paragraph 8.
92 Ibid., paragraph 24.
93 *IDFBlog*, "Special Report: Operation Protective Edge, 2014," *IDFblog*, www.idfblog.com/operationgaza2014.
94 See IDF, Tweets, IDF@Spokesperson, https://twitter.com/IDFSpokesperson.
95 Harriet Sherwood, "Israel and Hamas Clash on Social Media," *Guardian*, last modified July 16, 2014, paragraph 5, www.theguardian.com/world/2014/jul/16/israel-hamas-clash-social-media.
96 Ibid., paragraph 13.
97 Adam Horowitz, "Video: Diane Sawyer Misrepresents Photo of Gazans in Aftermath of Israeli Bombing as Israeli Victims of Missile Strikes," *Mondoweiss*, last modified July 9, 2014, http://mondoweiss.net/2014/07/misrepresents-aftermath-palestinian.
98 Ibid., paragraph 4.
99 *B'Tselem*, "Ruins in Beit Hanoun," August 2014, www.btselem.org/photoblog/20140810_beit_hanun.
100 Suhair Shabat, quoted in *B'Tselem*, "Suhair Shabat Describes Mortal Fear of Bombing, Leading Her to Take Her Children and Flee Beit Hanoun," last modified July 14, 2014, www.btselem.org/testimonies/20140714_gaza_suhair_shabat.
101 Jodi Rudoren, "Hamas Emerges Buoyant Despite Bloodshed and Devastation in Gaza," *New York Times*, last modified September 3, 2014, www.nytimes.com/2014/09/04/world/middleeast/israel-gaza-hamas-fatah-.html.
102 Ibid., paragraph 4.
103 Jonathan D. Haevi, "Hamas's Attack Tunnels: Analysis and Initial Implications," Jerusalem Center for Public Affairs, July 22, 2014, http://jcpa.org/hamas-attack-tunnels.
104 Mitch Ginsburg, "How Hamas Dug Its Gaza 'Terror Tunnel,' and How the IDF Found It," *Times of Israel*, last modified October 16, 2013, www.timesofisrael.com/how-the-tunnels-in-gaza-are-dug-and-detected.
105 Gavriele Fiske and Mitch Ginsburg, "IDF Blames Hamas for 'Terror Tunnel' From Gaza to Israel," *Times of Israel*, last modified October 13, 2013, www.timesofisrael.com/hamas-terror-tunnel-found-running-from-gaza-to-israel/#.
106 Shlmo Turgeman, quoted in Fiske and Ginsburg, "IDF Blames Hamas," paragraph 4.
107 James T. Conway, "The Moral Chasm Between Israel and Hamas," *Wall Street Journal*, last modified July 24, 2014, http://online.wsj.com/articles/james-t-conway-the-moral-chasm-between-israel-and-hamas-1406243128.
108 See, for example, Israel Defense Forces, "Israel Under Fire," IDFBlog.com, n.d., www.idfblog.com/facts-figures/rocket-attacks-toward-israel.

180 Public diplomacy and social media wars

109 See Nicholas Pelham, "Gaza's Tunnel Phenomenon: The Unintended Dynamics of Israel's Siege," *Journal of Palestine Studies* 41, no. 4 (2012): 6–31.
110 Israel Ministry of Foreign Affairs, "Behind the Headlines: Hamas Terror Tunnels," *Israel Ministry of Foreign Affairs*, last modified July 22, 2014, http://mfa.gov.il/MFA/ForeignPolicy/Issues/Pages/Hamas-terror-tunnels.aspx.
111 Ibid., paragraph 4.
112 Ibid., paragraphs 3–4.
113 Ibid., paragraphs 10.
114 Ibid., paragraphs 8–11.
115 Ibid.
116 James Verini "Gaza's Tunnels, Now Used to Attack Israel, Began as Economic Lifelines," *National Geographic*, last modified July 21, 2014, paragraph 22, http://news.nationalgeographic.com/news/2014/07/140721-gaza-strip-tunnels-israel-hamas-palestinians.
117 Ibid., paragraph 22.
118 The aura that swirled around Shalit iconography would have portentous consequences. For more on the role that visualities and remembrances of Shalit have played in Israeli–Palestinian relations, see Rachel Somerstein, "On Liminality and Loss: A Decade of Israeli and Palestinian Film," *Visual Studies* 29, no. 1 (2014): 94–98, DOI: 10.1080/1472586X.2014.862998. On the nationalistic, mythic importance of the Israel preoccupation with getting back missing Israeli soldiers, see Danny Kaplan, "Commemorating as Suspended Death: Missing Soldiers and National Solidarity in Israel," *American Ethnologist*, 35, no. 3 (2008): 413–427, DOI: 10.1111/j.1548-1425.2008.00043.x.
119 Israel Ministry of Foreign Affairs, "Behind the Headlines," paragraphs 17–20.
120 Israel Ministry of Foreign Affairs, "The Hamas Covenant: Selected Excerpts," last modified November 19, 2012, http://mfa.gov.il/MFA/ForeignPolicy/Terrorism/Palestinian/Pages/Hamas_Covenant-Excerpts.aspx.
121 Pfeffer, "Hamas is Losing On the Battlefield But Hitting Israel Where It Hurts," *Ha'aretz*, last modified July 24, 2014, www.haaretz.com/israel-news/.premium-1.606903.
122 Ibid., paragraph 3.
123 Ibid., paragraph 4.
124 Ibid., paragraph 4.
125 Ibid., paragraph 8.
126 *Ha'aretz*, "Watch: IDF Video of Soldiers Finding Weapons in a Gaza Tunnel," *Ha'aretz*, last modified July 24, 2014, www.haaretz.com/news/video/1.607026.
127 Naftali Bennett, quoted in William Booth, Sudarsan Raghavan and Ruth Eglash, "More Than 100 Palestinians Dead in Worst Day of Gaza Conflict," *Washington Post*, last modified July 21, 2014, paragraph 33, www.washingtonpost.com/world/israel-begins-heaviest-bombardment-yet-in-gaza-sending-residents-fleeing/2014/07/20/578ae882-0fe5-11e4-8c9a-923ecc0c7d23_story.html.
128 Eytan Buchman, quoted in ibid., paragraphs 34–35.
129 Verini "Gaza's Tunnels," paragraph 8.
130 Michael B. Mukasey, "Tunnels Matter More than Rockets to Hamas," *Wall Street Journal*, last modified July 20, 2014, http://online.wsj.com/articles/michael-mukasey-tunnels-matter-more-than-rockets-to-hamas-1405894408.
131 Tom Cohen, "CNN's Wolf Blitzer Goes into a Hamas Tunnel," *CNN*, last modified July 30, 2014, www.cnn.com/2014/07/28/world/meast/israel-gaza-tunnels-wolf.
132 Kerr, "How Israel and Hamas Weaponized," paragraph 7.
133 James Der Derian, quoted in Sylvia Varnham O'Regan, "A Battle for Hearts and Minds: Who's Winning Gaza's Social Media War?" *SBS*, last modified July 17, 2014, paragraph 51, www.sbs.com.au/news/article/2014/07/17/battle-hearts-and-minds-whos-winning-gazas-social-media-war.

134 Sherwood, "Israel and Hamas Clash," paragraph 3.
135 Ibid., paragraph 4.
136 Gon Ben-Ari, "Sex, War, Social Media and the Israel Imagination," *Forward*, last modified August 6, 2014 paragraph 3, http://forward.com/articles/203551/sex-war-social-media-and-the-israeli-imagination/?p=all.
137 Ibid., paragraphs 1–7.
138 Ibid., paragraphs 10–20.
139 Sherwood, "Israel and Hamas Clash."
140 Netanyahu, in Jod Rudoren, "Tunnels Lead Right to the Heart of Israeli Fear," *New York Times*, July 28, 2014, www.nytimes.com/2014/07/29/world/middleeast/tunnels-lead-right-to-heart-of-israeli-fear.html.

7 There are no "innocent civilians" in Gaza

Coping with post-human framings of the Gaza Strip

Let me begin this chapter by noting from the outset that I am one of those who believe that the State of Israel "proper," behind the Green Line, is an existential reality. Hamas spokespersons hurt the Palestinian cause when they talk or write about annihilating or dismantling Israel, and that is as problematic as arguing that there is no Palestinian ethnic community or nation-state.

The French historian Ernest Renan famously argued that national amnesia and collective public forgetting are all a part of national imaginaries and identity formation,[1] and the residents of Gaza who suffered through OPE are just some of those who have confronted this type of political revision. "There is no such thing as Palestinians ... they did not exist" then-Prime Minister Golda Meir confidently proclaimed in 1969.[2] Decades later, during the debates that took place over the meaning of OPE, Giora Eiland echoed these remarks when he argued that, in Gaza today, there is no such thing as "innocent civilians."[3]

If Palestinians in the diaspora have any hopes of helping their brothers and sisters in Gaza or in the West Bank then they need to critique this type of revisionism and they need to steadfastly defend viable plans for two-state solutions. They need not adopt utopian calls for one-state solutions that would marginalize Israelis, nor do they need to adopt nihilistic creeds for totalizing warfare that would do little to help with Palestinian dispossession. I have no interest in joining the ranks of those who try to gain some illusory ideological leverage by adopting utopian Palestinian schemes that involve massive transfers of populations that would take us back to the days before the Israeli "war of independence." In a fair world my own Palestinian relatives, who live on several continents, would have an unqualified right of return that would look much like the Israelis' right of return for Jews, but we do not live in a fair world. Disparate power relationships, and the lack of foreign interventionism, means that all of the parties involved need to place a premium on compromise. Not feigned compromise, but actual negotiations that involves some Israeli return of occupied territories.

Although I empathize with those who wish to protect a universal Palestinian "right of return" for all of those who suffered from the Nakba and their descendants, we need to keep in mind that this would mean that more than six million people would be allowed to return to Israel "proper" and the West Bank. The

Israelis, who have been keeping a keen eye on relative demographics since at least 1948, are not about to let this happen. The monthly reports of settler expansion, the destruction of Arab cemeteries (Mamilla, etc.), Palestinian homes in Jerusalem, and incursions into Gaza by Israeli military forces only complements the efforts of Israeli diplomats, who can always claim that ending terrorist threats is a precondition for serious negotiations. The Israelis, as one might imagine, get to decide the nature and scope of those perceived threats, and all of this circular logic means that only outside pressure can help with the implementation of any workable two-state solutions.

I respect the *realpolitik* limits of having to deal with nuclear powers like Israel and the United States, who often have politicians, military leaders, and empowered civil servants who can appropriate and co-opt human rights rhetorics and international humanitarian law (IHL) principles so they can effectively arm themselves for all types of lawfare. If pragmatic Palestinians want to live to see the day that they have their own nation-state, and not just the subservient PA, they need to adopt non-threatening rhetorics that resonate with so many international cosmopolitan or liberal communities. We need UN interventionism, and Arab peacekeeping forces from regional communities to ensure that fewer rockets are directed toward Israel. Only then can we break the impasse that allows the continued blockading of Gazan shores.

This type of roadmap for peace is not something that would be welcomed by Israeli forces that have the upper hand and see no need to relinquish any land. A host of other difficulties will confront those who want the recognition of a divided Jerusalem, the dismantling of some Israeli settlements in the West Bank, and the formation of a unified PA government that would include Fatah and Hamas parliamentarians.[4] This would be a modified version of the proposals that take us back to the "Green line," before the 1967 Six-Day War, and the Palestinians would guarantee the security of Israel by policing and stopping those who fire rockets into Israel. These theoretical plans are endangered each and every time some Hamas rocket is fired in the direction of some Israeli settlement or town.

Are there any signs at all, textually or visually, that this particular Israeli generation is going to give up the idea of keeping "Judea" and "Samaria" in the name of ending terrorist threats? The circulation of hegemonic rhetorics, that are produced by military, political, and social mainstream and social media outlets, ensures that Israeli national identity depends on seeing Palestinian resistance as a continuation of historical anti-Semitism, Holocaust denialism, and collective terrorism. Many Israeli decision-makers and publics like to argue that they are willing to negotiate for peace, but as I have noted throughout this book they have little reason to part with what they have.

From a post-structural or post-colonial standpoint one could argue that the Israelis seem to believe that they live their daily lives in a constant state of exception, and they are resigned to the fact that they are better off *not negotiating* with either the PA or Hamas. They can continue arguing that the 2005 disengagement from Gaza was a major concession, and this helps deflect attention away from their violent dispossessions on the West Bank. Given the power of their military, and the backing of the United States, why should Israelis compromise when no international communities—ICC, NGOs, single nation-states, etc.—dare interfere with their rhetorical defense of "Greater Israel"? After all, the West Bank, with all of its A, B, and C categories, has been domesticated, so why not continue to just wear down the Gazans to the point where they will be traumatized and leave the Gaza Strip? If the place becomes entirely uninhabitable, this can always be blamed on Hamas.

Interestingly enough, it appears that one of the few chinks in the Israeli psychosocial armor comes in the form of their own perceptional need to appear before the international community as counterterrorist leaders and the anchor for democracies in the region. This means that although the Israelis can physically act with impunity when they bomb Gaza or send in troops to go after the "terror" tunnels, they want to be perceived as backers of the "most moral" military forces in the world and not as reactionaries. This is why they use their hasbara to try to find a way of legitimating the *collective punishment of Gazans*, and they are now busily assembling the counterterrorist frameworks that will help accomplish that task.

For defenders of Israeli military exceptionalism, talking and writing about the "military" wing of Hamas will not suffice. In the immediate aftermath of the latest Israeli withdrawal from Gaza in early August 2014, former Major General Giora Eiland published a very revealing op-ed piece entitled "In Gaza, There is No Such Thing as 'Innocent Civilians.'"[5] Eiland was bothered by what he perceived to be the schizophrenic Israeli approaches to Gazan populations, who were treated as both members of an enemy state as well as the worthy recipients of Israeli food and energy. He viewed all of this as "absurd," and argued that regardless of how Operation Protective Edge (OPE) might turn out, the topic of the Hamas tunnels was just one facet of a much more complex "strategic" question that he believed needed to be answered, and answered consistently, by Israelis. That question, Eiland averred, revolved around the issue of whether Israel was going to avoid falling into what he called the "asymmetry trap," where Israelis failed to see that the "story" the Israelis were telling during OPE was very similar to the one that was once told during the intervention in Lebanon in 2006.[6] Yet Eiland may have underestimated the rhetorical power of the Israeli social media this time around.

Several weeks before the withdrawal of Israeli soldiers from Gaza there were countless internet commentaries from Israeli detractors that explained how all of the attacks on Hamas homes and infrastructures looked like the latest iteration of the Dahiya doctrine, but several analysts of Israeli decision-making responded that OPE had its own unique geopolitics that had little to do with that older doctrine. Yet Giora Eiland's op-ed provided one of many indicators that there seemed to be an uncanny convergence, and rehabilitation, taking place as older theories and twenty-first-century military practices melded together in some representative Israeli commentaries on civilian culpability in Gaza.

Since at least the time of the beginning of the second Intifada, Israelis had been searching for just the right rhetorics to deploy, and their framing of the "terror" tunnels seemed to do the trick. The threat magnification that came from talk of both Hamas rockets and the terror tunnels appealed to many supporters of Israeli policies outside of Israel and helped explain why they still worried about their survival and rights of self-defense.

Some readers may vehemently disagree with Giora Eiland's assessment and his framing of the current situation, but he should be commended for honestly expressing opinions that needed to be aired in order to be evaluated and critiqued. For example, he argued that in spite of the IDF's "impressive fighting," it looked as though the Israelis and Hamas by early August 2014 were in some sort of "strategic tie."[7] Eiland was convinced that this was because the wrong decisions had been made about how to fight this asymmetrical war. If anything, the Israelis were acting with too much restraint, and Eiland had a clear idea of what had gone wrong:

> What would have been the right thing to do? We should have declared war against the state of Gaza (rather than against the Hamas organization).... The moment it begins, the right thing to do is to shut down the crossings, prevent the entry of any goods, including food, and definitely prevent the supply of gas and electricity. In a war between states, each side is entitled to use its ability to pressure the other side. The fact that we are fighting with one hand and supplying food and energy to the enemy state with the other hand is absurd. This generosity strengthens and extends the ability of the enemy state of Gaza to fight us.[8]

As far as Eiland was concerned the Israelis were practicing a form of what international relations scholars call "moral hazard," where humanitarian aid simply prolongs a conflict. Was this the time when Israelis finally needed to admit that there were no civilians in Gaza?

Eiland realized that this might not sit well with some Israelis who considered themselves to be compassionate, so he prepared some ready-made answers to the traditional queries that might be posed by those who were reluctant to engage in totalizing forms of warfare. For example, he adapted to his audiences' cultural and ideological expectations by arguing that the Gazan residents should suffer because "this situation" was "just like Germany's residents" who were "to blame for electing Hitler as their leader." In the same way that the Germans had "paid a high price," so should the populations in Gaza.[9] In theory, the cutting off of any supplies would hurt those who should be punished for their transgressions. By being compassionate toward "those cruel people," argued Eiland, the Israeli authorities were "committing to acting cruelly towards the really compassionate people—the residents of the State of Israel."[10]

This twenty-first-century form of securitized argumentation had many twentieth-century antecedent genres—rhetorics filled with talk of harsh interpretations of just war doctrines, calls for totalizing war, worries about moral hazards from humanitarians, etc., and as I have been pointing out since Chapter 1 these types of arguments mushroomed after the beginning of the second Intifada and they resonated with many diverse Israeli audiences.

Only time will tell if other Israelis will openly express similar sentiments, and we will have to wait and see how many vocal diplomats, civil administrators, and members of the public will not only condone, but applaud, the collective punishment of civilian populations in Gaza. We got inklings of these attitudes in my earlier chapters on targeted killings, OPE, and social media weaponization.

What I will argue here is that Israelis perhaps sense that what is going on is a battle of wills, where the Palestinians in Gaza, as well as the members of Hamas, are performatively expressing the Arabic notion of "*samud*," of steadfastness, that simply infuriates many Israelis—who believe that they are the ones who are resolute. Arguments like Eiland's remind Palestinians that many Israelis wish that Gazans would just "move along" (Jacques Rancière), where one does not struggle and one acknowledges and gives in to the policing powers of the empowered.[11] In Palestinian–Israeli relational contexts, Israelis often argue that if stateless Palestinians wanted electricity, they would dump Hamas, or leave the Gaza Strip, or travel to places like Jordan, Lebanon, Egypt, Iraq or Syria. Left unsaid was the real possibility that they would always be treated as if they had second-class citizenship within what is marketed as a democratic, Zionist, and Jewish Israeli state.

The subtext here is that Israel, after 2005, was not only physically disengaging from Gaza, it was also unilaterally leaving behind the babble of utopian peace talks. Sadly, the implication here is that peace talks can be configured as the weapons of the weak, a form of lawfare where the proffering of either Palestinian one-state or two-state solutions was *always* going to threaten the survival of Greater Israel.

West Bank Palestinians, with their Palestinian Authority (PA) and their more "moderate" communities had individuals who occasionally could be reasoned with—and, as noted by many scholars, at times they even provided collaborators in the war against terrorism. In this bifurcated geographic imaginary, Palestinians living in Gaza seemed to be the standard barriers of a more militant, and a more strident, form of nihilistic Palestinian nationalism. They were forming what Benedict Anderson has called "imagined communities,"[12] and he specifically mentioned the great transcontinental truths and solidarities of believers in the "Islamic Ummah."[13] Some of the Palestinian versions may be more provincial and recognizable, but they were nevertheless tied to matters of honor, statehood, and victimhood.

The Israelis, however, were unwilling to countenance the idea of living next to the democratically elected "Hamas regime." This meant that Gazans were not citizens of any sovereign state, and this in turn implied that when they did not flee their homes during aerial bombardments they were automatically the legitimate targets of naval artillery, drones, or Israeli tanks.

Talk of "mowing the lawn" was just one of the idiomatic phrases that could be used to indicate that after compassion fatigue set in, the tourists would flock back to the Israeli beaches, the Gazans would continue to rely on the largesse of the UN, and the rest of the world would pass meaningless paper-tiger declarations and conduct investigations that went nowhere.

Many Palestinians, regardless of their gender, their social class, their political allegiances, or their religion, understand the symbolic importance of the Gaza Strip.

It may indeed by an "open prison," an area filled with dependent refugees, an experimental place for urban warfare, etc., but it is also the topographical land of Palestinian imaginaries, where the slightest gesture of defiance in the face of overwhelming Israeli military power transforms Gazans into today's Warsaw Ghetto fighters.[14]

The more that Israelis refuse to bargain with Hamas and find viable political solutions to these problems, the more that they face growing numbers of disaffected Palestinians who will continue to demand all sorts of "rights." The daily, varied performances of *samud*—that may come in the form of requests for electricity, calling for an end to blockades, voting for Hamas, staying in one's home in the face of danger, demanding Palestinian citizenship, or even treating refugee status as evidence of historical wounds—have everything to do with political identities in Gaza.[15]

Israelis can figure this steadfastness as support for terrorism, especially in cases where they refuse to discuss the possibility that they are still occupiers who need to recognize IHL rights. Eiland's claim that there are no civilians in Gaza can easily become an argumentative thread that is woven into previous tapestries with layered claims that there is no Palestine. Military attempts at cultural erasure just add more securitizing rationales to a surfeit of historiographies that already render invisible Palestinian heritages, land rights, and cultures.

All of this talk of cutting off Israeli largesse, and fighting with one hand behind one's back—that have disseminated over the years in Israeli circles in everything from Israeli Supreme Court opinions to the lay person's discussions of how to carry out Operation Cast Lead or OPE—can be linked to more legalistic or militaristic discourses about the use of "disproportionate" force when you are fighting such an obstinate people.

This mélange of cultural assumptions, political goals, and military strategizing is not new. Rhetorical commentary on the invincible nature of the Israeli Iron Dome missile defense system[16] becomes the latest manifestation of Ze'ev Jabotinsky's 1920s dream of Zionist colonies that would have the protection of *Die Eiserne Wand*, "the iron wall,"[17] that would be made of Jewish bayonets.[18] All of this talk of controlling food, electricity, buildings, etc., gives credence to Helga Tawil-Souri's claims that "Israel's increasingly globalized security–military–high tech industry" includes the "technological sealing of Gaza" as part of the transformation of the "mechanics of Israeli occupation" toward "frictionless" control that began with the first Intifada.[19]

Eiland's stance, that puts on full display some of the antipathy that animates many incursions into Gaza, is troublesome in many ways, including the fact that it makes it appear as if the military deployment of massive force, that may target civilian populations, is a humanitarian act because it is rationalized as a technique for saving Israeli lives. All of this assumes the priority of the usage of Israeli definitions of *jus ad bellum* and *jus in bello* principles that go against the grain of most global interpretations that indicate that protecting civilians should always be one of the first priorities of those who wage "just wars." Israeli "force protection" thus clashes with international arguments about civilian protection.

The worry here is that the erosion of traditional protections for civilians in Gaza, and the acceptance of Israeli interpretations of IHL or human rights law will have dire consequences for many denizens of the world, including those who live in the Gaza Strip. If we follow Eiland's logic, and blur the lines between the military armies of the world and their civilian populations, then we regress back to the colonial days when colonizers were retaliating against populations during declared "emergencies."[20] Palestinian hardline fighters, for example, could use this same operative logic and argue that the presence of any weapon in any Israeli home or settlement transforms that home into a targetable "infrastructure." This leads to cyclical violence and goes nowhere.

If we deny civilian status to Gazan populations, based on mythic visualities from the IDF and elsewhere, then we will be in danger of entering the murky realm of what Vik Kanwar calls "post-human humanitarian law,"[21] where weapons and their legal rationales are rendered visible while we hide the older interpretations of IHL, like the Geneva Convention that once protected noncombatants. As Christian Enemark has recently noted, the defense of some of these "post-human" ideas of military virtue are borne out by a desire to reduce risk to one's own troops, but this means a transfer of risk onto civilian populations.[22]

By magnifying the biopolitical importance of force-protecting Israeli soldiers and civilians, and by vilifying those who are considered to be part of the civilian "infrastructure," defenders of hardline policies see nothing wrong with declaring war on populations in place of individual Hamas rocketeers. These aggressive militaristic framings, that conceptualize the Gazan populations as a tragic but obvious enemy force, twist the principles of distinction, proportionality, necessity, or humanity in ways that highlight the need to prioritize the protection of the aggressors who send their naval artillery shells, their drones, and their tank shells in the direction of targets that they can always claim had human shields. Who, after all, is privy to the secret target lists that designate a person as a Hamas terrorist? Who can challenge the findings of the Israeli Secret Services or the IDL or anyone else who declares with impunity that this or that person has lost their civilian status by participating in hostilities?

Both American and Israeli writers of law reviews can fill up rooms with abstract discussions that justify the targeting of those who allegedly aid and abet terrorists, but they end up becoming state apologists when they simply parrot back the findings of Israelis who argue that they are the ones who have the expertise to separate out the "moderate" and "political" Palestinians from the "terrorist" and "militant" ones.

Sadly, Eiland's stance on civilians can also be used by many other rhetors who have other reasons for vilifying Gazan populations. Israelis are not the only ones who worry about Hamas and the spread of some forms of terrorism. Egyptians, for example, since President Abdel Fattah al-Sisi took control of

Coping with post-human framings 189

the government in Cairo, now echo some of the lamentations of American and Israeli observers when they remind us that Hamas is an offshoot of the older Egyptian Muslim Brotherhood, an organization that has been criminalized in Egypt.[23] This, as I note below, makes it more difficult to find political or economic solutions for what are consistently called "intractable" Gazan problems.

As I hinted at in previous chapters, it is also no coincidence that all of this discourse regarding the potential culpability of Gazan civilians is circulating at the very time economists, political scientists, demographers, and others are keeping an eye on the growing resource needs of more than six million Israelis. Rising incomes, and growing demands from mobile aspirants who want to improve their lifestyles, make it easier to contrast the activities of those who make deserts bloom with those dependent refugees and others who don't deserve any Israeli electricity.

Granted, the introduction of virtual and visual technologies during the twenty-first century will inevitably mean we will confront sea changes and paradigmatic shifts in the ways we think about civilian responsibilities and rights, but readers would be remiss if they overlook the ways that Israeli arguers want to have a major say in the directionality of those shifts. Instead of bowing to international pressures and accepting "hearts and minds" law of armed conflict interpretations that are population-centric, they openly defend more and more force-protection rules that try to prevent the spilling of the blood of Israeli soldiers.

Recently, in the wake of new revelations that William Schabas would head a new UN Gaza Inquiry Commission,[24] the Israelis have responded by preparing what they call the "legal iron dome," where they will be defending those who manned the aerial missile defense systems that are believed to be protecting millions from rocket attacks.[25] As I noted in earlier chapters, all of this gets caught up in a complex dynamic of lawfare and counterlawfare.

Given the realities of twenty-first-century geopolitics in the Middle East, few will take seriously the UN Human Rights Commission's Navi Pillay's well-intentioned call that Israel's (and the United States') Iron Dome technologies be shared with Palestinians in order to deter illegal aggression in this region. So if interdisciplinary critics are going to try to find non-violent solutions to Gazan problems, they need to come up with other alternatives at the same time that they deconstruct Israeli military doctrines and jurisprudential lawfare rhetorics.

Although there are a number of heuristic approaches that might be taken in efforts to align academics with these peaceful ventures, I would like readers to consider these six major arguments, or theses, as they contemplate how to prevent another recurrence of something like OPE. Simply labeling problems as intractable and "moving on" will not suffice, especially when we are bombarded with so many post-human rhetorics. I therefore advance what I realize will be some contentious claims:

1 Future Israeli, Palestinian, and international publics and elite decision-makers must recognize the ontological existence of both refugee and humanitarian crises in Gaza.

2 There must be recognition that international humanitarian legal rhetorics can be used and abused, and that some nationalistic interpretations of IHL hinder the spread of egalitarian human rights for the disempowered.
3 If the UN, EU, ICC, Arab League, etc. are going to help resolve the refugee and humanitarian crises mentioned above, they will need to apply the "responsibility to protect" (R2P) doctrine in Gazan contexts.
4 There must be some recognition by many global parties that Hamas needs to be viewed as a legitimate political entity.
5 Cosmopolitan critics of aggressive warfighting during Gazan incursions need to keep an eye on the potential effectiveness of the growing Palestinian boycott, divestment, and sanctions (BDS) campaign.[26]
6 Promotion of an efficacious two-state solution may be the only way to guarantee Palestinian citizenship and security for both Israelis and Palestinians during the rest of the twenty-first century.

All of these potential solutions are fraught with their own unique problems, but given the horrific day-to-day conditions in Gaza, and the legal defenses that are advanced by those who support continuous Israeli incursions, it is hoped that at least some empowered international decision-makers will overcome some of their compassion fatigue. They will need to see some of the telegenic coverage of what is happening in Gaza through a humanistic lens that encourages us to avoid the spilling of more Israeli and Palestinian blood. As I noted in Chapter 5, no one has a monopoly on the thanatopolitical politics of these tragic affairs, and the sooner we find ways of deterring all militarization of these conflicts, the better.

In the rest of this concluding chapter, I will discuss the lawfare and warfare features of each of these six theses, and along the way I will point out some of the Israeli responses to these initiatives. At the same time I will highlight some of the contradictions, potentialities, and limitations of these options, especially in situations where they invite us to take different stances on one-state and two-state solutions.

International decision-makers, Israeli recalcitrance, and the lingering refugee problem in Gaza

One of the perceptual dangers that comes from the aftermath of military incursions into Gaza is that they sometimes deflect attention away from the chronic problems of those who have been living in that region during more "peaceful" times.

As Ilan Feldman explained in 2007, those who study the Quaker and UN relief efforts after the formation of Israel know that humanitarian "distinctions came to have political significance within the Palestinian community, as people sought to claim a space for themselves in the post-Nakba landscape."[27]

The structural and material problems of the Palestinians living in the refugee camps, as well as the challenges that confronted those living in Gaza City and elsewhere, did not disappear as global audiences were presented with images of destroyed city blocks during OPE. We need to remember that during times of war, when heated passions are aroused by loss of loved ones, we tend to forget the complex, inherently politicized nature of the nominalism that is used to decide whether a situation even warrants the label of being a "humanitarian crisis." Just because the UN, or some major NGO like Human Rights Watch or Amnesty International, labels something a crisis does not make it so in the eyes of those who feel threatened by that type of speech act. Those who worry about what they view of the "politicization of human rights," explained Neve Gordon in 2014, now try to treat "human rights as a security threat," and some Israelis belittle the efforts of B'Tselem and other activist organizations that are considered to be as threatening as Hamas rockets.[28]

Those who attempt to securitize these Palestinian–Israeli debates can find many reasons for questioning the existence of a refugee crisis, its historical and contemporary causes, and its solutions. For example, critics of some of the decision-making of Palestinians living in Gaza can complain that UN efforts are often one-sided, and not in Israel's best interests. The conversations about the inherent unfairness of the Goldstone Report, or the dangers that are posed by using universal jurisdiction arguments to go after Israeli generals or politicians, can be supplemented by complaints that disaster relief organizations are often working hand-in-hand with the very populations that elect Hamas terrorists. Israeli Deputy Foreign Minister Danny Ayalon once raised the concern that "today the trenches are in Geneva in the Council of Human Rights, or in New York in the General Assembly, or in the Security Council, or in the Hague," and he invited exploring the possibility that "international human rights day has been transformed into terror rights day."[29] This type of lawfare, or Israeli "counter-lawfare," is used to underscore the point that for many Israelis it was bewildering to think that so many outside of Israel misunderstood enemy prevarications.

Readers need to see how some of this militarization and securitization talk can impact the lives of the Palestinian refugees who are living in the Gaza Strip. They, too, are suffering from the privations of war, but they were not leading an easy life before all of these incursions. This can be overlooked by those who complain about UN lawfare, that spills over into the blame games that are used to argue that the magnitude of Palestinian refugee problems are exacerbated, perhaps caused by, the biopolitics of the UN. Those who over the years have used ration cards, determined "need" categorization schemes, or made other "difficult distinctions" (Ilana Feldman) have influenced who received aid from the old American Friends Service Committee (the Quakers), or the UN Relief and Works Agency for Palestine Refugees in the Near East (UNRWA), that was established in 1950.

Talk of warfare can easily hide the elision of competing refugee genealogies as rhetors talk about aid dependency, terrorists allied with dispensers of aid, or the misidentification of those who are truly needy. How quickly some forget the role the UN played in the very formation of Israel, the redrawing of geopolitical boundaries, and the aid that Israelis have received from US and European shores since the late 1940s.

In some cases, recent attacks on the continued "dependency" of Gazan refugees can be viewed as very transparent, twenty-first-century ways of attacking the identity politics of Palestinian nationalists.[30] Anxieties about NGO and UN support for some Palestinian initiatives can be especially worrisome to those who believe they are already fighting an asymmetrical conflict where the Iron Dome protects today's Davids against the Palestinian Goliaths. The resonance of these dominant securitizing frames, and the existence of multi-causal discussions of refugee situations, can quickly regress into complaints about speech acts that deflect attention away from the role Israelis have played in the formation and maintenance of these refugee camps. Granted, they are not the sole social agents who could have helped ameliorate conditions, but talking about the limited nature of Israeli responsibilities in the aftermath of the "belligerent occupation" or "disengagement" does not help.

For those readers who might argue that few really dispute the fact that a refugee crisis actually exists in Gaza, let me provide just one typical example of a rhetorical fragment filled with all kinds of hermeneutics of suspicion, an essay produced by Asaf Romirowsky, who wrote in May 2014 on "the Real Palestinian Crisis."[31] This author starts by admitting that many diplomats and researchers have concluded that questions regarding the "right of return" have presented some of the thorniest issues in Israeli–Palestinian debates. Romirowsky begins by making a fair point, that Israelis cannot agree to an absolutely guaranteed right of return to all aggrieved Palestinians because that would "effectively destroy Israel as a Jewish state."[32] He then makes a categorical claim that is more controversial when he asserts that "the Palestinians have steadfastly refused to compromise on this issue." This self-serving remark ignores the fact that Palestinians are themselves divided on the question of whether to pursue one-state or two-state solutions.

Romirowsky's critique of an absolute right of return may indeed represent the posture of a vocal minority of Palestinians, but the vast majority of Palestinians realize that a qualified right of return for those displaced after the 1967 Six-Day War, or a guaranteed right to return to the West Bank or to Gaza, may be the best they can hope for given current circumstances. Most Palestinians, I would argue, realize that it is a fool's errand to try to reterritorialize Israel "proper," behind the Green Line.

Romirowsky's essay masquerades as some objective investigatory study of refugee and NGO abuses, but it is actually a typical diatribe that tries to magnify the existential security threats that allegedly confront Israelis. Here, the focus is not on Hamas rockets, but on the UN humanitarian organizations and the Palestinian aid recipients who are caught up in a vicious cycle of co-dependency. When one decodes Romirowsky's essay on the "real" crisis, one finds that what is really being targeted here are the refugee discourses that he sees as facilitating the maintenance of "Palestinian identity." In one key segment of his essay he notes that UN policies have contributed to a situation where "Palestinians are, individually and communally, refugees." As if this wasn't bad enough, Romirowsky implies that many of these Palestinians have become dependent on the

UN Relief and Works Agency for Palestine Refugees in the Near East, and that UNRWA has, over the years, established direct ties with terrorist organizations.[33] These fragmenting strategies are a not-so-veiled attempt at ridiculing the notion that Palestinians will ever have their own nation-state.

In many ways Romirowsky's rhetoric can be viewed as a variant of military humanitarian rhetorics that are growing increasingly popular as both elites and publics measure and evaluate the importance of "new humanitarian" aid in relation to nationalistic and militaristic goals. Instead of focusing attention on the deaths of thousands of refugees over the years, and the history of dispossession that has been chronicled by writers such as Avi Shlaim,[34] Simha Flapan,[35] Benny Morris,[36] and Ilan Pappé,[37] Romirowsky finds a way of complaining about what is "essentially a massive social welfare system serving millions of Palestinians, primarily in the West Bank, Lebanon, Syria, and Jordan."[38] This kind of rhetoric is then used to ask why other refugees, in other locales around the world, aren't treated in similar fashion.

While Romirowsky doesn't go so far as to argue that none of these Palestinian refugees are in dire need of aid, he does construct a securitizing narrative that implies that they do little to prevent their own dependency. Moreover, he accuses the UNRWA of providing more than "simple humanitarianism" and of playing a political role in Palestinian society as they work on furthering the cause of Palestinian nationalism. This, Romirowsky argues, constructs a type of dystopic co-dependency where the refugees become the UNRWA's *raison d'être*, while the refugees do little themselves to help prevent the exacerbation of "the refugee problem." All of this, explains Romirowsky, makes any Israeli–Palestinian peace process almost impossible.[39] While he doesn't go into great detail explaining how this impacts the ending of blockades, the prevention of incursions, etc., it does allow him to tell visitors of his blog site that the UNRWA has no incentive to resolve the refugee problem because that would mean the organization would become obsolete.

As usual, these types of securitizing rhetorics about refugee aid do contain a kernel of truth—this particular dependency has gone on for too long. At the same time, it may be fair to argue that the UNRWA has indeed become a political actor in all of these geopolitics. As Ilana Feldman has noted, these enduring refugee crises have involved "social resentments, cooperation, contestations that emerged from the intersection of humanitarian relief and difficult conditions,"[40] but that does not mean the refugees suffer any less from concrete and demonstrable crises. All of this human suffering, during times of peace and war, involve more than just the telegenics that Prime Minister Netanyahu was complaining about.

As Niva Gordon recently pointed out, what is really going on here is that motivated stakeholders have as their objective the limiting of the "scope and impact of rights work carried out by liberal human rights NGOs so as to enable primarily Israel and the United States to carry out military campaigns unhindered."[41] The recognition of a refugee crisis complicates matters for those who want unfettered Israeli militaries, because the continued presence of the

UNRWA increases the number of potential social agents who can witness alleged abuses of civilian populations and then report back to organizations like the UN, ICC, or EU.

Moreover, all of this talk of aid dependency sounds eerily familiar, especially for those who remember the stories that are told about the historical roots of some of these military humanitarian discourses or international relations rhetorics. Romirowsky's attack on the UNRWA is another permutation of the old moral hazard type of argument that I referenced earlier in this chapter, a trope that has been around since at least the time of the debates about choosing sides during the Biafra conflict with Nigeria.[42]

Like many debaters, Romirowsky tries to minimize the existential dangers facing the Palestinians by complaining about the ways the UNRWA categorizes and defines what it means to be a refugee. For example, the UNRWA adopts the position that any Palestinian can be characterized as a refugee whose "normal place of residence was Palestine during the period 1946 to 14 May 1948 and who lost both home and means of livelihood as a result of the 1948 conflict." What Romirowsky fails to mention is that part of the reason that some of these protean categories kept changing is that the Quakers and members of the UNRWA who were trying to dispense aid realized that restricting categorization meant leaving out "native" Gazans who owned farms and were not displaced, and that different generations of Palestinians became refugees for diverse reasons.

That said, Romirowsky does seem to recognize that the existence of the refugee camps has become a part of the storytelling that is used by Palestinians as they tell the world about privation, dispossession, life under occupation, and the horrors of military confrontations. As Jerome Slater argues elsewhere, this often bothers many Israelis who have crafted an "Israeli mythology" that assumes that many Palestinians during this time voluntarily left their lands or sold their property.[43] Yet for Romirowsky, what makes matters worse is the fact that the UNRWA keeps expanding the definition of refugee—and by his logic, the definition of a Palestinian—by stating that the children and grandchildren of those refugees become eligible for agency assistance if they are registered with the UNRWA, are living in the area of UNRWA's operations, and really are "in need."[44] Sympathetic readers visiting Romirowsky's website might arrive at this conclusion: If the refugee camps weren't there, there would be fewer UN folks treating a collective as if they were Palestinian, and if the Palestinians were less dependent they might leave and forget about their grievances.

Visualities in our post-human world often help us understand this type of argumentation, and in this case, Romirowsky, who is writing months before the beginning of OPE, seemingly has no interest in displaying the horrors of refugee life. His essay on the UNRWA is adorned with an image of a Palestinian woman flying one of many kites in a beautiful blue sky. The crafted, implied message is clear—happy and carefree generations of Palestinians don't mind being refugees, and the UNRWA revels in its role as dispenser of aid. What seems to bother Romirowsky is that this has meant that over a 60-year period of time, there have been few incentives for "refugees to resettle in Arab countries or elsewhere."[45]

This talk of resettlement in "Arab" countries is a variant of the old "Jordanian" solution to the Palestinian "problem."

There are several reasons why passages and framings of refugee situations like Romirowsky's need to be critically engaged and decoded. First of all, narratives like his complement the stories that are told by others about how there are "no innocent civilians." Second, all of this deflects attention away from Israeli social agency so that readers start to blame the victims and the aid agencies that try to come to their rescue. Third, this provides a revisionist history that makes it appear as though Palestinians want to be refugees and that they work with aid agencies to maintain the status quo. This is an attack on Palestinian indigeneity, a crafted mythic world that assumes that Palestinians have mobility, and that they are not humiliated by handouts.

Obviously dealing with the status of refugees in Gaza is not the only issue that would need to be resolved in any future Israeli–Palestinian negotiations, but it is clearly an important one. This is, as Rebecca Stein has pointed out, because of the ideological clashes of jarring images that occur when Israelis and their defenders think of the past, present, and future of Gaza. Far too many are convinced that without Israeli tutelage, all that will remain will be "uncivilized and fundamentalist Gaza."[46]

Reconceptualizing applicable IHL principles in Gazan contexts

At the same time that decision-makers and others critically analyze the Israeli refugee narratives, they need to keep an eye on the Israeli counterlawfare that is used to pre-empt and obviate the need for outside jurisprudential critiques of what is happening in Gaza. Readers by now may argue that I am exaggerating the rhetorical impact that all of this post-2000 Israeli discourse on lawfare and Israeli interpretations of the IHL have had on geopolitical affairs, but I challenge those skeptical readers to visit a popular American website like "lawfare"[47] and see how some of the contributors to this website on "hard national security choices" often defend Israeli decision-making as well as Israeli interpretations of the IHL. It is no coincidence that many of the American legal memos, jurisprudential positions on national security issues, executive orders, etc. contain a growing number of arguments and discursive fragments from Israeli texts. For example, the infamous David Barron and Marty Lederman drone memo, that tried to justify the targeted assassination of an American, Anwar al-Awlaki, contained explicit references to Chief Justice Aharon Barak's opinion in *Public Committee Against Torture* v. *the State of Israel (PCATI)*.[48] All of this ideological migration of military doctrines and unilateral legal decision-making, along with the veto power of the five dominant members of the UN Security Council, has threatened to render vacuous any talk of applying IHL principles for aggressive intervention in Gaza.

Israelis are aware of this, and they realize that as long as they can come up with *plausible* arguments regarding their "intentions" to avoid excessive civilian casualties, then they will be able to counter the critics who over and over again cite some of the same passages of the Geneva Conventions or other international texts that Israeli legal advisers probably know by heart.

My point here is that a series of image events—including the mass-mediated coverage of the second Intifada, the "disengagement" from Gaza in 2005, the 2006 Lebanese War, the lamentations about the "Hamas regime" in 2007, the defense of attacks on "infrastructure" during Operation Cast Lead, the massive attack on the claims and authors of the Goldstone Report, and the circulation of the results of Israeli inquiries into the *Mavi Marmara* flotilla incident—have emboldened Israelis who already believed in forms of *Israeli exceptionalism*. Their counterlawfare, as I indicated earlier in this book, has provided them with all of the swords and shields they need as they "mow the lawn" in Gaza.

Moreover, performing acts of counterlawfare is now almost an Israeli national pastime as Israeli military legal experts, civil officials, journalists, citizens, bloggers, etc. all join the ranks of those who recognize that gains on the military battlefields will mean little if they cannot protect "Samaria" and "Judea" by legitimating and legalizing the aerial attacks and incursions into Gaza.

In order to circulate, and to help instantiate, Israeli interpretations of the IHL, Israelis have trained phalanxes of military lawyers and young computer experts so they can use the jargon of IHL and human rights talk as they put together mainstream or alternative press missives on the justness and legitimacy of Israel's causes. This involves everything from the dissemination of articles from Jerusalem think-tanks authored by Israeli officers in the reserves to the tweets that are filled with more vernacular messages that appeal to younger audiences. The polling data out of Israel shows overwhelming support for incursions like Operation Cast Lead or OPE, and this provides one of many indications that all of this variegated counterlawfare appeals to both elites and lay persons in Israel. The dominant Israeli narratives and myths, that contain assertions that only Hamas violates the IHL, resonate with audiences who are used to believing they are living in a constant state of emergency that is not of their own making.

Some Israeli interpretations of the IHL look very much like any other state usage of just-war theorizing. Israelis, for example, try to prove that they have a right to go to war by talking and writing about their inherent self-defense rights and the fact that they had to use aggressive warfare as a "last resort." At the same time they can complain that their neighbors—Egypt, Lebanon, Syria, or Jordan—have not contained the spread of "Islamic" terrorism, and this in turn has forced one of the few democracies in this region to take matters in hand by using the "iron fist." They can of course also show that they wear a velvet glove when they have to when they display how they are following the IHL principles regarding *jus in bello* guidelines by distinguishing between soldiers and civilians or carrying out proportional raids where the military benefits they gain outweigh the incidental harms that come during the retaliation against terrorists.[49]

In order to get beyond the usual polarizing "tit-for-tat" argumentation that takes place when Israelis talk about "security" rights or Palestinians talk about "land" rights or "human rights," critics during the twenty-first century will need to provide more nuanced analyses that explain some of the ideological underpinnings of select and partial interpretations of international humanitarian law or human rights law. The work of researchers such as Marie-Bénédicte Dembour,[50] Costas Douzinas,[51] Stephen Hopgood,[52] David Kennedy, Martti Koskenniemi,[53] and Nimer Sultany will need to be deployed to illustrate what international interpretations are left behind, or obfuscated, when state actors proffer self-serving interpretations of the IHL that just happen to mesh with controversial military, nationalistic, or diplomatic nationalist goals. For example, instead of taking at face value some of the claims that were made by Israelis in the wake of events such as the commando boarding of the *Mavi Marmara* or the 2008–2009 campaign in Gaza, we would show how Geneva Convention fragments and other texts were being interpreted in ways that provided the IDF or the Israel Air Force with maximum flexibility.

As I noted in earlier chapters, select, motivated, and unilateral IHL interpretations by Israelis have been used to justify more force protection for their troops, less protection of civilians regarded as "infrastructure,"[54] the deployment of targeted assassinations, the maintenance of blockades, and the legitimacy of unilateral incursions into Gaza. Craig Jones and others made the insightful observation that it would be a mistake to underestimate the prowess, and the stature, of the Israeli lawyers who advise commanders and diplomats of the wisdom of deploying this or that interpretation of the IHL.[55] What makes all of this even more potent is the way rhetors in Sderot or Haifa can parrot back fragments of these sedimented *dispositifs* counterlawfare *epistemes*.

Obviously, engaging in harsh, "critical" and ideological oriented critiques of the IHL and human rights laws carries many inherent risks. After all, it is the essentialist, and perceived consensual, nature of some of these laws that is believed to act as some international brake, or constraint, on the actions of the world's greatest powers. Jerome Slater, for example, calls the IHL some form of reflection of the "common morality" of humankind, where just-war theories are derived from religious principles that come from both Western and non-Western cultures.[56]

One could also argue that the belief in the substantive existence of these jurisprudential principles helped the Israelis gain their freedom from the British during the late 1940s, and that human rights talk is obviously important for Palestinian discussions of the right to return, anxieties regarding land dispossession, the right to travel, the right to make a living, and the right to be free of Israeli sanctions and blockades, and so on. Thus the dismantling of Israeli rationales carries attendant risks for those who want to deploy their own rights talk and advance competing IHL interpretations.

It would be imprudent to argue that Israelis have no security interests or that they have no rights of self-defense, but it is their militarizing and securitizing interpretations of these rights and interests, and their promiscuous deployment of these unilateral claims, that will need to be continually interrogated during the rest of the twenty-first century. There is a difference between defending Israel "proper" and defending Eretz Israel. As Nimer Sultany has so eloquently observed, even classical liberal and Zionist rhetorics, that in the abstract look egalitarian and democratic, can become *exclusionary*, especially in situations where they are used in military, academic, and political circles to help legitimate many forms of discrimination and injustice.[57] Note, for example, the unwillingness to see that the very existence of Hamas, as either a political or military entity, has something to do with grievances that can be traced as far back as the Nakba. If Hamas did not exist, it would have to be invented in the Palestinian geopolitical imaginaries, because Israelis have no monopoly on displays of steadfastness.

In sum, I would argue that those who deploy IHL rhetorics in their contextualizations of what is happening in Gaza have to make sure that their valorization of these principles doesn't play into the hands of those who invert and twist these principles to rationalize the dispensation of state violence and distant suffering.

Engaging in radical critiques of human rights rhetorics and international humanitarian law discourses is no easy matter, for as Frédéric Mégret has explained, some of this "work on international law is haunted by the possibility/impossibility of human rights," or at least, some story of "virtue's fall from grace."[58] He understands some of the nuanced positions, and the complex arguments, of those who express skepticism when they see human rights law as some type of "anti-politics," that allows people to make claims about certain things being "inherently true without any of the dirty work of political confrontation."[59] Furthermore, Mégret sees why radical critics might find that human "rights too easily play into grand technocratic designs" that can be "suspected of being involved in hegemonic enterprises."[60] However, he worries about the nihilistic dangers that might come from too much suspicion, when radical human rights critiques dismantle the very rhetorical foundations that are needed to secure basic human rights for many of the world's denizens.

As readers can guess by now I am more of a functionalist than a legal formalist, and I do not mind employing a hermeneutics of suspicion any time any major world power, armed with nuclear and other dangerous arsenals, views itself as a victim and then uses boiler-plate IHL materials to constantly advance the position that it is acting aggressively toward "other" civilian populations in the name of military necessity. In the end, if members of the international communities want to stem the tide of cyclical violence in Gaza, they will need to be ready to interrogate what appear to be plausible interpretations of the IHL that have dire consequences for Gazan populations that suffer from constant interventions.

This leads me to consider a third possibility—that besides worrying about the symbolic importance of refugees' status and militaristic Israeli interpretations of the IHL, we should consider the potential of having state actors intervene in Gaza on the basis of implementing international communities' R2P.

The promise and perils of applying R2P principles in Gazan contexts

As noted above, scholars are divided on whether the IHL was historically formed by communities and nations who were interested in utopianism or apologetics, or whether these rhetorics enabled or constrained aggressive warfare, and there are those today who believe that the principles of what are called "responsibility to protect" doctrines provide some of the clarity and specificity that is allegedly missing in the messiness of IHL provisions. In theory, the promoters of core "R2P" guidelines for military humanitarian interventions talk about the limits of state sovereignty and the principles that would regulate outside interference by global powers that cannot be found in UN Security Council provisions or cannot be discovered in the more penumbral features of IHL or human rights law.

Like many ideographic phrases the term "responsibility to protect" gained traction during a specific historical period when members of well-intentioned democratic communities felt that in many parts of the world nation-states were either making war on their own people or were looking the other way when their populations were suffering from humanitarian crises. During the last decade of the twentieth century there seemed to be this shared sense that caring, cosmopolitan communities needed to be concerned about distant suffering and that they needed some argumentative warrant to "do something" in order to prevent the spread of human suffering. Over the years, countless writers and contributors to the blogosphere suggested that R2P doctrines be applied in cases of disaster relief, resource scarcity disputes, large-scale massacres, or even genocides.

The guiding notion behind this search for formalistic guidelines was the idea that if one could get some type of international consensus about the balancing of sovereign-state interests and the rules that would allow the foreign trumping of that sovereignty in dire situations, then this might help prevent—or at least mitigate—some of the post-War War II horrors that were witnessed by those who talked about "never again."

A critical genealogical study of the discursive origins of R2P doctrines might invite readers to go back to 2001, when the Canadian government helped sponsor an International Commission on Intervention and State Sovereignty (ICISS). The members of ICISS—led by Gareth Evans, Mahamed Sahnoun, Michael Ignatieff, and others—suggested that it was time that the rest of the world, and the UN, recognize the "responsibility to protect" concept.[61]

Trying to adapt some of this R2P language in Gazan contexts gets tricky, especially when baseline decisions have to be made about the status of what the Israelis call the "Hamas regime." For example, regardless of whether the members of the UN did or did not decide to intervene in Gaza, the mere fact that they felt they had the right to debate about possible intervention may have signaled that they were treating Hamas as a legitimate, and political, "state" entity.

At the same time, many commentators who have worked to promote the concept of R2P seem disinterested in applying these doctrines in Gazan contexts. Professor Aidan Hehir has pointed out that one of the problems with using "R2P advocacy" in recent Gazan contexts has to do with the fact that most prominent organizations that have been established to promote the idea of R2P—the International Coalition for the Responsibility to Protect (ICRtoP), the Global Center for the Responsibility to Protect (GCR2P), and the Asian Pacific Centre for the Responsibility to Protect (APCR2P)—have shown little inclination to intervene in this particular conflict. These organizations are used to using social media to call attention to alleged human rights violations, including those committed by state sponsors, and yet all of the usual talk of treatment of refugees or complaints about lack of medical aid or the committing of atrocities did not translate, before OPE, into concrete initiatives to help Palestinians in Gaza.[62] In spite of the fact that these three organizations have tackled crises in places like Burundi, Iraq, Kenya, Mali, Myanmar, Nigeria, and the Central African Republic, up until the fall of 2014 there has been a conspicuous absence of attention paid by these organizations to the situation in Gaza. Professor Hehir argues that if this "mute reaction" continues, then it will show that R2P critics are right when they argue that R2P guidelines are "selectively" used by "the West" when they decide who has, or has not, engaged in human rights violations.[63]

All of this has to do with a fourth controversial claim that I will advance in this chapter—that any resolution of the Israeli–Gazan conflicts will have to involve some recognition that Hamas has to be treated as a political, as well as military, entity. Configuring Hamas' members as nothing but terrorists may be an inherent part of the geopolitical "forensic architecture" of our post-human age,[64] but it hinders the possibility of ever helping humanize the Gazan populations that deserve to be treated as "protected" civilians.

The challenge of reconfiguring Hamas as a political, as well as military entity

A critical genealogy of the origins of Hamas would show how a host of symbolic and material conditions have contributed to the ebb and flow of interest in seeing Hamas configured as a viable Palestinian political organization. Countless numbers of Israelis could point to the old 1988 charter that mentions the destruction of Israel, and many view this as an example of how supporters or defenders of Hamas must be wishing for the destruction of Israel, but this is a mirror image of the Israeli arguments that have been used to argue that a Palestinian state never existed or never will exist. Again, as I noted above, all of this hyperbole may serve the cause of those who require countless rationales and justifications for their skirmishes and wars, but it goes nowhere and simply hinders the possibility of finding diplomatic solutions to concrete problems. Neither the Palestinians nor the Israelis are going away, and I think that most readers would agree that this type of vilification, from all sides, should not be used to justify the targeting of any civilians, including the people of Sderot or Gaza City.

Both Israelis and Palestinians celebrate the importance of being steadfast and obstinate in the face of life's trials and tribulations, and in order to even consider the possibility of treating Hamas as a political partner for negotiation our critical genealogies have to take us back to a time before the terrorism of the Stern Gang or the counterterrorism of the British after World War II. We could go back and follow the social agency of the precursor to Hamas, the Muslim Brotherhood, and see how Palestinians during that era worried about everything from the way that Anglo-Americans conceptualized the Levant to the oppressive colonial regulations of the British mandate system. Many of them, after the Balfour Declaration of 1917, realized they were having to cope with both Jewish Zionism as well as British imperial aspirations.

Long before today's Egyptians worried about Hamas and their policing of their 12-km-long border with Gaza, the Muslim Brotherhood sent representatives from Egypt in 1936 into Gaza with the aim of trying to help Palestinians in their struggles against the British and the Jewish immigrants. Professor Lorenzo Kamel argues that while members of this organization proudly provided that help, their ideologies often threatened state leaders, especially those who were trying to modernize or secularize their nations. In the 1950s and 1960s the Muslim Brotherhood had trouble surviving during the reign of Egyptian President Gamal Nasser for that very reason. Interestingly enough, it appears that at one time the Israelis *tolerated* the existence of the Muslim Brotherhood because the Israelis viewed them as an organizational entity that *counterbalanced* the power of the PLO.[65]

Hamas would be founded in 1987, near the beginning of the first Intifada. Sheikh Ahmed Yassin, the founder of Hamas, was born in Al-Jura (Sderot), and after an attack against Israel in 1989 that killed several Israel soldiers Yassin would be sentenced to life in prison. During this same period, some 400 Hamas members would be deported to Lebanon, and this movement of people and ideas ended up helping create ties between Hamas and Hezbollah. By 1991, Hamas created its own military branch, named Iz al-Din Qassam, and over the next several years they carried out a number of high-visibility terrorist attacks against Israelis in the West Bank.

It was during this same period that Hamas members started to talk and act like they sought the utter destruction of the Israeli state, as evidenced by the production of the 1988 Hamas Charter. The carrying out of suicide raids into Israel seemed to put on display the practical results of their philosophizing.[66] Given this chronology, that many Israeli decision-makers and intellectuals are familiar with, it becomes understandable why so many Israelis are loath to consider Hamas as anything but a non-political terrorist organization. One could argue that some of the British must have felt the same way when they had to watch as some members of the Stern Gang and other Israeli "freedom fighters" became Israeli political decision-makers after the "War of Independence."

In many ways it could be arguing that after the mid-1990s Hamas became both a real organization and a mobile signifier, a condensation symbol of evil that could be used by just about any Israeli politician, military leader, or jurist who desired to rationalize the detentions, deportations, targeted assassinations, building of "separation" walls, fences, etc. in the coming years. One popular argument against those who would characterize Israel as an apartheid state is that categorical legal distinctions are made by Israelis on the basis of security concerns, and not one's ethnic heritage. This security interest, in turn, depended on publics and elites who focused on Hamas.

Few Israelis shed any tears when in March 2004 an Israeli missile attack took out Sheikh Yassin. While the *Al-Jazeera* satellite channel showed grisly photos of the results of the missiles that killed "wheelchair-bound HAMAS figurehead Sheikh Ahmed Yassin as he exited the Islamic Association Mosque in the densely populated al-Sabra neighborhood in the center of Gaza City," a spokesperson for the IDF claimed that Yassin had been personally responsible for numerous murderous terror attacks that had resulted in the deaths of many Israel and foreign civilians.[67] All of this commentary was circulating during a period of time when Hamas was distributing social goods to desperate Gazan populations.

More seeds of distrust were sown between Palestinians living on the West Bank and those in Gaza when some Palestinians on the West Bank were recruited by the Israeli Secret Service and the IDF to try to infiltrate Hamas. This is just one of the elements that helps explain Hamas' victory in the 2006 legislative elections. By 2007 the Israelis must have felt that the more "moderate" members of Fatah in the PA had learned to accept the tutelage of the Israelis, and this could be contrasted with the actions of the Gazan populations that appeared to be irrational in their support for Hamas. After all, didn't the Israelis allow humanitarian aid into the "Hamas regime," and didn't the Knesset have members who argued against the cutting off of water and electricity to regions that were filled with terrorists enemies? Israelis could use these types of arguments to not only differentiate themselves from the Palestinians, but to differentiate between "good" and "bad" Palestinians. These are the old tried and true "divide and conquer" strategies that have served legions of other historical communities.

After Hamas' Ismail Haniyeh became the prime minister of the region, Israel's Prime Minister Ehud Olmert responded by imposing the infamous blockades. Professor Lorenzo Kamel explains that when the political wing of Hamas failed to help with the removal of the Israeli blockades and other restrictions, this undermined any attempt at finding pragmatic, non-violent solutions to Gazan problems and this empowered those who were leading Hamas' military wings.[68]

To be fair to members of the Hamas political wings, readers have to ask themselves this question: During the period between 2007 and the beginning of Operation Cast Lead in 2009, how many members of the "international community" worked at helping Hamas' political wing hold off the military wing? As some Israeli leftists have pointed out, foreigners could afford to stand on the sidelines and watch the Israelis fire away with impunity, but the Palestinians who had weapons in their hands were not about to stand idly by and watch the Israelis "mow their lawn."

What Professor Lorenzo and other experts in this area have tried to point out is that it is a mistake to think of Hamas as some single, militant entity, that has all of its members following the old 1988 charter. He and others have tried to counter the Israeli claims that Hamas has no interest in negotiating by spelling out the number of times that Hamas appeared to be trying to extend the olive branch but were rebuffed by Israeli negotiators.[69] Getting rid of Hamas will not "end" terrorism, as long the conditions that led to that terrorism are ignored.

Pragmatic members of Hamas' political wings, who worry about the suffering of their people in Gaza, have tried to find practical ways of making concessions and recognizing Israel's right to exist while defending Palestinian rights. "The differences between the party's platform [in 2006] and the Islamic Charter [of Hamas]," argued Menachem Klein,

> do not represent an attempt at deception or the empty and unconsidered use of words. They are the product of a change and modification of lines of thought as a part of a process which Hamas has become a political movement.[70]

This line of reasoning, as readers might imagine, is not accepted by many members of the Israeli Supreme Court, the IDF, the Israeli ministry, or anyone else who refuses to negotiate with Palestinian terrorists. In the name of "deterrence" the supporters of the most moral army in the world did not mind using annihilation rhetorics when they lumped together the military and political wings of Hamas.

Yet here it needs to be acknowledged that even those members of Hamas who belong to the political wing of that organization have sometimes acted as their own worst enemy. For example, there have been times when Hamas representatives ended up arguing with Egyptians over the opening of the Rafah crossing, or when they have feuded with fellow Palestinians from Fatah. Vacillating between the advocacy of one-state solutions and two-state solutions, members of the political wing of Hamas have let their hatred of Israelis overshadow their need to maintain a focus on the transcendent goal of providing at least some Palestinians with the legitimate rights associated with statehood.[71]

The Arab League has occasionally tried to help with the unification of Fatah and Hamas, and their members sometimes facilitate the Palestinian–Israeli peace talks, and I am convinced that some of this helps when they argue that a twenty-first-century "just" and "agreed" upon solution would include returning to the 1967 territorial lines. Peter Beinart, writing in *Ha'artz* in August 2014, explained that too many American and Jewish leaders were focusing on what was written during the 1980s in the Hamas charter. Instead of paying attention to the evolution of negotiated demands that could help these Middle Eastern communities move away from their cycles of violence, they wasted time recycling the ancient positions of older arguers. Beinart worried that Israel was not only trying to undermine Hamas, but was also working away at undermining Palestinian support for the two-state solution. He made what I believe is an insightful comment when he noted how all of this is also aimed at the containment of non-violent protest.

One of the key issues here has to do with the geopolitical parameters of what it means when one talks about the "State" of Israel. Some generalized commentaries that are used to attack Hamas also contain strategically ambiguous statements about whether we are talking about the policing of the old "Green" line and the "proper" State of Israel that occupies other territories, or are we talking about what some Israelis call "Greater Israel," where Israel includes "Judea" and "Samaria"? Beinart pointed out that Prime Minister Netanyahu was making things difficult for moderate Arabs in neighboring states as well as for Abbas when he kept insisting that Palestinians not only recognize Israel's right to exist, but they needed to recognize it as a Jewish state that included the occupied territories.[72] Moreover, Netanyahu was talking about an Israel that was defined architecturally and logically by the separation barriers and the "recovery" of "Judea" and "Samaria."

This not only made it difficult for liberal Zionists who wanted to support some sort of humanitarian assimilationist policies—it also encouraged Palestinian civilian populations to see that Netanyahu's rhetoric would configure them as stateless. This, Beinart argued, was why Israeli policies were unintentionally helping with Hamas' legitimation in Gaza. This defense of what might be called a variant of the "one-state" solution envisioned an Israel that would include both Jewish and Muslim populations, but the Palestinians would have to live their lives as subservient communities who recognized and accepted Israeli exceptionalism.

The importance of recognizing Hamas has been a topic that has also occupied the attention of leaders and denizens of neighboring countries. They realize that one of the most powerful of the rhetorical frames that Israelis circulate in United States and in international circles involves the crafting of a metanarrative that Hamas cannot be viewed as a legitimate "political" party or leader. Turkey's Prime Minister Recep Tayyip Erdogan and Foreign Minister Davutoglu have tried to counter some of this by using their NATO connections to argue that Hamas should be removed from the list of terrorist organizations in the United States and in Europe.[73] During an interview with Lally Weymouth, Prime Minister Erdogan contextualized the aftermath of the controversial 2006 Palestinian elections in ways that reminded *Washington Post* readers of the material conditions that contributed to the rise of Hamas in the first place:

> First of all, Hamas is not an arm of Iran. Hamas entered the elections as a political party. If the whole world had given them the chance of becoming a political player, maybe they would not be in a situation like this after the elections that they won. The world has not respected the political will of the Palestinian people. On the one hand, we defend democracy and we try our best to keep democracy in the Middle East, but on the other hand we do not respect the outcome of ... the ballot box. Palestine today is an open-air prison. Hamas, as much as they tried, could not change the situation. Just imagine, you imprison the speaker of a country as well as some ministers of its government and members of its parliament.[74]

Erdogan was not saying that Hamas was necessarily a good organization or that it didn't make mistakes—he was simply pointing out the restricted and myopic ways of defining democracies that exacerbated the problems in Gaza.

Occasionally Hamas representatives help their cause by openly espousing more pragmatic solutions to these difficult problems. For example, in January 2009, during a televised speech a senior Hamas Official, Ismail Haniyeh, expressed an openness to work on a diplomatic solution that looked nothing like the old 1988 Charter. He reiterated previous demands that any deal had to include the opening of Gaza's border crossings that linked Gaza to Israel and Egypt. Speaking from hiding in Gaza, he admitted: "We are not close to this path."[75] What he was pointing out, however, is that for many Gazans, who suffer from high morbidity and mortality rates, any lasting peace with Israel had to include at least the modification of blockades and the opening up of key border crossings.

Holding the (Green) line: the importance of gaining Palestinian consensus for two-state solutions

As noted above, it is my position that the best way to protect the civilians in Gaza is by having decision-makers and lay persons support the adoption of a viable two-state solution. In 2013 Simon Waldman lamented the fact that too many rhetors, since the time of the collapse of the Oslo Process and the failed talks at Camp David in 2000, have started to advocate a one-state solution.[76] Meron Benvenisti, writing in April 2009, noted that pundits who watched Middle Eastern affairs seemed to be witnessing "the binationalism vogue."[77] The advocates of these various one-state solutions would argue that the combination of Israeli insecurities, power, and objections to two-state solutions means that Palestinians would be better-off trying to assimilate and force Israeli decision-makers to grant equal rights to non-Jewish citizens of Israel.

The attractiveness of this type of approach is that it would provide a non-violent, incremental way of accepting the dominant Zionist and Jewish features of Israeli national identity while striving for the creation of a more egalitarian state. In other words, it would leverage Israeli beliefs in the democratic nature of their country, and use shame, guilt, embarrassment, or other tactics to put on display the mistreatment and inequality of Palestinians who were treated as second-class citizens as they suffered from Israel's two-tier legal system. In theory, embarrassed Israelis, trapped by their own egalitarian rhetorics, would then treat Palestinians in the same way they treat settlers and other Israelis.

The advent of all the violence and finger-pointing that was going on during OPE also created material and symbolic difficulties for those who advocate two-state solutions. For example, when a single missile landed near Tel Aviv in July 2014, and three-quarters of foreign airlines had to briefly avoid landing in Ben Gurion Airport, Raphael Ahren asked whether this was the "rocket that spelled the end of the two-state solution?"[78] The fighting in Gaza, in addition to causing all of the psychological and economic damage, was taking its toll on the political chances of reviving any future peace agreements. Ahren explained that some in Israel were articulating their concern that if a single rocket could bring Israel's international air traffic to a standstill, then how could Israel ever take seriously the possibility that they needed to hand over control of the West Bank to the Palestinians?

Israelis from the political right were convinced that if one took into account the West Bank's mountainous topography then one would see that it would be easy for terrorists to rain down rocket fire on the airport. Ahren did explain to readers of the *Times of Israel* that there were some Israelis with "*bona fide* security credentials" who still argued that in today's "day and age, the only way to really ensure Israel's safety is through diplomacy."[79] Again, this looked naive to the hardliners.

Some of the same Israeli polls that show overwhelming support for OPE also indicated that a little over 40 percent of those polled viewed a two-state solution as the best way of ending these conflicts.[80] This, however, may have represented some fading hopes. At one point during the latest round of fighting Akiva Eldar opined:

> The way things look today, Aug. 3, the military investment in the Gaza war failed to result in any diplomatic dividends to either of the two sides. Israel did not achieve its long-term objective, as expressed by the prime minister, i.e., the demilitarization of Gaza from fighting means, and Hamas failed to force Israel into lifting its lengthy siege of the Gaza Strip.... Even in the best-case scenario, the only partner with whom Israel might have reached a long-term arrangement in the occupied territories has been found irrelevant. In the worst-case scenario, Palestinian President Mahmoud Abbas has been portrayed to his constituents as a collaborator with Israel. Negotiations over a two-state solution now seem even more remote than they did on the eve of Operation Protective Edge.[81]

Note how the assumption here is that the presence or power of some single social agent, like Mahmoud Abbas, is treated as one of the keys to keeping the faith in two-state solutions.

I am convinced that many observers today have focused plenty of attention on the military advantages or disadvantages of having the Israeli military firing on Gaza civilians, but they often miss some of the political signals and rhetorical importance of these same attacks in diplomatic contexts. As noted above, there is plenty of anecdotal evidence that giving up on the two-state solution is exactly what many Israelis want, and they would be happy to live in a world of mobile, stateless Palestinians, where the only people holding steadfast are the ones who control the land, air, and sea of Gaza.

Other observers continue to hope for more peaceful resolutions to these Gazan conflicts. As Simon Waldman explains, "far from being dead, the two-state solution remains the only viable solution." This is because "Israelis and Palestinians do not share the same national narratives and have developed separate identities that make any talk of a binational solution superfluous and unrealistic."[82]

If binationalism was going to work, then this would have to involve the dismantling of rhetorics that configured all Palestinians as terrorists, and we would have to see over the years an Israeli Supreme Court that treated Palestinians in the same way that it treated Jewish settlers or Israeli citizens. Israeli jurists are used to talking about the egalitarian nature of their democracy, but they are often talking about the equality that exists between settlers living in occupied lands and those Israelis living in Israel "proper." Many Israelis have defined their national security interests in ways that try to naturalize and normalize the need for "separate" walls, laws, lands, etc. in ways that make it clear they would not welcome the majority of Palestinians into their country. As Waldman noted, this would threaten their national mythologies and their narratives, and most Israelis want to maintain both physical demographic majorities as well as metaphysical ideologies of Zionism and Judaism. One-state solutions might help a few tens of thousands of "good" Palestinians, but I don't think the endangered civilians of Gaza would be first in line when it came to handing out Israeli citizenship to the dispossessed.

Conclusion

I am sad to say that I do not believe that OPE will be the last time Gazans will appear on global video screens as the telegenically dead, and they will continue to serve as the *bêtes noires* of the Israelis who are interested in the defense of Eretz Israel. What the 2005 disengagement shows is that Israelis' *perceived* future interest lies in building up the settlements in the West Bank and expansionism in Jerusalem, and the incursions into Gaza are treated as militarily necessitous actions that protect both Israelis and other in the region from Hamas and other Palestinian terrorists.

As I write these words, the "biggest land grab in the occupied West Bank in 30 years" is taking place as the Israelis formally declared nearly 1,000 acres of territory near Wadi Fukin "state lands" and "no trespassing" signs are put up along with dozens of bright yellow plastic boards that are printed with the logo of the Israeli military's Civil Administration.[83] It also seems as though any Gazan conflict is some sideshow, while the real dispossessions are taking place on the West Bank.

As I've shown in several previous chapters, the Gazans are not rendered invisible in Israeli tales, but are instead configured as denizens of an uncivilized maze of underground tunnels and networks. As Prime Minister Netanyahu was fond of saying, Israelis were threatened from above by homemade rockets, and from below by the tunnels. The Gazan election of Hamas purportedly showed their dedication to terrorism, which "forced" the Israelis to attack the infrastructures and those who acted as voluntary shields.

Some of this may sound irrational to many of Israel's critics, but as I explained in Chapter 1, I am interested in explicating how Israelis used particular argumentative legal and military frames, and showing how just about any social, economic, political, or cultural facet of Palestinian social life can be linked by empowered Israelis to some perceptual security threats. Beliefs in "Israeli exceptionalism"[84] can easily trump the most evocative story of refugee deprivations.

Any hopes for long-lasting peace, that take into account both Palestinian and Israeli rights and interests, will have to involve the jettisoning of much of this unproductive talk of trying to destroy Israel or claiming that there is no Palestinian state. Neither of those nihilistic rhetorics gets us anywhere, and in the same way that the Palestinians have to put up with the fact that they will have to negotiate with someone like Netanyahu or members of the Likud Party, Israelis will have to openly admit they have to accept Hamas as a "political" entity and drastically cut down on the targeted killings of potential negotiating partners. Otherwise it will be clear that Israelis realize that time is on their side, and that their Iron Dome has obviated the need for any consideration of two-state solutions. If that is the case, then Gaza will continue to be characterized as a massive military experiment "ghetto," "prison," an Agamben "camp" or some twenty-first-century site of siege.

Ultimately, I believe that going forward Palestinians' only hope of seeing peace in the Middle East depends on foreign governments that no longer accept the Israeli rhetorics that militarize and securitize Gaza. Palestinian BDS campaigns may help in blogospheres with consciousness-raising about the privations in the West Bank and Gaza, but some of their members' advocacy of one-state solutions and utopian calls for the "right of return" for everyone does little to calm the fears of Israelis who regard this as "destroying" Israel. Far better to try to agree to protect the security of Israel "proper," work for the ending of blockades, and help with the formation of a united Hamas–Fatah PA government than allow Israelis to keep "mowing the lawn" and win their wars of attrition.

In sum, this book is intended to show that, indeed, there are still civilians in Gaza, and that all of us need to be able to understanding some of the assumptions behind all of this argumentation if we ever want to find peaceful solutions to what on the surface appear to be intractable problems. We need to avoid accepting the militarizing and securitizing grammars that treat occupations or wars as issues that always involve counterterrorist solutions, and one way of doing that is to be cognizant of the biopolitical and thanatopolitical features of the discourses that *enable, rather than constrain the* disproportionate use of force in Gaza.

Those who join Hamas are no angels, but trying to disconnect the firing of the rockets and the building of tunnels from the historical grievances that swirl around them does little to help us as we argue in the future about blockades, closures, fences, "separation barriers," indefinite detention, deportation, disengagement, etc. Palestinians and other readers need to also remember how the members of the UN, who write up their reports that infuriate so many Israelis, are not the only interpreters who are adept at circulating lawfare in all of these debates about the status of Gazan citizens.

Responsible decision-makers need to constantly interrogate Israeli readings of the law of armed conflict so that we can counter the efforts of those who would treat Gazans citizens as terrorist aiders and abettors. As Kristin Solberg would explain in an essay published in *The Lancet*, some of those who have died during OPE are the children, the disabled, and the ambulatory patients who had to watch as the al-Aqsa Hospital in Deir al Balah or the Al Wafa medical hospital were hit.[85] The thousands who have died in this and other Gazan conflicts should be protected by both Israelis and others who no longer believe that the circulation of warning leaflets, or the use of some "knock on the roof tactic,"[86] provides evidence that civilians are not being intentionally targeted.

Without an argumentative study that at least tries to understand, and unpacks, the assumptions behind so much of this warfare and lawfare, we can do little more than watch the rise and application of the next Dahiya doctrine. This, in the end, does little to help preserve the security of Israelis or the aspirations of Gazan civilians.

Notes

1 Ernest Renan, cited in Stathis Gourgouris, *Dream Nation: Enlightenment, Colonization and the Institution of Modern Greece* (Redwood City, CA: Stanford University Press, 1996), 239.
2 Golda Meir, quoted in Benny Morris, "Book Review: Palestinian Identity: The Construction of Modern National Consciousness," *Israel Studies* 3, no. 1 (1998): 266–272.
3 Giora Eiland, "In Gaza, There is No Such Thing as 'Innocent Civilians,'" *Ynetnews.com*, last modified August 5, 2014, www.ynetnews.com/articles/0,7340,L-4554583, 00.html.
4 Obviously some of the April 2014 rapprochement gestures between Fatah and Hamas caught the attention of many observers. See, for example, Jack Khoury and Barak Ravid, "Hamas, Fatah Sign Reconciliation Agreement," *Ha'aretz*, last modified, April 23, 2014, www.haaretz.com/news/middle-east/1.586924; John Judis, "Who Bears More Responsibility for the War in Gaza? A Primer," *New Republic*, July 25, 2014, www.newrepublic.com/article/118846/israel-palestine-history-behind-their-new-war. Judis is one of those commentators who asks readers to quit using the Hamas charter as an "excuse" to allow Israelis to rationalize the prolonging of the occupation.
5 Eiland, "In Gaza, There is No Such Thing."
6 Ibid., paragraph 1–2.
7 Ibid., paragraph 4.
8 Ibid., paragraph 5–6.
9 Ibid., paragraph 7.
10 Ibid., paragraph 10.
11 Jacques Rancière, "Ten Thesis on Politics," European Graduate School, 2001, www.egs.edu/faculty/jacques-ranciere/articles/ten-thesis-on-politics.
12 Benedict Anderson, *Imagined Communities: Reflections on the Origin and Spread of Nationalism* (London: Verso, 1991).
13 Ibid., 36.
14 See, for example, David Lindorff, "Now It's Israel's IDF Leveling Gaza," *Counterpunch*, last modified July 23, 2014, www.counterpunch.org/2014/07/23/now-its-israels-idf-leveling-gaza.
15 For an excellent discussion of the role that "samud" has played in humanitarian as well as political debates in Gaza since 1948, see Ilana Feldman, "Difficult Distinctions: Refugee Law, Humanitarian Practice, and Political Identification in Gaza," *Cultural Anthropology* 22, no. 1 (2007): 129–169.
16 One of the most interesting twists and turns of some of the lawfare in the Iron Dome debates took place when the UN complained about how the United States and Israelis were not sharing Iron Dome technologies with Gazans to protect them. For a typical

210 *Coping with post-human framings*

Israeli reaction to these types of arguments, see "Carl," "Lunatic Navy Pillay Condemns Israel and US for Not Sharing Iron Dome With Hamas," *Israel Matzav*, last modified August 1, 2014, http://israelmatzav.blogspot.com/2014/08/lunatic-navi-pillay-condemns-israel-and.html.

17 These historical linkages are not lost on all twenty-first-century observers. See Philologos, "'Iron Dome' has Roots in Zionist Past," *Forward*, last modified December 2, 2012, http://forward.com/articles/166817/iron-dome-has-roots-in-zionist-past/?p=all; Robert Stothard, "Politics of Asymmetric Fear in Israel," London College of Communication, April 15, 2013, http://robstothard.co.uk/files/2014/03/POLITICS-OF-ASYMETTRICAL-FEAR-IN-ISRAEL.pdf.
18 Jerome Slater, "Just War Moral Philosophy and the 2008–09 Israeli Campaign in Gaza," *International Studies* 37, no. 2 (2012): 44–80, 44.
19 Helga Tawil-Souri, "Digital Occupation: Gaza's High-Tech Enclosure," *Journal of Palestine Studies* 41, no. 2 (2012): 27–45, 27–28.
20 See Nasser Hussein, *The Jurisprudence of Emergency: Colonialism and the Rule of Law* (Ann Arbor, MI: University of Michigan Press, 2003); Mark Neocleous, "The Problem of Normality: Taking Exception to 'Permanent Emergency,'" *Alternatives* 31 (2006): 191–213.
21 Vik Kanwar, "Review Essay: Post-Human Humanitarian Law: The Law of War in the Age of Robotic Weapons," *Harvard National Security Journal* 2 (2011): 616–628.
22 Christian Enemark, *Armed Drones and the Ethics of War: Military Virtue in a Post-Heroic Age* (London: Routledge, 2013).
23 Richard Falk, "No Exit from Gaza: A New War Crime?" *Foreign Policy Journal*, last modified July 18, 2014, paragraph 4, http://richardfalk.wordpress.com/2014/07/16/no-exit-from-gaza-a-new-war-crime.
24 Yitzhak Benhorin, "Head of UN Gaza Inquiry Commission Called to Try Netanyahu at ICC," *Ynetnews.com*, last modified August 12, 2014, www.ynetnews.com/articles/0,7340,L-4557779,00.html.
25 *124News*, "Israel Prepares Legal 'Iron Dome,'" last modified August 14, 2014, www.i24news.tv/en/news/israel/40247-140814-israel-prepares-legal-iron-dome.
26 An excellent overview of the involvement of Palestinian activities in the growing BDS movement can be found in Sean F. McMahon, "The Boycott, Divestment, Sanctions Campaign: Contradictions and Challenges," *Race & Class* 55 (2014): 65–81.
27 Feldman, "Difficult Distinctions," 152.
28 Neve Gordon, "Human Rights as a Security Threat: Lawfare and the Campaign Against Human Rights NGOs," *Law & Society Review* 48, no. 2 (2014): 311–344.
29 Danny Aylon, quoted in Gordon, "Human Rights as a Security Threat," 331.
30 For an interesting letter to the editor of the *New York Times* that points out how many Arabs have at times doubted the existence of Palestinian nation-states as they critiqued the artificial boundaries crafted by English or French colonizers, see Kenneth Levin, "What Golda Meir Said About Palestinians," *New York Times*, last modified October 12, 1993, www.nytimes.com/1993/10/12/opinion/l-what-golda-meir-said-about-palestinians-766493.html.
31 Asaf Romirowsky, "The Real Palestinian Refugee Crisis," *The Tower*, May, 2014, www.thetower.org/article/the-real-palestinian-refugee-crisis. Romirowsky suggests that the readers also read the work of James G. Lindsay, *Fixing UNRWA: Repairing the UNs Troubled System of Aid to Palestinian Refugees* (Washington, DC: Washington Institute, 2009).
32 Ibid., paragraph 1.
33 Ibid., paragraphs 6.
34 Avi Shlaim, *The Iron Wall: Israel and the Arab World* (New York: W.W. Norton, 2000).
35 Simha Flapan, *The Birth of Israel: Myths and Realities* (New York: Pantheon, 1987).
36 Benny Morris, *The Birth of the Palestinian Refugee Problem* (New York: Cambridge University Press, 1987).

37 Ilan Pappé, *The Making of the Arab–Israel Conflict, 1947–1951* (London: Tauris, 1992).
38 Romirowsky, "The Real Palestinian Refugee Crisis," paragraphs 6.
39 Ibid., paragraphs 6, 7.
40 Feldman, "Difficult Distinctions," 148.
41 Gordon, "Human Rights as a Security Threat," 312.
42 For a critique of some of these moral hazard arguments, see Alex J. Bellamy and Paul D. Williams, "On the Limits of Moral Hazard, the 'Responsibility to Protect,' Armed Conflict and Mass Atrocities," *European Journal of International Relations* 18 (2012): 539–571, DOI: 10.1177/1354066110393366.
43 Slater, "Just War Moral Philosophy," 46.
44 Romirowsky, "The Real Palestinian Refugee Crisis," paragraph 8.
45 Ibid., paragraph 13.
46 Rebecca L. Stein, "Impossible Witness: Israeli Visual, Palestinian Testimony and the Gaza War," *Journal for Cultural Research* 16, no. 2/3 (2012): 135–153, 147. DOI: 10.1080/14797585.2012.647749.
47 See Lawfare, "Lawfare: Hard National Security Choices," n.d., www.lawfareblog.com.
48 See the David Barron and Marty Lederman memo that was attached to the Second Circuit Court's June 2014 decision in United States Court of Appeals for the Second Circuit, *The New York Times Company et al. v. The U.S. Department of Justice et al.*, June 23, 2014, www.aclu.org/files/assets/2014-06-23_ca2-revised-opinion-plus-drone-memo.pdf; Rania Khalek, "Obama Cites Israeli Supreme Court to Justify Killing Americans Without Trial," The Electronic Intifada, last modified June 24, 2014, http://electronicintifada.net/blogs/rania-khalek/obama-cites-israeli-supreme-court-justify-killing-americans-without-trial.
49 As I noted in earlier chapters, countless commentators who talk to the press have confusing ways of talking about various tenets of "just war" theories and principles, but an excellent overview of some of their strategic usages appears in Slater, "Just War Moral Philosophy."
50 Marie-Bénédicte Dembour, *Who Believes in Human Rights? Reflections on the European Convention* (Cambridge: Cambridge University Press, 2006).
51 Costas Douzinas, *The End of Human Rights: Critical Legal Thought at the Turn of the Century* (Oxford: Hart Publishing, 2000).
52 Stephen Hopgood, *The Endtimes of Human Rights* (Ithaca, NY: Cornell University Press, 2013).
53 Martti Kosenniemi, *The Gentle Civilizer of Nations: The Rise and Fall of International Law, 1870–1960* (Cambridge: Cambridge University Press, 2002); Martti Koskenniemi, *From Apology to Utopia: The Structure of International Legal Argument* (Cambridge: Cambridge University Press, 2005); Martti Koskenniemi, "Between Impunity and Show Trials," *Max Planck Yearbook of United Nations Law* 6 (2002): 1–35; Martti Koskenniemi, "Human Rights Mainstreaming as a Strategy for Institutional Power," *Humanity: International Journal of Human Rights, Humanitarianism, and Development* 47, no. 1 (2010): 27–58, DOI: 10.1353/hum.2010.0003.
54 Slater, "Just War Moral Philosophy," 75.
55 Craig Jones, "Frames of War: Targeting Advice and Operational Law in the Israeli Military," *Society & Space: Environment & Planning D: Society and Space* 33 (2015): 1–21, DOI: 10.1177/0263775815598103.
56 Slater, "Just War Moral Philosophy," 51.
57 See Nimer Sultany, "Liberal Zionism, Comparative Constitutionalism, and the Project of Normalizing Israel," in *On Recognition of the Jewish State*, ed. Honaida Ghanim (Jerusalem: Madar Center, 2014), 91–109, http://papers.ssrn.com/sol3/papers.cfm?abstract_id=2405372.

212 Coping with post-human framings

58 Frédéric Mégret, "The Apology of Utopia: Some Thoughts on Koskenniemian Themes, with Particular Emphasis on Massively Institutionalized International Humanitarian Human Rights Law," *Temple International & Comparative Law Journal* 27 (2013): 455–497, 456.
59 Mégret, "The Apology of Utopia," 456.
60 Ibid., 456.
61 The International Commission on Intervention and State Sovereignty, *The Responsibility to Protect* (Ottawa: Canadian Minister of Foreign Affairs, 2001), http://responsibilitytoprotect.org/ICISS%20Report.pdf.
62 Aidan Hehir, "A Propensity to Ignore? R2P Advocacy and the Crisis in Gaza," *E-International Relations*, July 15, 2014, www.e-ir.info/2014/07/15/a- propensity-to-ignore-r2p-advocacy-and-the-crisis-in-gaza.
63 Ibid., paragraph 8.
64 For more on the relevance of this concept of "forensic architecture" in Gazan contexts, see Eyal Weizman, *The Least of All Possible Evils: Humanitarian Violence from Arendt to Gaza* (London: Verso, 2011).
65 Lorenzo Kamel, "Why do Palestinians in Gaza Support Hamas?" *Ha'aretz*, last modified August 5, 2014, paragraphs 5–7, www.haaretz.com/opinion/.premium-1.608906.
66 Ibid., paragraphs 8–9.
67 Nigel Parry, "The 'Targeted Killing' of Sheikh Ahmed Yassin," The Electronic Intifada, last modified March 22, 2004, paragraphs 1–3, http://electronicintifada.net/content/targeted-killing-sheikh-ahmed-yassin/5033.
68 Kamel, "Why Do Palestinians," paragraphs 14.
69 For examples of what could be called the "lost opportunities" narrative, see Zeev Schiff, "Ex-Mossad Chief: Hamas Offered 30-Year Ceasefire in 1997," *Ha'aretz*, last modified March 30, 2006, www.democraticunderground.com/discuss/duboard.php?az=view_all&address=124x120581; Merav Michaeli, "Israel is Missing Another Opportunity for Peace," *Ha'aretz*, last modified January 2, 2012, www.haaretz.com/print-edition/opinion/israel-is-missing-another-opportunity-for-peace-1.405001. One intriguing permutation of what might be called the "Hamas is reforming" narrative includes the suggestion that Hamas tries to prioritize the targeting of military, instead of civilian, targets. Amos Harel and Avi Issacharoff, "Hamas' Change of Strategy: Rocket fire Directed at Israeli Military Targets," *Ha'aretz*, last modified June 20, 2012, www.haaretz.com/blogs/east-side-story/hamas-change-of-strategy-rocket-fire-directed-at-israeli-military-targets.premium-1.439939.
70 Menachem Klein, "Hamas in Power," *Middle East Journal* 61, no. 3 (2007): 442–459, 450.
71 Kamel, "Why Do Palestinians," paragraphs 18.
72 Peter Beinart, "Who are the True Jewish Allies of Hamas?" *Ha'artz*, last modified August 6, 2014, www.haaretz.com/opinion/.premium-1.609257.
73 Gallia Lindenstrauss and Sűfyan Kadir Kivam, "Turkish–Hamas Relations: Between Strategic Calculations and Ideological Affinity," *Strategic Assessment* 17, no. 2 (2014): 7–16, 8.
74 Recep Tayyip Erdogan, quoted in the *Washington Post*, "Palestine is an Open Air Prison," *Washington Post*, last modified January 31, 2009, paragraph 8, www.washingtonpost.com/wp-dyn/content/article/2009/01/30/AR2009013002809.html.
75 Ismail Hiniyam, quoted in Taghreed El-Khodary and Sabrina Tavernise, "U.N. Warns of Refugee Crisis in Gaza Strip," *New York Times*, last modified January 12, 2009, paragraph 7, www.nytimes.com/2009/01/13/world/middleeast/13mideast.html.
76 Simon A. Waldman, "Review Article: Exaggerating the Death of the Two State-Solution," *Middle Eastern Studies* 49, no. 3 (2013): 840–853, 840. For general background on two-state approaches, see Asher Susser, *Israel, Jordan, and Palestine: The Two-State Imperative* (Waltham, MA: Brandeis University Press, 2012). For examples of those who may have given up on finding any two-state solutions, see Edward

Said, "The One-State Solution," *New York Times*, last modified January 10, 1999, www.nytimes.com/1999/01/10/magazine/the-one-state-solution.html; Tony Judt, "Israel: The Alternative," *New York Review of Books*, last modified October 23, 2003, www.nybooks.com/articles/archives/2003/oct/23/israel-the-alternative; Virginia Q. Tilley, *The One-State Solution: A Breakthrough for Peace in the Israeli–Palestinian Deadlock* (Ann Arbor, MI: University of Michigan Press, 2005).

77 Meron Benvenisti, "The Binationalism Vogue," *Ha'aretz*, last modified April 30, 2009, www.haaretz.com/print-edition/opinion/the-binationalism-vogue-1.275085. See also Daanish Faruqi, *From Camp David to Cast Lead: Essays on Israel, Palestine and the Future of the Peace Process* (London: Lexington Books, 2011).

78 Raphael Ahren, "The Rocket That Spelled the End of the Two-State Solution?" *Times of Israel*, last modified August 10, 2014, www.timesofisrael.com/the-rocket-that-spelled-the-end-of-the-two-state-solution/.

79 Ibid., paragraphs 3–5.

80 Msrael Matzav Staff, "Poll: 91% of Jewish Israelis Support Operation Protective Edge," *Israel Matzav*, last modified July 30, 2014, http://israelmatzav.blogspot.com/2014/07/poll-91-of-jewish-israelis-support.html.

81 Akiva Eldar, "Gaza War Stifles Democracy in Israel," *Al-Monitor*, last modified August 23, 2014, www.al-monitor.com/pulse/ru/originals/2014/08/protective-edge-democracy-zoabi-idf-golan-levy.html#.

82 Waldman, "Exaggerating the Death," 150.

83 Isabel Kershner, "New Emblem of an Elemental Conflict: Seized West Bank Land," *New York Times*, last modified September 9, 2014, www.nytimes.com/2014/09/10/world/middleeast/after-land-seizure-west-bank-villages-symbolize-an-elemental-conflict.html.

84 For specific usages of the phrase "Israeli exceptionalism," see John Dugard and John Reynolds, "Apartheid in Occupied Palestine: A Rejoinder to Yaffa Zilbershats," EJIL Talk!, last modified October 2, 2013, www.ejiltalk.org/apartheid-in-occupied-palestine-a-rejoinder-to-yaffa-zilbershats.

85 Kristin Solberg, "Gaza's Health and Humanitarian Crisis," *The Lancet* 384 (2014): 389–390.

86 Peter Beaumont, "A Knock on the Roof, then Another Gaza Home Destroyed by Israeli Missile," *Guardian*, July 14, 2014, www.theguardian.com/world/2014/jul/14/gaza-home-destroyed-israel-shati.

Bibliography

Books

Agamben, Giorgio. *Homo Sacer: Sovereign Power and Bare Life*. Translated by Daniel Heller-Roazen. Stanford, CA: Stanford University Press, 1998.
Alam, M. Shahid, *Israeli Exceptionalism: The Destabilizing Logic of Zionism*. Basingstoke: Palgrave Macmillan, 2009.
Anderson, Benedict. *Imagined Communities: Reflections on the Origin and Spread of Nationalism*. London: Verso, 1991.
Anderson, David. *Histories of the Hanged: Britain's Dirty War in Kenya and the End of Empire*. London: Weidenfeld, 2005.
Azoulay, Ariella. *The Civil Contract of Photography*. New York: Zone Books, 2008.
Bayoumi, Moustafa. *Midnight on the Mavi Marmara: The Attack on the Gaza Freedom Flotilla and How It Changed the Course of the Israeli/Palestinian Conflict*. Chicago: Haymarket Books, 2010.
Benvenisti, Eyal. *The International Law of Occupation* Oxford: Oxford University Press, 2012.
Ben-Yehuda, Nachman. *Political Assassination by Jews: A Rhetorical Device for Justice*. Albany, NY: SUNY Press, 1992.
Black, Ian, and Benny Morris. *Israel's Secret Wars: A History of Israel's Intelligence Services*. New York: Grove Weidenfeld, 1991.
Byman, Daniel. *A High Price: The Triumphs and Failures of Israeli Counterterrorism*. London: Oxford University Press, 2011.
Catignani, Sergio. *Israeli Counter-Insurgency and the Intifadas: Dilemmas of a Conventional Army*. New York: Routledge, 2008.
Cohen, Amichai, and Stuart A. Cohen. *Israel's National Security Law: Political Dynamics and Historical Development*. New York: Routledge, 2012.
Condit, Celeste Michelle, and John Louis Lucaites. *Crafting Equality: America's Anglo-African Word*. Chicago: University of Chicago Press, 1993.
Dembour, Marie-Bénédicte. *Who Believes in Human Rights? Reflections on the European Convention*. Cambridge: Cambridge University Press, 2006.
Dinstein, Yoram. *The International Law of Belligerent Occupation*. Cambridge: Cambridge University Press, 2009.
Douzinas, Costas. *The End of Human Rights: Critical Legal Thought at the Turn of the Century*. Oxford: Hart Publishing, 2000.
Duncan, Gillian, Orla Lynch, Gilbert Ramsay, and Alison M.S. Watson. *State Terrorism*

and Human Rights: International Responses Since the End of the Cold War. New York: Routledge, 2013.
Elkins, Caroline. *Imperial Reckoning: The Untold Story of Britain's Gulag in Kenya.* New York: Henry Holt, 2005.
Enemark, Christian. *Armed Drones and the Ethics of War: Military Virtue in a Post-Heroic Age.* London: Routledge, 2013.
Faris, Hani A., ed. *The Failure of the Two-State Solution: The Prospects of One State in the Israel–Palestine Conflict.* London: I.B. Tauris, 2013.
Faruqi, Daanish. *From Camp David to Cast Lead: Essays on Israel, Palestine and the Future of the Peace Process.* London: Lexington Books, 2011.
Flapan, Simha. *The Birth of Israel: Myths and Realities.* New York: Pantheon, 1987.
Ford, Franklin L. *Political Murder: From Tyrannicide to Terrorism.* Cambridge, MA: Harvard University Press, 1985.
Foucault, Michel. *The History of Sexuality, Volume One.* Translated by Robert Hurley. New York: Vintage Books, 1990.
Gourgouris, Stathis. *Dream Nation: Enlightenment, Colonization and the Institution of Modern Greece.* Redwood City, CA: Stanford University Press, 1996.
Guiora, Amos. *Legitimate Target: A Criteria-Based Approach to Targeted Killing.* New York: Oxford University Press, 2013.
Hochberg, Gil Z. *Visual Occupations: Violence and Visibility in a Conflict Zone.* Durham, NC: Duke University Press, 2015.
Hopgood, Stephen. *The Endtimes of Human Rights.* Ithaca, NY: Cornell University Press, 2013.
Hussein, Nassar. *The Jurisprudence of Emergency: Colonialism and the Rule of Law.* Ann Arbor, MI: University of Michigan Press, 2003.
Kennedy, David. *Of War and Law.* Princeton, NJ: Princeton University Press, 2006.
Klein, Aaron J. *Striking Back: The 1972 Munich Olympics Massacre and Israel's Deadly Response.* New York: Random House, 2005.
Koskenniemi, Martti. *The Gentle Civilizer of Nations: The Rise and Fall of International Law, 1870–1960.* Cambridge: Cambridge University Press, 2002.
Koskenniemi, Martti. *From Apology to Utopia: The Structure of International Legal Argument.* Cambridge: Cambridge University Press, 2005.
Kretzmer, David. *The Occupation of Justice: The Supreme Court of Israel and the Occupied Territories.* Albany, NY: SUNY Press, 2002.
Levy, Gideon. *The Punishment of Gaza.* London: Verso, 2010.
Levy, Yagil. *Israel's Death Hierarchy: Casualty Aversion in a Militarized Democracy.* New York: New York University Press, 2012.
Lindsay, James G. *Fixing UNRWA: Repairing the UN's Troubled System of Aid to Palestinian Refugees.* Washington, DC: Washington Institute, 2009.
Lustick, Ian S. *Unsettled States, Disputed Lands: Britain and Ireland, France and Algeria, Israel and the West Bank-Gaza.* Ithaca, NY: Cornell University Press, 1993.
MacKenzie, Donald. *Inventing Accuracy: A Historical Sociology of Nuclear Missile Guidance.* Cambridge, MA: MIT Press, 2001.
Morozov, Evgeny. *The Net Delusion: The Dark Side of Internet Freedom.* New York: PublicAffairs, 2011.
Morris, Benny. *The Birth of the Palestinian Refugee Problem.* New York: Cambridge University Press, 1987.
Morris, Benny. *Righteous Victims: A History of the Zionist–Arab Conflict, 1881–1999.* New York: Vintage Books, 2001.

Netanyahu, Benyamin. *A Durable Peace: Israel and its Place among the Nations*. New York: Warner Books, 2000.

Opher, Adi, Michael Givoni, and Sara Hanif, eds., *The Power of Inclusive Exclusion: Anatomy of Israeli Rule in the Occupied Palestinian Territories*. Brooklyn, NY: Zone Books, 2009.

Pappé, Ilan. *A History of Modern Palestine: One Land, Two Peoples*. Cambridge: Cambridge University Press, 2004.

Pappé, Ilan. *The Making of the Arab–Israel Conflict, 1947–1951*. London: Tauris, 1992.

Pedahzur, Ami. *The Israeli Secret Services and the Struggle Against Terrorism*. New York: Columbia University Press, 2009.

Plaw, Avery. *Targeting Terrorists: A Licence to Kill?* Hampshire: Ashgate Publishing Limited, 2008.

Pugliese, Joseph. *State Violence and the Execution of the Law: Biopolitical Caesurae of Torture, Black Sites, Drones*. New York: Routledge, 2013.

Rapoport, David C. *Inside Terrorist Organizations*. London: Frank Cass, 2001.

Raviv, Dan, and Yossi Melman. *Every Spy a Prince: The Complete History of Israel's Intelligence Community*. Boston, MA: Houghton Mifflin, 1990.

Ron, James. *Frontiers and Ghettos: State Violence in Serbia and Israel*. Berkeley, CA: University of California Press, 2003.

Shlaim, Avi. *The Iron Wall: Israel and the Arab World*. New York: W.W. Norton, 2000.

Solis, Gary D. *The Law of Armed Conflict: International Humanitarian Law in War*. New York: Cambridge University Press, 2010.

Sontag, Susan. *Regarding the Pain of Others*. New York: Farrar, Straus & Giroux, 2003.

Susser, Asher. *Israel, Jordan, and Palestine: The Two-State Imperative*. Waltham, MA: Brandeis University Press, 2012.

Tilley, Virginia Q. *The One-State Solution: A Breakthrough for Peace in the Israeli–Palestinian Deadlock*. Ann Arbor, MI: University of Michigan Press, 2005.

Weizman, Eyal. *Hollow Land: Israel's Architecture of Occupation*. London: Verso, 2007.

Weizman, Eyal. *The Least of All Possible Evils: Humanitarian Violence from Arendt to Gaza*. London: Verso, 2011.

Book chapters

Comaroff, Jean and John Comaroff. "Law and Disorder in the Postcolony: An Introduction." In *Law and Disorder in the Postcolony*, edited by Jean Comaroff and John L. Comaroff, 1–56. Chicago, IL: University of Chicago Press, 2006.

Derrida, Jacques. "Autoimmunity: Real and Symbolic Suicides." In *Philosophy in a Time of Terror: Dialogues with Jürgen Habermas and Jacques Derrida*, interviewed by G. Borradori, 85–136. Chicago, IL: University of Chicago Press.

Foucault, Michael. "Technologies of the Self." In *Technologies of the Self: A Seminar with Michel Foucault*, eds. L.H. Martin, H. Gutman, and P.H. Hutton, 16–49. London: Tavistock, 1988.

Johnson, Paul. "The Cancer of Terrorism." In *Terrorism: How the West Can Win*, ed. Benjamin Netanyahu, 31–49. New York: Farrar, Straus and Giroux, 1986.

Shenhav, Yehouda and Yael Berda. "The Colonial Foundations of the State of Exception: Juxtaposing the Israeli Occupation of the Palestinian Territories with Colonial Bureaucracy History." In *The Power of Inclusive Exclusion: Anatomy of Israeli Rule in the Occupied Palestinian Territories*, ed. Adi Ophir, Michael Givoni and Sari Hanafi, 337–374. New York: Zone Books, 2009.

Sultany, Nimer. "Liberal Zionism, Comparative Constitutionalism, and the Project of Normalizing Israel." In *On Recognition of the Jewish State*, ed. Honaida Ghanim, 91–109. Jerusalem: Madar Center, 2014.

Weizman, Eyal. "Thanato-tactics." In *The Power of Inclusive Exclusion: Anatomy of Israeli Rule in the Occupied Palestinian Territories*, eds. Adi Ophir, Michael Givoni, and Sari Hanafi, 543–573. New York: Zone Books, 2009.

Scholarly articles and law reviews

Aldrich, George H. "Progressive Development of the Laws of War: A Reply to Criticisms of the 1977 Geneva Protocol I." *Virginia Journal of International Law* 26 (1985): 693–720.

Allan, Diana, and Curtis Brown. "Media's Messengers: The *Mavi Marmara* at the Frontlines of Web 2.0." *Journal of Palestine Studies* 40, no. 1 (2010): 63–77.

Amossy, Ruth. "From National Consensus to Political Dissent: The Rhetorical Uses of the Masada Myth in Israel." *Rivesta Italiana di Filosofia del Linguaggio* 6, no. 3 (2012): 1–15. DOI: 10.1080/14650040903486983.

Aouragh, Miriyam. "Everyday Resistance on the Internet: The Palestinian Context." *Journal of Arab and Muslim Media Research* 1, no. 2 (2008): 109–130.

Appadurai, Arjun. "Disjuncture and Difference in the Global Cultural Economy." *Public Culture* 2 (1990): 1–24. DOI: 10.1215/08992363-2-2-1.

Atran, Scott, "Genesis of Suicide Terrorism," *Science* 299 (2003): 1534–1539.

Azoulay, Ariella. "Declaring the State of Israel: Declaring a State of War." *Critical Inquiry* 37, no. 2 (2011): 265–285, DOI: 10.1086/657293.

Bar-Tal, D. and Dikla Antebi. "Siege Mentality in Israel." *International Journal of Intercultural Relations* 1, no. 1 (1992): 49–67.

Barak, Aharon. "International Humanitarian Law and the Israeli Supreme Court." *Israel Law Review* 47, no. 2 (2014): 181–189. DOI: 10.1017/S0021223714000041.

Bashi, Sari. "Controlling Perimeters, Controlling Lives: Israel and Gaza." *Law and Ethics of Human Rights* 7, no. 2 (2013): 243–282.

Bell, Colleen. "Hybrid Warfare and Its Metaphors." *Humanity* 3, no. 2 (2012): 225–247. DOI: 10.1353/hum.2012.0014.

Bellamy, Alex J., and Paul D. Williams. "On the Limits of Moral Hazard, the 'Responsibility to Protect,' Armed Conflict and Mass Atrocities." *European Journal of International Relations* 18 (2012): 539–571. DOI: 10.1177/1354066110393366.

Ben-Naftali, Orna. "A Judgment in the Shadow of International Law." *Journal of International Criminal Justice* 5, no. 2 (2007): 322–331.

Ben-Naftali, Orna, and Keren R. Michaeli, "'We Must Not Make a Scarecrow of the Law': A Legal Analysis of the Israeli Policy of Targeted Killings." *Cornell International Law Journal* 36 (2003): 233–292.

Berlin, Eric. "The Israeli Supreme Court's Targeted Killing Judgment: A Reaffirmation of the Rule of Law During War." *Michigan State International Law Review* 21 (2013): 517–546.

Bhungalia, Lisa. "Im/Mobilities in a 'Hostile Territory': Managing the Red Line." *Geopolitics* 17 (2012): 256–275.

Blondhem, Menaham and Limor Shifman. "What Officials Say, What Media Show, and What Public Get: Gaza, January 2009." *Communication Review* 12, no. 3, 205–214.

Blumenthal, Max. "Politicide in Gaza: How Israel's Far Right Won the War." *Journal of Palestine Studies* 44, no. 1 (2014): 14–28.

Bohrer, Ziv and Mark Osiel. "Proportionality in War: Protecting Soldiers from Enemy

Captivity and Israel's Operation Cast Lead: "The Soldiers are Everyone's Children." *Southern California Interdisciplinary Law Journal* 22 (2013): 637–691.

Bousquet, Antoine. "Chaoplexic Warfare or the Future of Military Organization." *International Affairs* 84, no. 5 (2008): 915–929.

Brenner, Y.S. "The 'Stern Gang,' 1940–48." *Middle Eastern Studies* 2, no. 1 (1965): 2–30.

Buchan, Russell. "The International Law of Naval Blockade and Israel's Interception of the Mavi Marmara." *Netherlands International Law Review* 58 (2011): 209–241.

Busse, Jan. "The Biopolitics of Statistics and Census in Palestine." *International Political Sociology* 9, no. 1 (2015): 70–89.

Caldwell, William B., IV, Dennis M. Murphy, and Anton Menning. "Learning to Leverage New Media: The Israel Defense Forces in Recent Conflicts." *Military Review* 89, no. 3 (2009): 2–10.

Cohen, Amichai, and Stuart A. Cohen. "Israel and International Humanitarian Law: Between the Neo-Realism of State Security and the 'Soft Power' of Legal Acceptability." *Israel Studies* 16, no. 2 (2011): 1–23.

Cohen, Matthew S., and Charles D. Freilich. "The Delegitimation of Israel, Diplomatic Warfare, Sanctions, and Lawfare." *Israel Journal of Foreign Affairs* 9, no. 1 (2015): 29–48.

David, Steve R. "Fatal Choices: Israel's Policy of Targeted Killings," *Mideast Security and Policy Studies* 51 (2002): 1–26. DOI: 10.4324/9780203485422.ch9.

DeLuca, Kevin Michael. "Unmoored: The Force of Images as Events." *Journal of Advanced Composition* 28, no. 3/4 (2008): 663–673.

Dugard, John, and John Reynolds. "Apartheid, International Law and the Occupied Palestinian Territory." *The European Journal of International Law* 24, no. 3 (2013): 867–913.

El-Sarraj, Eyad. "Suicide Bombers: Dignity, Despair, and the Need for Hope." *Journal of Palestine Studies* 31, no. 4 (2002): 71–76.

Fahmy, Shahira. "High Drama on the High Seas: Peace Versus War Journalism Framing of an Israeli/Palestinian Related Incident." *The International Communication Gazette* 76, no. 1 (2014): 86–105.

Farer, Tom. "The Goldstone Report on the Gaza Conflict: An Agora." *Global Governance* 16 (2010): 139–143.

Fassin, Didlier. "The Humanitarian Politics of Testimony: Subjectification Through Trauma in the Israeli–Palestinian Conflict." *Cultural Anthropology*, 23, no. 3 (2008): 531–558. DOI: 10.1111/j.1548-1360.2008.00017.x.

Feldman, Ilana. "Difficult Distinctions: Refugee Law, Humanitarian Practice, and Political Identification in Gaza." *Cultural Anthropology* 22, no. 1 (2007): 129–169.

Fenrick, William J. "The *Targeted Killings* Judgment and the Scope of Direct Participation in Hostilities." *Journal of International Criminal Justice* 5, no. 2 (2007): 332–328.

Frakt, David J.R. "Lawfare and Counterlawfare: The Demonization of the Gitmo Bar and Other Legal Strategies in the War on Terror." *Case Western Reserve Journal of International Law* 43 (2011): 335–356.

Gregory, Derek. "War and Peace." *Transactions of the Institute of British Geographers* 35, no. 2 (2010): 154–186.

Gordon, Neve. "Rationalising Extra-Judicial Executions: The Israeli Press and the Legitimation of Abuse." *International Journal of Human Rights* 8, no. 3 (2004): 305–324.

Gordon, Neve. "Human Rights as a Security Threat: Lawfare and the Campaign Against Human Rights NGOs." *Law & Society Review* 48, no. 2 (2014): 311–344.

Gross, Aeyal M. "Human Proportions: Are Human Rights the Emperor's New Clothes of the International Law of Occupation?" *The European Journal of International Law* 18, no. 1 (2007): 1–35.
Gross, Emanual. "Democracy in the War Against Terrorism: The Israeli Experience." *Loyola of Los Angeles Law Review* 35, no. 11 (2002): 1161–1216.
Gross, Emanual. "Thwarting Terrorists' Acts by Attacking the Perpetrators or Their Commanders as an Act of Self-Defense: Human Rights versus the State's Duty to Protect Its Citizens." *Temple International & Comparative Law Journal* 15 (2001): 195–246.
Gross, Michael L. "Fighting by Other Means in the Mideast: A Critical Analysis of Israel's Assassination Policy." *Political Studies* 51, no. 2 (2003): 350–368.
Gross, Michael. "Assassination and Targeted Killing: Law Enforcement, Execution or Self-Defence." *Journal of Applied Philosophy* 23, no. 3 (2006): 323–325.
Guilfoyle, Douglas. "The *Mavi Marmara* Incident and Blockade in Armed Conflict." *British Yearbook of International Law* 81, no. 1 (2010): 171–223.
Guiora, Amos. "Targeted Killing as Active Self-Defense." *Case Western Reserve Journal of International Law* 36 (2004): 319–334.
Guiora, Amos N. "Determining a Legitimate Target: The Dilemma of the Decision-Maker." *Texas International Law Journal* 47, no. 3 (2011): 315–336.
Hamdi, Naila. "Arab Media Adopt Citizen Journalism to Change the Dynamics of Conflict Coverage." *Global Medial Journal* 1, no. 1 (2010): 3–15.
Hammack, Phillip L. "Exploring the Reproduction of Conflict Through Narrative: Israeli Youth Motivated to Participate in a Coexistence Program." *Peace and Conflict: Journal of Peace Psychology* 15, no. 1 (2009): 49–74. DOI: 10.1080/10781910802589923.
Handel, Ariel. "Gated/Gating Community: The Settlement Complex in the West Bank." *Transactions* 39, no. 4 (2014): 504–517, DOI: 10.1111/tran.12045.
Hasson, Shlomo. "Gaza Enclave: Victim, Enemy, Rival." *Geopolitics* 15, no. 2 (2010): 385–405. DOI: 10.1080/14650040903486983.
Herzberg, Anne, and Gerald M. Steinberg, "IHL 2.0: Is there a Role for Social Media in Monitoring and Enforcement?" *Israel Law Review* 45, no. 3 (2012): 493–536.
Hijab, Nadia. "Reversing Defeat Through Non-Violent Power." *Contemporary Arab Affairs* 2, no. 4 (2009): 566–575. DOI: 10.1080/17550910903236717.
Hochberg, Gil. "Soldiers as Filmmakers: On the Prospect of 'Shooting War,' and the Question of Ethical Spectatorship." *Screen* 54, no. 1 (2013): 44–61.
Honig, Or. "Explaining Israel's Misuse of Strategic Assassinations," *Studies in Conflict & Terrorism* 30, no. 6 (2007): 563–577.
Humphreys, Stephen. "The Emptiness of Empire and Other Hazards of Theory." *International and Comparative Law Quarterly* 57, no. 1 (2008): 225–242.
Inbar, Efraim and Eitan Shamir. "'Mowing the Grass': Israel's Strategy for Protracted Intractable Conflict." *Journal of Strategic Studies* 37, no. 1 (2014): 65–90.
Jones, Craig. "Frames of War: Targeting Advice and Operational Law in the Israeli Military." *Society & Space: Environment & Planning D – Society and Space* 33 (2015): 1–21. DOI: 10.1177/0263775815598103.
Jordan, Jenna. "When Heads Roll: Assessing the Effectiveness of Leadership Decapitation." *Security Studies* 18 (2009): 719–755.
Joronen, Mikko. "'Death Comes Knocking on the Roof': Thanatopolitics of Ethical Killing During Operation Protective Edge in Gaza," *Antipode* (2015). DOI: 10.1111/anti.12178.
Kalb, Marvin A. and Carol Saivetz. "The Israeli–Hezbollah War of 2006: The Media as a

Weapon in the Asymmetrical Conflict." *The Harvard International Journal of Press/Politics* 12, no. 3 (2007): 43–66. DOI: 10.1177/1081180X07303934.

Kampf, Zohar. "News-Media and Terrorism: Changing Relationship, Changing Definitions." *Sociology Compass* 8, no. 1 (2014): 1–9.

Kanwar, Vik. "Review Essay: Post-Human Humanitarian Law: The Law of War in the Age of Robotic Weapons." *Harvard National Security Journal* 2 (2011): 616–628.

Kaplan, Danny. "Commemorating as Suspended Death: Missing Soldiers and National Solidarity in Israel." *American Ethnologist*, 35, no. 3 (2008): 413–427. DOI: 10.1111/j.1548-1425.2008.00043.x.

Kasher, Asa, and Amos Yadlin. "Assassination and Preventive Killing." *SAIS Review of International Affairs*, 25, no. 1 (2005): 41–57. DOI: 10.1353/sais.2005.0011.

Keller, Helen and Magdalena Forowic. "A Tightrope Walk Between Legality and Legitimacy: An Analysis of the Israeli Supreme Court's Judgment on Targeted Killing." *Leiden Journal of International Law* 21 (2008): 185–221.

Khalidi, Rashid. "1948 and After in Palestine: Universal Themes?" *Critical Inquiry* 40, no. 4 (2014): 313–331.

Klein, Menachem. "Hamas in Power." *Middle East Journal* 61, no. 3 (2007): 442–459.

Kober, Avi. "Targeted Killing during the Second Intifada: The Quest for Effectiveness," *The Journal of Conflict Studies* 27, no. 1 (2007): 76–93.

Kober, Avi. "From Heroic to Post-Heroic Warfare: Israel's Way of War in Asymmetrical Conflicts." *Armed Forces & Society* 41, no. 1 (2015): 96–122.

Korn, Alina. "Israeli Press and the War against Terrorism: The Construction of the 'Liquidation Policy.'" *Crime, Law and Social Change* 41, no. 3 (2004): 209–234.

Koskenniemi, Martti. "Between Impunity and Show Trials." *Max Planck Yearbook of United Nations Law* 6 (2002): 1–35.

Koskenniemi, Martti. "Human Rights Mainstreaming as a Strategy for Institutional Power." *Humanity: International Journal of Human Rights, Humanitarianism, and Development* 47, no. 1 (2010): 27–58. DOI: 10.1353/hum.2010.0003.

Kretzmer, David. "Targeted Killing of Suspected Terrorists: Extra-Judicial Executions or Legitimate Means of Defence?" *The European Journal of International Law* 16, no. 2 (2012): 171–212.

Kuntsman, Adi, and Rebecca L. Stein. "Digital Suspicion, Politics, and the Middle East." *Critical Inquiry* (2011): 1–10.

Lagerquist, Peter. "Shooting; Gaza: Photographers, Photographs, and the Unbearable Lightness of War." *Journal of Palestine Studies*, 28, no. 3 (2009): 86–92.

Lesh, Michelle. "Case Note: *The Public Committee Against Torture in Israel v. The Government of Israel* – The Israel High Court of Justice Targeted Killing Decision." *Melbourne Journal of International Law* 8, no. 2 (2007): 1–25.

Li, Darryl. "The Gaza Strip as Laboratory: Notes in the Wake of Disengagement." *Journal of Palestine Studies* 35, no. 2 (2006): 38–55.

Lindenstrauss, Gallia, and Süfyan Kadir Kivam. "Turkish–Hamas Relations: Between Strategic Calculations and Ideological Affinity." *Strategic Assessment* 17, no. 2 (2014): 7–16.

Litowitz, Douglas E. "Kafka's Outsider Jurisprudence." *Law & Social Inquiry* 27, no. 1 (2002): 103–137. DOI: 10.1111/j.1747-4469.2002.tb01109.x.

Luban, David. "Lawfare and Legal Ethics in Guantánamo." *Stanford Law Review* 60 (2008): 1981–2026.

Luft, Gal. "The Logic of Israel's Targeted Killing." *Middle East Quarterly* 10, no. 1 (2003): 3–13.

McMahon, Sean F. "The Boycott, Divestment, Sanctions Campaign: Contradictions and Challenges." *Race & Class* 55 (2014): 65–81.

Makdisi, Saree. "The Architecture of Erasure." *Critical Inquiry*, 36, no. 3 (2010): 519–559.

Mbembe, Achille. "Necropolitics," *Public Culture* 15, no. 1 (2003): 11–40.

Mégret, Frédéric, "The Apology of Utopia: Some Thoughts on Koskenniemian Themes, with Particular Emphasis on Massively Institutionalized International Humanitarian Human Rights Law." *Temple International & Comparative Law Journal* 27 (2013): 455–497.

Melzer, Nils. "Keeping the Balance Between Military Necessity and Humanity: A Response to Four Critiques of the ICRCs Interpretative Guidance on the Notion of Direct Participation in Hostilities." *New York University Journal of International Law and Politics* 42 (2010): 831–916.

Merom, Gil. "Israel's National Security and the Myth of Exceptionalism." *Political Science Quarterly* 114, no. 3 (1999): 409–434.

Milanovic, Marko. "Lessons for Human Rights and Humanitarian Law in the War on Terror: Comparing *Hamdan* and the Israeli *Targeted Killings* Case." *International Review of the Red Cross* 89, no. 866 (2007), 373–393.

Mirzoeff, Nicholas. "The Right to Look." *Critical Inquiry* 37, no. 3 (2011): 473–496.

Mitchell, W.J.T. "Picturing Terror: Derrida's Autoimmunity." *Cardozo Law Review* 27 (2005): 913–925.

Moghadam, Assaf. "Palestinian Suicide Terrorism in the Second Intifada: Motivations and Organizational Aspects." *Studies in Conflict & Terrorism* 26 (2003): 65–92.

Morris, Benny. "Book Review: Palestinian Identity: The Construction of Modern National Consciousness." *Israel Studies* 3, no. 1 (1998): 266–272.

Murray, Stuart J. "Thanatopolitics: On the Use of Death for Mobilizing Political Life." *Polygraph* 18 (2006): 191–215.

Naaman, Dorit. "Brides of Palestine/Angels of Death: Media, Gender, and Performance in the Case of Palestinian Female Suicide Bombers." *Signs* 32, no. 4 (2007): 933–955.

Neocleous, Mark. "The Problem of Normality: Taking Exception to 'Permanent Emergency.'" *Alternatives* 31 (2006): 191–213.

Orgad, Shani. "Watching How Others Watch: The Israeli Media's Treatment of International Coverage of the Gaza War." *Communication Review*, 12, no. 3 (2009): 250–261.

Parks, W. Hays. "Part IX of the ICRC 'Direct Participation in Hostilities' Study: No Mandate, No Expertise, and Legally Incorrect." *New York University Journal of International Law and Politics* 42 (2010): 769–830.

Pelham, Nichals. "Gaza's Tunnel Phenomenon: The Unintended Dynamics of Israel's Siege." *Journal of Palestine Studies* 41, no. 4 (2012): 6–31.

Plasse-Couture, François-Xavier. "Effective Abandonment: The Neoliberal Economy of Violence in Israel and the Occupied Territories." *Security Dialogue* 44, no. 5/6 (2013): 449–466.

Pratt, Simon Frankel. "'Anyone Who Hurts Us': How the Logic of Israel's 'Assassination Policy' Developed During the Aqsa Intifada." *Terrorism and Political Violence* 25 (2013): 224–245.

Pugliese, Joseph. "The Tutelary Architecture of Immigration Detention Prisons and the Spectacle of 'Necessary Suffering.'" *Architectural Theory Review* 13, no. 2 (2008): 206–221. DOI: 10.1080/13264820802216841.

Schabas, William A. "Gaza, Goldstone, and Lawfare." *Case Western Reserve Journal of International Law* 43 (2010): 307–312.

Bibliography

Schmitt, Michael N. "Deconstructing Direct Participation in Hostilities: The Constitutive Elements." *International Law and Politics* 42 (2010): 697–739.

Shahoub-Kevorkian, Nadera. "Human Suffering in Colonial Contexts: Reflections from Palestine." *Settler Colonial Studies* 4, no. 3 (2014): 277–290. DOI: 10.1080/2201473X.2013.859979.

Shany, Yuval. "The Law Applicable to Non-Occupied Gaza: A Comment on *Bassiouni* v. *The Prime Minister of Israel*." *Israel Law Review* 42 (2009): 101–116. DOI: 10.1017/S0021223700000467.

Shapiro, Shlomo. "No Place to Hide: Intelligence and Civil Liberties in Israel." *Cambridge Review of International Affairs* 19, no. 4 (2006): 629–648. DOI: 10.1080/09557570601003361.

Siapera, Eugenia. "Tweeting #Palestine: Twitter and the Mediation of Palestine." *International Journal of Cultural Studies* 17, no. 6 (2014): 539–555. DOI: 10.1177/1367877913503865.

Sifman, Limor. "An Anatomy of a YouTube Meme." *New Media and Society* 12, no. 2: 187–203.

Slater, Jerome. "Just War Moral Philosophy and the 2008–09 Israeli Campaign in Gaza." *International Studies* 37, no. 2 (2012): 44–80.

Solberg, Kristin. "Gaza's Health and Humanitarian Crisis." *The Lancet* 384 (2014): 389–390.

Somerstein, Rachel. "On Liminality and Loss: A Decade of Israeli and Palestinian Film." *Visual Studies* 29, no. 1 (2014): 94–98. DOI: 10.1080/1472586X.2014.862998.

Stahl, Adam. "The Evolution of Israeli Targeted Operations: Consequences of the Thabet Thabet Operations." *Studies in Conflict & Terrorism* 22 (2010): 111–133.

Stein, Rebecca L. "Impossible Witness: Israeli Visuality, Palestinian Testimony and the Gaza War." *Journal for Cultural Research* 16, no. 2 (2012): 135–153. DOI: 10.1080/14797585.2012.647749.

Stein, Rebecca L. "StateTube: Anthropological Reflections on Social Media and the Israel State." *Anthropological Quarterly* 85, no. 3 (2012): 893–916.

Stein, Yael. "By Any Name Illegal and Immoral." *Ethics & International Affairs* 17, no. 1 (2003): 127–137. DOI: 10.1111/j.1747-7093.2003.tb00423.x.

Strand, Trude. "Tightening the Noose: The Institutionalized Impoverishment of Gaza, 2005–2010." *Journal of Palestine Studies* 43, no. 2 (2014): 6–23.

Sultany, Nimer. "The Legacy of Justice Aharon Barak: A Critical Overview." *Harvard International Law Journal Online* 48 (2007): 83–92.

Sultany, Nimer. "Activism and Legitimation in Israel's Jurisprudence of Occupation." *Social & Legal Studies* (2014): 1–25. DOI: 10.1177/0964663914521449.

Sydor, Elizabeth. "*The Gatekeepers*." *Oral History Review* 41, no. 1 (2014): 139–141. DOI: 10.1093/ohr/ohu001.

Tawil-Souri, Helga. "Digital Occupation: Gaza's High Tech Enclosure." *Journal of Palestine Studies* 41, no. 2 (2012): 27–45.

Tomba, Massimiliano. "Another Kind of *Gewalt*: Beyond Law, Re-Reading Walter Benjamin." *Historical Materialism* 17 (2009): 126–144.

Vagts, Detlev F. "*Ajuri* v. *IDF Commander in West Bank*." *The American Journal of International Law* 97, no. 1 (2003): 173–175.

Vatter, Miguel. "Eternal Life and Biopower." *CR: The New Centennial Review* 10, no. 3 (2010): 217–240. DOI: 10.1353/ncr.2010.0035.

Vennesson, Pascal, and Nikoas M. Rajkovic. "The Transnational Politics of Warfare Accountability: Human Rights Watch Versus the Israel Defense Forces." *International Relations* 26, no. 4 (2012): 409–429. DOI: 10.1177/0047117812445450.

Waldman, Simon A. "Review Article: Exaggerating the Death of the Two State-Solution." *Middle Eastern Studies* 49, no. 3 (2013): 840–853.
Weizman, Eyal. "Lethal Theory." *Open* 18 (2009): 53–78.
Wolfsfed, Gadi, Paul Frosh, and Maurice T. Awabdy. "Covering Death in Conflicts: Coverage of the Second Intifada on Israeli and Palestinian Television." *Journal of Peace Research* 45, no. 3 (2008): 401–417.
Zerubavel, Yael. "The Death of Memory and the Memory of Death: Masada and the Holocaust as Historical Metaphors." *Representations* 45 (1994): 72–100.
Zuker, Lian, and Edward H. Kaplan. "Mass Casualty Potential of Qassam Rockets." *Studies in Conflict & Terrorism* 37, no. 3 (2014): 258–266. DOI: 10.1080/1057610X.2014.872024.

Legal cases

Supreme Court of Israel. *Abu Baker* v. *Defense Ministry*. HCJ 6133/03 (2003).
Supreme Court of Israel. *Adalah-Legal Center for Arab Minority Rights in Israel and Others* v. *General Officer Commanding Central Command, Israeli Defence Force and Others*. HCJ 3799/02 (2005).
Supreme Court of Israel. *Ajuri* v. *IDF Commander in the West Bank*. HCJ 7015/02. (2002).
Supreme Court of Israel. *Al Bassiouni* v. *Prime Minister*. HCJ 9132/07 (2008).
Supreme Court of Israel. *Mayor of Ad-Dhahiriya* v. *IDF Commander in West Bank*. HCJ 178/06 (2006).
Supreme Court of Israel. *Dweikat* v. *The Government of Israel*. HC 390/79 (1979).
Supreme Court of Israel. *Public Committee Against Torture in Israel et al.* v. *Government of Israel et al.* JCJ 769/02 (2006).

Military publications

Dunlap, Charles J. Jr., "Lawfare: A Decisive Element of 21st-Century Conflicts?" *Joint Forces Quarterly* 54, no. 3 (2009): 34–39.
Eiland, Giora. "The Third Lebanon War: Target Lebanon," *Strategic Assessment* 11, no. 2 (2008): 16.
GOC Southern Command, *Transcript of GOC Southern Command Regarding the Finds of the Investigation of the Demotion of the Buildings in Rafah (10–11.Jan.02), IMRA*, January 28, 2002, www.imra.org.il/story.php3?id=9932.

Official state and international legal documents

Goldstone, Richard, Christine Chinkin, Hina Jilani, and Desmond Travers. *Report of the United Nations Fact-Finding Mission on the Gaza Conflict, United Nations General Assembly*. New York: United Nations General Assembly, 2009.
International Commission on Intervention and State Sovereignty. *The Responsibility to Protect*. Ottawa: Canadian Minister of Foreign Affairs, 2001. http://responsibilityto-protect.org/ICISS%20Report.pdf.
Palmer, Geoffrey, Alvaro Uribe, Joseph Ciechanover Itzhar, *Report of the Secretary-General's Panel of Inquiry on the 31 May 2010 Flotilla Incident, July 2011*. http://blog.unwatch.org/wp-content/uploads/Palmer-Committee-Final-report.pdf.

UN Fact-Finding Mission. *Report of the United Nation Fact-Finding Mission on the Gaza Conflict*. New York: United Nations General Assembly, 2009.
UN Human Rights Council. *Report on the International Fact-Finding Mission to Investigate Violations of International Law, Including International Humanitarian and Human Rights Law, Resulting from the Israel Attacks on the Flotilla of Ships Carrying Humanitarian Assistance*. New York: UN Human Rights Council, 2010.
Zurayk, Rami, Anne Gough, Ahmad Sourani, and Mariam Al Jaajaa. *Food Security Challenges and Innovation: The Case of Gaza*. Rome: Food and Agriculture Organization, 2012.

NGO and think-tank publications

Amnesty International. *Israel and the Occupied Territories: State Assassinations and Other Unlawful Killings*. New York: Amnesty International, 2001.
Amnesty International. "Document: Israel and the Occupied Palestinian Territories – Israel/Gaza Conflict," *Amnesty International*. Last modified July 25, 2014. www.amnesty.org/en/library/asset/MDE15/017/2014/en/5b79b682-8d41-4751-9cbc-a0465f6433c3/mde150172014en.html.
B'Tselem, *Policy of Destruction: House Demolitions and Destruction of Agricultural Land in the Gaza Strip*. Tel Aviv: B'Tselem, 2002. www.btselem.org/download/200202_policy_of_destruction_eng.pdf.
Human Rights Watch. *Razing Rafah: Mass Home Demolitions in the Gaza Strip*. New York: Human Rights Watch, 2004. www.hrw.org/reports/2004/rafah1004/rafah1004text.pdf.
Human Rights Watch. *"I Lost Everything": Israel's Unlawful Destruction of Property During Operation Cast Lead*. New York: Human Rights Watch, 2010.
Roy, Sara. *The Gaza Strip: The Political Economy of De-Development*. Washington, DC: Institute for Palestine Studies, 1995.
Stein, Yael. *Israel's Assassination Policy: Extra-judicial Killings*. Tel Aviv: B'Tselem, 2001.
Ulutaş, Ufuk. *A Raid from the Sea: The Gaza Flotilla Attack and Blockade under Legal Scrutiny*. Istanbul: SETA Policy Brief, 2011. http://arsiv.setav.org/Ups/Pdf/SETA_Policy_Brief_A_Raid_from_the_Sea_Ufuk_Ulutas.pdf.
Van Esveld, Bill. *Rockets from Gaza: Harm to Civilians From Palestinian Armed Groups – Rocket Attacks*. New York: Human Rights Watch, 2009.

Miscellaneous internet materials

B'Tselem, "Demolition for Alleged Military Purposes." B'Tselem. Last modified January 1, 2011. www.btselem.org/razing/rafah_egyptian_border.
Dunlap, Charles, Jr. *Law and Military Interventions: Preserving Humanitarian Values in 21st Century Conflicts*. Washington, DC: Kennedy School of Government, 2001. http://people.duke.edu/~pfeaver/dunlap.pdf.
European Institute for International Law and International Relations. "Israel's Dahiya Doctrine: Terror Tactics to Ensure Colonial Domination of Gaza." Last modified July 31, 2014. www.eiilir.eu/politics-strategies/topics/actual-topics/128-israel-s-dahiya-doctrine-terror-tactics-to-ensure-colonial-domination-in-gaza.
Goodman, Hirsh. and Dore Gold. *The Gaza War 2014: The War Israel Did Not Want and the Disaster It Averted*. Jerusalem Center for Public Affairs, 2015. http://jcpa.org/pdf/The-Gaza-War-2014-Site.pdf.

Gregory, Derek. "Virtual Gaza." *Geographical Imaginations*. Last modified July 27, 2014. http://geographicalimaginations.com/2014/07/27/virtual-gaza.

Gunneflo, Markus. "The Targeted Killing Judgment of the Israeli Supreme Court and the Critique of Legal Violence." *Selected Works of Markus Gunneflo*. January, 2012. http://works.bepress.com/cgi/viewcontent.cgi?article=1007&context=markus_gunneflo.

Heller, Kevin Jon. "Can Israel Cut Off Water and Power to Gaza." Opinio Juris. Last modified July 27, 2014. http://opiniojuris.org/2014/07/26/can-israel-cut-water-power-gaza.

Jones, Craig. "Frames of War: Targeting Advice and Operational Law in the Israeli Defense Force." War, Law, and Space. 2013. https://warlawspace.files.wordpress.com/2013/09/jonesc-frames-of-law-blog.pdf.

Mondoweiss. "End the Gaza Massacre, Boycott Israel: What Eve Ensler, Angela Davis, Judith Butler, Chandra Talpade Mohanty and More are Demanding." Alternet. Last modified August 9, 2014. www.alternet.org/world/end-gaza-massacre-boycott-israel-what-eve-ensler-angela-davis-judith-butler-chandra-talpade.

Stothard, Robert. "Politics of Asymmetric Fear in Israel." London College of Communication. Last modified April 15, 2013. http://robstothard.co.uk/files/2014/03/POLITICS-OF-ASYMETTRICAL-FEAR-IN-ISRAEL.pdf.

Sultany, Nimer. "Repetition and Death in the Colony: On the Israeli Attacks on Gaza." Critical Legal Thinking. Last modified July 11, 2014. http://criticallegalthinking.com/2014/07/11/repetition-death-colony.

Weizman, Eyal. "Introduction to the Politics of Verticality," Open Democracy. Last modified April 24, 2002. www.opendemocracy.net/ecology-politicsverticality/article_801.jsp.

Visual artifacts

Blumenthal, Max. "Israelis Celebrate IDF Flotilla Attack." YouTube. Last modified June 6, 2010. www.youtube.com/user/mblumenthal#p/u/18/ZWha0aMGIlQ.

Idfnadesk, "IDF Pinpoint Strike on Ahmed Jabir, Head of the Hamas Military Wing." YouTube. Last modified November 14, 2012. www.youtube.com/watch?v=P6U2ZQ0EhN4.

Idfnadesk. "12 Examples of Hamas Firing Rockets from Civilians Areas," YouTube. Last modified July 31, 2014. www.youtube.com/watch?v=IUrDAEgisXM.

Moreh, Dror. Interview with Richard Peña, NYFF Select Committee Chairman, Film Society of Lincoln Center, "NYFF Press Conference: *The Gatekeepers*." YouTube, Last modified October 17, 2012. www.youtube.com/watch?v=jczwdsmIvNo.

Moreh, Dror. *The Gatekeepers*. Mac Guff Ligne, Cinephil, and Dror Moreh Productions, 2012.

Index

Abbas, Mahmoud 3, 26, 43, 94, 113, 146, 204, 206
Agamben, Giorgio 82, 208
Ajuri v. *IDF commander in the West Bank* 108
Al Bassiouini v. *The Prime Minister of Israel* 25
Al-Helou, Yousef 148
Al-Jabari, Ahmed 3, 156–8, 160
Al-Jura 107, 201
Al-Qassam Brigades 158, 166
Al-Shifa Hospital 148, 160
Al-Sisi, Abdel Fattah 130, 188
Almog, Doron 39–40, 68
Amnesty International (AI) 69, 85, 135, 192
Anderson, Benedict 186
apartheid 34, 162, 201
Arafat, Yasser 8, 69, 76–7, 147
armed conflict 7, 9, 10, 13, 21, 36, 66, 69, 78, 81, 83–4, 87, 110, 146, 156
assassinations 12, 23, 57, 66, 71–2, 76–8, 81, 83, 88, 91, 93, 197, 201
autoimmunity 79
Aylon, Amil 55
Aylon, Danny 191
Ayyash, Yahya 72–3
Azoulay, Ariella 124

B'Tselem 7, 20, 32, 40, 69, 164–6, 191
Balfour Declaration 201
Baker, Farah 147–50
Barak, Aharon 5, 22–4, 31, 53, 68, 75, 78, 80–94, 108, 195
Barak, Ehud 69–70, 72, 75
Barron, David 195
Basic laws 5, 33, 69
Begin, Menachem 72
Beit Hanoun 164–6

Bell, Avi 137–8
belligerent occupation 3, 7, 31, 39, 104–10, 151, 169, 192
Benayahu, Avi 145
Benjamin, Walter 6, 21
Benvenisti, Meron 205
Berda, Yael 101, 116
Bhungalia Lisa 104
biopolitical 2, 24–5, 70, 76, 79, 86, 90, 102, 118, 124, 169–88, 208
blogosphere 25, 11, 25, 44, 49, 103, 125–6, 146, 151, 153, 173–4, 199, 208
Blum, Gabriella 159
Blumenfeld, Laura 69
border zones 39, 31
Bousquet, Antoine 17
Boycott, divestment, and sanctions movement (BDS) 25, 190, 208, 210
Breaking the Silence 7, 27, 121–2
Buchan, Russell 36
buffer zones 7, 15, 34, 39–42, 106, 112
Bush, George W. 112
Butler, Judith 6, 11, 27

Caldwell, William B. 153–4
Camaroff, Jean 21
Camaroff, John 21
Chaoplexic warfare 17, 51
Chinkin, Christine 43–6
Clausewitz, Carl von 20, 151, 173
clicktivism 150
Cohen, Amichai 5
Cohen, Jack 133
Cohen, Matthew 7, 68
Cohen, Stuart 5
condensation symbol 13, 49, 101, 201
counterinsurgency doctrines (COIN) 7, 85, 106, 123, 150–1

Index 227

counterterrorism (CT) 6, 8, 11, 19, 70, 106, 201
critical genealogical studies 1, 9, 13, 26, 33, 59, 71, 73, 79, 91, 149, 172, 199
critical rhetorical studies 4, 10, 68

Dahiya Doctrine 6, 12–13, 42, 47–52, 59, 139, 158, 174, 184, 209
Danon, Danny 144
de jure 77, 116
decapitation 70, 73, 78–9, 93
Deleuze, Gilles 16
DeLuca, Kevin 11
Dembour, Marie-Bénédicte 197
Der Derian, James 173
Derrida, Jacques 6, 11, 27, 79–80
Diamond, Eitan 138
diaspora 7, 13, 91, 109, 182
Dichter, Avi 68, 75–7
digital vernacularism 144
direct participants (in hostilities) 22, 45, 53, 81–5, 90, 135
Dinstein, Yoram 137
disengagement 15, 17, 25, 33, 35, 67, 73, 86, 100, 103–5, 107, 110–14, 116–17, 126, 137, 144, 153, 166, 169, 183, 192, 196, 207–8
dispositifs 10, 31, 49, 90, 104, 137, 197
disproportionate 37, 45, 47, 50, 52, 120, 139, 152, 154, 169, 187, 208
distinction 46, 54, 82, 84, 86, 125, 132, 152, 159, 188, 190–1, 202
Douzinas, Costas 197
Dunlap, Charles, Jr. 20

Eakin, Britain 37
ecocide 106
Efrati, Eran 16
Eiland, Giora 38, 49–52, 182, 184–8
Eisenkot, Gadi 49–50, 52
Enemark, Christian 188
epistemes 10–13, 15, 49, 125, 148, 197
Erdogan, Recep Tayyip 204

Facebook 16, 132, 138–9, 144, 147–8, 157–8, 161, 173–4
Fahmy, Shahira, 37
Falk, Richard 23–4, 139
Feldman, Avigdor 81
Feldman, Ilan 190–1, 193
Flapan, Simha 193
fog of war 16, 53, 131, 173
forensic architecture 15, 200
Forowicz, Magdalene 22–3, 82, 87–8

Foucault, Michel 10–11, 44, 118
Frankel, Naftali 161
Freilich, Charles 7, 68

Gatekeepers, The 24, 34, 53–9
Gaza Strip 6, 17, 24, 35–6, 38–41, 52, 66, 82, 89, 100, 103, 105–11, 113, 115–16, 120–2, 137, 147, 164, 166–7, 174, 182, 184, 186–8, 191, 206
Gehl, Rob 152
Geneva Conventions 1–2, 9, 21, 23, 33, 43, 46, 82, 110, 136–7, 168, 188, 191, 196–7
Givoni, Michal 33
Glick, Caroline 162, 179
Goldstein, Brooke 19–20
Goldstone Report 8, 13, 24, 34, 42–53, 59, 63, 191, 196
Goldstone, Richard 11, 13, 43, 44, 46, 49, 53
Gordon, Neve 11–12, 21, 77, 191, 193
Gregory, Derek 11, 19, 91, 94
Gross, Aeyal 1
Guiora, Amos 74

Haganah 4, 72, 96
Hajjar, Lisa 74, 93
Halutz, Dan 68, 75, 77
Hamas 2–209; Charter of 1988 200–3, 205; regime 4, 8, 25, 37, 102, 104, 107, 110, 126, 128, 147, 171, 186, 196, 199, 202
Hamastan 113–14
Hanifi, Sari 33
Haniya, Ismail 166, 172
Hannibal Directive 152, 176
hasbara 1, 8, 26, 68, 145, 162, 175–6
hauntology 80
Havey, Shimon 15
Hehir, Aidan 199–200
Herzberg, Anne 146
Hezbollah 5, 7, 13–14, 18, 32, 34, 43, 47–52, 59–60, 66, 90–1, 126, 129, 139, 145, 152–4, 201
Hochberg, Gil 35
Hopgood, Stephen 197
Hroub, Khaled 156
human shields 3, 6, 14, 25, 43, 45, 53, 83–4, 89, 92, 123, 131, 137, 163, 167–8, 188
Humma, Majdi Abu 56–7
Humphreys, Stephen 22

image events 11, 133, 196

Index

Inbar, Aefraim 20
infrastructure 2, 7, 9, 15, 18, 25, 42–4, 47–8, 51, 53, 87–8, 92, 121, 123, 131–3, 136, 138–9, 137, 157, 171, 184, 188, 196–7, 207
institutional impoverishment 100
Intifada; First 66, 67, 93, 100, 147, 187, 201; Second 3, 7, 12, 23–4, 26–7, 31, 32, 39–40, 58, 67, 69, 71, 73–5, 79, 91, 96, 102, 107, 109, 121, 128, 131, 136, 145, 184–5, 196
International Commission on Intervention and State Sovereignty (ICISS) 199
International Criminal Court (ICC) 42, 68, 86–7, 150, 184, 190, 194
International humanitarian law (IHL) 1–2, 5, 9–10, 17, 22–3, 31, 33, 37–8, 40, 43–6, 49, 52, 60, 68–9, 81, 82, 84–8, 93, 95, 104, 108, 122–5, 135–7, 140, 146, 150, 152, 155, 159, 183, 187–8, 190, 195–9
inverted empathy 1
Irgun 72
Iron Dome 8, 25, 93–4, 123, 126–9, 131, 140, 150, 157, 187, 189, 192, 208–10
Iron wall 187
Israel Defense Forces (IDF) 2–3, 5, 7–10, 12, 15–18, 23, 31–2, 35, 40–2, 44–6, 48, 50, 52, 54–5, 67–8, 70, 76, 78, 83–4, 86–7, 89, 91, 93–4, 98, 101, 103–4, 107–8, 114, 120–1, 123–36, 138, 142, 144–7, 149, 153–9, 161–3, 167–74, 185, 188, 197, 202–3
Israel High Court (IHC) 5, 8, 10, 24, 33, 38, 52–3, 66–8, 75, 77, 80–2, 89, 93
Israeli exceptionalism 8, 27–8, 33, 54–5, 86, 196, 204, 207, 213

Jabari, Ahmed 3, 156–8, 160
Jabotinsky, Ze'ev 187
Jilani, Hina 43–4, 46
Joint Special Operations Command (JSOC) 11, 158
Jones, Craig 197
Joronen, Mikko 136
Judea 5, 10, 32–4, 66, 74, 82, 95, 103, 111, 183, 196, 204
jus ad bellum 9, 87, 168, 187
jus in bello 9, 49, 87, 135, 187, 196

Kamel, Lorenzo 107, 201–2
Kanwar, Vik 188
Kasher, Asa 86–7
Keller, Helen 22–3, 82, 87–8

Kennedy, David 197
Kerr, Dara 157–8, 172
Khalidi, Rashid 4
Klein, Menachem 203
Kober, Avi 32
Kokhavi, Aviv 15
Koskenniemi, Martti 197
Krauthammer, Charles 1–2, 6, 151
Kretzmer, David 93

Law of armed conflict (LOAC) 2, 21–2, 40, 76, 84, 86, 131, 135–6, 146, 161, 163, 189, 208
lawfare 1, 3–5, 7, 9, 15, 19–24, 41, 68, 71, 77, 87–92, 94, 106, 110, 135, 150, 155, 163, 171, 174, 183, 189–91, 195–7, 208–9
Lederman, Marty 195, 211
Leibovich, Avital 155, 158–9
Levy, Gideon 31–2, 38, 88–9, 114, 117, 153
Li, Darryl 7, 39
liquidations 66–71, 73–4, 77–8, 81–3, 86, 88–91
Livni, Tzipi 115
lost opportunities genre 59, 69, 77, 111, 212
Luban, David 22
Luft, Gal 78–80

MacKenzie, Donald 129
Mandelblit, Avichai 110
Manor, Eviatar 8
Masada complex 31, 60, 72
Mavi Marmara 24, 34–9
Mbembe, Achille 14–15
Mégret, Frédéric 198
Meir, Golda 26, 72, 133, 173, 182
Mendel, Yonatan 26
Menning, Anton 153–4
Mirzoeff, Nicholas 133, 151
Mitchell, W.J.T. 79
Mofaz, Shaul 113
moral clarity 1–2, 4, 11, 125, 151
moral hazard 185, 194
Moreh, Dror 24, 34, 53–9, 64
Morozov, Evgeny 149–50
Morris, Benny 4, 193
mowing the grass 20, 107, 174, 186, 208
Mukasey, Michael B. 172
Murphy, Dennis 153–4
Muslim Brotherhood 130, 189, 201

Nakba 26, 58, 72, 107, 124, 140, 144, 182, 190, 198

necropolitics 14, 104
Netanyahu, Benjamin 3, 7, 15, 18–19, 32, 35, 38, 42, 68, 101, 115, 125, 128, 130, 133, 135, 144–6, 148, 161, 169, 171, 174, 193, 204, 297
network-centric warfare 80, 145

Olmert, Ehud 48, 114–15, 202
Operation Cast Lead 8, 13, 25, 31, 33, 42–5, 47–8, 52–3, 60, 71, 87, 124–5, 145, 150, 154–6, 159, 172, 187, 196, 202
Operation Pillar of Defense 3, 18, 116, 129, 131, 144–5, 150, 156–60, 172
Operation Protective Edge (OPE) 1, 4, 6–7, 10, 18–19, 25–6, 32, 35, 40–1, 56, 71, 87, 102–3, 107, 116, 120–40, 144–50, 161, 163–4, 167, 172–3, 184, 206
Ophir, Adi 33
Oren, Michael 56
Oslo Accords 8, 69, 109, 205

Pakistan 9, 11, 90
Palestinian Authority (PA) 3–4, 21, 66, 100, 114, 138, 183, 186
Pappé, Ilan 193
Phillips, Karl Hudson 37
Pillay, Navi 189
Pink Line 40
post-heroic 32, 60, 70
post-human 16, 88, 145, 182–209
post-structuralist 11, 13, 15, 20, 80, 90, 183
precision warfare 46, 69, 74, 92, 155, 168
proportionality 9, 52, 54, 68, 81, 87, 88–8, 93, 125, 152, 159, 188
Public Committee Against Torture in Israel et al. v. Government of Israel et al., The, (PCATI) 22, 24, 27, 71, 78, 80–3, 85, 87–2, 95, 195
Pugliese, Joseph 17, 90
purity of arms 1, 71

Rafah 5, 40, 130, 165, 170, 203
Rancière. Jacques 186
real time 10, 147, 158, 174
Red Alert Israel 18–19
Red line 106
Reisner, Daniel 75–6, 209
Renan, Ernest 182
responsibility to protect (R2P) 6, 7, 25, 190, 198–200

rhetorical vignettes 34
Romirowsky, Asaf 192–5
Roy, Sara 42
rules of engagement (ROE) 9, 18, 21, 40–1, 76, 122

Sabah, Muhammad 164–5
Sabra massacre 68
Samaria 5, 10, 32–4, 66, 74, 82, 95, 103, 111, 183, 196, 204
Samud 186–7, 209
Sawyer, Diane 163–4
Schabas, William 189
Schmitt, Michael 84, 90
Sderot 3, 107, 124, 128, 197, 200–1
Shalit, Gilad 3, 153, 157, 169, 180
Shenhar, Yehouda 101
selfies 1–2, 132, 145, 151, 173–4
separation barrier 5, 7, 22, 32–4, 93, 204, 208
Shaar, Gil-ad 161
Shaked, Ayelet 138–9
Shalom, Avraham 56, 59
Shamir, Eitan 20
Sharon, Ariel 3, 7, 32, 39, 55, 68–9, 72, 75, 77, 88, 111–13, 116
Shlaim, Avi 193
Shehadeh, Salah 87
Shin Bet 7, 24, 53–9, 67, 69, 73, 75–7, 89, 92, 105, 114, 130, 157
Shuja'iyya 16, 42, 163
Siboni, Gabriel 49, 52, 158
situational awareness 8, 115, 146
Slater, Jerome 194, 197
soft power 5
Solis, Gary 76
Sontag, Susan 151
Sourani, Raji 139
Spielberg, Steven 72
state terrorism 34, 46
Stein, Rebecca 1, 10, 25, 71, 124–5, 144–5, 173, 176, 195
Steinberg, Gerald 146
Stern Gang 201
Strand, Trude 100–1
suicide bombers 7, 73, 76, 79, 82, 93, 108–9, 151
Sultany, Nimer 92, 197–8
Sydor, Elisabeth 54, 58

targeted killings (TKs) 3, 5, 7, 12, 20–5, 60, 66, 70, 72–4, 78, 87–95, 97–9, 104, 129, 138, 147, 159, 186, 208
Tawil-Souri, Helga 17, 158, 187

Tel Aviv 3, 32, 52, 56, 108, 114, 158, 205
telegenic: dead 15, 144–5, 148, 169, 171, 190, 207; warfare 1, 16, 18
territory: disputed 5, 31, 162; occupied 5
Thabet, Thabet 12, 71
thanatopolitical 2, 9, 11, 14, 24, 53, 58, 70, 73, 79, 102, 104, 112, 131, 138, 151, 157, 171, 190, 208
thano-tactics 90, 94, 117
Travers, Desmond 43–4, 46
tunnels: smuggling 39, 126, 130, 167, 170; terror 2–3, 25, 40–1, 120, 123, 126, 133, 139, 166, 168–72, 174, 184–5
tutelary architecture 17
two-state solutions 2, 4, 24, 31–2, 54–5, 60, 70, 74–5, 100, 107, 109, 112, 123, 182–3, 186, 190, 192, 203, 205–6, 208, 212

Ubaida, Abu 144
United Nations Gaza Inquiry Commission 189
United Nations National Relief and Works Agency for Palestine Refugees in the Near East (UNRWA) 43, 106, 191, 193–4

Waldman, Simon 205–7
Warsaw Ghetto 187
weaponized social media 2, 145, 147, 157, 161
Weissglass, Dov 111–12, 114
Weizman, Eyal 11, 15–16, 74, 76, 90, 94, 103, 117
World Food Program (WFP) 106

Yadlin, Amos 75, 86–7
Ya'alon, Moshe 68–70, 131, 156
Yassin, Ahmed 201–2
Yesh-G'vul movement 77
Yifrach, Eyal 161
Yishai, Eli 52–3
Yishuv 23, 72–3
YouTube 3, 25, 37, 127, 142, 147, 150, 152–3, 155–9, 171

Zionism 55, 201, 207
Zoabi, Haneen 38